John Rosselli's wide-ranging study introduces all those singers, members of the chorus as well as stars, who have sung Italian opera from 1600 to the present. Where did they come from? How were they trained? What did they earn, and what pressures shaped their careers?

Singers are shown slowly emancipating themselves from dependence on great patrons and entering the dangerous freedom of the market. The castrati who dominated eighteenth-century opera turn out to be more conscientious and professional than their previous reputation as extravagant, vain creatures has suggested. The book examines the sexist prejudices against them and against women singers – who in the early days of opera were presumed to be courtesans and sometimes were. But for women, opera provided one of the very few professional and economic opportunities.

SINGERS OF ITALIAN OPERA

SINGERS OF ITALIAN OPERA

THE HISTORY OF A PROFESSION

JOHN ROSSELLI

Reader Emeritus in History, University of Sussex

CAMBRIDGE
UNIVERSITY PRESS

Published by the Press Syndicate of the University of Cambridge
The Pitt Building, Trumpington Street, Cambridge CB2 1RP
40 West 20th Street, New York, NY 10011–4211, USA
10 Stamford Road, Oakleigh, Melbourne 3166, Australia

© Cambridge University Press 1992

First published 1992
First paperback edition 1995

Printed in Great Britain at the University Press, Cambridge

A catalogue record for this book is available from the British Library

Library of Congress cataloguing in publication data
Rosselli, John.
Singers of Italian opera: the history of a profession / by John Rosselli.
p.   cm.
Includes bibliographical references and index.
ISBN 0 521 41683 3 (hardback)
1. Singers.   2. Opera – Italy.   3. Singing – History.   1. Title.
ML460.R68   1992
782.1′023′45 – dc20   91–40160   CIP   MN

ISBN 0 521 42697 9 (paperback)

VN

To Anne and François Duchêne

CONTENTS

ILLUSTRATIONS

PREFACE

Singers of Italian Opera follows on from my *The Opera Industry in Italy from Cimarosa to Verdi. The Role of the Impresario* (Cambridge University Press, 1984). Because I was then moving into virtually uncharted territory, I limited myself in that book to the period 1780–1880 and to a fairly well-defined group of people. With more experience, and the benefit of others' work on an area that has drawn increasing interest in recent years, I have now ventured to study a much larger, more amorphous group over nearly four centuries. The Introduction explains the scope and method of the book.

Two technical points. First, I have stated in French francs sums paid in Italy between 1800 and 1914. The lira of the Napoleonic Kingdom of Italy, that of Piedmont from 1814, and that of the united Kingdom of Italy from 1860 were all officially at par with the franc, a currency familiar in much of the world; minor fluctuations can be ignored. After 1914, when inflation played havoc with earlier parities, sums paid in Italy are given in lire. To ensure comparability, I have also rendered in francs some amounts paid in eighteenth-century Italy; this entails reading back from exchange rates of about 1800, a procedure justified in chapter 6.

Secondly, the subject throws up in acute form the problem that discussion of groups of mixed gender always raises in English. From the start, singing has been an unusual profession in being made up of roughly equal numbers of women and men. Is one always to be saying 'his or her'? I have cut the knot by using either 'he' and 'his' or 'she' and 'her'; unless the context makes it clear that only one gender is meant, these words should be taken to include both.

A book of this kind leaves one with a large debt to many people, above all to archivists and librarians, too many to name; I am grateful to them all. Lorenzo Bianconi has all along helped me, in spite of his own busy schedule, with valuable information and advice; so have Julian Budden, Sergio Durante, Michael Henstock, Malena Kuss, Nicola Mangini, Mary Jane Phillips Matz, Giovanni Morelli, Fiamma Nicolodi, Pierluigi Petrobelli, Juan Andres Sala, Morris Vitalis, and Thomas Walker. Kenneth A. Stern let me use

xiii

his Ph.D. thesis on Giuditta Pasta; I have had help with documentation from Paolo Da Col, Juan Pedro Franze, Nicola Lucarelli, Sylvie Mamy, Alessandro Roccatagliati, Guido A. Tedeschi, Colin Timms, and Roberto Verti, and informative interviews with Carlo Maria Badini, then superintendent of La Scala, the singers Elena Arizmendi, Nino Meneghetti, and Luigi Vellucci, the teachers Paolo Mirko Bonomi and Luciana Piovesan-Bernardi, the conductor-manager Tony Amato, the retired trade union official Professor Umberto Bruno, and (on his recent concern with video opera rather than his earlier management of Covent Garden) Sir John Tooley. I thank them all warmly, while taking sole responsibility for what follows.

The research on which the book is based was carried out with the help of a grant from the Economic and Social Research Council, and of leave from the University of Sussex. What I owe my late wife Eleanor Timbres Rosselli cannot be stated, though it might be sung.

ABBREVIATIONS

AcMu	*Acta Musicologica*
ACS	Archivio Centrale dello Stato, Rome
AMZ	*Allgemeine Musikalische Zeitung*
AnMu	*Analecta Musicologica*
AR MI	Archivio Ricordi, Milan
ASBO	Archivio di Stato, Bologna
ASCR	Archivio Storico Capitolino, Rome
ASCR FC	Archivio Storico Capitolino, Rome, Fondo Capranica
ASMO Mus	Archivio di Stato, Modena, Archivio per Materie, Musici
ASN	Archivio di Stato, Naples
ASR	Archivio di Stato, Rome
ASV	Archivio di Stato, Venice
ATLaF	Archivio del Teatro La Fenice, Venice
ATRP	Archivio del Teatro Regio, Parma
BARCH BO	Biblioteca dell'Archiginnasio, Bologna
BASCR	Biblioteca dell'Accademia di S. Cecilia, Rome
BAV	Biblioteca Apostolica Vaticana
BCI SI	Biblioteca Comunale degli Intronati, Siena
BE MO	Biblioteca Estense, Modena
BLP NA	Biblioteca Lucchesi-Palli, Naples (in BN NA)
BNF CV	Biblioteca Nazionale, Florence, Carteggi Vari
BN NA	Biblioteca Nazionale, Naples
BTBR DC	Biblioteca Teatrale del Burcardo, Rome, Donazione Capranica
BTBR	Biblioteca Teatrale del Burcardo, Rome
BU BO	Biblioteca Universitaria, Bologna
CMBM BO	Civico Museo Bibliografico Musicale, Bologna
DBI	*Dizionario biografico degli Italiani*
DNB	*Dictionary of National Biography*
EaMu	*Early Music*

ES	*Enciclopedia dello Spettacolo*
ISVP	Istituto di Studi Verdiani, Parma
JAMS	*Journal of the American Musicological Society*
LPA NY	Library of Performing Arts, Lincoln Center, New York
M&L	*Music and Letters*
MCCV	Museo Civico Correr, Venice
MOA NY	Metropolitan Opera Archives, New York
MTS	Museo Teatrale alla Scala/Biblioteca Livia Simoni, Milan
NRMI	*Nuova Rivista Musicale Italiana*
Piancastelli	Collezione Piancastelli, Carte Romagna, Biblioteca Comunale, Forlì
Piancastelli Autog.	Collezione Piancastelli, Autografi, Biblioteca Comunale, Forlì
RIDM	*Rivista Italiana di Musicologia*
RMI	*Rivista Musicale Italiana*
TNG	*The New Grove*, ed. S. Sadie, London, 1980

by a lone singing voice in place of polyphony, and the further vogue for pastoral.[9]

The new form can be seen emerging from older ones in the earliest opera still current today, Monteverdi's *L'Orfeo* (1607), where the first two acts run to decorative madrigal singing. But by the same composer's *Il ritorno d'Ulisse in patria* (1640) the single voice poignantly used to dramatic purpose, already heard when the Messenger announces to Orfeo the death of Euridice, has become the standard mode of utterance.

Il ritorno d'Ulisse was first performed in one of the public opera houses of Venice; the first of these had opened only three years earlier. Elsewhere at that date, for instance in Rome, an opera was still an occasional entertainment given by a great man (say the cardinal nephew to the current pope) in his own palace, to which he would invite local nobles and distinguished foreign visitors: productions were lavish and there was no question of any of the audience paying. The owners of the new Venice theatres too were noble families who used them in part to enhance their political standing, but they were also interested in making (or at any rate in not losing) money: they accordingly let their theatres by the season to impresarios who, at least in theory, took the risks, hired the singers and musicians, and stood the loss if there was one. In practice the impresario was and remained semi-dependent on the theatre owners, who would subsidize him up to a point but also control him; he served them as a buffer. This system, already in place at Venice in the mid seventeenth century, was in its essentials still how most operas were put on in Italy by the time Puccini made his way with *Manon Lescaut* in 1893. Relations among the various parties to so complex a business as opera had altered in the intervening 250 years, but gradually and without any clean break.[10]

This was true of a great deal else in the daily round of the singing profession. When a break did come it broke with the past twice over, so marking a deep divide.

First, at a date not easy to pin down but somewhere between 1885 and 1914, the old distinct Italian singing profession merged – except, for a time, in Italy itself – into a highly mobile international profession which is still with us. Until then there had been, all over what westerners were pleased to call the civilized world, a recognizable Italian opera staffed by people who sang little else: outside France, always resistant to its influence, it was *the* opera; in fashionable London seasons everything, down to so Germanic a work as *Der Freischütz*, went on being sung in Italian until 1887. National opera (German or Russian or Czech or even English) coexisted with it, but that was all. After the break, a singer with pretensions to an international career was more and more likely to bridge several schools: today, according to the veteran baritone Gino Bechi, it is all but impossible even in Italy to put on at the same time two equally good *Rigolettos* with Italian singers alone.[11]

Secondly, hard on the heels of this change came the downfall of opera in the theatre as a popular entertainment: it was supplanted, in Italy as elsewhere, by the cinema, later by radio and television. Broadcasting and gramophone records, on the other hand, meant the diffusion of opera (and of singers' reputations) by new means. Taken together, these changes blurred still further the outlines of a distinct Italian profession.

To cope with a story of slow development giving way to rapid change, the book is organized as follows. Four chapters, arranged in broadly chronological order, deal with the growth of the singing profession, first in its initial period of dependence on ruling princes and great nobles, and then in its working of a market, both national and international. This takes the story down to about 1850, a moment of crisis which, for reasons to be explained, marks the beginning of decline both for Italian opera and for the distinct Italian profession. Three chapters then look at aspects of singers' professional lives throughout the period so far covered, and – where change was late in coming – somewhat beyond. Two final chapters, again chronological, pick up the story about 1850 and bring it up to the present, in less detail as the strictly Italian profession loses its clear shape.

Another reason for sketchier coverage of the past thirty or forty years is that in this recent period documentation becomes harder to find. There is plenty of gossip, but little of the written evidence on which the book as a whole rests – memoirs (depended upon only gingerly), letters, official records, above all contracts and other legal documents, where people may be found setting down facts, decisions, or opinions to get something done rather than to impress the public or posterity.

Oral history – based on the spoken recollections of people who took part in the events studied – can be illuminating. But in opera it is of doubtful value. Opera singers move about a great deal; they and the partners they deal with engage in many similar transactions which are easily confused (did such and such an incident take place in Dallas, or was it in Rio? Did X demand £1,500, or only £1,000?) All this quite apart from the pressures of publicity and the demands of self-esteem that may lead memories to distort, perhaps unconsciously. Though I have interviewed a few people, both among singers and in opera management, I have in the main relied on the historian's normal methods. Written evidence has its pitfalls, but, as those will know who have turned up their own thirty-year-old letters, it keeps its healthy capacity to surprise.

I

MUSICIANS ATTENDING

'Opera singer', entered in one's passport under 'occupation', will not surprise frontier officials today. It is a recognized profession. But there was no such profession when opera emerged as a new entertainment about 1600, or when the first public opera house opened in Venice in 1637, or for three or four decades after that: operas were too few to demand most of anyone's time.

In the early seventeenth century not even 'singer' was as yet a clearly defined trade. Many singers played instruments: some accompanied themselves (and some composed their own music), while others switched between singing and playing. The commonest Italian term for them all was *musici*: they were what was meant by the first stage direction in *Twelfth Night*, 'Enter Duke, Curio, lords, musicians attending.'

Barbara Strozzi, for instance, limited herself to composing and singing her own music to her father's friends at his home in Venice – they and he were members of a sort of literary club, at once learned and freethinking; she never appeared on the stage, though her father wrote the words of one of the most successful of early operas. Giulio Caccini was famous as singer and lutenist; he composed his own music, which was seen as new because of the prominence it gave the single voice, and he wrote one of the first operas; his daughters too sang and composed. Others who figured in early opera were members of the choirs attached to great men's chapels; others again were actors or actresses who could sing, like Virginia Andreini, drafted in an emergency to create the title part in Monteverdi's *Arianna* of 1608.[1]

What the early singers of opera had in common was their dependence on patrons of the highest social status. Among these were sovereign princes, chiefly the rulers of the many Italian and German states, but also free-floating royals like Queen Christina of Sweden after her abdication, when she settled in Rome. Others were the aristocrats who controlled the opera houses of republican Venice and Genoa, and the cardinals and other leading members of noble Roman families (most of them related to a present or recent pope) who put on occasional operas in their town houses: early in the next century the young Handel was to work for both kinds, first for a Roman prince, then for a theatre owned by a Venetian noble family. These were not unlike rulers in their wealth and pretensions. A few lesser nobles could influence singers' fortunes because of their official position or their social ties.

What made singers dependent on such patrons was the character of opera through most of the seventeenth century, a spectacular mixed genre that demanded great resources, had originated in courts, and served as 'a public demonstration and representation of authority'.[2] But opera was born into a time of scarce resources: its rise coincided with a deep and long-lasting economic crisis that particularly damaged Southern Europe. Italian industries lost much of their share in international trade; though historians have tended to lighten the unrelieved dark picture they formerly painted of industrial decay within Italy, especially in a privileged capital city such as Venice, there is no doubt that families once active in trade came to depend more on the produce of their landed estates; in nearly all things, territorially based nobles took the lead. This meant that even public theatres with a semi-commercial form of production had to be controlled by families that supplied doges and cardinals.

To understand the social world in which opera developed from 1600 we should look at a few court singers who were active about that time, some of whom never sang in the new genre. The court of Ferrara in the 1580s was celebrated for its musicians. The best of them, for example the three singers who made up the original, celebrated 'concert of ladies', performed 'secret music' of a refinement intended for the ears only of the ruler and a chosen few. They and their successors came for the most part from the families of prominent artists or merchants, though one at least was the daughter of a minor noble. But at court they were not just performers: they were expected to make 'agreeable conversation' as well as music, and to behave like ladies and gentlemen.[3]

For musicians like these, working for a court posed special problems. A ruler interested in music (from whatever motive) provided an opportunity for those musically gifted to advance themselves as courtiers; but the more prominent and regular their musical performances, the more they needed to establish and maintain their courtly credentials.

This was far from easy. Everyone at court was in theory the ruler's servant: the greatest noble might have the privilege of handing him his nightshirt. On the other hand the ruling ideology, most famously expounded in Baldassarre Castiglione's *Il libro del cortegiano* (*The Courtier*), placed high value on noble birth, as well as on accomplishments that ought to seem effortless, that is, non-professional. In a hierarchical-minded age, the ruler's servants spent much time asserting their precedence over others and cultivating a code of honour. Then the late sixteenth-century fashion for a new kind of virtuoso music, designed to bring out individual voices and to be appreciated by an audience, left the soloist exposed: performing in public, especially if you were a woman, might carry unwanted associations of the fairground or the courtesan's dwelling. You also needed to master the language of intimate court exchanges, a blend of high-flown compliment and teasing: it was conventional and must not be taken literally.

All this helps to explain why some well-known singers in these years behaved as they did – why they were keen to achieve noble status, to uphold it if they already had any semblance of it, and to be seen to be patronized by the great, as far as possible on equal terms. To attain any of these ends was worth a good deal of verbal self-abasement.

Giulio Cesare Brancaccio, the star bass singer at the Ferrara court around 1580, was an impoverished noble, conscious of his 'servile' position as a salaried artist and eager to show himself a soldier and courtier. In this he was little different from the first Orfeo in Monteverdi's opera of 1607, the tenor Francesco Rasi, likewise the son of a noble family that had come down in the world: Rasi did his best to have himself treated as a nobleman by the court of Mantua, or at least authorized to eat with the chamberlains rather than with the musicians; the ruler, he pointed out, had once let him take a horse from the ducal stable.

Rasi was not mistaken in seeing court service as a path to noble or other high status. A court was an inward-looking world where to be around, to give satisfaction, and to avoid offence could make the fortune even of the relatively humbly born. The three original ladies of Ferrara all married courtiers; one was murdered by her jealous husband, but that too was a hazard of sixteenth-century court life.[4]

A musician might serve the ruler in non-musical ways. Giulio Caccini was recommended to the court of Modena in 1588 as a possible superintendent of gardens and a dab hand at rearing citrus trees: 'he has excellent handwriting as well, and is apt for every kind of service'. The debutant singer Angela Zanibelli, daughter and niece of Ferrara court singers, was serving as a weaver or embroideress in the household of the city's virtual ruler, Marquis Enzo Bentivoglio, while being trained to read music and to sing; she was lent out to the Duke of Mantua in 1607 for performances of Marco da Gagliano's opera *Dafne* and other works.[5]

This kind of all-purpose service lasted longer in German than in Italian courts, no doubt because in Germany Italian musicians remained for many years a luxury found chiefly in court establishments. Between 1650 and 1692 several castrati gave the Electors of Saxony non-musical service, one as historian-propagandist, another as inspector of the pheasant runs and the lesser chase, a third as steward of the Electress Dowager's household, yet another as a purchasing agent; the last two were ennobled. This kind of post meant immersing oneself in every aspect of a court life where (in 1665) wolf-baiting in the castle yard was followed that evening by a pastoral dance. It also meant security for one's declining years (within limits) and prestige of a kind not to be got by music alone: Clementino, another famous castrato, let it be known in 1689 that he was serving the Elector of Bavaria 'in a capacity other than that of *musico*, and that if he sings now and then he does so as a pastime, not professionally'.[6]

Just how important the right standing at court could be to a singer – especially to a woman – may be seen from the careers of Adriana Basile and her daughter Leonora Baroni.

Adriana, already famous in her own city of Naples, agreed in 1610 to serve Duke Vincenzo of Mantua (strictly speaking, his wife and daughter-in-law) at his court. Some three months' complex, at times ill-tempered correspondence ensued before Adriana, her husband, and her brother set out for Mantua. The business turned on a provision in the original agreement (reached through an intermediary) that the Duchess and her daughter-in-law would write to the Vicereine of Naples asking her to order Adriana to go: the point of this was to maintain Adriana's *reputatione* and the respect in which her family was held, and to make her 'more greatly honoured'. The Mantuan court was at first unwilling to deliver, but Adriana held out, even in the face of threats, and in the end got her way.

The issues seem to have been these. The Viceroy and Vicereine were reluctant to see Adriana leave Naples, and needed to be squared by a request from a fellow-sovereign; the Duke at first wished to avoid putting his wife's own *reputatione* on the line; Adriana expressed qualms, probably genuine, about dangers to her health from the Mantuan swamps (she had never travelled before) and to her chastity from persons unnamed, no doubt from the Duke himself: by holding out she was in effect saying 'I am no common woman singer, I am a lady and an artist of standing in *this* court, and I must be acknowledged as such in your court as well'.[7]

The lesson was well learnt by her equally famous daughter: before permitting her old friend Cardinal Mazarin to bring her to the French court Leonora insisted that the Queen Regent should invite her, and should request the cardinal who was her patron to let her go. In her retirement she was annoyed when people brought up her singing days, 'repeating a number of times "What pointless pleasantries! What insipid praise! Who wants to remember all that?"[8]

Long before, Adriana's husband – a minor Calabrian gentleman – had been made a baron by Duke Vincenzo and given a landed estate; Adriana herself had queened it on a visit to Naples, declining to call unless called upon first; she had exchanged with the next two dukes of Mantua a string of those little notes, wisps of flattery and teasing often accompanying or giving thanks for minor presents, that seem all but pointless but that in fact worked (like the dropping of visiting cards in the 1890s) to confirm status and social ties: a practice kept up by some other women singers of the seventeenth and early eighteenth centuries in equally vapid correspondence with royal or noble persons. After fifteen years Adriana lost the favour of the then duke and duchess; getting no reply to several letters, she finally asked: had she ever refused to do her job as a musician? For the sake of serving her patron, had she not again and again forgotten herself, her own condition, and her husband's birth? It was all in vain.[9]

Yet she had been uncommonly careful to preserve her status. Neither she nor her daughter seems ever to have sung in opera, at any rate in public; both confined themselves to chamber singing – refined and private. But ennobled though they were, Adriana could be frozen out; Leonora in retirement found that for at least one Roman lady she was still a *persona* rather than a *dama*.[10] A generation after Leonora, the famous castrato Giovanni Francesco Grossi, who did sing in opera (he was known as Siface from his best-known part), 'much disdained to show his talent to any but princes': it was a way of keeping up his status. But it did not help him when he engaged in an 'affair', presumably sentimental rather than physical, with a noblewoman, and let it be known: her kinsmen ambushed and murdered him.[11]

A generation before Adriana's story, a Florentine nobleman had urged Caccini not to let himself be 'bought' by some Genoese patrons: it might mean being called in the middle of the night by a servant shouting 'Come, come with your theorbo, my lord wants music'; such servitude would be burdensome to a man 'habituated, through the courtesy of our [Florentine] gentlemen, to dealing with them almost as an equal'. Much virtue in that 'almost'. In the 1640s the famous Roman castrato Marc'Antonio Pasqualini could be seated at dinner with nobles because such was the will of his patron Cardinal Antonio Barberini, but the nobles did not like it and one of them, a visiting Frenchman, insulted the singer.[12]

Such attitudes died hard. In 1708 the Countess of Sunderland wanted to invite to her country house a visiting Italian soprano and her husband, 'provided they would not be above dining with the servants, or by themselves. . . . I don't think any singing will make amends to me for dining and supping with 'em every day, but if I could have 'em without that trouble, it would be a great pleasure.'[13]

These examples tell us much about the difficulties even the most talented singers faced in their dealings with patrons – difficulties compounded when they began to appear before paying audiences.

Those who put on the first opera to be given in a public theatre – *Andromeda*, at the Teatro San Cassiano, Venice, in 1637 – were a troupe with at its core a family: Francesco Manelli, his wife and son; they supplied the score, the management, and much of the singing. But far from being regular opera performers, they had started, Manelli as a church singer and his wife in the service of a great Roman noble; though they appeared in a few more Venetian operas, Manelli in 1638 joined the choir of St Mark's, and seven years later all three took service at Parma, the parents as court singers, the son in a leading church choir. Even their 'public' opera had been an offshoot of a semi-private performance organized by a nobleman in Padua.[14]

Their careers sum up nearly all the possibilities then open to singers. Membership in a church choir (in Italy open only to men) was ideally a lifelong post, often attained through a kind of apprenticeship. Service with a great nobleman or a ruling prince was more exposed to the hazards of war, mortality, and whim, but it too could be lifelong; it might mean singing in chamber or church, and now and then in semi-private opera, though exceptionally a church singer – an Italian priest singing in the Imperial Chapel in Vienna, for instance – would decline to appear in opera, pleading religious scruples that were not widely shared.[15]

Singing in a public theatre meant, from the start, working for an impresario, who might, like Manelli, himself be a musician; or a partnership of artists and moneyed men might contract to put on a season. But, as we have seen, impresarios were in practice dependent on nobles – those who owned the theatres and those who had invested in the ownership of boxes.[16]

These forms of employment all depended on patronage, direct or indirect – if not of a ruler or a great family, then of a high-ranking churchman or religious institution. The one thing the Manellis did not try was the 'blessed liberty' described a little earlier by their colleague Monteverdi. A young bass then living in Venice – Monteverdi reported – had declined to serve the court of Mantua (short of an unreasonably high fee) because, without being on any establishment, he could pick up a living from singing as a freelance in the many Venetian religious festivals.[17] But 'blessed liberty' could too easily mean being left at liberty, unemployed and unprotected.

Singers' need for protection is clear from many of the arrangements for opera seasons in Venetian public theatres as we next observe them, around 1660–70 – a time when ostensibly commercial production by impresarios was well established.

Protection means patronage; but, as the term 'protection racket' still shows us, it can also hold the threat of reprisal if the dependent person does not do what the patron wants. In seventeenth-century Italy great men were prepared to use threats, and sometimes to act on them. When the Duke of Mantua's agent told Adriana Basile that princes such as his master did not care to let anyone make fools of them, she 'burst out weeping bitterly, saying "If the Lord Duke wants to have me killed or raped he can do so, I know, I believe it, but rather than go and serve anyone I will bear all these ills", and so saying she fainted dead away'.[18] Adriana may have been giving a bit of a performance at an awkward moment in negotiations, but her choice of terms is significant.

The Duke of Savoy, asserting in 1667 his right to recall two of his singers from leave part way through the Venice carnival season, threatened to make one of them, the castrato Giovanni Antonio Cavagna (Cavagnino), 'feel the effects of our rightful indignation' if he should try to shift to another patron: 'princes like us have long arms'.[19] The following year, the same Duke of Savoy took on another castrato, Antonio Rivani (Ciccolino), who had been in the service of Queen Christina in Rome and had taken advantage of her absence in Germany to flit; Christina ordered her agent to get Rivani back: 'if he does not sing for me, he will not sing for long for anybody'.[20] As late as 1697, a singer who worked for the Margrave of Brandenburg-Ansbach as his agent in Italy claimed to have given orders in Venice for a rival singer-agent, lately dismissed, to be beaten up if he spoke of the Margrave without due respect.[21] No wonder yet another castrato – petitioning for his job back after having been dismissed over a misdemeanour – described his sovereign as 'my God on earth'.[22]

Yet we should not be overimpressed by what was in part a conventional language of bluster and submissiveness. Patrons did not have it all their own way. They had to reckon with other patrons, and could sometimes be played off against one another. Good singers also had rarity value. The problem for them around 1660–70 was that opera, the most lucrative employment, was itself still rare: only Venice as yet had regular seasons in competing public theatres. For those who were willing to base themselves permanently in Venice, a career singing secondary parts in opera was just beginning to be possible and, it seems, to look more attractive than service in St Mark's choir, though one could also combine the two. The best singers, however, needed –

if they were to make the most of their opportunities – to combine service elsewhere (in Rome or under a ruling prince) with occasional Venetian engagements.[23]

That patrons should have to reckon with other patrons was nothing new. A century earlier, around 1570, the then Duke of Mantua – father of Adriana Basile's first employer – in recruiting for his chapel was having both to negotiate with ecclesiastical grandees and to face musicians' demands for competitive salaries; dealings were protracted and often broke down over money.[24] These transactions had to do mainly with permanent posts. The coming of opera, and the growing vogue for lavish musical entertainments on special occasions, both religious and secular, meant a particular demand for virtuoso singers: patrons therefore engaged in diplomatic dealings when they needed to borrow such artists or were able to lend them out. Trading singers and other musicians became an object of foreign policy.

Cardinal Mazarin, for the sake of putting on Luigi Rossi's *L'Orfeo* in Paris in 1647, mobilized France's allies among the Italian princes – several members of the Medici ruling family in Tuscany, and the Duke of Modena; he was able to recruit singers from France's old Barberini connection in Rome even though a new pope had lately driven the Barberini from power and made an alliance with Spain, because the Pope now had other reasons for appeasing the French crown.[25]

At a slightly less exalted level, the Grimani family, owners of what they were determined should be the leading theatres in Venice, formed political ties with Prince Mattias de' Medici, one of Mazarin's Florentine allies, and then with the dukes of Savoy: they were thus able from time to time to import for their carnival seasons leading musicians in the employ of those princes. The fracas over Cavagnino's Venice engagement in 1667, already mentioned, was legally a matter of how the singer's contract with the Venice impresario could be reconciled with his obligations to his permanent employer in Turin, but it was settled on political grounds: the Grimani at first tried to keep him on for the whole of the carnival season, but they evidently concluded that the danger of upsetting the Duke of Savoy outweighed the loss of profit from letting Cavagnino go; they withdrew their objections and the Venetian government overrode the contract.[26]

Something like a parody of these diplomatic exchanges was mounted in 1685 by the Duke of Mantua. He challenged the Elector of Saxony to a duel for enticing away the famous Margherita Salicola. The Elector declined to receive the challenge (it did not recite his titles quite correctly); duels between rulers, he pointed out, were known as wars, but since Mantua and Saxony were hundreds of miles apart, such a solution was impracticable. This was, all the same, an international crisis of sorts, calling for mediation by a third state, Bavaria: a compromise was patched up according to which Salicola would stay in Dresden for a short while and then go back to Mantua; she stayed ten years none the less.[27]

The last gasp of this kind of diplomacy came in the war of Spanish succession (1701–14). One of the Grimani, Cardinal Vincenzo, as Viceroy of Naples in the Habsburg interest was able to borrow the Duke of Modena's leading male soprano and to keep him on beyond the stipulated date; though his requests were always couched in the most gracious language, he was in the unusually strong position of representing the power of Austria at a crucial moment in the war.[28] This, however, was a throwback. Singers as bargaining counters in international relations were a seventeenth-century device, the result of scarcity of both virtuoso singers and suitable engagements.

Yet even in these conditions singers – good ones at any rate – were not defenceless. They could and did appeal from one patron to another, typically to a sovereign or to a great noble; or they could use their own patron as leverage against another employer. Examples abound. Cavagnino, whom we saw being threatened with the Duke of Savoy's 'long arm' in 1667, appears to have been a master prevaricator and intriguer. Faced with a similar problem in negotiations for the previous carnival, that of 1666 (the Duke wanted him to return before the end of the Venice season), he had suggested to the impresario that they should accept the condition and then, once the season was under way, turn round and plead that it would alienate the public; he also tried to bid up his fee by alleging that the competition – the Vendramin family, owners of the main rival Venetian theatre – were offering him one-third more money, and were using the Venetian Ambassador in Turin to promote their cause.[29] In the summer of 1666 he was in Milan, apparently lent out to the Spanish governor for an opera, and tried to enlist his master's authority to have himself cast in the lead part; when the Duke's anger broke over him in carnival 1667 he sought the protection of a member of the ducal family and of a Turinese noble.[30]

Cavagnino may have been an unpleasant individual; he had, it seems, tried to shoot another musician at Turin and been pardoned. But he was almost forced into prevarication by the scarcity of desirable engagements: only in a Venice carnival season could he earn 150 doubloons, the equivalent of his annual Turin salary (and that was nearly three times what most of his fellow-members of the Turin chapel earned); no wonder negotiations for this irreplaceable boon went on for nine months.

Typical grounds on which singers appealed from one patron to another were mishaps or misdemeanours that would get them into trouble: being late for an engagement because of wartime conditions; taking up an outside engagement without the patron's express leave, though this was said to have been promised; coming back from a previously authorized trip to Vienna (made in the unfounded hope of landing a job in the Imperial Chapel) without informing the patron or asking his permission.[31]

Patrons, indeed, were specially touchy about being asked for permission to take almost any important step, whether it affected their interests or not. Rather than displease the Abbé Vincenzo Grimani by a refusal, the soprano Domenico Broglia got out of a proposed Venetian engagement by alleging that he had given up singing; if he then wished to sing in Venice again, he would have to get Grimani's consent, even though there was no contractual obligation and his own patron was a Florentine noble.[32] Patrons also liked to be complimented on the proper occasions. Some of this was not so much substance as show – pomp and demonstration of the ties of dependence and submission.

If a singer was to be released temporarily from an established post to take an engagement elsewhere, patrons liked to be asked by a fellow-patron, and sometimes made trouble if they were not. On the other hand singers were themselves keen to be asked for or recommended by a person of high rank, either (like Adriana Basile) to preserve their status, or to enhance it: one singer in the Parma service wished to be paid as much for an engagement with the Modena opera house as he had lately received on another outside stint, but was willing to come for less if the Duke of Modena made a request for him direct to his master. Such a request was also thought by some artists to be the best way of ensuring that their salary from a court establishment was continued during their leave: the more usual course was to suspend it (they were after all not working for it, and were earning higher sums elsewhere), but now and then it might be continued as an act of grace.[33]

Were there no singers who worked in Venetian theatres without feeling the need for protectors? There may have been some, working perhaps in the 'blessed liberty' of the city all the year round and earning from both theatre and church engagements. Francesco Zanchi, a singer-instrumentalist, discussed a proposed engagement in 1654 as though the issue between him and the impresarios (one of them a nobleman) was the contractual terms and nothing else.[34]

Two women singers who appeared in Venice had noble protectors. Giulia Masotti, an expensive Roman prima donna, in 1666 used a member of a Venetian noble family as her defender and agent on the local market place, while herself haggling over terms in an unabashedly commercial way. Seven years later she sang in Vienna, was presently taken on as chamber singer, and settled down in the imperial establishment for at least the next quarter-century, marrying a violinist along the way: this was perhaps a withdrawal into a quieter world after the hurly-burly of Venetian opera.[35]

Anna Venturi made her Venetian debut in the previous carnival season (1665) at the behest of the nobleman Benetto Zorzi and in the face of reports that at a previous engagement in Verona she had sung persistently out of tune; Zorzi then withdrew her when the audience made its disapproval clear.[36] We seem to be hearing about a seventeenth-century equivalent of Citizen Kane and the 'singer' he forced on leading opera houses (he wanted to remove the quotation marks). What Zorzi's hold on the impresarios was we do not know: it may have been financial, political, or personal, perhaps all three.

Within twenty years, it began to be more feasible for singers to specialize in opera. By the 1680s, Venice was no longer the only place offering regular seasons. A number of towns now had theatres open to a paying public though often closely controlled by ruling princes or great nobles; there were also more opportunities in foreign courts. At Modena the court theatre was paralleled by a public theatre in the town, run by a nobleman in close touch with the Duke. In Tuscany the Grand Prince Ferdinand (heir apparent to the throne) ran opera seasons at his country villa, besides closely concerning himself with public opera houses in Leghorn and Florence; he had a keen taste for music, and treated the singers in his employ with royal affability – bland enough, but none the less reproved by his bigoted father the Grand-Duke, who urged him not to make himself cheap.[37]

Singers advertised as dependent on these two princes and on the Dukes of Mantua and Parma appeared between 1684 and 1710 along a 'ducal circuit' in all the towns just named, as well as in Venice and other major Italian cities; some of them also took engagements in Vienna and other German capitals. They included stars like Grossi (Siface) and Salicola, as well as others only slightly less well known. This was not the first time that something like an opera troupe had gone round parts of Italy. For a few crucial years (1644–53) a loose group of mainly Roman singers who called themselves Febiarmonici took the new Venetian opera to Naples, Milan, and other Italian towns, so helping to establish it as the national style; but they did not hold together for long. The 'ducal circuit', on the other hand, opened a run of seasons all over Italy that grew almost without interruption for the next couple of centuries.[38] The circuit proper fell away with the illness and death of the Grand Prince Ferdinand and the troubles of the War of Spanish Succession. But by this time – the first two decades of the eighteenth century – other changes were under way that made protectors more decorative and less inescapable. They were only half-masked by a continuing use of the language of flattery and submission.

First, singers were now generally identified as such rather than as undifferentiated musicians or – except in some laggard German courts – as embroideresses, head gardeners, or stewards. The singer who accompanied herself on lyre or harp – essentially a chamber musician – was now a figure of the past, though the composer who could sing and teach singing, as a rule in private, remained the Italian norm down to Rossini and Donizetti.

Secondly, leading singers' names now appeared as a rule in the libretto that served as programme – a new departure that brought out their contribution to the success of an opera.

Thirdly, the multiplication of theatres and seasons – along the 'ducal circuit' and elsewhere – made it easier to move about, even for singers who belonged to a princely establishment. A singing teacher recommending a girl pupil in 1683 asked for help in placing her either with the Duke of Modena 'or elsewhere, as for instance in Venice, or with some other prince', implying a fairly wide range of choice; the Duke's own agents in the last years of the century were giving news of potential recruits from Venice, Vienna, and Rome, while some of his singers were themselves working away from base for the carnival season. The impression is, not as yet of a market, but of a semi-controlled network.[39]

Finally, rulers' ability to employ and control 'their' singers was severely affected in these years by wars – those of the League of Augsburg (1688–97) and Spanish Succession (1701–14), which brought Habsburg and Bourbon armies into Italy. Most of the North Italian states were invaded or overrun; the Duke of Modena had to flee his state from 1702 to 1707; in the latter year the Gonzaga dynasty at Mantua was overthrown. In emergencies the rulers were too busy or financially too hard pressed to keep up their musical establishments: they would either fail to pay them for years on end, or set them free to make a living where they could. Some rulers – those of Mantua in particular, later followed by those of Modena and Parma – began to issue patents ostensibly taking into service as 'their' singers men and women who never came onto the payroll: this seems to have been a straight swap of prestige advertising for the patron against high-sounding protection for the artist. Rulers, however beleaguered, still wanted to be treated as patrons, but although singers kept up the old obsequious language they felt freer in practice to do what suited them.

This may be seen by following the careers of a number of singers. Diana Aureli and her husband or lover the impresario Averara, an ex-abbé, were allowed by the Duke of Savoy to seek engagements elsewhere when war overtook him in 1690. They first went to a string of Italian towns, then negotiated with several German states in turn. When Bavaria could not have them because of the war the Duke ordered Diana to come back for an oratorio; they put off returning to Turin on various pretexts and instead skipped to Berlin and then Hanover. The Duke, though angered at first, tried to use Diana as leverage to get military help from the German states; he eventually granted her leave and extended it. She and Averara for their part seem to have followed a policy of not alienating the Duke altogether: they professed total obedience, but in practice went where they chose, negotiated through Savoyard nobles and representatives for a high salary on their return, and meanwhile made all the money they could – understandably, since the Duke was paying Diana little or nothing. It worked: Diana stayed on the nominal payroll from 1697 to 1710, still able to call herself the Duke's *virtuosa* while singing at most times away from Turin.[40]

A similar title issued by the Duke of Mantua in 1688 was helpful to Maria Maddalena Musi, not because it theoretically brought in a (lowish) salary but because the ducal patent was a kind of passport; she could also use the Duke in practice as her agent. In the following two years, though she invariably asked for his 'benign permission' and thanked him profusely for his goodness to her 'worthless self', she ran her own negotiations; the Duke either underwrote her choice or did something positive to help her, for instance by keeping the Grimani theatre in Venice in play until she was able to settle with the rival Vendramin theatre. In later years he seems to have put his foot down only once, when she tried to use his authority to break one contract and enter into another; she still hoped to enlist his influence (under the guise of asking his advice) to make sure that she was paid for singing in Milan, something she had grounds for being anxious about.[41]

This Duke of Mantua – last of his line – treated several other well-known singers in this way, not as actual dependants but as artists who ran their own careers while ostensibly getting his consent, and who meanwhile wore his title like a pair of sandwich boards. Women – for instance Margherita Salicola and Barbara Riccioni – were prominent among them, perhaps because they could as yet work only as chamber or opera singers and such music-making was particularly affected by the wars: their chance of actual court appointments was, just then, slim.[42]

At Modena the issuing of patents to singers who were never on the strength can be documented from 1721, the year when the Duke cut down his actual musical establishment.[43] But through the previous thirty years Modena's patronage had been gingerly and ambiguous.

On the one hand leading court singers – Grossi (Siface) in 1686 and the prima donna Ottavia Monteneri in 1689 – were told politely that they must sing in the Modena town theatre run by a noble impresario because the Duke regarded this as equivalent to his own service; Monteneri's husband was left at liberty to negotiate a fee with the impresario – a nominal freedom when there was no alternative, hence no leverage other than Monteneri's standing with the Duke. Yet two other court singers had their preferences consulted when outside engagements were arranged; one of them, Marc'Antonio Origoni, may have been allowed to dispose of carnival seasons as he wished.[44] A final contrast: in 1713 the leading soprano Diamante Scarabelli, then in the Modena service, was forbidden by the Duke to sing anywhere because she had broken an engagement to sing at Genoa; the authorities in Milan, where she was engaged for carnival 1714, assumed that she would not be coming and took on someone else, but she arranged to sing in Rome for the Queen of Poland instead. Between 1695 and 1718 Scarabelli was nominally a dependant of the Duke of Mantua, the Viceroy of Naples, and the Duke of Modena in turn, but in fact she sang mainly in the public theatres of Venice and Bologna and of other North Italian towns. Her dependence seems to have been largely ornamental.[45]

By the 1710s, with the old 'ducal circuit' broken up, fewer singers styled themselves *virtuosi* of this ruler and that. The practice itself was obviously growing more decorative and less meaningful, until in 1732 a comic opera libretto could parody it by describing various singers as 'chamber *virtuoso* to HM the Queen of Japan amid the imaginary spaces . . . *musica*, unbeknown to her, in the service of the Grand Mogul . . . accidentally in the service of a master she hasn't yet found'.[46] It dwindled gradually down to the 1780s; for women singers in particular it meant emancipation.

This is not to say that patrons vanished. Nobles went on recommending singers for opera engagements; they went on asking each other to persuade this or that singer to enter into or fulfil a contract. Rulers did much the same, as they were to go on doing well into the nineteenth century. Singers now and then tried to enlist a ruler's help in their contractual dealings with impresarios, as when the ageing tenor Francesco Guicciardi, a long-standing dependant of the Duke of Modena, wished the Duke's secretary to intervene and tell those who had had the bad taste to prefer another tenor that 'that is not how princes' servants are to be treated'.[47] But where patrons directed an opera singer's career they now did it almost wholly through influence and persuasion.

There were several reasons for this besides the disruption brought about in court establishments by the wars. First, opera by 1700–20 was established as the regular and foremost entertainment of many towns of Northern and Central Italy, and of many courts throughout Central Europe and the Iberian peninsula, as well as in London. Engagements multiplied: the better the singer the less she need depend on an established post. By the 1750s even a good debutant singer could afford to ignore the chance of a place in a church choir: of one such young man, a correspondent of the great musicologist Padre Martini wished he could be reported as 'following the ecclesiastical path', but in fact he had just sung in opera at Turin and Piacenza 'with fair success, so his father has it in mind . . . to set him to a theatrical career'. Even those who did take church posts were impelled by economic necessity or professional pride to ask repeatedly for leave to sing in opera; if it was not granted they were apt to resign.[48]

Artists themselves still had a use for patrons. Unknown young singers needed to be introduced, a process taken to its extreme by a well-known singing teacher on behalf of his pupil: 'Madama Sarò [Sarraut?] . . . has recommended him to the Abbé Turchi, who is on very good terms with the Duchess of Atri, to whom Maestro Piccinni greatly defers.'[49] A nobleman could still try to push a young woman singer with whom he was having an affair, though this could be counter-productive if the singer was mediocre: in such circumstances a comic opera, later successful, was booed off the stage in the Venice carnival of 1768.[50] Leading singers enjoyed flattering attentions from governors and ambassadors, such as having them stand godparents to their children or being lent a carriage for the afternoon promenade,[51] but this was a salon patronage, not unknown today and of limited significance.

The kind of dependence which in the mid seventeenth century had marked the relation of a Marc'Antonio Pasqualini to the Barberini family, of a Cavagnino to the Duke of Savoy, and of many other singers to other patrons, was no longer to be found by about 1730–40, at any rate in Italy and among successful singers. This was shown by the contrasting treatment given two leading castrati. In 1721–3 Giovanni Ossi, a dependant of the princely Borghese family, by way of fee for singing at two Rome theatres was given a claim on the rents that the Borghese owed for their theatre boxes. In 1737 the impresario of the new Teatro San Carlo, Naples, refused to pay Giovanni Carestini until two great nobles, both his declared 'protectors', paid the arrears on their boxes – implying that Carestini was, in the old way, an extension of his patrons' personality. This time the King at once ordered Carestini to be paid – though he also told the nobles to pay their arrears.[52]

A second main cause of change was that the spread of public theatres, and the coming of regular opera seasons in many other towns besides Venice, affected patrons themselves. There was less need for expensive semi-private productions in a ruler's or nobleman's palace: the great man could still oversee what went on in the public theatre, as owner, boxholder, or member of the official supervisory board; he could use this position to confirm his social status, while leaving the impresario to act as a financial and social buffer. This implied some willingness to let contractual relationships override ties of protection and dependence.

The shift was gradual over a long period and not always consistent, but its beginnings can be observed in the attitude of successive viceroys of Naples.

In 1700 Maria Maddalena Musi was singing at Naples, with a contract for three operas, when the season was interrupted by the death of the King of Spain. The Viceroy asked her in December to stay on till the summer, when opera would resume; she would do so only if she was paid her full fee for the cancelled season plus a retainer. At this the Viceroy was furious; he paid Musi a third of her fee and ordered her to leave Naples within four hours; she took refuge with a great noblewoman, who successfully interceded to have her allowed more time.[53] We see here a mixture of contractual dispute (itself caused by the vague wording of contracts, which did not as yet provide for such contingencies) and of the ruler's exercise of arbitrary power, tempered by the influence of another patron.

In 1729, at the end of a season marked by rivalry between two great castrati, Antonio Bernacchi and the much younger Carestini, another Viceroy asked Bernacchi to stay on for one more year: he agreed to do so if a woman singer who was his pupil also stayed on and if Carestini was not re-engaged. The Viceroy was willing, but a pro-Carestini party objected; the Viceroy washed his hands of the business and left it all to the impresario; Bernacchi told the impresario 'he was a man to be sought after; he was not the man to put himself forward; he had no wish to stay in a country where he was unwelcome'; he tore up the draft contracts and left Naples.[54] Here ruler and patrons express partisanship, but the singer is free to contract an engagement or not, as the mood takes him.

Naples was the slowest of the Italian governments to accept the shift from status to contract in the making and breaking of singers' engagements and the settlement of financial questions. Just before the Napoleonic take-over it was still forbidding all benefit nights for singers and then allowing individual exceptions; this was deliberate policy, so that artists could be seen to depend on the king's will.[55] All the same, there had been a shift: opera singers' terms of employment were by then contractual, even at Naples; the fuss about benefits was a rearguard action.

Italian rulers (or officials on their behalf) through the eighteenth century and right down to the 1850s went on using arbitrary power to discipline singers and other theatre personnel if they had misbehaved. This meant, typically, sending artists to gaol or putting them under house arrest for a few days if they had refused to sing on grounds judged to be unreasonable; sometimes it meant bringing them to the theatre under guard to perform. But there was a strong ritual element to these measures: they were meant to show who was boss.

The usual practice was for singers under arrest to be released, the more important ones as soon as they had performed, the minor ones on their expressing contrition, as a rule within twenty-four hours or so. In a 'bad' case – at the end of a difficult Parma season in 1816 the tenor Alberico Curioni whistled back at the hostile audience – the singer was confined to the fortress for eight days and then expelled from the duchy. Even in Naples, however, the arbitrary methods preferred by government officials went together with some respect for civil law: a prima donna whose salary had been withheld by the management could simultaneously be made to sing by the threat of arrest and allowed to take the original dispute to court – where she won.[56]

In some late eighteenth-century Central European courts, however, the old-fashioned notion of artists as mere servants lingered on. No Italian ruler of the 1770s could have behaved like Frederick the Great of Prussia, who tried to prevent the soprano Gertrud Elisabeth Mara from ever leaving Berlin, still less like Prince Nicolaus Esterhazy – virtual ruler of his Hungarian estates – who gave an Italian tenor fifty lashes for drunken misconduct on stage.[57] The reason was not that Italian rulers were kinder but that opera in Italy was much more developed: it allowed singers a wide field of employment; if they were given too much trouble they could go elsewhere.

Committing oneself indefinitely to a patron still brought security of a kind – always dependent on the patron's financial solvency and open to the chance that his heir might be uninterested in music. But it was one thing to spend a lifetime on the books of the Naples royal chapel, as the leading castrati Caffarelli and Giuseppe Aprile did (with a steady income, artistic as well as financial insurance against old age, and meanwhile plenty of leave to sing in opera elsewhere); it was quite another thing virtually to exile oneself to a remote Hungarian plain where there was no alternative to the patron's will: few other than very minor Italian singers stayed at Eszterháza for more than a year or two.[58]

There had, however, been a change of manners among the Italian upper classes. If not kinder, they had grown more urbane. The great librettist Metastasio in old age asked his brother if he really thought their grandparents – men and women of the mid seventeenth century – had been better off, living as they did in 'times when jealousy, revenge, violence, treachery, enforced by poison, snares, and hired killers, were the highest virtues of men of high rank'.[59] He was pointing to a Europe-wide gentling, particularly marked in Italy. He himself had done most to instil into Italian opera ideals of civility and grace; he had started his work at the end of the period 1700–20, when not only was singers' dependence on patrons waning but opera itself was moving away from the direct representation of court life (both in its serious and its comic aspects) and splitting into two branches, one devoted to abstract emotions known as 'affects', the other to the comedy of ordinary life.[60] As opera shed its function of mirroring court life, so singers need no longer pretend to be courtiers. Membership of a profession was now enough to bring, if they were successful, wealth, fame, and – with prudent management – status for themselves or their descendants.

1 Marianna Benti Bulgarelli, Metastasio's friend, for whom he wrote the part of Dido. By Pierleone Ghezzi (Biblioteca Apostolica Vaticana Ottob. Lat. 3116 f. 144)

2 Gioseppino, a young castrato, son of a Rome midwife. By Pierleone Ghezzi
(Biblioteca Apostolica Vaticana Ottob. Lat. 3117 f. 160)

3 The castrato Valeriano Pellegrini, by Pierleone Ghezzi (Biblioteca Apostolica
Vaticana Ottob. Lat. 3116 f. 162)

4 Paolo Boi, a Neapolitan who specialized in teaching professional women singers. By Pierleone Ghezzi (Biblioteca Apostolica Vaticana Ottob. Lat. 3115 f. 137)

5 Anfronio (real name Mozzi), a comic bass who sang at the Teatro Capranica, Rome (1722), at the age of eighty. By Pierleone Ghezzi (Biblioteca Apostolica Vaticana Ottob. Lat. 3114 f. 121)

6 Punning caricature of the baritone Antonio Tamburini (Tambour-i-nid), by
Dantan. (Collezione Piancastelli 638.82, Biblioteca Comunale, Forlì)

7 The prima donna Maria Giustina Turcotti (flourished *c.* 1730–40). Caricature by Antonio Zanetti (Fondazione G. Cini, Venice, Istituto di Storia dell'Arte)

2

CASTRATI

For a century or more, castrated male singers dominated Italian opera. This well-known fact has long been an embarrassment.[1]

That people should have castrated substantial numbers of boys, not in antiquity or in another continent but in early modern times and at the heart of Western Christendom, arouses fear, distaste, sometimes a prurient interest. That at least is how most onlookers have reacted since the mid eighteenth century, both in Italy and outside. Comments have been jocular or hostile, concerned with the eccentric and the grotesque. Jokes have kept the castrati safely on the margin of everyday life. Awareness of our own feelings should help us to see that, on the contrary, they were for many years accepted at the heart of social life in the courts and towns of Italy, and played some part in that of areas under Italian cultural influence, particularly southern Germany and the Iberian peninsula.

About the castrati there is much we do not and cannot know. We cannot hear their voices; the few recordings made in the infancy of the gramophone only hint at a sound now lost. We cannot interrogate them; this is true of many people studied by historians, but even when there were still castrati living, scholars were too embarrassed to ask them searching questions.[2] We do not really know how they were operated on or what the operation did to human characteristics other than the voice. Nor do we always know who were or were not castrati; so we can make only a rough estimate of how many there were at any time.

Such knowledge as we have is largely back to front: it comes from the late eighteenth century, when castrati were on the way out. Much of it comes from a few sources like the musicologist Charles Burney, who visited Italy in 1770. He and other travellers reported Italians as deeply ashamed of the practice; they built up a myth according to which Naples was the centre of opera, with its orphanages (*conservatorii*) the chief source of musical education, and its surrounding Kingdom of Naples the main provider of castrati, whom they saw as in the first place opera singers: castrati singing in church choirs Burney dismissed as 'the refuse of the opera houses'.[3] Yet if one thing is clear about castrati it is that most of them were church singers, who might or might not sing from time to time in opera.

Nor do we know much about the physiology and psychology of castrati. Some things are clear. Males castrated before puberty had high voices, lacked secondary sexual characteristics such as facial and body hair and early baldness, and were more likely than ordinary males to grow to an unusual height. Some – not all or even most – attained an unusual vocal power, range, and length of breath, because an enlarged thoracic cavity combined with an undeveloped larynx allowed a mighty rush of air to play upon small vocal chords. The resulting tone, in the best singers, was felt as extraordinary, at once powerful and brilliant; it did not sound like what we hear from most counter-tenors. At the extreme, Farinelli united this power and brilliance with highly-trained flexibility and a range said to be above three octaves (from C to D in altissimo): no wonder a woman in a London audience exclaimed – the story is apt though perhaps untrue – 'One God, one Farinelli!'[4]

Other characteristics are as unclear now as they were in Burney's day. Writers of the time were content to repeat a farrago of notions drawn from ancient authors such as Hippocrates: castration cured or prevented gout, elephantiasis, leprosy, and hernia; castrati tended to have weak eyes and a weak pulse, lacked fortitude and strength of mind, and had difficulty in pronouncing the letter R.[5] Burney, from personal knowledge, denied that castrati were cowards or lazy, but could not supply a full alternative account.[6] Males castrated before puberty clearly cannot father children; but the question was often raised: can they none the less experience the sexual drive and engage in sexual intercourse? The only 'authority' available then or now on the practice of castration is outstandingly muddled: its implied answer is at one point 'yes', at another 'no'.[7] The answer 'yes' was current in the ancient world and in early modern Europe; twentieth-century medical opinion, for what it is worth, tends to say 'no'.[8]

It seems best, then, to forget the clichés that litter books on opera, and look at the whole phenomenon of castrati afresh.

The rise of opera coincided with but in no obvious way caused that of the castrati. If anything, the taste for the castrato voice antedated opera. Nor did it at once dominate the new form. A castrato sang the prologue and two female parts in Monteverdi's *L'Orfeo* at Mantua in 1607,[9] but the lead part was sung by a tenor. Of Monteverdi's two other surviving operas, *Il ritorno d'Ulisse in patria* (1640) uses normal male voices, but *L'incoronazione di*

Poppea (1642) allots the two male leads to castrati. Vocal casting then and for another 200 years was determined by which singers were available: castrati, it seems, were not yet always at hand or perhaps always wanted.

There seems to be no evidence of castrato singers in Western Europe before the 1550s. Some of the earliest came from Spain, perhaps because of previous Moorish rule there. One entered the Papal (Sistine) Chapel choir in 1562, though he and others were not formally described as castrati until 1599. At St Peter's the Pope officially authorized the recruitment of castrati in 1589.[10]

By the early seventeenth century there were castrati employed all over Italy as the court singers of ruling princes, in chamber or chapel or both. They also flourished in Germany – first in southern capitals (Munich, Stuttgart, Vienna), then, by mid-century, in Dresden. So far as we can tell they were all Italians or at any rate had been castrated and trained in Italy, except for some in Germany who were locally produced and who seem to have been employed only in their ruler's chapel; Spaniards faded out. From then on castration for artistic purposes remained a practice known to be carried on almost exclusively in Italy and associated with Italian music. It had spread quickly. Why?

The explanation has to be looked for in church. Women were forbidden (in line with St Paul's teaching) to utter there. This was a necessary but not a sufficient cause, since boys and falsettists (male altos) could sing the higher parts. Contemporary comments show that people became dissatisfied with choirboys because they were no sooner trained than lost, with falsettists because their sound came to seem weak and reedy; the castrato voice in contrast was described as 'natural' and 'genuine' (*sincera*) – terms obviously applied to the quality of sound rather than to the means that produced it.[11]

People were besotted with the high, in particular the soprano, voice: its special value called for the exotic powers of castrati. This value may have lain in an association with youth: in opera, castrati were to sing the parts of young heroes. It may also have had to do with superiority. 'Soprano' means 'higher', a notion not taken lightly by a society that was at once hierarchical-minded and used to displaying hierarchical order in forms perceived by the senses. A composer in charge of a church choir, writing when the system had been going for a long time, assumed that higher voices took precedence of lower – and that a 'natural' alto (a castrato) must as a rule take precedence of a falsettist.[12] This superiority found practical expression in the new public opera houses: the fees paid to high voices in leading parts (castrati and women) were almost invariably higher than those paid to tenors and especially to basses. In church choirs the matter was complicated by seniority, but there too the high voices (castrati and tenors) were generally paid better than basses, the commonest male voices.[13]

We still need to explain why a preference, even a craze, for high voices should have led ordinary people to undertake (and people in authority to condone) so drastic a step as castration. One possible answer is that the cultivation of the solo voice in the new genres of the early seventeenth century – opera, cantata, and oratorio – required a new professionalism uncalled for in the age of polyphonic music that had gone before; and that the castrati – thanks to unbroken study from childhood, less hampered by social custom than the education of girls – were best able to meet this new demand.[14] This is of some help. Yet we still need to ask: was the step taken as drastic as we think?

We have noted the severe economic crisis that struck Italy about 1620. The city of Venice apparently managed to keep much of its industry going in spite of increasing rigidity and lack of competitiveness. In many other places, however, deindustrialization – followed by war and by the two great plagues of 1630 and 1656 – confirmed the upper classes in their retreat into landholding as their main source of income; sometimes the retreat was accompanied by a new imposition of feudal tenures or by a strengthening of entails to safeguard the line of descent. With it went an increase in the numbers of monks and nuns, probably most marked in the period 1580–1650: by the 1670s they seem to have accounted for some 5 per cent of the population in Florence and Catania, for about 9, 10 or 11 per cent in decayed Central Italian towns such as Siena, Pistoia, and Prato; in more populous cities – Venice, Rome, Naples – the proportion was lower but absolute numbers higher, with monks alone numbering well over 3,000 in Rome, 4,000 in Naples.

For rich families, getting a son or a daughter into a monastic order cost less than setting up the son in an official career or than marrying off the daughter; in a lean time it could bring privileges such as tax concessions. For many middling or poor people a child who became a monk or a nun held out the hope of security in troubled times, not just for the individual but for the family. Such decisions about a child's future were a matter of family strategy. Material explanations of this kind need imply no denial of the intense religious feeling common in baroque Italy – itself stirred by the sense of danger and decline. These conditions broadly held through the whole of the seventeenth and the first half of the eighteenth century.[15]

Monks, according to a late eighteenth-century German writer, were 'so to speak, castrati who had not been operated upon'.[16] They were celibates, not always of their own choice. A castrato could be thought of as an enforced celibate with an unusual chance of securing for his family an income, perhaps a fortune. There were castrato monks who sang in or directed church choirs: one took part – though only after Mazarin had spent six years using diplomatic pressure on the Pope – in the Paris performance of Cavalli's opera *Ercole amante* (1660), singing the part of a woman disguised as a man.[17] Some other castrati became monks late in life; many more became priests. But no vows were needed for the castrato's 'vocation' to have something in common with that of the monk.

We need to stand as far as we can away from modern assumptions. Central to these is the right of human beings to sexual fulfilment. The tradition of Christian asceticism began to decline even in Southern Europe from the mid eighteenth century; it is nearly lost. But around 1600 it was still strong. Renunciation of sexual life could seem not just possible but ideal. Sexuality could anyhow be a burden when (as happened in at least parts of Italy) celibacy was on the increase between 1600 and 1750 owing to economic hardship and the efforts of families to safeguard property,[18] while the vigilance of those same families probably did much to prevent sexual relations outside marriage. Celibacy was a means to birth control. According to a foreign observer in eighteenth-century Naples, the practice of castration 'attracts no notice in a country where the population is huge in relation to the amount of work available'.[19] To become a castrato – still more, to make your son become one – need not in these conditions seem a total misfortune.

Nor was it a step condemned by the Church. Theologians held that we are caretakers, not owners, of our bodies. Most thought castration licit only to save life, on medical advice and with the boy's consent. A minority, however, held that on a balance of advantage castration for artistic purposes could be licit if the benefit to the community (to the effectiveness of church services or the supposed needs of rulers) outweighed the damage to the individual. Among Italian theologians it was discussed until about 1750 as a matter finely balanced between 'probable' and 'more probable' opinions, and even when opposition began to build up Pope Benedict XIV advised (1748) against a proposal that castration should be forbidden by all bishops – essentially on prudential grounds: it was better to avoid disturbance and work for a compromise that would bring about gradual change.[20]

The operation itself may have been relatively mild and safe. We know little about it. According to the dubious source already mentioned, the testicles might be removed, or they might be caused to wither through pressure, maceration, or the cutting of the spermatic cord; none of these methods amounted to the horrific 'total castration' (removal of the penis as well as of the testicles) said to have been inflicted mainly in Africa on slaves intended for Turkish and Persian harems, and to have killed most of them. An account of the cost of castrating a Modenese boy, drawn up – probably in the 1670s or 1680s – by an experienced person, assumed 'about thirteen days' as the time needed for the operation and the period of convalescence.[21] This does not suggest a very grave wound. People gossiped about operations that had supposedly failed to castrate a boy fully. One such is documented: the boy had been 'castrated on one side only', so that as he turned fourteen his voice broke.[22] We do not hear of deaths caused by castration. They may have occurred, and may have gone unreported in times when early death, and death through medical error, were common. But the impression one gets is that the operation was a routine one.

This impression is strengthened by the wording of apprenticeship contracts between boys' families and teachers, of boys' own applications for financial help in having themselves castrated, and of comments on them in government archives. In the seventeenth and early eighteenth centuries, there was little attempt at euphemism or concealment; some persons in authority had no compunction about approving or even paying for castrations.

Many contracts survive that bind young Italians to a singing teacher as, in effect, apprentices; the system will be examined in chapter 5. Some of these notarial contracts (public documents, to be deposited in an official archive) openly set as a condition that the boy should be castrated.

The parents and uncle of Paolo Nannini, of Viterbo, in 1671 undertook to have him castrated within a few weeks at the teacher's expense, so that he 'may learn music and keep his voice'.[23] A contract of 1697 effectively sold an eight-year-old Apulian boy to Nicola Tricarico (a well-known contralto singer of comic parts) who was to have him taught by his brother, a canon and cantor of Gallipoli Cathedral; the boy's father, it explained, had 'resolved, for the greater benefit of [himself], of his family, and of [his son] to have him perfectly taught the profession or art of ornate singing, and in due time to have him castrated', but he lacked the necessary means: the decision to have the boy operated on was left to the Tricarico brothers to make sometime in the coming six years, clearly depending on the promise he showed in the meantime.[24] A much later contract of 1773 provided that the teacher would pay for the castration of Domenico Bruni, son of an Umbrian building worker; Domenico became one of the last famous castrato opera singers. The teacher, incidentally, was musical director to the religious confraternity of which the boy's father was a member, so this was almost a family affair.[25] A slightly different type of contract, an eighteenth-century one providing for a boy to be taught and boarded at the school attached to the basilica of San Francesco in Assisi, stated that if the boy was to be castrated the father should pay.[26]

In yet another type of contractual arrangement, the ten-year-old Gaetano Majorano's grandmother gave him in 1720 the income from two vineyards so that he could study grammar and especially music, 'to which he is said to have a great inclination, desiring to have himself castrated and become a eunuch'; the boy was to become famous under the name Caffarelli. A little later, the retired castrato Filippo Balatri named, in a poetic 'will', the surgeon who had operated on him as a boy; he did so in a spirit of burlesque rather than denunciation.[27]

Openness and family strategy were combined in the fortunes of the Melani family of Pistoia. Domenico Melani was appointed bellringer of Pistoia Cathedral in 1624, when the eldest of his seven sons was one year old; he kept the job for the remaining twenty-five years of his life. Of the seven sons – all born within fifteen years of his appointment – at least three were castrated and became singers; three more became composers or singers and there is some question whether one of them may not have been a castrato too. Only the fourth son's marriage produced children and perpetuated the family; this son inherited the bellringer's post. Several of the musician sons had distinguished careers; some engaged in international diplomacy, and the next generation climbed into the Tuscan nobility. There were also two Melani cousins, born about the same time as the seven brothers, who became castrato singers. It is inconceivable that the cathedral authorities in Pistoia did not realize what their bellringer's family was up to.[28]

Of another church establishment, the music school attached to the collegiate church of Santa Maria Maggiore, Bergamo, we know that in 1650 it paid a substantial sum to have one of its choirboys castrated; the surgeon was one of its own string players and the payment was authorized by the governing council of the important charity that was responsible for the school.[29]

After all this it is not surprising to find an orphaned Roman boy in 1613 reported as having voiced 'a great desire to have himself castrated' so that he could serve the Duke of Mantua. Another Rome agent in 1661 told the then Duke of a promising boy of thirteen, not yet castrated – but 'that can be done'.[30]

Later in the century, at least two boys petitioned the Duke of Modena for financial help in getting themselves castrated; one got it, the other probably got it, and an account detailing the costs of castration (for which boy is unclear) gives the fee for the operation as five doubloons 'in conformity with what was done on other occasions by order of His Most Serene Highness'.

Both boys stated that they were afraid of losing the quality of their voice if it was allowed to break; both pleaded poverty. Silvestro Prittoni asked discreetly 'to be made to be without those instruments' that 'might' cause his voice to break. Rinaldo Gherardini stated his resolve 'to have himself castrated through Your Highness's goodwill, so as to make progress in [the singing] profession and give much better service both to Our Lord and to Your Highness'; he also wished to become a priest, and implied that this was suitable in terms of family strategy by pointing out that he had two married brothers. When the Duke authorized payment of four doubloons to Silvestro 'for the aforementioned purpose' the only precaution used was to state in the order to the treasurer that it was issued 'for reasons known to us'. Rinaldo spent his life in princely service; Silvestro appeared in opera in Venice at least once, singing a small part.[31]

This kind of frankness became less acceptable in the course of the eighteenth century. More castrations were explained as having been necessitated at an early age by illness or by an unspecified 'need'. A favourite cause was the bite of a wild swan or a wild pig. According to a well-known satire of 1720, the hangers on of a castrato opera singer would explain away his condition with one or other of these tales, and in 1784 the Franciscan biographer of Farinelli sent round a questionnaire virtually asking to have his subject's voice explained in the same way; the cause he was supplied with was a fall from a horse. By the mid nineteenth century the surviving castrati of the Sistine Chapel had apparently all fallen victim to pigs.[32]

Yet even in a more shamefaced age boys could still allege that they had consented to, even begged for castration. The eleven-year-old Angelo Villa did so in 1783, and – even in a Lombardy where 'enlightened' reform was at its peak – succeeded in having his teacher and adoptive father Pietro Testori let off five years' hard labour; Angelo went on to make a fair career in opera under the name Testori.[33] We need not take the boys' petitions at face value. But they – and their acceptance by rulers – show that for many years castration was almost a routine matter, calling at best for perfunctory concealment.

What sort of people allowed their sons to be castrated? We do not know. Most of the boys operated on – it is reasonable to suppose – came of modest but not necessarily poverty-stricken families. Farinelli's parents were said to be of noble descent, but impoverished; his father was a minor government official. Other castrati were the sons of tradesmen, of a shoemaker, of a midwife, of an immigrant German timpani player, of a wandering valet-cum-fencing and dancing master.[34] Yet others, as we have noted, were the sons or grandsons of winegrowers or building workers. These few known examples probably define the range of social origin among the very many we do not know about.

They came from all over Italy. The Kingdom of Naples as the main source of castrati is a legend – the result of overconcentration on the Naples conservatories, where indeed most pupils came from the hinterland. Recent research has shown that castrati were trained in many other institutions, typically orphanages or choir schools attached to important churches, monasteries, or seminaries; many studied privately with individual teachers.[35]

How many castrati were there at any one time? We cannot tell with any precision: all the statistics we have raise insoluble problems. What we can do is to use such figures as there are (for Rome) to work out some notion both of castrati numbers in particular areas and of changes over time.

On a conservative estimate, some 100 or so castrati were probably living in Rome in 1694, nearly all of them primarily church singers, of whom eighty or ninety were active; in Rome choirs high voices outnumbered low in a ratio of about four to three. Half a century later, in 1746, the ratio was significantly reversed: higher voices were already harder to find, total numbers had fallen, and, within the total, the number of castrati had fallen faster than that of normal male voices. Allowing for a greater number of opera singers by this date without a church connection, we may guess that there were then living in Rome some fifty or sixty castrati – at best, two-thirds or so of the 1694 total. Nor should we take the 1694 numbers to represent a peak: some Rome choirs were already in decline in the latter half of the seventeenth century. We might therefore guess at a total (and probably an historical maximum) of 120 or so castrati in the Rome of about 1650.[36]

Rome was not necessarily typical. Fragmentary evidence from Bologna suggests that castrato numbers there may have peaked rather later, sometime between 1670 and 1720.[37] What is beyond doubt in Bologna as well as Rome is that castrati declined, both in absolute numbers and as a proportion of all singers, from about 1740; there remains a possibility, even a strong likelihood, that the decline had set in earlier.

Besides Rome and Bologna, important centres for the employment of castrati were the great pilgrimage churches at Padua, Loreto, and Assisi; capital cities with both court and religious establishments (Turin, Milan, Parma, Modena, Florence, Naples); many religious institutions up and down the peninsula; and Venice with its public opera houses. There were, besides, court establishments in many seventeenth-century European states (even in England, where the castrati in Queen Catherine of Braganza's chapel disappointed Pepys),[38] later followed by opera houses.

All that can be said is that at any time between about 1630 and 1750 there must have been living several hundred castrati, nearly all Italians, with a marked decline setting in about 1740–50. In Naples, Rome, Bologna, and Venice (all but the first with less than 160,000 population in the seventeenth and eighteenth centuries) and in some smaller towns (Padua, Assisi, Loreto) there were groups of castrati large and stable enough to be a feature of everyday life.

The career pattern of castrati changed over time, but slowly. Castration, actual or in prospect, implied a total commitment to the singing profession: as an eleven-year-old applicant to one of the Naples conservatories put it, 'since he is a eunuch, music . . . is the only profession to which he wishes to apply himself'.[39]

So as to concentrate on his training, the pupil generally boarded with a teacher or an institution. Castrati had, in comparison with other male singers, an early start and a period of training uninterrupted by puberty – though whether this allowed them a longer career as fully fledged professionals is unclear; the advantage lay in the chance of steadily developing musical knowledge and vocal agility. Another advantage was the favourable treatment they got in religious institutions such as the Naples conservatories, originally orphanages, and other schools up and down the peninsula. Because they were deemed essential to the church functions on which the schools relied for part of their income, they were relatively cosseted and were sometimes admitted to free places even though not orphans, or else had their admission fees reduced.[40]

Whether in an institution or not, these boys were being trained for careers as, in the first place, church singers. The church work they were destined for was in part liturgical routine, but also oratorio, which in some towns until about 1750 was 'the most accessible and pervasive genre of dramatic music' on offer.[41] From then on, opera engagements multiplied and opera became more feasible as a chief occupation for some; Rome and most of the Papal States, where women were forbidden to appear on stage down to 1798, supplied engagements for young castrati to sing women's parts.

How the change affected the outlook of castrati on the threshold of a career may be seen from the cases of Felice Altobelli and Bartolomeo Pierotti.

Altobelli in 1736 had been studying for two years in Bologna with the great musicologist Padre Martini; he ran out of money, could find no local post because there were already too many male sopranos in the city, and was sent by his teacher, with a strong recommendation, to the Franciscan school at Assisi; there he spent eight months, just enough to learn to read music in several clefs, before the offer of a theatre engagement at Verona enticed him away. Here opera looks like an overmastering diversion from a course presumably meant to lead to a church post.

Pierotti in 1755 had just finished seven years' apprenticeship to a well-known teacher and wished to go to Bologna 'to seek his fortune', but also wished 'first to be assured of a place in a chapel' there. Since Bologna was by then the chief market for opera engagements we may assume that opera was Pierotti's goal; for a singer described as having a 'middling' but 'pleasing and flexible' voice, a post in a chapel had become something to fall back on.[42]

The changing balance between church and theatre in the careers of castrati can be documented in two different ways: by looking at the patterns of some individual careers – necessarily those of the best-known – and by asking how groups of more modest singers divided their time.

Two famous early castrati based in Rome, Loreto Vittori and Marc'Antonio Pasqualini, both served full twenty-five-year terms as members of the Papal Chapel; both were composers as well as singers; both sang from time to time in opera, always given under monarchical or noble patronage and before an invited audience; both generally worked in Rome in the service of the Barberini and other papal families, occasionally abroad when one or the other was lent out to a foreign magnate. The mainspring in the career of each was Barberini patronage: if they absented themselves from the chapel, as they often did, it was as a rule because a pope or papal favourite chose to use them in an opera (or indeed to take one of them hunting, as Cardinal Antonio Barberini took Pasqualini) rather than in church. Through the influence of opera-minded popes, Urban VIII Barberini or Clement IX Rospigliosi, other well-known castrato chapel singers were given leave in the mid seventeenth century to appear in operas for some of which Rospigliosi or his nephew had provided the text; one, Giuseppe Fedi, sang a woman's part. Now and then the chapel services were suspended because of these and like absences.[43]

Such behaviour was shortly to be disapproved by more austere popes; but we should not see the careers of Vittori, Pasqualini, or Fedi as divided between religious and secular. The operas they appeared in were often on sacred subjects; their careers were integrated, first by allegiance to a patron, and secondly by the interpenetration of religion and spectacle characteristic of baroque Rome.

Some other castrati based or trained in Rome at this time followed a similar career pattern, mainly abroad. Giovanni Andrea Angelini Bontempi sang first in St Mark's, Venice, and then for some thirty years in the chapel of the Elector of Saxony, where he became for a time deputy to the great Heinrich Schütz as kapellmeister and composed three operas. Seven castrati who entered the chapel of the German Jesuit college in Rome between 1617 and 1645 found partly overlapping employment in the Imperial Court Chapel in Vienna, and, in Rome, in the Papal Chapel, in Barberini-patronized operas (some also given in Paris), and in the service of Queen Christina of Sweden, which included singing in a dramatic oratorio or near-opera. Once again opera appears as an incident, though an important one, in careers taken up largely with church music and the service of princes.[44]

In these decades, the 1640s and 1650s, opera in the Venetian style was making its way in many parts of Italy. Venetian opera meant works on non-Christian themes, often treated so as to bring out their erotic aspects, with women singers in some of the leading parts and performed in 'mercenary' conditions, that is, before a paying audience. Castrati took part in them, though some of the most highly regarded castrati objected at first to doing so, especially those who served the leading chapels and magnates of Rome and Naples. 'Every castrato singer was held to be infamous' – so a well-informed gossip explained the reluctance of three singers from the Naples royal chapel to take part in Cesti's *La Dori*, an opera of Venetian type – 'if he mixed in those companies in the public mercenary theatre'. What the three objected to seems to have been not a 'mercenary' performance (it was being given in the Viceroy's palace) but 'mixing in those companies', particularly having to deal with women singers some of whom were still courtesans, the prima donna in this 1675 *La Dori* being a notorious example.[45] A few years later, in Rome (where women on stage were in practice tolerated now and then in the semi-privacy of noble palaces), papal officials objected to the loan of a contralto from the Sistine Chapel to the Duke of Bracciano, not because he was to sing in opera but because he would appear alongside two women.[46]

This helps to explain why some famous seventeenth-century castrati never sang in a theatre. Even Matteo Sassani (Matteuccio), a royal church singer at Naples, Madrid, and Vienna from 1684 until 1711, did not appear in opera until 1697 and then only for scattered seasons.[47] At his stage debut he replaced Grossi (Siface), who had just been murdered. Grossi's career showed how a celebrated castrato could now take advantage of the network of theatres that had developed in the last third of the century. The high fees available to leading castrati began to push the balance of their activities further towards opera.

Francesco Pistocchi apologized in 1702 for having to miss Holy Week at San Petronio, Bologna, where he was due to sing, because he was obliged to stay on in Milan and sing in opera during the coming visit of Philip V of Spain, then ruler of the state: 'believe me, though staying on is extremely profitable to me, it hurts me to the very soul, but one must be patient'.[48] We need not doubt Pistocchi's sincerity, but priorities were changing. The slightly younger Nicola Grimaldi (Nicolino) began (but for a brief operatic appearance at the age of twelve, in a small part) as the leading church singer in Naples; from the age of twenty-four his triumphs in the operas of Alessandro Scarlatti set him on an international stage career that included five years in London. Yet he kept on with his church and chamber singing and concentrated on it exclusively in the last eight years of his life. When he was in Naples he would give an oratorio at his house on St Joseph's day, to celebrate the branch from the Glastonbury thorn bush (supposedly grown from the staff of St Joseph of Arimathea, who buried Christ) which he had been given in England.[49]

These two and, in the next generation, Carlo Broschi (Farinelli) and Gaetano Majorano (Caffarelli) did most to establish the legend of the castrati as virtuosos astounding above all for their performances in opera.

From about 1680 to 1700, increasing vocal specialization in the theatre brought in the reign of the castrato as leading man (*primo uomo*) with at his side a female soprano of increasingly high range. At the same time opera split into two branches, serious and comic: serious opera with its heroes drawn from ancient history or myth was recognized as the medium for the best castrato voices to work their astonishing powers. Castrati appeared now and then in comic opera, but (outside the Papal States) not as a matter of routine.

In spite of the greater chances opera now held out, some leading castrati still took trouble to keep on their regular salary from a church choir, however many leaves they took abroad (like Caffarelli, a lifelong member of the Naples royal chapel), while others' church engagements were brief and intermittent. Even in the period of decline some castrato opera stars (like some normal male singers down to the late nineteenth century) regarded a church appointment as insurance.

Gaetano Guadagni, a sixteen-year-old pupil in the choir of St Anthony's, Padua, was dismissed in 1746, soon after his appointment, because of his unauthorized absences on theatre engagements. He tried for a year to get himself reinstated, still kept up with his old teacher, and won his place back after eighteen years (during which time he had created Gluck's Orfeo); he accepted a moderate salary, and it was understood that he would still from time to time sing in opera outside Padua. After another eight years he retired to Padua for good and from then on was continuously active both in the chapel and in the musical life of the town, not just as a singer but as a composer and an artistic innovator inspired by 'enlightened', perhaps masonic ideals.[50] Somewhat later, Domenico Bruni achieved the same end while avoiding conflict with the cathedral choir of Perugia: appointed to it in

1792, when he was already famous, he did not for some years sing there but, by agreement, made over at least half his salary to a substitute; this amounted to a trade-off of a small profit for Bruni against reflected glory for the choir. He eventually sang with the choir during his comfortable retirement.[51]

The choirs themselves came under increasing pressure from theatres, at different times according to the spread of opera in their recruitment area. Venice with its six or seven public opera houses was the front line of competition. The choir of St Mark's between 1660 and 1725 – we have seen – was already losing some of its importance as a creative musical centre. Nearly forty regular members of its choir (of all voice types) sang in Venice opera seasons as well; most were singers of less than the first rank, for whom a post in the choir, combined with the chance of local theatre engagements in secondary parts, held out the prospect of a reasonable living. When first-rate castrati were appointed they went off on an extended series of leaves or else, like Pistocchi and Stefano Romano (Il Pignattino), shortly departed altogether; since visiting stars were needed for high days such as Christmas, these two came back at fees, for a single appearance, equivalent to between an eighth and a quarter of a choir member's annual salary.[52]

In Rome, the rearguard action of two popes held back public opera houses and even for a time closed them down. But by 1728–9 the Papal Chapel was recruiting three castrati all of whom had spent the previous few years singing in opera, at least some of the time in women's parts or in comic opera. Two of the three went on appearing in Rome opera houses at various times in the 1730s, but always – more respectably – in serious opera and in men's parts. This gave a paying audience – part clerical, part aristocratic, part tourist – the indulgence the Barberini had assumed for themselves and had granted certain other noble patrons by allowing chapel singers to appear in non-'mercenary' opera performances. On one occasion the Pope himself overrode objections and granted the best known of these castrati leave to appear at the Teatro Argentina 'so that the city should not lack for respectable entertainment, of a kind that generally fends off others more perilous'.[53]

Pressure of competition must have been great when the authorities at St Peter's had to threaten dismissal for any singer who absented himself without leave to sing in opera; the threat was directed particularly at sopranos and the critical time was carnival, which by then had established itself as the busiest and most fashionable season for opera in most Italian towns.[54] At mid-century, Pope Benedict XIV forbade all church singers who were clerics (including all members of the Sistine choir) to appear on stage.[55] With the spread of public theatres and secular opera librettos, a career straddling church music and opera could no longer be integrated, anyhow for those formally committed to a religious life. In baroque Rome, many activities could be held religious, because religion entered into everything; but the old baroque synthesis had broken down.

The Pope's action did not deter church singers outside Rome from putting further pressure on their employers. In the 1740s and 1750s the chapel at Loreto had to grant repeated leaves to fifteen of its singers (seven of them castrati) to sing in opera. Most of these sang in minor seasons in nearby towns such as Camerino or Fermo, with an occasional foray to Perugia or Rome (still within the Papal States); two sopranos went further afield and eventually departed to German courts. The singers who entered the Loreto chapel from about 1760 had, most of them, locally circumscribed theatre careers, though the soprano Gerolamo Bravura won but – because of the Napoleonic wars – could not take up an engagement in London; he eventually disappeared into Moravia. The practice of granting leave to sing in opera went on through the whole of the nineteenth century; the last castrato to take advantage of it, Eugenio Boccanera, sang minor parts at La Scala and Florence in 1813 and 1817 and then left for the Perugia Cathedral choir.[56]

The choir of Santa Maria Maggiore, Bergamo, sometime about 1700 began to allow its singers annual leave during a local autumn holiday so that they could perform elsewhere, whether in opera or in church functions. By 1779 it was reduced to offering any good young soprano the whole of carnival off 'and even much of Lent if he wants to work in the theatre'; the traditional autumn holiday was still available as well, up to All Saints' Day, and the soprano could have All Saints off too if he had an opera engagement 'so long as he provides the church with some weak tenor [*sic*] as a substitute'. Moreover, his salary would be continued through all his leaves.[57] Nothing could illustrate more clearly the dearth of good castrati, the spread of opera, and the decline of church music in the latter half of the eighteenth century.

Gifted castrati now found their career pattern leading them most of the time round the opera houses – but there were very few gifted castrati left. Of the dwindling numbers that still entered church choirs, many were singers of, at best, modest competence: not all of them 'the refuse of the opera houses' (some, as we have noted, still appeared in local theatres of equally modest pretensions), though others fell below the standards even of seasons at Camerino. And all this happened before the coming of the French in 1796, the temporary banning of castrati from the opera stage, and the Napoleonic dissolution of many monastic orders (and choirs) on top of those already dissolved by 'enlightened' sovereigns. The withdrawal of the ban, and Napoleon's cultivation of the great Girolamo Crescentini, could make no difference. G. B. Velluti went on until 1830 as virtually the only castrato still before the European opera public, and the only one for whom leading composers still wrote parts (Rossini in *Aureliano in Palmira*, 1813, Meyerbeer in *Il crociato in Egitto*, 1824), though in faraway Montevideo the little-known Marcello Tanni, who with his brothers and sisters had found a niche there, sang in opera for one more year after Velluti had fallen silent.[58] The few castrati operated on after 1796 could have as their destination only a small group of Rome choirs.

Even successful castrati had to reckon with the time when they would no longer be able to perform satisfactorily. Church posts were long-term appointments and offered as a rule the prospect of some kind of pension – though even here wars could stop payment for years. Castrati who worked for rulers could become in effect civil servants, like Angelini Bontempi, who in his thirty years at Dresden became an official historian; even Farinelli's position at the Spanish court (1737–59), shorn of legend, was that of a master of the revels who also sang for the King in private.[59] For a few, diplomacy was another resource: Atto Melani, son of the Pistoia bellringer, acted in various courts for his employer Cardinal Mazarin and, later, for Louis XIV; Domenico Cecchi (Il Cortona) is said to have carried out more shadowy missions for the Emperors Leopold I and Joseph I, and was eventually allowed a sinecure as pension.[60] These diplomatic tasks concerned, as much as anything, the personal relations and intrigues of sovereigns, and are not easy to tell apart from the rest of the singer's obligations as a ruler's dependant. Leading castrati were probably thought suited to them because they got about and mingled with the great, and also because, like monks, they had no children to advance.

Serving a ruler over a long period did not necessarily bring exalted position. For Farinelli in Spain it did mean the Order of Calatrava, wealth, portraits that showed him as a near-regal figure, and – at a new reign – honourable discharge followed by luxurious retirement to a villa outside Bologna. There he went to a good deal of trouble to secure privileges reserved for nobles, in particular that of having Mass said in his house; the portraits in his gallery included one pope, two emperors, one empress, five kings, two queens, two crown princes, one crown princess, and one royal prince, most of them his former patrons and all hung in his billiard room.[61]

For the little groups of castrati who performed sacred music for Louis XIV and his successors it meant something more modest. They never sang in opera, though some appeared in Paris concerts (as did starrier castrati who were passing through). Several lived together, quietly and comfortably, in a house one of them had built at Versailles about 1704; there were still castrati living there in 1748. Both among this group and, about 1780, among a later group of Versailles castrati, several left each other their modest property in their wills, after providing a small income for their one servant.[62]

This kind of quiet routine, ending in tidy testamentary dispositions, was perhaps more typical of castrati in retirement than the eccentricity and display attributed to them by legend. True, even some famous singers ran through the vast sums they had earned and, like Pasqualino in 1752, stunned everyone by dying penniless.[63] A commoner fate was that of the Cavaliere Valeriano Pellegrini (Valeriani), a Veronese who sang in the Papal Chapel, travelled Europe in the service of various rulers, lost his voice, became a priest, and died destitute in 1746, aged eighty-three, after having for some years lived on charity.[64] The teacher Pier Francesco Tosi had had a successful career in London and Germany, but by his death in 1732 that was long past; his most valuable possessions were a bed, a shotgun, and a silver watch, and his net estate amounted to little.[65]

A number of successful singers, on the other hand, lived well on estates or in large town houses which they had bought with their savings: Matteuccio, Nicolino, Francesco Bernardi (Senesino), Pistocchi, Caffarelli, and Giovanni Manzoli, as well as Farinelli and, later, Bruni and Velluti. Some (Matteuccio, Caffarelli) acquired titles; Bruni, after some initial resistance by the nobility of his home town of Fratta, was admitted to patrician rank in the town council and eventually made gonfaloniere (a post akin to mayor); his contemporary Cristoforo Arnaboldi bought former noble lands from the revolutionary government of the Cisalpine Republic, so enabling his nephew later to marry into the restored Piedmontese aristocracy.[66]

Nephews and nieces were indeed the usual beneficiaries, though Pistocchi, in a fussy will, left his considerable estate to his servant of twenty-four years, Angelo Maria Sarti, on condition that he added the name Pistocchi to his; in the nineteenth century some Sarti Pistocchi were eminent lawyers in Bologna.[67] This stipulation was a practice found here and there when a castrato had no nephews to carry on the family name; Domenico Bruni settled half his landed property on his niece, provided that not only would her husband take on the surname Bruni but all their children would be given names beginning with D.[68]

Because castrati underwent long training, sometimes including a fair literary education, some developed bookish interests which they could pursue into retirement. In the early eighteenth century the celebrated Antonio Maria Bernacchi, as well as the less prominent Gaetano Berenstadt and Andrea Adami, were all bibliophiles and dealers in books. This was still a luxury trade, addressed to a tiny public and manageable as a sideline; Berenstadt's relation to his patrons was not markedly different whether he provided singing, books, or (another line of his) antiques.[69] The leading singers Francesco Bernardi and Filippo Elisi (described as a well-bred person) corresponded with the celebrated musicologist Padre Martini and with his colleague Girolamo Chiti; Elisi helped Martini with his researches in libraries.[70]

For men of this stamp, teaching was an obvious resource, both during and especially after a singing career. It could be carried on at all levels, from the authoritative position of Bernacchi at Bologna or, later, of Crescentini at the Naples conservatory to modest small-town instruction in keyboard playing as well as singing: many castrati could double as instrumentalists. Bernacchi in retirement stood at the centre of Bologna musical life, head in effect of a small singing school who lived in each other's pockets (he liked to refer to his pupils as his 'brigade'), taken up with the internal politics of the Accademia Filarmonica, friend of Padre Martini, correspondent of Metastasio, general busybody and go-between. Crescentini's position and salary at Naples were so exceptional as to make for undying hatred between him and the director of the conservatory, the composer Niccolò Zingarelli.[71]

A more representative career combining singing, teaching, and a position at the heart of urban musical life was that of Antonio Maria Giuliani (1739–1831). He was based throughout at Modena, where he served the cathedral choir for over half a century as singer and then as director. He had previously served the Duke, in his chapel as first soprano and in his orchestra as harpsichord player, while also taking occasional opera engagements at Venice and elsewhere: on the opera market he was a minor but no doubt reliable artist, who sang as primo uomo in small towns and secondo uomo in bigger ones. Before directing the cathedral music he spent a quarter-century as chief répétiteur of the leading Modena opera house, and composed one opera for it. He also taught the harpsichord in several noble households. Through his long life he accumulated a large library of books and prints; he is said to have been highly cultivated, particularly in French literature, and much loved and respected in the town.[72]

Many castrati became priests – not in itself very significant (of other than education) in the Italy of the seventeenth and eighteenth centuries, which was full of unbeneficed clerics. To become a monk was a more decisive step, a withdrawal from the world that, as they grew older, attracted a few of these childless men. Nicolino did not become a monk but, at the end of a blameless life, had himself buried in a Franciscan habit in a specially austere service. Balatri did enter a monastery in Bavaria after learning of his brother's death. He stuck to it, but Giovanni Antonio Predieri and Pistocchi flitted in and out of the Franciscan and Oratorian orders: Predieri, a distinguished composer, singer, and teacher, was a restless, difficult person, while Pistocchi (who was said to have brought 'gaiety' into the community) may have been no more than lonely – as an Oratorian he did not take vows, and was entitled to leave.[73] A touch of melancholy recurred among some castrati: the celebrated Gasparo Pacchierotti regretted near the end of his long life not having realized earlier 'that all that once moved my weak senses was mere vanity and illusion'.[74]

What then remains of the stereotype of the castrato as opera star, colossally vain, extravagant and temperamental? It had some basis, though a slender one. The tension of singing in public – of bringing off an extraordinary performance wholly dependent on one's own powers – makes artists susceptible: in the late seventeenth and eighteenth centuries castrati were the most prominent singers, and had their share of susceptibility. A few castrati really were 'impertinent and haughty': such behaviour was held to account for Siface's murder, while Caffarelli was the original badly behaved castrato – vulgar, quarrelsome, and exhibitionistic (in 1741 he was put under house arrest for making obscene gestures on stage, joking with the audience at the expense of his fellow-singers, and refusing to join in ensembles).[75] Most castrati, however, seem to have been of average conscientiousness or better. Even the physical stereotype of the gigantic, clumsy castrato with over-developed thorax and breasts was not universal or perhaps even common: all we can say is that some fitted it, some did not.

The contradictions between the stereotype and what we know of the real thing are best explained by a deep ambiguity in contemporary attitudes, not unlike the ambiguity with which the dominant groups in European society have at various times looked upon alleged inferiors who seemed in some way potent or attractive – Jews, say, or women. As with Jews and women, a good many castrati played into these attitudes, no doubt to propitiate hostile neighbours but with the effect of confirming them in their hostile stance.

Two startling seventeenth-century examples show how far ambiguity could go. Angelini Bontempi's theoretical work on music, based on contemporary philosophical formulas, likened the power of song to that of semen – this from a singer whose own generative power had been destroyed before it could appear.[76] Bontempi may have been parroting clichés and blinding himself to their significance, but this cannot have been true of our next witness. A monody entitled *Il castrato* set a text in the first person, a cascade of double-entendres based on the common notion that castrati could perform sexually all the better for the loss of testicles, and deploying the usual imagery of tree trunks, cannonballs, keys, etc.; the person who sang it was a castrato, well aware of how unfounded it was.[77]

Those who wished to insult castrati had means ready to hand. 'Castrone' was the pejorative term used by satirists – by Salvator Rosa in the mid seventeenth century, and by Giuseppe Parini in the late eighteenth.[78] 'Cappone' (capon) was a variant. 'Coglione' meant both 'testicle' and 'fool': Zingarelli, reminded by Crescentini that their salaries in the Naples conservatory were equal, snapped back 'You're right, Maestro, you've found in Naples those you left outside'.[79] Yet even satirists could be ambiguous. Another satire of Parini's begins by declaring his abhorrence of 'a singing elephant' who on stage emits 'a thread of tone'; it then attacks the castrato's corrupt parents, warning them (inaccurately) that their son will turn against them, so that they will go begging while he sits, singing and belaurelled, by the side of kings – his defects apparently now forgotten.[80] Parini himself wrote the libretto of *Ascanio in Alba* (set by Mozart for castrati among others) and left uncompleted the libretto of an opera seria that would likewise have required castrati.

To a minor composer of the 1740s the castrato G. B. Mancini was 'that castrone' (because he was supposed to have slandered the composer and owed him money), but the same letters sent polite greetings to 'il signor Antonio [Bernacchi] and his pupils'.[81] 'Some of my best friends are castrati' sums up this attitude. Not even Padre Martini or his fellow-musicologist and friend Chiti were free of it. A castrato copyist who did a poor job was only showing the ignorance typical of his kind, he had 'left his humanity behind in his castration'; when a young singer showed himself lacking in courtesy 'one must', Martini wrote, 'feel sorry for him because he is a castrato, but much more because he has sung women's parts on stage'. Yet both Martini and Chiti were close friends of castrati.[82]

Castrati themselves joined in the fun. Balatri in his burlesque autobiography referred to himself as a 'cappone' – rhyming with 'castr . . .' [*sic*]. Senesino (Francesco Bernardi) when in England exchanged suggestive doggerel with the poet-librettist Paolo Rolli: the burden of it was that other castrati were capons but Senesino was a 'cock' pursued by English 'hens'; he pretended to have been worn out by all the girls who 'hanker after my tree that gives no fruit', so that he could no longer 'hoist a sail', etc.[83] Rolli began it; Senesino may have felt obliged to respond in kind, like a heroine of Shakespearian comedy joking about maidenheads before an audience for whom loss of maidenhead was, in their own families, far from a joking matter.

The most surprising instance of this kind of humour occurs in Metastasio's letters to Farinelli. Metastasio was a man of delicate feeling, a precise user of language, and a great friend of Farinelli, whom he called his 'twin'. Yet his letters now and then included sexual jokes mild enough in themselves but scabrous when addressed to a castrato. If he was pestered by his 'twin' to write an opera libretto, he suspected Farinelli of being pregnant, 'for that is never a masculine longing'; if he was asked to cut one of his earlier librettos, he described the task as 'circumcision' and then as 'castrating oneself with one's own hand'; if he used the expression 'the flesh is weak' he hinted that this must not be taken to mean that he was impotent.[84] Farinelli's letters are lost: we do not know what he made of the jokes. They were not inadvertent.

As he continually voiced tender affection for this 'twin' Metastasio now and then pretended to fear that their love for one another might be thought sinful.[85] This was mere teasing. But the sexual lives of castrati were matter for gossip right through the seventeenth and eighteenth centuries. Many were said to have affairs, homosexual or heterosexual. We need not rehearse most of these stories: their truth cannot be determined. They are, however, of interest as symptoms. We may also be able once or twice to understand something of the emotional lives of castrati.

Many castrati, especially famous ones, were said to have had affairs with women. Giusto Ferdinando Tenducci married an Anglo-Irish girl of good family who later gave birth to two children; the marriage was in the end annulled at her family's instance. More interestingly, two less well known castrati were allowed to marry in Germany, Bartolomeo Sorlisi in 1668 and Filippo Finazzi in 1762, after much official and theological deliberation – Finazzi only because he had broken both legs; they stayed married.[86] We are used to the sexual feelings popular singers can rouse; those least suitable as sexual objects may rouse the strongest feelings. Baroque Europe had its groupies. But the position of women in it suggests a more complex answer.

Of Matteuccio, a Neapolitan diarist wrote that he was 'loved by all, particularly by the ladies, as much for his being a handsome young man and a eunuch as for his sweet and sonorous voice'.[87] The diarist may have meant something boring about eunuchs being thought safe and hence available for sexual intrigue. But when we recall the assumption under which Pepys operated, let alone a late seventeenth-century Neapolitan – that almost any woman was available for fumbling at the first opportunity – we may well imagine that some women found a castrato's company restful, and some fell in love with him.

In the theatre a woman performer – of all women a target for sexual advances – might fall in love with a castrato because he could give her musical guidance as well as affection. Caterina Gabrielli, a prima donna who later showed great sexual and personal independence, is said to have fallen in love with Guadagni during rehearsals for her debut at seventeen, and to have been physically transformed from a thin, fretful girl into a beauty.[88] A similar teacher–pupil relation probably explains the ménage à trois that Giuseppe Jozzi formed with the young German singer Marianne Pyrker and her sponging husband, a violinist.[89] The novelist Stendhal, who knew a great deal about the opera world at the turn of the eighteenth and nineteenth centuries, explained this kind of relationship by the superior musical attainments of the castrati: 'Out of despair, those poor devils became learned musicians; in concerted pieces they kept the whole company going; they lent talent to the prima donna, who was their mistress. We owe two or three great women singers to Velluti.'[90] What 'mistress' meant we cannot tell; it probably stood for real feeling.

For the castrati, the chief hazard in life was probably loneliness. A family of brothers, sisters, nephews and nieces was not always enough, and anyhow might be far away. Balatri's autobiography records a bittersweet return to Pisa: father, mother, elder brother, and nurse fall on his neck, but the brother asks if there is a present for him, the servants expect large tips, the town, after Vienna, seems empty and poor.[91]

A castrato sometimes formed a close relationship with a young man – often a favourite pupil – whom he treated as an adoptive son. What we hear about such ties generally amounts to malign (and unverifiable) gossip. One case is well documented, anyhow on the surface.

Pistocchi seems to have had no close relations who could inherit the family name, something that mattered to him. In 1701–2, shortly after he had got back to Bologna from a long engagement in Germany, he formed ties with no fewer than three potential adoptive heirs. He was then in his early forties, at or just past the peak of a career that had made him one of the most famous singers in Europe. He had brought with him from Germany a young pupil, the violinist 'Rinaldo' [Reinhold?] Bulmein, whom he referred to as 'my Rinaldo', 'my son Rinaldo'; when he had to be away from Bologna he would write back to make sure that Rinaldo was getting all he needed by way of money, schooling, and (if need be) shoes and socks.[92]

About the same time, however, Pistocchi started sharing a house (largely built and furnished by himself) with a slightly younger man, Francesco Antonio Oretti, a doctor of philosophy and medicine and a lecturer at Bologna University. He lent Oretti's father – another doctor, of noble status – and Oretti himself 'considerable sums' without charging interest, so that they could deal with unspecified but urgent family needs; in 1702, the year when the father died, Pistocchi was also making the son an allowance. In 1704 Oretti junior entered into a contract establishing total community of property between him and Pistocchi. In it he acknowledged Pistocchi as his 'brother' and residuary legatee. If Oretti died first, leaving legitimate children, Pistocchi was to stand to them in the relation of father; he was to provide them with dowries or with shares in the estate (determined by the Oretti family entail); he was to look after Oretti's widowed mother or make her a fixed allowance. For the rest, he was free to do as he wished with the estate, and to pass on the joint surnames; if he chose to bequeath both estate and surnames to a descendant of the Oretti family in the female line it would be much appreciated, but he was not bound to do so.[93]

The third person who entered Pistocchi's life about 1701–2 was the servant Angelo Sarti. After 1704 the story shows gaps. Rinaldo went back to Germany. Oretti went on teaching at Bologna University; he was to outlive Pistocchi by twenty years, but meanwhile he and his declared 'brother' may have fallen out. In 1715 Pistocchi became for a time an Oratorian. His will, drawn up in 1725 and revised shortly before his death the following year, mentions neither Rinaldo nor Oretti. The residuary legatee was Sarti. One of his qualifications, perhaps the most important, was that he had children. Pistocchi's 'descendants' might at one time have been patrician Oretti Pistocchi; they were now to be bourgeois Sarti Pistocchi.

Besides pledging Sarti to have masses said for him (twenty-four a year for twenty-four years – as many years as Sarti had been in his service), Pistocchi bequeathed some valuable objects, about the precise disposition of which he was a good deal bothered, to three well-known castrati. A few years on, Tosi was to leave such estate as he had to a younger castrato, whose proxy for legal purposes was a relative of Bernacchi.[94] The closest ties of some castrati may well have been with other castrati. It was, after all, natural for birds of such uncommon feather to flock together.

By the time of Pistocchi's death it appears from a slightly earlier satire on the opera world that younger castrati were beginning to make excuses for their condition.[95] Shortly afterwards, Voltaire began his recurrent satires on castration as an institution, part of his attack on the Catholic Church. By Burney's visit to Italy in 1770 the sense of incongruity and shame appears to have been general among the educated. But the immediate reason why castrati numbers were already in full decline was a series of decisions by Italian parents not to have their sons operated upon even though they had fine treble voices; these decisions were taken while Voltaire wrote, about 1730–40 (and some may have been taken earlier), by people few of whom had ever heard of Voltaire or of any other satirist or 'enlightened' thinker, but whose equivalents in 1630–40 had opted for castration without seeing it as a problem.

It is always difficult to explain why people do not do something; they may not even be aware of having made a choice. One general cause of parents' behaviour was probably the economic revival that began about 1730: though in a limited way, prospects for their sons were improving. In parts of Italy important demographic changes took place about the turn of the seventeenth and eighteenth centuries that are just beginning to be studied: kinship ties were becoming looser, so that large lineage groups within which people had intermarried were splitting into virtual nuclear families.[96] Smaller family units may have allowed greater care for the individual destiny of sons – no longer subordinated to the fortunes of the lineage as a whole.

Probably the most important cause was the gradual decline of Christian asceticism, manifested through the eighteenth century in the falling membership of the religious orders. If a decision to make one's son a castrato meant for most people a decision to make him a church singer – a more drastic, greedier, or riskier version of enrolling him in a monastic order, – such a choice became less attractive as choirs dwindled or vanished. This, together perhaps with some sense that the enlightened and educated were beginning to disapprove, helps to explain why the number of castrati fell just as employment in opera was expanding. To gamble a son's virility on success as an opera singer was immensely risky; to stake it on his finding a tenured post as a church singer had been reasonably likely to bring him and his family a lifelong return, both in financial security and (while the ideal of Christian asceticism still held) in status. It is thus fitting that the handful of castrati who survived into the early twentieth century should have been concentrated in a few ancient church choirs at the heart of Catholic Christendom.

3

WOMEN

One notable group of singers was for many years barred from the full freedom of the market. Women ought not to be on the stage at all: so many people thought, not just in Italy but throughout seventeenth-century Europe. Those who did make a public show of themselves were all suspected of being courtesans; some were.

If they behaved like courtesans, governments anxious to keep 'peace within families' might arrest them, expel them, put them into convents. When they gradually established themselves as skilled musicians they remained suspect: they still flouted the first rule of the society, woman's dependence on man. Yet the female voice, if beautiful enough and skilfully enough handled, triumphed over prejudice – not without cost.[1]

Exposure to men was the trouble – not just to men in the audience but to fellow-workers in the theatre. In Italy as in other Mediterranean countries, respectable women were meant to be seen, if at all, at home or in a few public places, especially in church, accompanied by relatives or duennas: a rule whose severity deepened the further south you travelled. What this meant for women singers as late as 1740 was spelt out by the Naples official in charge of theatres: 'they have never been held to be respectable, since the singing profession carries with it the harsh necessity of dealing with many men: composers, instrumentalists, poets, and music-lovers; anyone who witnesses all this coming and going in and out of a woman's house readily concludes that she is immoral, whether she actually is or not.'[2]

This alludes to the practice of holding early rehearsals at the prima donna's lodging: more respectable no doubt than for her to traipse out to places dominated by strange men, but the men attending the rehearsals were not the kind a well-behaved woman was meant to receive, to say nothing of the 'music-loving' admirers.

'As I am a singer by profession' – Zeffirina tells her husband in a late eighteenth-century comic opera, *I due castellani burlati* – 'I can't afford to snub anybody, I must receive them all in my house.' 'And your husband?' he asks. 'My husband? My husband isn't there.' 'I understand – he has to spend all his time at the coffee-house.' Elsewhere in the same work a German tourist complains of women singers as gold-diggers who employ a procuress and have robbed him of his snuffbox.[3] These unattached or loosely attached women were held to be frivolous if not dangerous. Their freedom of action, incidentally, made them useful as leading characters in many plays and comic operas: the social position of Fiordiligi and Dorabella in Così fan tutte – displaced and unprotected – becomes clear if we take them to be singers between engagements.

The attitudes the librettist took for granted in his audience had not changed much since Renaissance times, when the licentious poet Aretino described women's learning to sing, play instruments, and write poetry as 'the very key that opens the gates of their modesty'.[4] Nor was the publicity attendant on these skills the only trouble. The virtuoso performance of music, according to a monk writing about 1700, brought honour and what we should call social mobility; it suited all ages and conditions but not women, 'since, being in itself a sweet and soothing art, it would add magical spells to their attractions'.[5]

In banning women from the Roman stage the popes merely kept up for another century and a half a practice common throughout early seventeenth-century Europe, from Shakespeare's theatre to the court of Louis XIV, where women singers were unusual down to the 1650s and men danced women's parts into the 1680s.[6] Only in the next century did the Roman practice come to seem strange to visitors who knew nothing of the skilled female impersonators in Chinese opera, Japanese kabuki, or South Indian kathakali. The surprise expressed by late eighteenth-century visitors points to the relative autonomy northern European women of the middle and upper classes had attained: their sexuality was no longer felt as so hazardous as to be constantly watched and denied any public display.

In Italy women singers had established themselves in late sixteenth-century courts, and singing actresses in touring commedia dell'arte companies; yet the example of Adriana Basile and her daughter shows the lengths to which the best artists might go to maintain their respectability, above all by never singing in opera. To sing at court held some dangers; to appear on the public stage meant, as in antiquity, that you were taken to be a high-class prostitute.

The requirements of early opera and the order of priorities that ruled the casting of women's parts did something to put this notion into operagoers' minds, though it is not easy to tell how far the genre moulded itself to existing prejudices, how far it shaped new ones. Operas such as Cavalli's dealt in a swooning eroticism; they required of women singers qualifications listed by a commentator in 1663 – beauty, rich clothes, attractive singing, appropriate acting, pretty well in that order – rather than dazzling technical feats.[7] A couple of decades earlier, Luisa Sanches, a Rome-based singer who hoped for a Paris engagement from Cardinal Mazarin, had listed her qualifications as her age (eighteen), her ability to play instruments and to sightread, her looks and her morals (both good), her languages, her memory; quality of voice came seventh, next to last. A woman singer in this period was at least as much looked at (and wondered at) as heard.[8]

One requirement of early opera the full burden of which is hard for us to understand was that women must often perform in men's clothes. The age of unisex is peculiarly unfitted to grasp what this meant.

On the one hand audiences enjoyed the spectacle of women dressed up as men and men dressed up as women (sometimes of a woman acting the part of a man disguised as a woman, such as Achilles dodging the Trojan War); this seems to have been part of a cult of sexual ambiguity that affected vocal casting as well, particularly in opera of about 1630–1750, where a soprano hero often sang opposite a contralto heroine, or (as in some of Cavalli's operas) a tenor nurse confronted an impudent valet sung by a young woman. On the other hand the sight of a woman showing herself to be a forked animal was felt to be so erotic as to border on the obscene. Transvestism had been condemned by various Church fathers as no better than fornication, a condemnation repeated by a priest writing in 1750; no doubt it added a guilty thrill to the audience's enjoyment.[9] This feeling persisted in Italy down to the early 1950s, when men still hooted at women if they wore slacks in town or rode a moped astride.

How a woman singer felt at wearing such scandalous dress before hundreds of male eyes is documented only here and there. Vittoria Tesi, a famous singer who created many travesti parts, and the opposite of a shrinking violet, in 1738 refused for a time to sing any more of them on the grounds that 'acting a male part is bad for her health'.[10] This was perhaps a way of saying that the psychological strain was bad for her morale – terms not then available.

Clearer hints come from a later period when the convention was fast going out of date in opera, though it still flourished in music-hall and pantomime. Nelly Marzi, singing the soprano part of the page in *Un ballo in maschera* at Buenos Aires in 1875, was partly excused for an unsatisfactory performance on the grounds that any woman making her debut in male attire 'is bound to be much affected by anxiety at being the target for everyone's gaze'.[11] A little earlier, the American Ginevra Guerrabella (Genevieve Ward), singing the same part in Cuba, insisted on wearing puffed-out trunk hose, high boots, and a cloak so as to conceal not just her legs but her whole person. At her benefit a rumour got about that she was to appear in the last act 'sin botas', without boots; she refused, and had to outface a riot of catcalls and cries of 'sin botas!'. 'I was' – she later recalled – 'a singer, and I was not going to bring myself down to that level. The women will understand.'[12]

Women singers in the early days of opera, then, existed as objects of male expectancy, at once dubious and entrancing. They were not seen as straightforward professional musicians: the general opinion was that they could not acquire the highest musical skills because under the social proprieties of the day they could not take lessons from men other than their relatives. But this opinion too had at least as much to do with what was expected of them as with the chances actually open. Good teaching – we shall see – was not as hard for women to come by as people liked to make out. Male commentators, however, througout the seventeenth and much of the eighteenth century went on talking about them as what we should call sex objects.

Change was gradual: a Bolognese nobleman could discuss two women singers in 1728 wholly in terms of beauty and 'spirit'; three years later he first discussed another prima donna's voice, and only then went on to describe her as 'aged twenty-two, very courteous, tall, with a shapely waist, thin rather than fat'.[13] By 1751 the impresario of the San Carlo, Naples, opined that in a company of singers at least one of the women should be 'an object not unsightly'.[14] This was to concede that one or two more might be employed strictly for their vocal and dramatic skills.

The San Carlo was the temple of serious opera: by the mid eighteenth century this genre called for technical feats such as to make personal attractions dispensable, and artists more obviously professional. But in other theatres the years from about 1740 to 1800 were the boom time of comic opera. In Naples the soubrettes of the dominant genre – the Despinas and Zerlinas – were the performers repeatedly arrested or expelled by the authorities, usually for love affairs or attempted marriages with young noblemen: beauty and verve were still their chief qualifications. They also appear to have been singled out, under regulations of 1734–9, as presumed courtesans who in theory must reside in the suburbs but were exempted so long as they had an opera contract; there was a nasty moment about 1740 when (probably owing to rivalry between government officials for control over this group of people, and perhaps over protection money) 'resting' singers were threatened with having the regulations applied.[15]

Comic opera as an exclusive speciality died out soon after the Napoleonic wars. But such was the ill repute of women singers in general that even the dazzling technicians of serious opera had to be recommended (when it was at all possible) for the excellence of their morals and conduct. In the 1760s Metastasio and the composer J. A. Hasse were at pains to recommend the gifted German soprano Elisabeth Teiber on these grounds, with much emphasis on the 'sacrifice' she was making for her family's sake in venturing on the Italian stage; as late as 1841 Donizetti recommended Almerinda Granchi (for whom he had written a leading part) as 'of good conduct'.[16]

'Prostitute' is not always a clear category. It could be mere obloquy, as when the father-in-law of Adriana Ferraresi del Bene, the original Fiordiligi in *Così fan tutte*, denounced his son for having 'prostituted [her] in concerts and theatres'; he meant that she had sung in the opera houses of Florence and London.[17] The term could readily, perhaps automatically be linked with the stage, as when a Naples diarist of 1671 described the prima donna Giulia (Ciulla) Di Caro as 'actress singer musician whore'.[18] Yet Ciulla (1646–97) undoubtedly was a courtesan; she was also a singer rather than a 'singer' of the kind later patronized by Citizen Kane. Her story shows the possibilities open to a Neapolitan woman singer in the late seventeenth century.

She was the daughter of a cook and a washerwoman; at fourteen she married the assistant to a dentist who worked in the crowded open space outside the viceregal castle at the heart of Naples. Her job was to draw the customers to the dentist's booth by singing in both Neapolitan and Italian; with her fine voice and looks she soon was being kept by members of the nobility, and her husband was paid off and dispatched to Rome, though she seems not to have broken off all relations with him.

Ciulla then took singing lessons (whether for the first time or not is unclear) and made her opera debut in the Naples public theatre, where through the next four years she sang parts requiring technical competence. Because of her continuing sexual adventures she was several times threatened with expulsion from Naples and at least once expelled. In 1675 she went on what seems to have been a tour of several leading Italian towns, accompanied by a large train including a castrato (who may have been her singing partner) and a bravo. She returned a widow; rumour – unsubstantiated – said she had had her husband killed. She sang again, this time at the Viceroy's, but soon afterwards, whether owing to the rumour or to a scurrilous pamphlet naming her lovers, she was arrested and put into a conventual home for fallen women. She was got out eighteen days later by a young man from a rich family, who presently married her even though he too had to undergo two months' imprisonment.

Ciulla, it seems, had made a vow to the Madonna that if she could marry she would be faithful to her new husband; she gave the Madonna all her jewels, lived with her Carluccio in quiet suburban ease, and gave birth to her only child, a daughter, when she was thirty-eight.[19]

Ciulla's story may suggest why a young woman with a good voice might sometimes have to choose between becoming a courtesan and becoming a nun. The two professions have at times been poetically linked as extremes that meet on some metaphysical level, but we know of actual cases. A sister of Francesco Rasi, the original Orfeo in Monteverdi's opera, was sent by the Duchess of Modena to study singing with Giulio Caccini in Florence, but because she turned out to have little talent Rasi put her into a nunnery.[20] A generation later, in 1650, Anna Maria Sardelli, a courtesan-singer if ever there was one, was said to be on the point of experiencing a conversion and taking the veil. She did not; instead she went on to mixed adventures that saw her shot at and stabbed offstage and, as Cleopatra in Cesti's *Il Cesare amante* (1652), helped by Caesar to undress in an erotic duet on the way to the bath.[21]

A few years earlier, in 1641, a singer in a leading Rome church choir was interested in a possible opera engagement at Ferrara for his daughter Veronica Santi, whom he had been training; he clearly hoped to make money that way, but proposed later to make her a nun. The trouble, as the leading composer Marco Marazzoli reported to Ferrara, was that the girl's training was 'wholly ecclesiastical'; all she had was a good voice and good intonation: 'For the rest everything is still to do, but what troubles me is her great modesty; in singing, a free and easy manner is needed and, may I say, a touch of effrontery; none of this is to be found in Veronica; she is so modest that even her father loses his temper and preaches impudence to her.'

A third possibility was that if Veronica's modesty was beyond cure and her singing remained 'somnolent and nun-like' she might be a waiting woman to the wife of the effective ruler of Ferrara. Her plainness, Marazzoli pointed out, 'could only be satisfactory to that lady', an obvious reference to what might otherwise have been a career as a courtesan; the term was after all related to 'court' and, in Italian, was the feminine of 'courtier'.[22]

The career seen as ideal, that of wife and mother, was closed to many girls in seventeenth-century Italy because their parents could not afford a dowry. Of Francesco Rasi's ten surviving brothers and sisters, four were nuns (and two were monks, two more priests). Admission to a nunnery also required a (more modest) dowry, but this could be waived for a girl able to sing, play an instrument, and teach music; in the next century Padre Martini was still being asked to suggest candidates.[23] Before 1680 or thereabouts a woman singer could make a regular career only in a court, with the implications so strenuously fought off by Adriana Basile. Between that and the nunnery lay an ambiguous zone where a woman might get occasional lucrative opera engagements, at the cost of being deemed a courtesan or else of having again and again to be certified as respectable.

Hence a general need for highly placed male protection. A number of women singers could be straightforwardly described as courtesans; these by definition had their protectors. The others needed protectors to establish (what for many of them was probably true) that they were not courtesans. Even then the celebrated Anna Renzi – the original Ottavia in Monteverdi's *L'incoronazione di Poppea*, – though hymned as 'chaste' in a lavish publication in her honour, was automatically written down as 'courtesan' by an operagoer scribbling in his programme.[24]

With the outright courtesans contemporaries did not mince words. The agents who recruited singers for princes wrote of one of them 'she sings well enough to please Your Highness, and she is besides the kind of woman one can sleep with by lamplight'; collectively their offerings were 'merchandise'.[25] Charles II's agent in Florence, an imperfectly anglicized Italian, wrote proposing a sixteen-year-old girl, bred up to music by one of the Medici princes, 'that att this present, ist in a resonable Perfection, and ist Excellent voice ... and besyde, the Gerle is no vere Ogly ... and as I think a Mayde, butt for this, I will not Promise'. The King, he thought, would like her better than Cecca (Anna Francesca) Costa, a courtesan-singer Charles had presumably known during his Parisian exile; so the character of this 'merchandise' is clear.[26]

Courtesan-singers' careers were short, a few years at most. Some were virtually non-existent: we are here dealing with 'singers' under a convention like the one that lets high-class call-girls appear in today's newspapers as starlets or models.

'Singers' are none the less worth a glance: their doings helped to set a tone. We do not hear of any opera appearances by La Giorgina (Angela Voglia), perhaps because contemporaries in the Rome of the 1680s were too busy chronicling how she was surprised at Queen Christina's (who had saved her from arrest) with a canon of St Peter's, how the Duke of Mantua and the Spanish Ambassador competed to buy her from her stepfather (with the loser having the stepfather beaten up), how the Ambassador won and took her off to Naples on being made viceroy, ultimately to Spain.[27] La Giorgina did sing in private, but the only singing recorded of another Roman, Vittoria or Tolla di Bocca di Leone, was her serenading the widowed Queen of Poland (whose son was keeping her) under the royal balcony while dressed as a man; on this occasion, a warm night in 1700, a jealous nobleman tried to disfigure her, and a year or so later yet another Roman, Costanza Maccari, who sang opera at least once in the noble palace for which Handel was to compose, really was disfigured. Meanwhile Tolla's story included an alleged miscarriage, extensive travel, an on-and-off engagement with the Duke of Mantua (often mixed up with singers and 'singers'), and an explosion of sonnets satirizing her doings.[28]

In these same years of the late seventeenth century, at least two courtesan-singers with greater musical pretensions forwarded the burgeoning career of the composer Alessandro Scarlatti. One of his two singing sisters, then the mistress of a high official, probably helped to get him appointed director of the Naples royal chapel in the teeth of the local musical establishment; the outcome was scandal, resignations, and, for Melchiorra Scarlatti and other 'whore actresses', the choice of expulsion or a convent.[29] Giulietta Zuffi, who sang in Naples on and off for eight years – with at least two appearances in Scarlatti operas, once alongside the great Siface, – was best known for having spent a night with the inevitable visiting Duke of Mantua; he spent the following night with the seconda donna of the opera company, so showing a sense of precedence. Giulietta had had affairs with a great nobleman and an impresario and had been the cause of a duel, but when she was caught with a foreign diplomat with whom the government was in dispute she was given the usual choice of expulsion or a convent. She left. Here was a woman whose technical competence must have been adequate at least, but whose career was perceived by a contemporary diarist in terms for which the literal sense of 'pornography' ('writing about prostitutes') is suitable.[30]

Giulietta was expelled in 1687. Two years later the wars broke out which over a quarter-century did much to loosen the bonds of patronage, especially for women singers. Leading singers of these years such as Diamante Scarabelli – we have seen – could afford in practice to ignore the rulers on whom they nominally depended, though old habits of mind died hard and it was later rumoured that Diamante, for all her independence and professionalism, had been converted late in life by an ascetic musician who lived like a hermit and performed miracles.[31]

No one, however, seems to have described Scarabelli or her leading contemporaries as courtesans. That term was now confined to the practitioners of the new comic opera which in the 1700s was beginning to split off from the old erotic-courtly opera. There is no point in going over their stories, a repetitive matter of affairs with nobles or ruffians or both, affrays, pregnancies, attempted elopements, male disguises, arrests, expulsions, brief and at times scandalous confinement in nunneries. They are documented because the police took a close interest: we hear little about other comic opera soubrettes who may have led humdrum professional lives; even the authorities acknowledged now and then that one of them was chaste and well behaved.[32]

In Italy stereotyped behaviour was on the whole welcome; it still is. There is a sense that these flighty, irresistible charmers of Neapolitan comic opera with their mothers given to scrounging and intrigue (often thought to be *mammacce*, fictitious mothers) were playing an expected part.

Once in a while we get a glimpse of something more individual. Francesca Mignatti's story suggests how ill repute may, to some women, have been liberating.

She was a Bolognese who sang in Naples in 1708, got into the usual scrape (a judge's son, she claimed, had promised marriage), and was punished by having police stationed in her apartment. Hence scandal: the neighbours demanded that she should leave, among them a duke who lived on the floor above. The Viceroy's equerry and theatrical factotum, a Bolognese count, offered to help her if she kept quiet and did not mention his name, 'but she', as he reported, 'instead of following my instructions, sat continually on the balcony making fun of everybody and even of the duke, and saying "the equerry is going to do this and say that and the other on my behalf", etc.'. The count, angered, withdrew all help; she then left Naples, as he thought in despair. But it is at least as likely that Mignatti had grounds for not wanting to put herself under an obligation to the count, and was making the most of things by haranguing the populace.[33]

The lives of four singers who made their debuts between 1708 and 1716 show how the social climate was changing, at least for women at the top of the profession, even as Mignatti went through her raree-show.

Faustina Bordoni and her exact contemporary Vittoria Tesi were among the foremost singers of their time, the one known for a new kind of dazzling agility, the other for vigorous expression as well as for virtuosity; the less famous Anastasia Robinson, an Englishwoman partly brought up in Italy, sang the second woman's part in a number of Handel and Bononcini operas. Rosa Ungarelli, older than these by a few years, was the leading exponent of the new comic intermezzo.

All four dealt with noblemen on an equal footing. Faustina, like Ungarelli, seems to have managed from the start without a noble protector; though she went on enjoying the usual decorative monarchical titles, she ran her career professionally, caused no sexual scandal, married the composer Hasse, with whom she had a long partnership, and was received 'like a lady' in the most aristocratic Roman houses.[34] Tesi, in her frank letters to her nobleman lover (a young monsignor), was scornful both of her fellow-singers and of certain courtiers: 'I'm used to dealing with intelligent people, I can't get accustomed to these baboons, full of ignorant pride.' After her retirement she lived in Vienna in the palace of the music-loving Prince of Sachsen-Hildburgshausen, not as a dependant but as a respected friend, while the husband she had long before picked up as a convenience (a former barber) kept the faro bank.[35] Anastasia Robinson seems to have been the first singer, actress, or dancer to marry an English peer, though the marriage was acknowledged only on his deathbed; a letter of hers shows a good education and a command of easy ladylike persiflage.[36]

Rosa Ungarelli went about for years with her partner Antonio Ristorini, performing the two-handed comic intermezzos (*La serva padrona* the only one remembered today) that were the vogue in the first half of the eighteenth century. A naive entry in a contemporary diary shows her holding court during an engagement at Pistoia in 1725:

many gentlemen went to visit her. She certainly is a free and easy woman; I need only say that she is a singer, and there are no simpletons among them. This woman has done well in Pistoia, and so has Signor Antonio . . . she bagged the most unlikely people; the presents she got, though, were all of things to eat and drink, because nowadays money is scarce and few can afford to give it – and the woman was ugly; God help us if she had been beautiful, for she had an inimitable manner, and a way of acting out emotion that couldn't have been more expressive.

A Pistoia lawyer known for his meanness – the diarist reported – was the favourite; he acted as one of the impresarios for the season and gave Ungarelli more presents than anybody. Nowhere is there any hint that Ungarelli was a courtesan or gave anything in return for what must after all have been fairly modest presents of wine or chocolate, apart perhaps from dazzling smiles, lively conversation, and a still livelier stage performance.[37]

In the next few decades doing without a patron still meant taking a risk, but perhaps one that could be lived with. The leading prima donna Anna Maria Peruzzi was temporarily out of voice when she sang in Milan in 1733: some in the audience shouted insults at her, and, according to a visiting nobleman (the same man who had tried to 'protect' Francesca Mignatti in Naples a quarter-century earlier), 'She has to hear them and keep quiet because she has no protection, whether from the Governor, the court, or anyone else with power; hence she is exceedingly mortified.'[38] What this really shows, however, is that the middle-aged commentator with his long-standing habit of 'protecting' singers was working on old assumptions; the young prima donna was able to ride out the storm without him or others of his kind, uncomfortable though the experience no doubt was.

Within opera seria there was an instructive change in the treatment of women singers at the two leading Italian monarchical theatres. At the San Carlo, Naples, in 1737 they were not allowed to make visits in the boxes unless escorted by the official who supervised the theatre; at the Regio, Turin, in 1788 the custom was for the prima donna to be entertained during the ballet in this or that lady's box, outwardly as an equal, and the heir to the throne told Gertrud Elisabeth Mara (a London-based singer who specialized in Italian opera) that he would have taken her for an English lady.[39]

A witness on an international scale to the change in the position of leading women singers was Caterina Gabrielli, whose genius for declamation kept her career going from 1747 to 1782. Her father was cook to a Roman prince; she was reputed to have had affairs with the Austrian Chancellor and the ruling Duke of Parma (whom she supposedly called 'you damned hunchback' when he grew jealous and tried to beat her), not to mention the Spanish and French ambassadors to Vienna; the Frenchman hid in Caterina's apartment to catch the Spaniard; he then wounded her slightly – she kept the sword as trophy. Yet her round of engagements in London, Vienna, and St Petersburg depended only incidentally on her affairs with great men; in her dealings with the authorities she was readily defiant.[40]

Not that her career was free from tension; her missed performances, blamed at the time on 'caprice', seem to have been due in part to gynaecological problems, perhaps also to the strain of asserting independence in a still hierarchical-minded society. But there is about it something curiously modern, down to the contrast Metastasio discerned between her consciousness of her artistic worth and her 'extreme timidity'[41] (which suggests Callas) or the two views taken of her by the Burneys, father and daughter: to Charles she seemed, at forty-five, 'the most intelligent and best bred virtuosa' he had ever met, who bore herself with 'all the grace and dignity of a Roman matron' and could talk like a well-educated woman on all sorts of topics; Fanny noticed chiefly, as Gabrielli left the theatre, one servant carrying her train, another her little dog, another her parrot, and another her monkey.[42] The modern opera star – part hard-working artist, part creature of publicity – had arrived; like some modern opera stars, Gabrielli spent her retirement quietly with a woman companion (her sister and former partner) and unmarried.

In the nineteenth century the legal position of women singers was ruled by different versions of the Napoleonic code, which had been adopted in nearly all the Italian states. According to the more pedantic writers on theatrical law, this meant that a woman could not sign contracts without her husband's consent (or, if an unmarried minor, her father's). Though the code allowed married women in business to act on their own, this – according to the pedants – could not apply to singers, because the 'dangers and seductions' of the theatre, the 'nomadic' and peculiarly independent character of the singer's life, threatened family life and morality; on these grounds a husband would even be entitled to break a contract he had previously approved.[43]

Against this, the legal writer with most practical experience of the opera world asserted that in Italy, unlike France, a woman did not need her husband's consent to sign a theatrical contract on her own – as most singers appear to have done; the contract would be void only if it could be shown that by failing to get his consent she had harmed the family; if the husband allowed it to run for some time or drew income from it he could be assumed to have tacitly endorsed it. This interpretation seems to reflect what went on most of the time.[44]

Even strictly interpreted, the Napoleonic code safeguarded the earnings of separated women, as English law (before the Married Women's Property Act of 1882) did not. A fair number of nineteenth-century women singers were separated, legally or not, often from husbands who were themselves singers. The reason, according to Antonio Ghislanzoni, the librettist of *Aida*, was much like that later assigned for the instability of marriages between Hollywood stars – marriage to a fellow-singer was at risk from disparity of talent and the need to travel: 'One goes to Lima, the other to St Petersburg, and good night for ever!'[45] Marriage to men not connected with the theatre may have worked better.

The early nineteenth-century cult of morality and respectability touched singers – up to a point. In 1848 a Naples journal alleged that unmarried women singers wished only to get married, and married ones to remain faithful to their husbands.[46] The incidence of separation alone shows that this was too sweeping. The article did, however, point to a change of tone. The last known document to refer to singers (the usual minor comic opera performers) as 'public women' dates from 1809.[47]

Whether, in the rest of the century, minor women singers could always afford to be monogamous or choosy (or always wished to be) is open to doubt. There must have been many like Adelaide Carpano, now remembered only because her accompanist, who happened to be the thirteen-year-old Rossini, burst out laughing when she let out a squawk; a woman with more beauty than voice, she was at that time the mistress of a nobleman-impresario and had hopes of a career, but nine years later, when she was living with the famous tenor Giovanni David, she was willing to settle for any part, however minor, in the season in which he was to appear.[48] In general, however, discretion in both behaviour and comment was now somewhat greater than in the eighteenth century.

Among singers, episodes like the multiple pregnancies of the unmarried Giuseppina Strepponi (Verdi's future companion and wife) and the tone in which they were discussed among theatre people suggest that the real early nineteenth-century requirement was to avoid a public scandal.[49] The language used among themselves by these theatre people, some women included, was still pretty free; Giuditta Grisi, the original Romeo in Bellini's opera, was noted for her swearing. But more respectable appearances were kept up in dealings with the rest of the world. It seems unlikely that any librettist of 1840 could have written, even for private circulation, a poem like one by a predecessor of a century or so earlier. Vittoria Tesi, it records, after singing to a company of friends in the grounds of the Prince of Sachsen-Hildburghausen's villa, went into the woods to relieve herself, inadvertently cleaned herself with some nettles, cried out in pain, and was then seen rubbing her bottom against the fresh grass of a nearby field, amid general laughter. 'O happy grass!' the poem concludes.[50]

Changes at once subtler and more profound than this came over the position of leading women singers by the early nineteenth century. They were now fully accepted as professional musicians. With the disappearance of the castrati, and before the cult of the powerful tenor had set in, women came to dominate Italian opera; and they dominated it by vocal and acting skills, only in the most marginal way by physical attraction. Good looks in a prima donna were not despised, but no longer were they required in at least one member of a company. Proof of this was the career of the Rossinian contralto Rosmunda Pisaroni. Nothing could improve on the description by the British Ambassadress in Paris, Lady Granville:

magnificent, wonderful, *entraînante* Pisaroni. Hideous, distorted, deformed, dwarfish Pisaroni. She has an immense head, a remarkably ugly face. When she smiles or sings her mouth is drawn up to one ear, with a look of a person convulsed in pain. She has two legs that stand out like sugar-tongs, one shorter than the other. Her stomach sticks out on one side of her body, and she has a hump on the other, not where stomachs or humps usually are, but sideways, like panniers.

With all this, she had not sung ten minutes before a Paris audience was in ecstasies. . . . Every word is felt, every sound is an expression. Zuchelli's singing with her and after her made one feel, 'What is he at? what is he mumbling? why don't he sing? why don't he feel?' I came home quite enchanted.[51]

The Napoleonic period, too, brought forward a number of upper-class singers whose families had fallen on hard times: the great Giuditta Pasta, for one, creator of the part of Norma; in her Paris seasons she was partnered by the contralto Adelaide Schiassetti, daughter of a Napoleonic general. The two of them were close friends of the novelists Stendhal and Mérimée and their intellectual group; later on Pasta became friends with nationalists, whose outlook she shared.

Pasta was irreproachable in her conduct; she felt strongly the need to shield her only daughter from the world of the theatre, to the point of entrusting her for some years to a young Englishwoman, a member of an old Roman Catholic gentry family who was also one of the wholehearted women devotees Pasta tended to attract. Pasta's marriage to an amiable lawyer (a minor tenor in his younger days) was, so far as we can tell, happy, notwithstanding their persistent habit of role reversal: their letters to each other and to Pasta's mother regularly refer to Giuditta as a man and to Giuseppe as a woman, each with a suitable nickname. Those were pre-Freudian days when such adjustments (including pleasantries about Giuditta's 'virile voice' of command and Giuseppe's happiness as her 'slave') could be enjoyed without guilt.[52]

In a more general sense the best women singers could now play a masterful role. If they were good enough they had not only earning power but wide social acceptance. Far from being suspect and dependent on a protector, they could be independent breadwinners. Luigia Boccabadati supported not only her children but her separated husband, a minor impresario; after her death one of her singing daughters took over as provider.[53]

Such independence could be costly. A young debutante singer in the small town of Porto San Giorgio in 1870 had – a local music teacher reported – 'a very fine voice and great accuracy . . . but, to turn her into an artist, one would have to take her away from her parents and make her live like an artist – that is, either undergo hardship or sell herself'.[54] The celebrated Erminia Frezzolini, after parting from her husband, a well-known tenor, declined an offer to go and live with her sister, because she thought her brother-in-law would try to control her: 'you know how much I've suffered through life over our father, whom I loved. It's better to live alone than to be tyrannized over from morning till night'. Father and brother-in-law as well as husband were singers, but this did not prevent Erminia from feeling that men, especially one's male relatives, always wanted things their own way and ended by criticizing and turning upside down women's best motives.[55]

Nor did professional independence do away with the problems of women's sexuality at a time when their right to self-determination in this area was nowhere acknowledged. Anna de la Grange, a Frenchwoman who sang in Italy around 1850, was plagued with a campaign of anonymous letters from a disappointed suitor, addressed to her friends and to herself and containing 'horrors'.[56]

Worse befell Adelaide Tosi, who made an early success in Naples. She had an affair with the composer Saverio Mercadante which ended badly, and took up with a Neapolitan prince. The former lovers met again in Madrid, where both were contracted for the opera season. Mercadante's reports to a friend in Naples, which he asked should be spread abroad without his name being mentioned, are a monument of insane southern jealousy. Tosi, he writes, flopped because she got drunk and lost her voice:

and now in all the drawing-rooms, cafés, bars, shops, streets everyone shouts aloud 'Tosi is a whore, she failed in her duty, she got drunk, she had herself fucked all night by her Pr[ince], and we had to pay without being able to enjoy an opera we like so much.' The ladies swear they will no longer receive her, and meanwhile she's in bed not even able to speak, and God knows when she'll be able to appear again.

Tosi is 'ugly, dirty, slovenly', she sings out of time, her voice is gone in all registers, all she has left is 'runs like a trombone's, trills like the sound of the carts that carry hemp at Lake Agnano, mordents like the bite of a mad dog' – and so on. It is hard to tell whether any of this had a basis; probably Tosi did run into vocal difficulties. Two years later, she appeared in a new Mercadante opera, with the composer in attendance; he was still resentful, though in quieter vein. One more year, one more collaboration. This time we have no private letters. By then Mercadante had married somebody else; his jealous fit may have evaporated. At all events there is no sign that he objected to writing fresh parts for Tosi.[57]

Meanwhile, however, his Madrid letters could have destroyed her reputation in Naples. They were meant to, and they remind us how exposed a woman singer still was when her personal or vocal difficulties could be turned to account by a man bent on sexual revenge.

8 Scene from an unidentified eighteenth-century opera in a Venice theatre. Note the closeness of the stage boxes to the singer, and the two masked figures carrying on a conversation. (Museo Civico Correr, Venice)

9 The beginnings of exotic costume: Giuseppina Grassini as Zaira in Peter Winter's opera (early nineteenth century). (Museo Teatrale alla Scala, Milan)

10 Giuditta Pasta as Anna Bolena in Donizetti's opera, 1830. (Painting by Brulon, Museo Teatrale alla Scala, Milan)

73

11 The sisters Barbara (left) and Carlotta Marchisio as Arsace and Semiramide in Rossini's *Semiramide*. An example of 1860s costume design. (Museo Teatrale alle Scala, Milan)

12 Scene from *La sonnambula*: the heroine walking over a perilous bridge above a millrace. Italian popular print (Civica Raccolta Stampe A. Bertarelli, Milan)

13 *Lohengrin*, a popular opera for many years sung in Italian by Italian singers.
Popular print (Civica Raccolta Stampe A. Bertarelli, Milan)

Teatri Italiani.   Il "Simon Boccanegra" al teatro della Scala. (Disegno del signor Ximenes).

14 A grandiose late nineteenth century staging: Verdi's *Simon Boccanegra* (revised version) at La Scala, Milan, 1881. (Civica Raccolta Stampe A. Bertarelli, Milan)

15 Giuseppina Gargano (flourished *c.* 1880–90), probably as Lucia di Lammermoor in the mad scene. By A. Pietra (Civico Museo Bibliografico Musicale, Bologna)

4

THE COMING OF A MARKET

'You've been told that I don't much like it here,' one of the composer Carissimi's ex-pupils wrote to him from Vienna; '. . . if it wasn't for the money I certainly wouldn't stay another hour.'[1] A healthy interest in the cash nexus could sway even a singer taken up mainly with church music, as this one was, even as early as 1639.

Wanting to draw a good salary, however, is not the same thing as working a market. Before singers could enjoy the benefits and run the risks of a market, certain conditions had to be met, not singly but together. Most of them were in place sometime between the 1750s and the 1780s; the rest followed in succeeding decades. After the 1848 revolutions, governments and law courts were increasingly reluctant to interfere with freedom of contract among those engaged in market dealings, a reluctance confirmed in the new united Italy from 1860. Opera singers of about 1800 were thus already creatures of the market, and the new state of things was confirmed as the nineteenth century wore on.

What is a market in opera singing? The conditions that define it may be set out as follows.

First, there must be at any one time a substantial amount of both supply and demand: an array of singers and theatres, affording on either side a number of levels of quality, pretensions, and fees, with enough opportunities for supply to meet demand (and vice versa) at each level.

Secondly, payment must generally be made in cash, because only cash makes possible rapid comparisons of value between one sector of the market and another.

Thirdly, theatres and singers must be able to communicate and singers to move about readily; news of jobs and singers available must travel fast: in a complex and dispersed business like opera, a network of go-betweens is probably needed.

Finally, singers and their employers must both be free from serious non-economic constraints when they make their choices; contracts must be explicit and contractual relations governed by ascertainable laws or rules, with some assurance that these will be enforced, and that disputes over their interpretation will be settled by means both sides can accept.

None of this is to suggest that a market will ever be perfect, that it will be free from fluctuations or imbalances in supply and demand (hence in employment opportunities or fees), or that everyone will be satisfied with its workings.

Rather than the mere existence of theatres, demand from an array of opera seasons makes a market. Some Italian towns quickly took to regular seasons; others were much slower. Venice, the pioneer, had an almost unbroken run (generally in several competing theatres) from the 1640s; some leading Southern Italian towns did not get going till the early nineteenth century. An example roughly characteristic of the more important Northern and Central Italian towns is that of Reggio Emilia: three or four scattered seasons in the 1640s; a fairly steady run of seasons, with occasional years missed out (chiefly because of wars), from 1668 to 1743; regular annual seasons from 1748 to 1771; two seasons a year as the norm from 1772.[2] A sleepier town like Perugia seems to have had only scattered opera performances until a permanent theatre was built in 1723; there were then frequent seasons, with occasional breaks, and two competing seasons after the opening of a rival theatre in 1781.[3]

We shall not be far out if we assume a general quickening of activity in 1700–20, regular seasons in many places from the 1740s, and a further intensification from about 1770 or 1780. This meant not only more opera houses in more towns, but, in the larger towns, more seasons: spring and autumn, and on occasion summer, seasons joined carnival, which in most places was the traditional high spot of both the theatrical and the social year. Lent was annexed (at first for 'sacred drama' – opera on a biblical subject) from the 1780s. These seasons were dovetailed together, so that a singer could and, increasingly, expected to move straight from one to another; even July and August, slack seasons in most of Italy, could be put to use either in a season coinciding with a trade fair or in a supposedly cool place such as London.

In this sequence outbreaks of peace are significant, particularly the ending of the War of Austrian Succession in 1748: it marked the onset of almost a half-century without wars fought on Italian soil – a virtually unprecedented boon – and made possible increasing traffic along a now dense Italian opera network. Communications opened up elsewhere as well. Besides keeping up their previous travels to Central Europe, the British Isles, and the Iberian peninsula, Italian singers by the second half of the century were regularly active in Russia and Scandinavia, and, by about 1840, in Turkey, mainland Greece, and the Americas.

Supply of singers cannot be measured. What is revealing is that as late as 1700 there was no salary structure for opera. A list drawn up in that year of six women singers available for a season at Bologna – all described as 'among the best' – names fees of 80, 100, 200, 260, and 500 doubloons.[4] Fees, it is true, were not then the only mode of payment: these would have been supplemented by payment in kind. Yet a range as wide as this suggests that no one quite knew what to ask, because singers free to take part in public performances were as yet too few to compare, and the question was complicated by some artists' drawing benefits from a patron. In the same year the prima donna Barbara Riccioni, invited by the nobleman in charge of the Turin opera season to take a smaller fee than she had asked for on a previous occasion, appealed to the Duchess Regent of Savoy: she would – she declared – take whatever the Duchess thought right.[5] This device (still used by Sicilian car park attendants) shows that prices are thought to be set less by a generally understood structure than by the status of the person paying. Full market pricing probably did not come in until singers were paid almost wholly in cash.

In the seventeenth century cash was both hard to come by and regarded as less honourable than payment in kind. Its scarcity went with economic backwardness: even kings and great nobles often found it easier to lay hands on buildings, flour, wine, firewood, or jewels than on coin; salaries were often paid late; nearly everyone was in debt. This state of things both enforced dependence on a patron who could supply the essentials of life and showed it to advantage: besides enjoying relative security, employees could be housed, fed, and clothed while they waited for their arrears of pay and hoped that no real disaster would strike. Such bargains were on offer particularly in the courts of Central Europe, and went on attracting minor Italian singers down to the 1780s; if, besides providing food, wine, and firewood, one's employer was 'a court that pays in cash rather than promises', it might justify accepting a modest salary.[6] In Italy the same principle held good, but musicians in church and court establishments more often received (or failed to receive) cash in lieu of lodging and food allowances.

At the level of gold chains, diamond-studded snuffboxes, silver plate, and silk stockings, payment in kind was reckoned more honourable than cash. Because Loreto Vittori was one of the foremost singers of his time, it was advisable to reward him with a present (*regalo*) rather than with money for singing in a court pageant at Parma in 1628; in the next generation the equally famous Anna Renzi, the original Ottavia in *L'incoronazione di Poppea*, was denied admission to Parnassus by a contemporary author because, unlike Vittori, she sang in public theatres for money: hers was a 'mercenary' art.[7] About 1670 the Pope and the Duke of Savoy took the trouble to buy jewelry for singers and musicians who in Rome at least seem to have been paid wholly in kind.[8] As late as the 1750s Metastasio was rewarded entirely in gold and silver objects by the courts of Spain and Portugal for adjusting librettos; when he provided a new one his letter of thanks delicately failed to mention that the valuables sent him in acknowledgment enclosed 400 doubloons: to be specific might have been beneath the dignity of the Imperial poet laureate, famous throughout Europe.[9]

By then payment of opera singers mainly in cash, always the rule in the great commercial capital, London, had spread to most places; the transition was probably gradual and cannot be traced in detail. Payment in kind was already being made fun of in 1724 – a sign that it was being questioned – in the comic intermezzo *L'impresario delle Canarie*, attributed to Metastasio: the prima donna demands sherbet, coffee, sugar, tea, the best vanilla chocolate, three kinds of tobacco, 'and at least two presents a week'.

Not that ostentatious presents from the great ceased to be part of leading singers' reward. The 'large silver bowl filled with sonnets all bordered with lace and gold fringe, enough to garnish a dress' that was presented on stage to Maria Maddalena Musi in 1694[10] – it came on behalf of the Grand Prince of Tuscany – had many successors: sonnets, flowers, jewels. Singers in Italy were to go on receiving such gifts down to about 1870 (in South America for a while longer), particularly on their benefit nights. That the habit died so hard shows – in opera as in sport – how a personal tie between performer and audience could run alongside the cash nexus. By about 1800 gifts were still worth having, but in Italian theatres their money value no longer made up a large part of singers' pay; the way they were presented suggests that their main function was to show esteem, as public as could be.

Throwing into the auditorium sonnets in the artist's honour (perhaps printed on silk), an Italian custom through most of the eighteenth and nineteenth centuries, was a form of conspicuous devotion. Having them delivered to the singer on stage by trained doves was an embellishment – perhaps novel at Venice in 1764, still heard of at Urbino in 1816, undoubtedly old hat on its last known appearance at Buenos Aires in 1875; it could be combined with more material gratification when the doves were made to carry gold or silver coins as well.[11]

Arrangements for benefits dramatized the relationship between the singer and the upper classes for whom the opera season was at the heart of social life. As the author G. M. Ortes explained in a private letter of 1768, the success of a benefit depended not just on how well the artist was thought to have sung but on her personal character and manners: some who had been well applauded on ordinary nights did badly because for one reason or another they were held in contempt. Special circumstances could now and then come into play, such as a feeling among the audience that a new, gifted singer was being paid an inadequate fee.[12]

The first step for the artist to take was to appeal to feelings of esteem among opera subscribers and other leading citizens by having a printed slip delivered to their houses. A surviving example from the contralto Rosmunda Pisaroni, distributed at Bologna in 1818, explained that at her forthcoming benefit she was to sing an extra scena and aria by Rossini: 'Not this slight addition, but that vivifying genius that animates every individual on this illustrious soil, leads her to flatter herself that the night in question will bring her honour; and that will be the highest prize for one who never did or will neglect any pains to make herself worthy of your benevolence and sympathy.'[13]

After such an exordium it was only fitting that the lady should be found standing in the foyer as the audience arrived, wearing full costume and with a bowl by her side into which well-wishers deposited offerings in cash; more personal presents – flowers, lace, jewels, perhaps cash as well – went straight to the beneficiary's lodgings. During the Napoleonic period the singer at times took her collecting bowl round the boxes, perhaps a token of the new parvenu manners. At Rome in 1808 this seems to have been thought too pressing a call; back went bowl and singer to the foyer, until in the 1830s the whole practice began gradually to die out in leading Italian theatres.[14] It had vanished by about 1870, together with sonnet-throwing: in a small town like Bagnacavallo, near Ravenna, the impresario could still, as late as 1900, arrange for leaflets bearing a few words of praise for the prima donna to be scattered at a convenient moment, but even at Bagnacavallo no one any longer troubled to make them into sonnets.[15]

Archaic practices like this one had their last days of glory in South America. At Ferrara in 1722 a cardinal leaned out of his stage box and handed a purse full of gold coins to the chief comic soprano on stage, just as she was singing the words 'Give alms to a poor pilgrim'; he thus combined two favourite baroque devices, a public show of beneficence and playing about with theatrical illusion.[16] The cardinal's gesture was forgotten, but its spirit lived on: at Buenos Aires in 1875 a prima donna's admirers saw to it that she should, when on the point of singing the Jewel Song in *Faust*, find an actual diamond tiara in the casket instead of the usual paste property. This was only a piquant moment in a benefit night that included a rain of flowers, doves flying and beribboned, diamond and turquoise hair brooches openly presented on stage, and, as a final apotheosis, a transparency bearing a congratulatory inscription flanked by banners with, beneath it, the diva's portrait and a heap of all the flowers she had received: an occasion outdone in Carácas some twenty years later when the *progresista* President of the Republic, his wife, his sons, his daughters, and the impresario all made the prima donna separate public gifts of diamond jewelry.[17]

Besides luxury articles, payment to singers in the early days of opera took the form of travelling and living expenses; for a Roman woman singer who appeared in Venice in the 1650s these expenses added about 50 per cent to her fee, but a good deal less to the fees accorded the highest-paid singers.[18] Even when opera was being given in a public theatre it was customary to provide singers from out of town with lodgings, often in the theatre proprietor's or the impresario's house. Travelling expenses were high, especially for singers going to a faraway place such as London: the leading castrato Senesino (Francesco Bernardi) was advised in 1729 that a fee of £1,000 for the season would leave him out of pocket unless he got travelling expenses and a benefit as well.[19]

Provision of board and lodging flowed from the relation of patron to dependant, with the impresario – if he played host – acting as a kind of head butler on behalf of the noble proprietors or boxholders. It fell away very gradually as cash payment grew more important. Thus the impresario of the Teatro Capranica, Rome, in 1732 was still providing his singers with meals and a cook, but that of the San Carlo in 1760 felt able to do away with the customary provision of lodgings for soloists, perhaps because, with the tourist boom in Naples, comfortable hotels and rooms were now easier to find.[20]

Such provision had long given rise to complaints on all sides, never so much as in the 1690s, when the Grand Prince of Tuscany virtually billeted singers on Leghorn merchants. One merchant complained that the prima donna he had been told to put up had arrived with a sister, a brother, and a servant, all exceedingly hungry; he produced accounts to show that this was more than his resources could bear.[21] As opera seasons became more common, lodgings were paid for by the impresario, but by the 1820s the practice had come to seem a nuisance: singers, according to an experienced man, complained on arrival that 'nothing was suitable, the rooms were inadequate, the furniture unspeakable, the outlook gloomy, the distance excessive, the floors uneven'.[22] By 1848, though in fact still resorted to here and there, the custom of putting up soloists was pronounced dead by a leading agent.[23] It lingered on for humble members of the chorus; a lodging-house keeper complained that when eight or ten women and a small child occupied a room during the Senigallia fair of 1836, with the little town packed out, the child wet the mattress.[24]

Cash payment went together with the arrival of professional agents who supposedly worked on artists' behalf and relieved them of a percentage of their earnings.

They had been preceded, from the earliest days of opera, by amateur go-betweens – noblemen, priests, tradesmen, or members of the musical profession; some of these expected a reward, so the line between amateur and professional is not always clear. Rome was to begin with the chief centre for the training of singers and the traffic in opera engagements; early in the eighteenth century it was displaced by Bologna, itself to be displaced, about a hundred years later, by Milan. At Bologna – but not only there – unmistakable professional agents operated from about 1770; some of them doubled as costume hirers or jewellers. A token that opera had become a highly organized business was the launching in 1764 of annual published records of seasons along the Italian opera circuit, taking in many North and Central Italian towns and some in other parts of Europe; their chief purpose was to serve as casting directories, and they went on appearing until theatrical journals (often run by agents) took over in the 1820s.[25]

What had happened was a gradual intensification and speeding up of the traffic in news about singers, contracts, and seasons rather than a sudden burst. Surviving correspondence of 1675 shows the twenty-year-old Abbé Vincenzo Grimani using a kinsman then in Rome to get detailed information about possible singers for the Grimani theatre in Venice and to negotiate with them, not only with stars such as the prima donna Maddalena or the young castrato Grossi (Siface) but with a singing female dwarf for whom comic parts might be written. The kinsman was eventually authorized to offer Maddalena a contract at fifty doubloons more than Grimani had resolved to pay any singer, because he was keen to meet the Venetian taste for novelty, and besides 'I am competing with others and that makes me particularly anxious'; the same anxiety led him to insist that a certain bass, a priest who had already been heard in a rival Venice theatre, should be inquired about very discreetly, 'so that if he is good and we need him we shan't get into a lot of bargaining over [his contract]'. Grimani considered himself well informed: one castrato proposed to him was unlikely to amount to much, 'since I've never heard his name mentioned'.[26] Later managers shared all these sentiments.

Exchanges like those between Grimani and his kinsman went on continuously, until agents and directories were needed to keep up with the volume and speed of business. Physical and postal communications had themselves speeded up, again gradually: a journey from Rome to Venice by chaise in 1665 took – in good weather – twelve days; in the early 1840s, still without benefit of railways but thanks to improved roads and bridges, it took half the time.[27]

Relatively clear and secure contractual relations took shape at about the same rate as cash payment and speedier communications. Contracts for mid seventeenth-century Venetian opera seasons were brief and left much unsaid. They did not name the works to be performed, rarely mentioned starting dates (as the season was always carnival the finishing date was known to be Shrove Tuesday), and, when they exceptionally went into arrangements for payment, used vague phrases such as 'during the run' or 'within the first week of Lent'. Nor did most of them state what would happen if the season was interrupted by war, plague, fire, or government action – frequent enough hazards, – though one contract of 1659 unusually and presciently stated that a season interrupted from such causes should be paid for in proportion to the length of time it had run.[28]

Maria Maddalena Musi's set-to with the Viceroy of Naples, already mentioned, shows what unpleasantness could arise from such gaps in the wording of contracts. By about 1730 the question of payment dates had been dealt with, at least in some theatres. Here, singers' fees were now paid in four instalments at set dates before and during the run – the usual system from then on, with occasional variants. Seasons interrupted through *force majeure* were to be paid for in proportion to the number of performances given – an obvious answer, and one already glimpsed in commercial-minded London (1709) as well as in Venice, but in more backward cities like Naples and Rome it had taken the better part of a century to emerge;[29] even then, in Rome, the headquarters of legal and bureaucratic pettifogging, the death of a pope four days before the end of the 1769 carnival season could still bring about confusion and lawsuits.[30] In general, however, such interruptions could be referred to by the 1750s as 'the usual fortuitous causes'; by the 1760s there were printed forms for contracts, embodying these and other conventions; by the 1780s the forms were in general use.[31]

Modern devices such as printed forms did not of course secure artists against defaulting impresarios who might leave them unpaid in mid season – another fairly common hazard. Star singers from the 1660s to the 1880s tried to safeguard their fees by exacting a banker's guarantee or the right to have first call on any government subsidy – at the expense of minor artists, stage staff, and other creditors. This was a form of privileged dependence on patrons.[32]

Demanding a guarantee in advance did show more foresight than the still older habit of appealing to some great nobleman to exact privileged payment, by fair or other means, from an impresario who had already defaulted: at Faenza in 1738 the bass managed to get paid through the influence of a local aristocrat, but by the time the composer of the opera appealed to a still more powerful nobleman at Bologna the impresario had taken himself and his property into sanctuary in a church.[33] Holding out for a guarantee, however, was not in principle very different. It assumed that leading singers could use their rarity value and their connections to jump the queue. Some of them clung to it even at the cost of unpleasantness: the tenor Luigi Mari, knowing that the Modena impresario in 1826 was running out of money, would not sing unless allowed a guarantee; the authorities put him in gaol but presently gave way.[34] As late as 1888 the famous tenor Roberto Stagno had a guarantee from several local businessmen when he sang in Buenos Aires, a city whose Italian impresarios were if anything more reliable than their equivalents back home.[35]

Eighteenth-century governments did do something to protect all opera personnel from the risks of the business. Venice in 1753–6, soon followed by others, made impresarios and theatre owners deposit caution money: in the event of bankruptcy all employees and creditors would have some redress – though the accounts of a failed season at a Venetian theatre in the 1760s show that leading singers still managed to get paid a much higher proportion of what was owed them than did lesser creditors.[36] Flawed though it might be, the requirement of caution money helped along the coming of a market by bringing into its transactions a measure of order and certainty. A market is not the same thing as a free-for-all: an impersonal legal framework designed to lessen the worst effects of irresponsibility or fraud was a modern development, unlike the use of arbitrary power to dictate the conduct of managers or artists.

Arbitrary power, it is true, went on being brought to bear on the detail of opera seasons down to the mid nineteenth century. Yet one can sense a gradual shift to more impersonal relationships between patrons and artists. The greater professionalism of women singers did much to bring it about. It came together with the spread of short opera seasons run by impresarios along an ever denser network: this entailed greater mobility and steadier reliance on contract.

The career of the great Caterina Gabrielli illustrates this. In deciding to spend a year or two in a foreign capital she seems not to have faced the choice between taking a fee (high but giving no security) and taking 'service' that had exercised, a generation earlier, the equally famous Francesca Cuzzoni:

Gabrielli's negotiations with Madrid show that whether she was contracted to the court or to the theatre impresario was a matter of convenience.[37]

By the time Gabrielli retired in 1782 the market largely ruled the development of singers' careers, though German courts, as usual archaic in their ways, were still recruiting such figures as a female soprano intended exclusively for chamber singing, or a castrato who would be expected to sing in church, chamber, and theatre alike, with the chance of a seven-year engagement.[38] Even Italian courts kept a few singers on the establishment into the first half of the nineteenth century, but at Modena, for instance – a court which had employed some of the finest singers of the late seventeenth century, – they were now obscure minor artists some of whom had at best sung small parts in the town theatre.[39] More successful artists had not the slightest interest in tying themselves down, though a title as chamber singer to one of the Italian rulers was still thought worth having: Giuseppina Strepponi, Verdi's future wife, was keen in 1843 to be thus nominally attached to the ex-Empress Marie-Louise, then Duchess of Parma.[40]

From the middle decades of the eighteenth century down to the First World War (later still in small towns and in Southern Italy) singers dealt in the first place with impresarios.

An Italian impresario was essentially a middleman, someone who put together an opera season as a concessionaire appointed by the theatre owners, and then moved on to do the same job somewhere else. Though he took a financial risk – and some impresarios failed – in theatres of any pretensions he depended on the owners, the boxholders, or the government for a subsidy. An impresario might be an ex-singer, more often a choreographer, but he need not be a musician or a man of the theatre at all; some were shopkeepers for whom an opera season was one trading venture among others.

Why did opera not develop a system like that of the Italian straight theatre, which for centuries was run by actor-managers at the head of permanent touring companies? An opera troupe headed by a singer-manager is not only conceivable; as we have noted, there were such troupes in the earliest days of public opera, but they then faded out except at the humblest levels of comic opera (and again, from about 1870, in operetta and in the specialized field of opera performed by children).

In 1652, 1726, and 1729 we know of management partnerships between a singer and one or more impresarios to put on a season in which the singer would appear; there were probably many more. These ran from a straightforward investment of money by a leading singer in her own season to a more modest singer's acceptance of boxes (which she could hope to let out) as, in effect, her fee. Both types were on occasion to be found at later times, mostly in minor theatres and in small towns, but as a rule they lasted for one season only.[41]

In Venice during the middle decades of the eighteenth century singers, musicians, and dancers regularly got together to form joint-stock companies (*imprese a carato*) for the sole purpose of running an opera seria season during the two-week Ascension Fair, and on occasion to run a longer (but modest) autumn and carnival season. The Ascension Fair ventures were speculative in two ways. First, they might be set up in the hope of securing one of the (as a rule two) theatres allowed to open at that time, rather than because of an arrangement already made with the owners. Secondly, the partners were to receive a share (*carato*) in any profit left over once the costs of the season had been met: the shares, though expressed as sums of money, signalled proportions rather than actual amounts. A more complex form allowed the partners to take on other artists who would be paid a straight fee. Leading singers such as Gaetano Guadagni joined some of these partnerships.[42] We know about these ventures because they generated notarial documents, but we do not hear about their results; some projected seasons did not happen. The fair probably lent itself to ventures of this kind because it was short and, in a good year, was thronged with tourists: a group of singers, dancers, and musicians with little capital might hope to make money quickly before they could over-extend themselves.

Why more permanent troupes managed by singers did not develop is a matter for speculation. Opera seasons longer than two weeks – we may suppose, – or more ambitious than a minor comic opera season, were too expensive for artists to take on: both the initial capital requirements and the potential losses were too great. The disastrous results of some early attempts to run Venice carnival seasons through artists' partnerships (one of them, in 1638, involved two singers, the composer Cavalli, a poet, and a choreographer) may have given the arrangement a bad name.[43]

Singers, then, once the market was fully in place were nearly always employees contracted for a season to an impresario who was himself a transient figure. This was generally true in Italy, and in a number of operatic outposts abroad – London and the Iberian peninsula, Vienna, later Greece and Constantinople, later still the Americas. In eighteenth-century Germany there were Italian impresarios, some of them itinerant, who for a time came close to being artist-managers; the men who launched *Don Giovanni* in Prague were of this type, but even they could expect to last only as long as their concession from the theatre owners. By and large, singers had every reason to behave as individuals concerned with maximum financial gain rather than with notions that could not be translated into cash, such as loyalty to an institution. The general attitude was summed up by a prima donna's father, who declined on her behalf an engagement said to confer 'honour' even though it did not pay very well: he was, he said, 'concerned with reality, not with chimaeras'.[44]

The 'reality' of the market was profitable for successful artists – those who could stand the pace of the Italian opera calendar with its seasons following each on the heels of the last, and its demand that they should be prepared continually to learn and rehearse a new work in three weeks. But already in 1766 we hear of two of the market's victims.

Francesco Piccoli, a tenor aged thirty who specialized in comic parts, had spent the past three years singing in Germany, Corfu, the Kingdom of Naples, and Romagna – most likely minor engagements. He then turned impresario, contracted to put on an opera season in the North Italian towns of Vicenza and Crema, lost a lot of money, and fled to Parma. There he tried to find a post as a church singer, but such posts were now scarce. He started looking once more for a part in comic opera – any part, whether of the first, second, or third rank; meanwhile he joined forces with another singer, probably a castrato, who after five years in the profession was frankly looking for no more than an *ultima parte*, the smallest part in an opera seria.[45]

There were to be many more like these two, struggling in and out of the profession down to recent times, some of them on the verge of starvation: a state of things probably at its worst in the latter half of the nineteenth century. If the price of patronage was submission to the great, in Italy as in Britain the price of market freedom was insecurity and, for singers of no more than average attainments, constant downward pressure from competition in an overcrowded trade.[46]

5

TRAINING

Almost since opera began, people have complained about singers' training, and the complaints have changed little. Standards – it has been said again and again – are in decline for various reasons: newfangled methods harm voices; singers are encouraged to make their debuts too soon, cutting short their training to the injury of their careers; new kinds of music put them under further damaging strain; so do new modes of transport that encourage flitting from place to place. The complainants, often themselves teachers of singing, have contrasted this state of things with a previous golden age; they have often claimed for themselves the secret of the only right method, which they have presented as quite unlike their competitors'. These complaints cannot all be true. Some prove to be baseless; others – too subjective to be true or false – no doubt spring from a human tendency to value most highly the joys experienced in one's youth.

Where we know something of how performers were trained from 1600 on, we are likely to be struck by the conservatism of the opera world, the slow change in its methods and attitudes, and the willingness of teachers to reproduce one another's techniques while claiming to be original.[1] This ought not to surprise us: singing, a bodily feat, does not lend itself with ease to analysis or perhaps to radically new methods; teaching and learning are always likely to be personal and in some degree incommunicable.

A further difficulty is that historians of music have concentrated on institutions such as the four Naples conservatories that flourished in the seventeenth and eighteenth centuries, because institutions leave behind them piles of documents that can be studied. The result can be misleading. The institution at the heart of Italian society down to recent times – one that had neither a charter nor regular documentation – was the family. Relationships that seem to us impersonal, such as those between a ruler and his people or a college and its students, were thought of as family ties on a larger scale, and people behaved accordingly.

English-speaking people find it hard to enter into Italian family feeling.

They have been used, probably for centuries, to small nuclear family groups which children leave in their late teens if not sooner. Italian family relationships even today, after industrialization, are more ramified, more intense, and more lasting (which need not mean more benign).[2] For most of our period they were stronger still, and were centred on the virtually undisputed power of the father.

Before the Napoleonic codes came into force there was no official coming of age; adult sons, as well as unmarried daughters, were bound to obey their fathers and to contribute to their parents' maintenance in exchange for the cost of their upbringing, unless the father issued a legal 'emancipation' setting them free to act on their own in financial matters. As we might expect, these imperatives were sometimes flouted in practice; yet when the tenor Giuseppe Tibaldi had enjoyed eighteen years' successful career in various parts of Europe he thought it worth while to get from his father in 1771 an 'emancipation' acknowledging that he had paid back the cost of his training and keep and had long been financially independent.[3] The bass Giuseppe Frezzolini in 1839 contracted with his daughter Erminia, a soprano then on the threshold of a great career, for a life annuity of 3,000 francs as his reward for having trained her; he has been denounced in our own time as an exploiter, but he was intensely proud of Erminia's success and was only carrying forward into the new age of contract what had long been enforced by custom or, under the *ancien régime*, by government dictate.[4]

Where a father died early, elder brothers could take his place. The baritone Natale Costantini, about to create the leading part of Ezio in Verdi's *Attila* (1846), had – as he thought – repaid his brothers for his keep, but one of them was in financial trouble and was pressing for help; Natale grumbled – he was about to get married, his profession was risky – but owned that he would do something. He then married, and almost immediately died. His widow, a minor singer, had the use only of a quarter of his estate; she none the less felt that before she resumed her career she needed to square his brothers, who were still pressing their claims for the cost of Natale's maintenance as a boy.[5]

Like any other trade, music came down by inheritance. Many singers were trained chiefly by their parents or uncles, themselves musicians. In the seventeenth century teachers and pupils were most likely to be church singers who made an occasional foray into opera, like the Melani family, already mentioned for the parents' bold castration strategy. The family of Alessandro Scarlatti (1660–1725) – brothers, sisters, children, grandchildren – included opera singers and composers; they intermarried with a similar, less well known family, the Uttinis, and a woman member of this kin group gave birth in 1813 to Giuseppe Verdi.[6] There were the Giordanis (father, two sons and two daughters, mid eighteenth-century composers and singers), and among nineteenth-century groups made up of singers only – some of them married to composers or impresarios, – the Mombellis (father, mother and two daughters), the Garcías (father, stepmother, two daughters, and a son), the Brambillas (three sisters and a niece), the Boccabadatis (mother, three daughters, son, son-in-law, granddaughter). These were all famous; more obscure family groups, typically made up of father, daughter, and son-in-law, or husband, wife, and wife's brother, took the comic operas that flourished from about 1740 to 1830 round Italian towns large and small, and sometimes abroad.

When musicians were trained within the family we are unlikely to hear about it in any detail, because people seldom needed to write anything down. A 1724 caricature does show a young castrato singing a female part in Rome with his uncle prompting from the wings; according to the caption, the uncle 'sang more than his nephew'.[7] A few young women with a violinist father or a pianist brother began by learning an instrument well enough to become skilled musicians, and picked up singing almost by the way: this was true in the eighteenth century of Gertrud Elisabeth Mara, in the nineteenth of the sisters Barbara and Carlotta Marchisio; in Connecticut early this century it was true of the child Rosa Ponzillo (later Ponselle), though here the quasi-parental figure was the local church organist, an Irish spinster who did not teach singing.[8]

At the opposite extreme, some Italian singers throughout the history of opera have remained *orecchianti* (literally 'earers') unable to read music, like the 23-year-old bass who in 1690 made a successful debut at the leading Venice theatre, demonstrating 'a very fine, full, sonorous voice with every quality'; he had had no formal training but was now eager to learn.[9] All the same, he must have had some kind of start, if only through performing on street corners and in the yards of wayside inns, where, according to foreign visitors down to the late nineteenth century, some remarkably well-tuned singing was to be heard.[10] One who began in this way, Brigida Giorgi Banti, learned in the first place from her father; by the 1780s, still illiterate, she was a leading singer in Paris and London: 'Hearing an air once played over, and that but indifferently, she sang it most divinely.' That so-called artists should have to be fed tunes 'like canaries' distressed theoreticians but did not prevent some, like Banti, from making a great name.[11]

She and her fellows presumably moved from unconscious imitation of their elders to somewhat more formal lessons, still held in the interstices of daily life and perhaps outdoors. Much later, in the 1930s, an eight-year-old boy from a poor family in the hills behind Venice made his first conscious efforts at singing when a friend's mother announced, as she did from time to time, 'I'll give five eggs to whoever sings the best high note.' Gastone Limarilli went on to a fair career as a tenor, though only the insistence of his future father-in-law, an amateur violinist, made him take lessons.[12]

Singers were less apt to be born into the profession than trumpeters or violinists, because singing more than instrumental playing depends on bodily gifts that need not run in families. But even when aspiring singers went outside their own family for their training, the patriarchal habits of Italian society made the relation between teacher and pupil close to that of father and child.

The obvious way for this to happen was for the teacher to adopt the child. A few eighteenth-century examples are known; they suggest that for a member of the theatre world to take on a child of eight, nine, or ten for training as a future singer or dancer need not require more than a private, informal contract, if that. Angelo Villa, the eleven-year-old castrato whom we saw defending his adoptive father, had been taken on in this way.[13]

Such children came of poor families. Adoption was not always easy to tell apart from an outright sale of a girl into prostitution – an arrangement legally sanctioned by the sixteenth-century Venetian Republic in cases of absolute need; about 1750, setting a girl on the path to a singing or especially a dancing career by handing her over to a member of the profession still struck Venetian officials as little better.[14] As late as the 1830s, an adult but unmarried woman performer sometimes went about with a *mammaccia* or *babbaccio* – a 'mock-mother' or 'mock-father' whose actual relationship with her was unclear, and who might be a varying blend of guardian, agent, teacher, sponger, and pimp.

On quite another level, a young singer might acquire a devoted father substitute who watched over his finances, his contracts, his voice production, his professional conduct, and even his dealings with servants, as the middle-aged Rossini watched over the Russian tenor Nicola Ivanoff, keeping it up for six years until Ivanoff was able to fend for himself.[15] Rossini's devotion was intense, the young man perhaps a surrogate for the children he never had. But even without being as devoted as this, a teacher commonly took on a paternal role and referred to his male pupils as 'sons'; two nineteenth-century prima donnas can be found addressing their teacher or ex-teacher as 'papa'.[16]

Until the coming of modern music colleges in the late nineteenth century, even teachers in conservatories behaved in patriarchal fashion, keeping some students as lodgers in their own homes, treating their conservatory pupils as their dependants, allowing some to shuttle between home and school, and placing others in the church choirs for which they were responsible.[17] As late as the 1880s a well-known teacher of singing, Francesco Cortesi, put up his students, Americans among them, in the Florence block of flats he lived in (and owned); even if they lodged two floors below him all he need do was call out of the window to get them to come up, perhaps three times a day, for a lesson or to accompany a visiting professional who had dropped in to seek advice. The lessons themselves were a mix of formal teaching and familiar conversation: 'it takes', one American pupil reported, 'an Italian teacher an hour to give a half-hour lesson' – and this was much more helpful than the relentless cash-conscious pressure the young man had experienced from teachers back home.[18]

For many singers, generally men, the father-child relationship was embodied in the apprenticeship contracts that provided them with training, down to Caruso and Gigli and perhaps even nearer our own day.[19]

Such contracts solved the chief problem facing most teachers and most students in a poor country: few students could afford to pay; even from those who could pay something a well-known Naples teacher about 1840 had to accept payment half in cash, half in IOUs to be cashed once the pupil got a contract with an opera house.[20] The solution was for the teacher to instruct, put up, and feed the student without charge (and sometimes clothe him as well, a notable expense in early modern times, when most people had only one suit of clothes); in exchange he would get a percentage of the pupil's earnings over a fixed term of years, usually coinciding with the apprenticeship itself. On occasion the boy's family was to pay something towards his keep. Contracts along these lines can be traced as far back as 1591.

Their terms were generally as follows. The teacher was to exercise a parent's authority, especially when the boy lodged with him; one contract let him decide whether to have the boy castrated. The apprenticeship was to last for a fixed term, with fifteen years an unusual extreme, three years a possible arrangement for pupils who had already had some training, ten or twelve years a common one for young castrati who got free places in the Naples conservatories, and six years the term most often named for private study with an individual teacher. The share of earnings assigned to the teacher in several early contracts was half, but later on we find wide variations. Where the boy's family was in an unfavourable bargaining position the teacher might take the whole of his pupil's earnings during the apprenticeship period, or agree only to give the family something at his own discretion; Caruso's teacher, on the other hand, who did not give his pupil room and board, was to receive a quarter. Schools like the Naples conservatories got something by hiring out their pupils for religious functions; a late eighteenth-century school at Parma, whose purpose was to train chorus singers for the ducal opera house, took one-fifth of their earnings if they sang elsewhere.

If the pupil broke the contract by leaving early, he or his family was contractually obliged to pay a penalty, and could be sued if he failed to do so; the examples known to us suggest that in practice the two sides were likely to make a compromise settlement out of court. Rather than break his contract, a successful young singer might buy it out by agreement, as Domenico Bruni did in 1783, and Caruso in 1899; – it cost him 20,000 francs.[21] Finally, some contracts provided for arbitration by experts if the teacher should default, for instance by going abroad – a common occurrence in the peripatetic world of Italian opera.

What was the quality of the human relations between teacher and apprentice? We do not know. Probably they varied as much as those between father and child, which in early modern Italy could be harsh – not just because individuals had character quirks but because society underwrote assertions of authority.

Such a contract – we do know – encouraged the teacher to become in effect his pupil's agent. In the precocious semi-commercial world of Venetian opera a priest-teacher can be found as early as 1665 hiring out the services of two girl pupils to an impresario for an annual sum; what he paid the girls was left for him and them to agree.[22] These singers failed, but a pupil who held out the possibility of gain could be fought over.

Geminiano Raimondini, a castrato probably aged about fifteen or sixteen, was contended for in 1706 by the composer-teacher Antonio Gianettini, who had him under six-year contract, and a Venice merchant with theatrical interests; each tried to influence Geminiano's engagements as a budding opera singer; each brought up reinforcements – the exiled Duke of Modena, patron to both teacher and pupil, and Geminiano's brother; Geminiano at one point shuttled between the two contenders, but eventually went back to his teacher, in whose new opera he sang a part more substantial than he had originally been offered. We seem to observe a tussle for control of a gifted young musician's future, of a kind known in our own day, with the young man perhaps exploiting the situation to his advantage.[23]

Girls who aimed at a singing career did not (with a few exceptions) enter into apprenticeship contracts: it was thought improper for them to have dealings with men not their relatives. Even when mixed conservatories were set up in the early nineteenth century on the French model, the regulations ensured that women's and men's classes were held separately, even (in Turin) many hours apart, so that the two sexes should never meet; in the Spanish-influenced south women were admitted as external students only, or not at all.[24] Only in our own century have genuinely mixed institutions come to be tolerated. Because they were kept in near-purdah, it has been said, women singers before 1800 were less well trained than men, in particular less well than castrati.

There is some truth in this. The Church was vigilant, at least in Rome and at official level; this mattered because in the seventeenth and eighteenth centuries teachers, music teachers included, were many of them clerics, and the institutions in which girls could learn music were nunneries or orphanages. A particularly austere pope decreed in 1686 that no female living in a convent or orphanage was to learn singing from a man, even if he was related to her, and the prohibition was renewed in 1705.[25] Much later, in 1850, a Rome composer of sacred music was applauded by a Vatican official for having withstood invitations to teach women during the short-lived Roman Republic of the previous year.[26]

The four Venetian orphanages whose girl singers and orchestras won European fame through the reports of travellers and the works of their teachers (Vivaldi among them) had strict, by and large successful rules aimed at ensuring that their young women would never turn professional. Men who married orphans had to sign a legal undertaking to that effect; external students were barred from singing lessons. As a result Venice was graced by housewives who were virtuoso singers in private.

These rules could be enforced only on the territory of the Venetian Republic. The orphanages now and then took a few Italian pupils sent by German rulers to learn singing, on condition that they would go back to Germany once they were trained. Among ordinary pupils, Lelia Achiapati and Maddalena Lombardini married professional musicians and sang in opera away from Venice; one or two ex-pupils managed to appear on stage in Venice itself – near the end of the century, when three of the orphanages were bankrupt and all were about to disappear. The orphanages were central to Venetian music; they trained many brilliant singers; they sometimes put on opera (to audiences of women, plus the male board of governors); the sacred music that they performed for mixed audiences in the late eighteenth century was 'in the opera style'; but their rules kept them on the margin of the opera profession.[27]

Convents in general maintained choirs and taught singing to some of their inmates; one purpose of teaching girls to sing in *ancien régime* Italy was that it could qualify them to become nuns without having to provide a cash dowry. But, like the Venice orphanages, convents turned away pupils once they had appeared on stage, even if the stage was that of a court theatre; this happened in 1688 to Diana Aureli, whom the Duke of Savoy had sent to a Milan convent known for its good musical training.[28] A century later in Rome, when the monastic tradition was in decay, Angelica Catalani was convent-trained in both singing and piety; both were exemplary in her later life as a celebrated prima donna. 'I do love to sing to my God!' she would exclaim, but her anecdotes of convent life disconcerted her English acquaintances: she recalled how she had brought up rabbits and then turned them into the dormitories with dogs, 'and when the dogs caught and tore them to pieces they jumped and squealed so you would have died laughing'.[29]

Some women found teachers who were neither nuns nor members of their immediate families. Often these were priests or monks who worked as composers and choirmasters. In Florence in 1600 one such monk taught two sisters of Francesco Rasi, the first Orfeo.[30] A century or so later in Bologna – by then the chief centre of musical training – the Franciscan Angelo Predieri taught girls as well as boys in the homes of respectable families. His pupils may not have been intended for the stage (one of his boy pupils became the great musicologist Padre Martini), but then and later in the eighteenth century several Bologna teachers specialized in teaching would-be women professionals, for whom they might write arias or whole operas when the time came to make their debut. In Rome a caricature of 1725 shows Paolo Boi or Buoi, a Neapolitan who 'taught all the professional women singers [*femmine cantarine*]'. These teachers all seem to have visited pupils in their homes.[31]

A Naples court case of 1737, the result of a dispute over non-payment of fees, involved a minor composer, Antonio Palella, who had been teaching at least two unmarried women pupils. Each of the women lived with her married sister, their brothers-in-law being a doctor and a fencing master. One of the young women was far enough advanced in her training to get a contract to sing in opera at Corfu; this prompted her to call in a second teacher to train her in soft, pathetic singing (*modi cantabili*). The case, with other musicians, a barber, and a laundrywoman all appearing as witnesses and all known to one another, affords a glimpse of a lively world where teaching for women was common even if regular payment was not.[32]

Yet there remained obstacles. The fears entertained by girls' relatives were confirmed by two elopements, both dating from the 1730s: Stefano Lapi and Francesco Maggiore, young teachers in Venice and Naples, each ran off with a woman pupil (Maggiore with two), leaving a wife and at least one child behind.[33] The Franciscan Predieri's teaching was attended by malicious gossip; later on his pupil Padre Martini strongly discouraged a fellow-Franciscan from teaching a girl.[34] Women's place in Italian society was such that a professional relationship could only with difficulty avoid a sexual taint.

This was true above all where a girl pupil lodged with a male teacher under the kind of apprenticeship contract normal for boys. The anonymous comic intermezzo *La canterina* (set by Haydn in 1766) has a budding singer and her mother living with a composer under such an arrangement. This was a variant of a theme common in eighteenth-century comedy, the elderly guardian with a pretty ward (as in *Il barbiere di Siviglia*). Whether it mirrored reality among eighteenth-century women singers we do not know. The one known example of a woman pupil who lived with her teacher under an apprenticeship contract dates from the late 1840s; it is far from reassuring.[35]

Luigia Bendazzi (1826/7–1901) was the daughter of illiterate parents in Ravenna; a maternal uncle, better off and better educated, paid for her to have some training in Milan (he later sued to be paid back with interest). In 1849 she was taken into the household of Federico Dallara, a Bologna composer, teacher, and répétiteur, with whom she may already have been studying; the arrangement was sanctioned in the following year, when Luigia was about to make her debut in opera, by a contract giving Dallara all the rights of a parent. Luigia's career prospered; she had a powerful dramatic soprano voice and was the original prima donna in Verdi's *Simon Boccanegra* (1857). But until 1859 she went on living with Dallara and his wife Annetta, who followed her on nearly all her engagements. Two occasions when she travelled without them, in 1856 and 1859, gave rise to surviving correspondence; it throws a weird light on the relationship.

'I owe you everything, everything,' Luigia wrote in 1856 to those she called 'papa' and 'mama'; 'only you exist for me in this world.' Away from them she felt lonely and ill; after a time she started signing herself 'Gigetta Dallara'; she depended on Federico to cope with all her affairs; her natural parents she denounced as infamous beggars and scroungers (there had probably been wrangles with them over money), her fellow-artists as scoundrels. Her daily letters show her obsessed with Federico as with an unsatisfactorily detached lover, which he perhaps was; Annetta she called 'mama' but also, sometimes to her face, 'sow, slut, whore', and she repeatedly fantasized either pulling out Annetta's pubic hair or showing off her own. These 1856 letters suggest a neurotic tangle fit to bear out the worst fears of those who objected to apprenticeships for girls. By 1859 things had calmed down. Though she was still unendingly grateful, Luigia's success seems to have brought her independence; meanwhile her parents and the Dallara household had been reconciled. She now signed herself 'Gigetta Bendazzi'. Later in the year she established her right to manage her own finances, with Dallara's consent, and not long afterwards she married another minor composer. The marriage may even have been happy.

Singers who went through an apprenticeship, formal or informal, did not necessarily have long to wait before they appeared in public. Boy pupils might sing in church; in the early eighteenth century several castrati who were to become famous (Bernacchi, Farinelli, Carestini, Gizziello) all made their formal stage debuts at fifteen or sixteen. Two generations later, Crescentini sang comic opera, in a small town, when not quite fourteen; his ostensible debut came two years later when he sang a woman's part in Rome.[36]

Comic opera singers of the same period could be just as young. Verve and address made up for a light voice; a comic talent could let an artist switch between acting and singing, not just when opera as a form was getting under way. Angela Zannucchi (La Brescianina) scored a great success in Venice in 1720 when she was thirteen; it seems not to have been her debut. A boy who in 1758 sang a maidservant's part in one minor Rome theatre (presumably as a treble) a few years later was acting lovers' parts in *commedia dell'arte* at another, and doubling as hairdresser.[37]

Even in the late nineteenth century, when tragic opera became dominant and vocal writing grew heavier, some well-known singers launched out after no more than a sketchy training. The Hollywood cliché of the young man whom a teacher overhears serenading a girl and whisks off to a great career is not quite baseless. It happened in 1875 to the Rome carpenter Francesco Marconi; his debut as a tenor in the following year was a resounding success.[38]

Another young artisan who needed no long preparation was the blacksmith Titta Ruffo. Through occasional influences – a brother who studied piano and flute, a lodger whose earnings in a pottery works went into singing lessons – he discovered at sixteen a tenor and at eighteen a baritone voice; the first time, if he is to be believed, his moonlit singing of the Stornello from *Cavalleria rusticana* brought out the neighbours, applauding. He then had a few months' unsatisfactory spell at the conservatory (while he still hammered away at the forge), three months' private lessons with a well-known singer, which he could not afford, six weeks' free lessons from a fellow-townsman in Milan while he made the rounds of the agents, before he secured two auditions that launched his career.[39]

A singer as famous in her day as Titta in his, Giuditta Pasta, emerged from a training that sounds no less casual: debut at 18 after lessons, not prolonged, from three teachers, one of them an uncle who was an amateur cellist; about a year's professional work in London and Paris, with tentative and varying results; another period of study, clearly beneficial, occasioned by pregnancy and lasting no more than a few months; a season appearing opposite the veteran soprano Giuseppina Grassini, who influenced her; a second debut in

Paris that showed, according to a review, 'all the difference . . . between a schoolgirl and a virtuosa'.[40] Later, in 1870, the young Vittorio Carpi, son of a Jewish business family that objected to his choice of career, worked seven hours a day for just under a year to learn singing and music theory from scratch; this was enough to launch him as a baritone, though – he later acknowledged – he was still unready as a stage performer.[41]

A singer's training, these examples suggest, did not have to be steady, prolonged, or clearly distinct from the first steps in a career. Singers went on learning, in part from experience, in part from bouts of further study or 'finishing' (*perfezionamento*) with a maestro or an older singer – the mature Giuditta Pasta, for instance, who did not engage in regular teaching but gave advice on interpretation, of the kind we now formalize as a 'master class'. Pasta's great contemporary Maria Malibran claimed to have exercised her own 'awkward' (*rebelle*) voice on the final aria from *La Cenerentola* for six years and still not to have got to the end of it.[42]

On the other hand singers' accounts of their own careers run to moments when the voice suddenly blossomed out, taking its owner by surprise. The Italo-Argentine bass Nino Meneghetti, who was still singing strongly in 1989 after a career of over forty years, recalled that when very young he had taken lessons as an amateur but had been unsure of his range and, even after identifying himself as a bass, had great trouble working out the passage between registers; he found it while cycling in the country, and from then on was able to sing in an open voice throughout.[43] The somewhat older tenor Mario Del Monaco, who numbered singers and other musicians in his family, had a similar experience. He had a period of conservatory training but felt that his voice was being spoilt in a search for elegance; he then found a private teacher, a singer with no operatic credits (other than a dog called Radames), who miraculously evened out his scale by 'opening up his throat'.[44] With an act as physical as singing one cannot be sure how far such discoveries may have come of earlier practice or of a silent maturing process: an athlete may find from one day to the next that he can after all run a four-minute mile.

One thing singers and teachers have always agreed about is that not even the most dedicated student should exercise his voice for more than a few hours a day: seven or eight hours' practice, not unknown among instrumental players, is out of the question. What then was the trainee singer's schedule?

The earliest account we have of class routine, in Rome about 1640, does allot four hours a day to formal singing practice – concentrated in the morning, with work on theory and counterpoint to follow in the afternoon: an hour for 'difficult things', an hour to practise trills, an hour for passage work (coloratura), an hour before the looking-glass to control posture and facial expression. There were also occasions for singing in church and for testing one's voice against an echo outside the city gates.[45] How all this worked in detail we can only guess. The pupils most likely practised in class one at a time, so that no one exercised his throat a full four hours.

First-hand evidence, though it dates from 250 years later, encourages us to think so. The young American baritone already quoted as reporting that 'it takes an Italian teacher an hour to give a half-hour lesson' explained that the mixture of singing practice and chat made for relaxation. He seems to have been giving a benevolent account of what a coarse satire by another Anglophone pupil described as standing about all day for a nominal one hour's lesson, among a motley group of students who each sang for ten minutes at a time.[46]

The seventeenth-century cliché had been that a 'mercenary' (paid) teacher must always be watching the clock and thinking of rushing off to his next lesson.[47] The patriarchal relation between a teacher and his pupils, however, may well not have varied much over time, especially when the teacher was on his own home ground. We could most likely project back into the eighteenth or even the seventeenth century the vignette we have of a well-known teacher, Francesco Lamperti, about 1890 – seated 'in slippered feet with a rug across his knees, mittens on his hands, a shawl about his shoulders', an admonitory baton ready to 'drub the arms and shoulders' of the careless among the students who crowded round him, listening to and learning from each other's exercises.[48] Timetables, we may conclude, were flexible and need not be taken literally except perhaps in modern conservatories; the few we have mention at most a total of two hours' singing practice a day.

What then should aspiring singers do the rest of the time? Those who were studying theory and an instrument had no trouble filling the day; where the timetable was institutional, classes, down to the early nineteenth century, were apt to start at 6 or 6.30 a.m., not only in Italy – a time derived from the early rising habits of the monks who for many years ran the schools. But, as we have seen, many Italian singers at all times had little or no formal musical training.

When faced with one such – a girl of eighteen who proposed to engage herself as prima donna on the strength of having sung in a few private concerts – the celebrated Bologna teacher Lorenzo Gibelli (1719–1812) is reported to have said that anyone wanting to become a perfect singer must

besides enjoying a fine, well-tuned voice, know all that concerns music and the essentials of her own language and of acting, and should also have furnished her mind with knowledge of the civil, political, and religious history of the peoples of the world, of the civilization and customs of different social classes, if possible of all times, not to mention enough philosophy to teach her the course of human passions.[49]

A tall order. Gibelli was a former horse trainer whose noble employer had seen to his informal general education; the more formal, musical part of it had been entrusted to the great scholar Padre Martini. He may have been making a conventional set speech rather than outlining a realistic programme. Did many of his own pupils follow it? Probably not.

Throughout the nineteenth and twentieth centuries Gibelli's successors were to lament Italian singers' want of general culture.[50] Surviving letters show that, especially before 1850 or thereabouts, many were weak in spelling and grammar, though some who did well and lived to a good age, like the contralto Adelaide Borghi-Mamo (?1820–1901), educated themselves as they went along. The great and much travelled Adelina Patti knew Italian, English, French, German, and Spanish, but none of these languages did she write correctly; in English she went on to the end with phrasing like 'he better be careful'. As late as 1950 the correspondence of the well-known baritones Tancredi Pasero and Afro Poli contained elementary misspellings; a little earlier, in 1938, a minor singer's specially printed repertoire listed *Cavalleria della rosa* – as though Mascagni had rewritten *Der Rosenkavalier*.[51]

Attempts to make singers into educated ladies and gentlemen were in practice left to the conservatories of the post-Napoleonic period. Earlier singers – and a good many later ones who had little formal schooling – concentrated on training their voices, with music theory and an instrument as optional extras. How did they set about it?

This is a peculiarly difficult question. Singers themselves have said little beyond recording their own moments of discovery, or singling out a teacher for praise or blame. Teachers, many of them authors of treatises, have had plenty to say; but even when they say the same things (as they often do) it is hard to tell whether they mean the same. For example: nearly all treatises warn students against shouting and against excessive ornamentation. But did shouting in Handel's day mean the same as in Puccini's? Would ornamentation judged excessive in 1620 still be thought so in 1720? In 1820? The very authors who warn readers against excess go on to commend a generous range of ornaments. Such questions are in part unanswerable before the age of recorded sound.

We do know from treatises that what was being said in the seventeenth century was still being said in the late nineteenth and even (by 'the rare modern spokesman of Italian tradition') in the late twentieth.[52] More boldly, one scholar has concluded that the actual 'aspects of purely technical vocal emission remained unchanged from 1550 to about 1836'.[53] He may well be right; but there can never be proof.

The treatise most influential within the Italian tradition, most often copied and paraphrased, was Pier Francesco Tosi's *Opinioni de' cantori antichi e moderni* (1723). Tosi was a castrato whose career, mainly outside opera, was at its peak about 1690. His book embodied a good deal of earlier doctrine, reaching back to the 1600s and beyond. Although, like most such authors, he seemed to decry the present and uphold past practice, he was really bent on instilling 'a superior concept of good performance'. Change might be under way, but it was slow and gradual, achieved by a 'general compromise by which singers and composers presided over the development of musical trends which were rejected in theory as much as they were pursued in practice'.[54]

The steps Tosi thought essential to make a good singer make up a sort of decalogue:

1　Beginners should learn to sing the scale, softly, a note at a time, and perfectly in tune; the higher notes should be brought in only gradually.

2　They should learn to hit semitones, and to distinguish nine 'commas' into which the interval between one tone and the next was reckoned to be divided (Tosi assumed the untempered scale; voice and violin alike must be able to distinguish D♯ from E♭). They should also learn to hit any interval readily.

3　They must learn to make the voice 'limpid and clear', avoiding both nasal and throaty emission – both 'most horrible defects' and, if persisted in, ruinous.

4　They must learn to unite the two registers of the voice – chest and head – without a perceptible break (Tosi confusingly called the head voice 'falsetto', but did not mean what we mean by the term; he warned students against forcing the chest register into the upper notes).

5　Students should learn to pronounce words clearly, vowels in particular; the best vowels to practise were open ones – Italian *a*, broad *e*, and broad *o*, especially *a*.

6　They should practise in front of a looking-glass to observe good posture (standing while singing was always best) and to avoid grimaces; the best way to hold the mouth was, most of the time, in a shape akin to one's smile.

7　Once past the first stage, they should practise high notes to maintain and extend the upper range of the voice.

8　They must learn to support held notes, keeping them steady and avoiding excessive 'fluttering' (*svolazzar*, presumably tremolo).

9　They should practise *messa di voce* – holding a note and moving gradually from very soft to very loud and back again.

10　They should start vocalization – moving rapidly from note to note, without words, and leading on to the practice of ornaments, which Tosi insisted should be worked out and semi-improvised by the singer, not written down by the composer.

Tosi had a great deal more technical advice about ornaments – trills (of several kinds), appoggiaturas, mordents, staccato ornaments, slides, cadences. It was important to keep time in these; in general, however, students were to cultivate rubato, the art of bending the tempo phrase by phrase (within an overall steady tempo) for the sake of expression. Breath control was likewise important, though Tosi did not go into physiological detail.

For students' musical and general education Tosi had limited aims. They should learn to read music, in all the seven clefs then in use: many singers could not, and hence found transposition difficult. They need not go far into the study of an instrument, beyond learning to accompany themselves at the keyboard, or into counterpoint or composition. They should at least be able to read their own language, though, as Tosi owned, many had yet to learn the alphabet; a knowledge of Latin grammar would be a help in church music. They should lead temperate lives and cultivate good manners, both in society and in professional relationships; manners included not covering other singers' voices in ensemble, and not doing what Maria Callas was much later to complain of in Fiorenza Cossotto – holding a note which both were singing in a duet longer than had been agreed.

Finally, Tosi inculcated the need for constant study, especially 'mental study', and for imitation (not copying) of the best singers, so as gradually to attain 'good taste'. No less important, aspiring singers should, as a means to true expression, listen to their own hearts. This was essential to the cantabile or pathetic style, which Tosi held to be in regrettable decline; not that it inhibited him from stressing above all the need to practise ornamentation. Expression was not the same as acting ability: this was good, but singing ability was rarer and must come first. Tosi, child of a time when opera was not yet the dominant form, recognized three styles (church, chamber, opera) and did not give the theatre pride of place.

The general effect Tosi aimed at is best summed up by a later amateur. Elizabeth Grant of Rothiemurchus, a witty Highland landowner, took lessons about 1818 from Mrs Bianchi Lacey, widow and former pupil of the Italian composer Francesco Bianchi. Her teacher's voice, though fading – Mrs Grant recalled, – was 'round and true and sweet in the upper notes, and the finish of her whole song, the neatness of every passage, the perfect expression she gave to both music and words ... gave to me a different notion of the *art*'. Mrs Bianchi Lacey's teaching followed Tosi's decalogue; her stress was on meaning, true intonation, even emission, few but neat graces, 'the whole got up so perfectly as to be poured forth with ease, any effort, such as straining or forcing the voice or unduly emphasising a passage, being altogether so much out of taste as to produce pain instead of pleasure'.[55]

If we look at treatises written before and after Tosi's we find a notable overlap. Late sixteenth-century treatises agree in discouraging excessive ornamentation, above all in pathetic strains. So does Giulio Caccini in the influential preface to his *Nuove musiche* (1601), where, like Tosi, he deplores music that treats voices in instrumental fashion, gives particular importance to meaning, and commends 'a certain noble negligence [*sprezzatura*]' making singing akin to speech. (Caccini's one eccentricity was to commend vocalizing on the letters *i* and *u* for higher voices; most writers thought these vowels harmfully narrow). Other treatises of the early seventeenth century followed Caccini and anticipated Tosi on such matters as scales, intonation, intervals, vowels, rubato, breath control, *messa di voce* (with variants in the placing of loud and soft), keeping time in ornamentation, and the wisdom of not extending the upper range too fast. The composer Monteverdi, in a letter, spelt out the need to unify the registers; authors of treatises assumed it. Caccini, it is true, admitted the use of two voices, 'natural' and 'artificial' (*finta*), but he may have meant something else. There were some technical changes over time in ornaments and their nomenclature; in general, however, Tosi summed up a great deal of past practice.[56]

After Tosi, the next most influential treatise, by G. B. Mancini (1774), virtually reproduced his advice. In the following year Vincenzo Manfredini took Mancini to task for overrating the importance of achieving a good trill: such ornaments were apt in cadenzas and a few other places, but were inessential compared with 'singing to the heart'. Since the 1750s, Italian audiences had turned against singing so laden with multiple ornaments as to break up the vocal line; the da capo aria, with the chance it offered to throw off such ornaments in the repeats, was in decline. Manfredini's polemics reflected these changes, but although he paraded his modernity his and Mancini's advice did not differ greatly.[57]

Two treatises of about 1810 – one by the great castrato Girolamo Crescentini – and another of 1821 again repeated most of Tosi's points. Crescentini stressed what we should call smooth legato phrasing, and placed great importance on words and expression; 'singing', he wrote – echoing Caccini after more than two centuries, – 'must be an imitation of speech'. As late as 1823 a 'simple method' for musical beginners was still going on about Tosi's seven clefs and the commas of the untempered scale; these, however, had shrunk from nine to three.[58]

The best-known treatises of the late nineteenth century, those of Lamperti (1864), Leone Giraldoni (1864), Panofka (1866), and Delle Sedie (1874), all by well-known teachers and all published in more than one edition, still contained a large helping of Tosi. By then, however, a new influence had come into the field, that of Manuel García the younger – an Italian-trained Spaniard operating in Paris and London, and a celebrated teacher whose treatise appeared in 1840. He was the first to enlist into voice teaching the prestige of modern science.

In his pursuit of anatomical knowledge García is said to have lowered a small mirror into his own throat on the end of a pencil. He later developed an instrument called a laryngoscope, and his publications – followed by many more down to our own day – went in detail into the workings of larynx and pharynx, diaphragm and thorax, as well as into the nomenclature of sushyoidian muscles and the like, all of which it was now important for aspiring singers to know about; they should also use that other new scientific instrument, the metronome. How much practical difference all this made to their training is unclear. García did bring in some new ideas. He worked out a fussier classification, with three registers (chest, middle, and head) instead of two, and two timbres (clear and dark). Controversially, he held that notes should be attacked with a sudden though slight opening of the throat (*coup de glotte*). Yet a great deal of what he had to say went back to Tosi and beyond. The old saws about mouth position, intonation, support, *messa di voce*, unifying of registers, ornaments, and expression were largely unchanged. The vowels prescribed for exercises were no different now that their anatomical foundations had been explained.[59]

García and his followers indeed set out laboriously in print what might have been better shown in class. Delle Sedie used forty-seven new signs to denote emotional expression, from 'sob' to 'reproach' and from 'profound sorrow' to 'defiance of adversity', which he applied even to a single syllable. As late as 1970 a treatise by the leading teacher Nanda Mari provided sixteen pages of anatomical illustrations and a six-page physiological glossary.[60]

All the nineteenth-century teachers lamented the decay of singing; some deplored the noisy, allegedly harmful music of their own day. Imbimbo (1821), whose pupils and readers were bound to be singing Rossini, warned them against him and pointed to the older graces of Cimarosa and Paisiello. Lamperti and Panofka, whose pupils undoubtedly would be singing Verdi, harked back to the true melodiousness of Rossini; they deplored the vogue (well over thirty years old when they wrote) for tenors to sing in their chest voice throughout their range.[61]

What is one to make of it? Treatises are one thing, singers' experience another, and what the audience hears a third. Parroting of Tosi may not always have meant much.

Take singers' freedom – indeed duty – to ornament the composer's melodic line. In the eighteenth century they were co-creators, and Tosi and his followers said as much (though Tosi added that women singers, for want of a proper musical education, generally needed to have their ornaments written down for them). Rossini, however – a Janus figure, at once codifier of the past and shaper of the future, – took to writing down ornamentation for everybody. After his death in 1868 a letter of his was circulated to a number of leading singers for comment.

In it Rossini had denied that singers could create an opera; only the composer and librettist could do that; singers could but interpret; any ornaments they contributed did not amount to creation, and might be damaging. Four singers then at the height of their careers in effect had to agree; the best they could do was to point out the value of interpretation in ensuring an opera's success. The older, retired, singers Giulia Grisi and Antonio Poggi, who in their day had probably done some creative ornamenting of their own, replied politely but did not comment. It looked as though singers' creative role was over.[62] Yet a later singer, Fernando De Lucia, can be heard on early gramophone records indulging in what to our ears seems a great deal of free ornamentation and pulling about of tempo and line; he carried it further than most contemporaries but was not unique.[63] What singers learn and do has probably always depended on a coming together of the doctrine and practice admired at the time, neither of them readily communicated in words.

Singing teachers anyhow came in many varieties. Directories of 1907 and 1909 listed – not exhaustively – fifty-seven in Milan and thirty-seven in Rome.[64] Some were well known; others may have been more like the Italian 'charlatans' described as preying on the gullible in the United States about 1880–90 – 'scientific' teachers who demonstrated with dolls and a pickled larynx, another who claimed that 'an aged monk in Italy was the last one surviving who knew these wonderful secrets of vocal art' and had confided them on his deathbed. Good teachers in Italy, on the contrary, relied on tradition and worked empirically: 'This is right, that is wrong.'[65] Doubtless a fruitful method, but not one we can easily get at.

We can at least take soundings in a few places – the classes run (for non-Italians) by an influential teacher of the late nineteenth century, the colleges that developed in Italy on the French model, the choral societies that grew alongside them, and the rehearsal room where a modern teacher counselled a young singer.

Mathilde Marchesi, described by a former pupil as 'the ideal Prussian drillmaster . . . a thorough musician . . . an indefatigable worker', was the daughter of an impoverished Frankfurt merchant; she eventually married a Sicilian noble who had a middling career as a baritone. She herself sang in opera just once, in an emergency; the reasons she gave for her failure to make her expected stage debut in Milan sound fishy, though she did well with opera arias in concert. Essentially she was a teacher, schooled by García, whose methods she upheld in a long career pursued mainly in Vienna and Paris. She taught both in state conservatories and privately; her private students were expected to leave their monthly fee discreetly in a vase, but non-payment was quickly noticed.[66]

She taught women only; though her pupils sang mainly in Italian opera, a list of eighty-four 'prominent' ones includes not one Italian. Marchesi wrote that her good pupils stayed with her at least two years; some of the best needed three or four to overcome initial difficulties and build up their voices. (Some, however, like Melba, came to her already trained and in need only of less than a year's 'finishing').[67]

What she called the old Italian bel canto method remained for her the one true school; her pupils were also to study piano, declamation, and dramatic art. The best of them were noted above all for pure intonation. Late in her career, when she may have been taking on too many, an informed critic complained that she turned out 'neat *voci bianche* [white voices]' by the score.[68] The fault, if it was one, was not that these voices were small: as was said at the time by another German trained in Italian opera, the great dramatic soprano Lilli Lehmann, 'One can sing with a small voice, if it but sound nobly'.[69] But Marchesi may have pursued one of Tosi's goals, elegance, at the cost of another, expressiveness. A former pupil, Emma Eames, recalled that Marchesi made her students avoid pronouncing words above middle F, so that their high notes gave 'the impression of ventriloquism'. Eames herself struck Bernard Shaw as casting 'propriety like a Sunday frock' over the stage.[70] Marchesi's teaching, on a sound, traditional base, signalled the coming of the ladylike ideal.

The ideal was not absent from nineteenth-century Italian music colleges either. These colleges were launched by the Napoleonic governments on the model of the Paris Conservatoire, itself a product of the French Revolution. Their general purpose was to make up for the disappearance of the old orphanages and of many of the schools run by the monastic orders. The state or municipal authorities that subsidized them were concerned chiefly to train singers for the local opera chorus, as well as musicians for the local orchestra or band. The new or newly reformed colleges of Milan, Bologna, and Naples got under way in 1804–8, later followed by those of Parma (1820), Turin (1827), Venice (various attempts from 1811 culminating in 1876), and others. Their individual histories varied; they are here referred to as conservatories, a title the best of them attained at different times.[71]

For aspiring singers the new schools became a path to a career chiefly in the late nineteenth and twentieth centuries, when the old patriarchal system of musical training was beginning to weaken and compulsory universal education to make some headway. Women singers had most to gain, because of the restrictions placed on girls' musical training in the past; even in the colleges singing was at first the only subject open to them (piano and harp were presently allowed as well, string instruments not till the very end of the nineteenth century or later). The Milan conservatory – the most ambitious foundation, launched in the capital of the Napoleonic Kingdom of Italy – almost from the start turned out not just chorus singers but successful prima donnas: Giuseppina Strepponi (later Verdi's wife) and the Brambilla sisters. Milan was, as usual, a pioneer, this time in admitting girls as internal students – something that had previously been done only at the Parma chorus school, another institution launched under reforming French influence. Bologna at first compromised – girls were to have individual lessons at home but take part in school rehearsals, while, as we know, southern colleges would at best admit them (in Naples from 1817) only as external students.

After unification in 1860 Italy became a late conquest of the movement for uplifting the masses through choral singing, which had been going in northern Europe for several decades. Young people with good voices, a love of singing, and no money could now join one of the new workers' choral societies, or, in some towns, the new municipal 'people's music schools' – spare-time classes limited to choirs and wind bands. But if the young were to be inspired with a sense of beauty and kept from 'other, less pure stimuli' – the words are those of Antonio Ghislanzoni, the Milanese writer and librettist of *Aida* – you had to catch them in the first years of elementary school. Trainee schoolteachers, as one well-qualified examiner found in 1877, could do no more than sing in unison and by ear: the teaching of choral singing must therefore be made a separate discipline imparted in the conservatories. And so, by the end of the century, it was.[72]

For singers these changes opened some new prospects, not all of them bright. Very poor boys from non-musical families occasionally made a start as members of a choral society. Francesco Tamagno, the original Otello in Verdi's opera, was one of fifteen children of a small *trattoria* keeper in Turin, ten of whom died of cholera or tuberculosis; as a child he got up at 4 a.m. to help his father. Like other members of his choral society he paid a teacher ten cents (1d) a week, and practised while standing on the river bed under one of the bridges. He entered the Turin music college but left after a time when the director told him he could only become a chorus singer (like Del Monaco later on, another stentorian tenor, he had problems with the placing of his voice which took him years to overcome).[73]

Yet another tenor, Galliano Masini, son of a pasta factory worker at Leghorn, left school at eight and worked at a series of manual jobs before becoming a docker and joining the dockers' choral society. A few months later he got a small part at the local opera house; somebody then paid for lessons, at one of which Masini arrived so black from unloading coal that the teacher said 'Right, today we'll rehearse *Otello*.' Finally the head of the dockers' trade union (and president of the choral society) provided money to send him to Milan to study; there he found a teacher who charged nothing – though we may guess that Masini signed the traditional undertaking to pay out of future earnings. A year later he made his debut in his home town, amid a burst of local enthusiasm. He then had a notable career; to the end he was a quick study but, it seems, still musically illiterate.[74]

Few other well-known singers seem to have come up through choral societies. What the rise of choral singing accomplished was to provide jobs in ordinary schools for conservatory graduates who could not make it in opera as soloists – the goal, well into this century, of most Italian singing students – and who did not care to settle for the raffish atmosphere of the pre-1918 opera chorus. As late as 1877 the chorus was still the destination of most singing students at the Naples conservatory – in this respect a shadow of the eighteenth-century institutions that had turned out so many stars;[75] but change was on the way.

At the Venice conservatory, for which names and statistics of graduates between 1881 and 1976 have been published, eighty-three out of 993 graduated in singing (ten of them from a course specifically aimed at training teachers). Significant changes appear to have taken place in the 1940s. Until 1948 all the graduates in singing were women; since 1943 there have been graduates in a separate discipline of choral singing (not included in the figures just given); only since 1944 do we find students who became well-known soloists, among them Katia Ricciarelli and Maria Chiara, though there was in 1901 a recent graduate who was leading contralto in a front-rank theatre – she seems not to have lasted.[76] Only in recent times – we may conjecture – has it come to seem essential for intending opera singers to have a full musical education; this led to the splitting off of the choral singing which until then had been, for women students in particular, a likely path to a teaching job. But other conservatories for which information is less accessible may have developed differently.

The memoirs of singers who trained in the decades up to the 1930s, like Titta Ruffo, Giuseppe Borgatti, Beniamino Gigli, Giacomo Lauri-Volpi, and Mario Del Monaco, treat their conservatory experience as one incident among others in their training, notable chiefly for encounters with an individual singing teacher, good or bad.[77] This suggests how difficult it is to persuade students of singing (and perhaps music students in general) of the need to acquire a broad education.

Successive reforms over the past 150 years have tended to bring more non-vocational subjects into the curriculum of what were to begin with narrowly professional schools. At Bologna, for instance, knowledge of the 'principles' of Italian grammar was made an entrance requirement in 1839, previous elementary schooling was demanded in 1885 (after a failed agitation for the introduction of literature classes), a declamation course started in 1891; a reform in 1905–8 brought in Latin, musicology, and music history. These and parallel changes in other conservatories were at length codified in a royal decree of 11 December 1930, which is still in force. It set the minimum age of entry for intending singers (which until then had fluctuated between twelve and twenty) at sixteen for women and eighteen for men. Besides singing, piano, music history and aesthetics, and general musical culture, they were to study Italian, history, geography, poetic and dramatic literature, and 'stage art' (*arte scenica*); this last included aspects of production as well as operatic acting.[78]

How much difference all this has made is hard to gauge, like so much else in education. People concerned with Italian music teaching are still lamenting the want of general culture in their students. On the other hand the level of formal schooling in the population at large is much higher than it was even half a century ago: what is felt as a want may be relative.

In the end we are driven back on the encounter between the individual student and the individual teacher. Francesco Cortesi, the Florence teacher who in the 1880s took on Francis Walker – the young American baritone already quoted – after Walker had had distressing experiences with American teachers and with an expensive Italian, decided after careful examination that the voice needed placing; he made Walker sing single notes and scales, the scales always sung legato with the breath supporting the tone throughout, and, in place of the García-inspired 'pressing down on the larynx' which earlier teachers had required from middle C on up, made him sing C in free open tone to overcome 'mental obstruction' – this even though the tone had at first to be 'torn out'. He also made him sing bass rather than high baritone. Walker felt that his voice was regaining health, but Cortesi in the end made it politely clear that although he could become a good teacher, he was unlikely to achieve an operatic career; the reason seems to have been the common one that the voice was just not strong enough. These dealings between a sensitive Henry Jamesian American and an affable Italian professional seem exemplary for competence and honesty on both sides.[79]

In the late 1940s, the young Argentinian Eléna Arizmendi had had two singing teachers neither of whom suited her, one of them the famous soprano Maria Barrientos (who, Arizmendi felt, tended too much to make her reproduce her own light coloratura voice). She failed an audition at the Teatro Colón, but was heard there by Luigi Ricci, a well-known Italian teacher and répétiteur. He took her on for three months and so improved her singing as to make her ready for a charity recital with Gigli; this in turn led to a Colón debut and a notable though brief career. What did Ricci do? He emphasized phrasing and the meaning of words. He worked a good deal on smoothing the passage between the registers and the middle of the voice, around G. He made little of high notes, saying they would come of themselves, but encouraged vocalizing. He sounds just like Tosi.[80]

Such experiences remain uncommunicable. What is certain is that among the men and women who have gone to singing teachers there have always been plenty of the untalented. They have perhaps been at their worst since the cult of the loud high note set in about 1850. Here is a vignette set down in 1959 by an experienced teacher: 'Shouting is not just a defect, it is an illness, a kind of obsession that seizes future opera singers. . . . the neck swells, the complexion takes on a fine purplish red tone, the head seems about to part from the body.' Yet, she added, if you tell aspiring singers to calm down and waste less energy, the chances are that they will only go off to another teacher.[81]

6

PAY

Singers as 'merchandise': the word – applied to other than courtesans – can be traced back to 1750.[1] It signals the coming of a market. From then on, what singers were paid can be studied. Most were paid in cash; we can therefore hope to compare the sums they earned, both over time and between one singer (or one town, theatre, or season) and another. The task is far from easy: the terms on which singers were paid (by the season, the month, the performance) and the currencies they were paid in are seldom directly comparable. Yet it is worth while: people's chief motive for competing to sing in opera was to make money.

To a San Francisco woman who gushed at a party 'Oh, Mr Gigli, aren't you thrilled when you hear all that applause?' the tenor replied 'Signora, I'm happy when I get the money.'[2] Among singers of Italian opera this was a traditional response. Most would have subscribed to a joke code worked out in 1831 by some Naples musicians: article 151 read 'The best [artist] is the one who earns most.'[3]

There were good reasons for this. In Italy, down to the late nineteenth century a traditional agricultural country, the ideal was to own land, enjoy a leisured existence, and perhaps do voluntary work. Paid work, especially when done at the behest of others, was inferior; it was best to get it over with by earning as fast as possible. Attitudes elsewhere in Europe were not greatly different, though in Britain the shift from regard for 'an independence' to the 'religion of work' came earlier, with industrialization. In backward Rome, lawyers acting for a prima donna argued successfully as late as 1829 that singing was a 'liberal' art akin to university lecturing rather than a 'mechanical' art carried on by physical labour; its 'noble' status was shown by singers' receiving an 'honorarium' by the season rather than a daily wage.[4] But their victory was soon reversed. Singing, after all, meant physical exertion by people who hired out their services. They could be ladies and gentlemen only after they had made a lot of money and retired – or their children or nephews could do it for them by marrying into the nobility.

Contemporaries were in no doubt about this. Adam Smith in 1776 set down the 'exorbitant rewards' of opera singers and other theatre people as 'founded upon these two principles: the rarity and beauty of the talents, and the discredit of employing them in this manner', which cut down the labour supply: uncommon though 'the talents' were, they were not as rare as people thought. Half a century later the manager of the King's Theatre took it for granted that 'a woman of character and education' could go on the stage only when driven by 'the hope of emolument'.[5] Nor was male singers' vocation more highly regarded. Even when 'discredit' grew less, as it did in the nineteenth century, a touring singer's life still meant risk and inconvenience. 'Emolument' made up for them.

Were the rewards as 'exorbitant' as Adam Smith thought? The overpaid singer has been a cliché almost since the beginnings of opera. If Dante came back, he would – according to a satirical poem of 1841 – get eighteenpence, while a leading tenor was worth 'the salary of six Ministers'.[6] Gossip still deals in the fabulous sums paid to star singers. Even opera, however, has its economic rationale. In its rough way, the market judges a leading singer to be six times as hard to replace as a cabinet minister – or whatever the multiple may be; in eighteenth-century Turin, the leading castrato at the royal theatre might earn in the carnival season as much as the prime minister made in a year.[7] What Adam Smith did not go into – probably because he had in mind the London opera season, a singular luxury – was the existence in opera of a wide scale of fees, some of them very low. Only a year after he wrote, a Naples critic was bewailing the glut of singers and performances and the low pay that went with them.[8]

Seventeenth-century opera as given in the public theatres of Venice and Naples – to judge from fragmentary evidence – paid all its singers at rates that were thought well worth having, without huge differences between the amounts earned by the leads and by minor singers. This fits in with the large casts employed at the start – twenty-four in Cavalli's *Didone*, twenty-one in Monteverdi's *L'incoronazione di Poppea*, of which many were episodic but few negligible. Even when cast numbers had fallen somewhat, accounts for a season at the Teatro San Bartolomeo, Naples, in carnival 1684 show nine singers who were paid between 160 and 700 scudi each, with four of them clustered between 500 and 700 and five between 160 and 265. The composer (Alessandro Scarlatti) got 500 and five instrumental players between them 660; this put them on a more nearly equal footing with leading singers than composers and orchestras were to be in future.[9]

By about 1720, with the proliferation of operas now divided into serious and comic, there were more companies but with yet smaller casts, dependent on a few singers of transcendent virtuosity or of unusual comic gifts. Whittling down of casts went on until in 1838 Donizetti's *Maria di Rudenz* needed only what its impresario termed a 'modern company' – a prima donna, a tenor, a baritone, and a secondary woman singer, along with two small part singers and a chorus.[10] All this made for wider differentials.

The period between the spread of efficient steamships and railways in the 1860s and the triumph of the cinema during the First World War probably saw, in real terms, the highest and the lowest rewards ever earned by singers. At a time of falling prices (1873–96) and low direct taxes, a few internationally renowned singers could earn unprecedented fees in the Americas and in Cairo, on occasion in Italy itself. Yet the multiplication of Italian opera houses – some of them catering for artisans, shopkeepers, minor officials – meant that, like many other industries, opera now had a 'slop end' based on cheap production methods, where wages were driven down.

The highest paid opera singer in history, in real terms, was probably the soprano Adelina Patti. Her doll-like looks and pure, even vocal emission masked a notable competence in running her career and a will of iron.

At the height of her fame she commanded 10,000 francs per performance in Italy; not that Italy could often afford her. On her concert and opera tours of the United States and Mexico between 1881 and 1892 she received (in 1881–2) an average of $4,646 (over Fcs 23,000) per performance, some of which presumably went to her agent and to supporting singers, but the bulk to her, and she did at least as well on later tours. Yet her pay was not 'exorbitant': she was, in present-day jargon, a 'bankable star'. Her concerts took far more money at the box-office than those of her rival Christine Nilsson, not to mention theatre tours by Sarah Bernhardt and Henry Irving; when she appeared with other star singers in an 1889–90 opera tour the takings on Patti nights regularly exceeded $10,000, an unheard of sum and well above the average for the season ($7,731). It was the reward not only for unique vocal gifts and skills but for her care in managing her health and ensuring that she always appeared at or near her best. Even during a slump in 1893 she was able to write from Cincinnati: 'Business is *frightfully* bad this season, and *nobody* makes money in the theatrical line excepting myself, what there is to be made Patti makes it'.[11] It was true.

While Patti was earning these sums, the prima donna at Assisi in carnival 1890 was to sing for Fcs 10 (8s) per performance, the tenor and baritone for Fcs 6 (4s 10d) each.[12] Assisi was a small place, but even in Milan the leading mezzo at the Teatro Castelli in 1875 – admittedly a beginner singing in a third-rank theatre – earned Fcs 200 in two months; as she was contracted to sing five times a week, this worked out at under Fcs 5 per performance.[13] Even at a leading theatre like the Apollo, Rome, in the same year the nine worst paid comprimari (as secondary singers were now termed) earned under Fcs 1,000 each for a season of 60 performances, while the leading tenor made Fcs 47,737 and the prima donna Fcs 39,000. These sums may be compared with the daily wage of a builder's labourer in Milan in 1860 (Fcs 0,81) or the price of a kilo of bread, which in the late nineteenth century hovered about half a franc.[14] The Assisi wage of Fcs 6 a performance was occasional, not daily, and it had to meet travelling expenses and the cost of minor articles of costume.

The reason for such low pay was the obvious one – glut. Theatres and seasons had multiplied, but singers and would-be singers had multiplied faster still. The increase can be roughly measured. Theatrical journals and directories sometimes gave numbers of people active in each vocal category. Where they listed names we have to allow for an element of advertising: entries were paid for, if only by subscribing for a copy. Hence the figures may leave out some who declined to pay, and include some on the fringes of the profession; they are none the less broadly indicative.

Table 1 gives numbers of singers said to be available in Milan in 1861, 1897, and 1925. The 1861 figures (which do not include names) are of singers actually unemployed in July, a slack time; other singers (in smaller but unspecified numbers) were reported to be available at Bologna and elsewhere. The 1897 and 1925 figures, however, are taken from directories purporting to list all the (named) singers on the books of agents in Milan, by those dates the virtually exclusive market-place; they cover both well-known names and beginners, and although some were foreigners based in the Americas or in Spain they all sang the Italian repertoire.

The 1861 figures are therefore not directly comparable with the later ones. They are included to show how the ratio between the different vocal categories remained unchanged over time. Sopranos were always the most crowded; they were all listed as prima donnas, which all might hope to be, in small towns: a 1940 directory listed fifty would-be Butterflys, forty-four Violettas, and forty-two Toscas.[15] But although the table exaggerates the contrast between 1861 and 1897, and none of its figures can be regarded as precise, the general trend it shows is almost certainly correct: a steep rise in the last third of the nineteenth century, thanks to the spread of popular and small-town opera seasons, and a moderate fall by the mid 1920s, presumably because of competition from the cinema.

In 1913, when the opera habit was at or near its peak, 131 Italian towns were listed as having had opera seasons, among them such dots on the agricultural landscape as Papozze, in the marshes of the Po delta, and Linguaglossa, below Mount Etna.[16] Not even this number of seasons (many

Table 1. *Solo singers available in Milan*

	1861	*1897*	*1925*
Sopranos	78	371	222
Contraltos/mezzos	15	181	64
Tenors	49	270	189
Baritones	25	156	129
Basses	22	102	57
Comic basses	8	26	14
Total	197	1,106	675

Sources: Gazzetta Teatrale di Milano, quoted in *Teatri Arti e Letteratura*
(Bologna), 15 July 1861; *Annuario dell'arte lirica e coreografica italiana*, Milan, I,
1897–8; *Annuario dell'arte lirica italiana*, 1925.

of them short) could keep all members of the profession employed at decent
wages. Already in the late 1850s the Italian-trained baritone Charles Santley
noted that the busy carnival season kept supply and demand in rough
balance, but at other times 'the fight' for engagements 'became deadly': some
of his fellows had to perform when driven literally 'to the confines of
starvation'.[17]

There had long been men and women on the fringes of the profession so
poor and, it may be, so untalented that they sang for no more than their
board. One such contracted in 1758 to sing small parts in comic intermezzi at
a minor Rome theatre: besides his meals he got the use of a horse to bring him
from his native Abruzzi and back, and of a pair of shoes to wear on stage.
Later, in 1837, a bass appealed to a leading impresario for any sort of
engagement, even in the chorus, for the mere cost of his food.[18]

Other singers did little better because they worked for managements that
lived from hand to mouth and sometimes failed, leaving the company unpaid.
These need not be fly-by-night operators. In bad times, such as the 1680s were
in Venice because of a long war with Turkey, even the leading aristocratic
theatre owners ran short of money. Their singers and musicians had to accept
payment in boxes which they might let to members of the public: in effect they
joined in an improvised management cooperative, and shared out the risks of
the season. Similar arrangements can be found in eighteenth-century Rome
theatres, especially in the famine year 1764. They became a normal way for a
company to salvage, if it could, earnings threatened by an impresario's failure
in mid-season.[19]

From the late nineteenth century, opera seasons in small towns were often run from the start by a musicians' cooperative because no impresario would take them on. At Montecosaro, a tiny hill town in the Marches of eastern Italy, the mayor in 1885 offered a subsidy of Fcs 80 and free use of the theatre, adding as a come-on that his fellow-townsmen were 'mad about music'; the singers and musicians would share out whatever they could take at the box office.[20] Much then depended on a mixture of skill and luck; at best, take-home pay was modest.

At worst, when both managers and singers were of the humble kind (but not necessarily bad at their job), both could be in distress. The small Teatro La Fenice, Naples, from the 1820s to the 1840s gave twice-daily opera performances, at first of comic opera based on local clown figures, later of serious works such as *Norma*. In such theatres the Naples authorities allowed managements to forgo paying the caution money that was normally required as insurance for their employees' wages, so long as the artists under contract agreed; the law also permitted creditors to attach wages at source. Singers' earnings were low in any case: in 1840 a second woman was being paid just over Fcs 6 per performance, a comic bass just under Fcs 7. Even these earnings were at times stopped either by management failure or by creditors swooping to collect old debts. When the company in 1834 refused to appear because their wages were being attached, the theatre owner (the only person who seems to have made money out of this and other minor Naples seasons) argued that there was little point in making them sing by police action:

what is the use of compulsion brought to bear on voices that put off the audience [*attaccano la sensibilità*] when the singers perform without spirit and without opening their mouths properly, because – for want of resources – they have not been able to sit down to a meal earlier in the day?[21]

From about 1860, even established singers in leading theatres had to cope with impresarios who defaulted, literally overnight. The causes were intertwined. Subsidies fell, especially in former capital cities stripped of their monarchical courts. Agrarian depression cut boxholders' incomes. The new Italian state did away with the paternalistic discipline imposed by its predecessors. The courts now upheld the sovereignty of contract, and went so far as to rule in 1903 that none of the caution money put down by an impresario who had later defaulted could be used to compensate artists left unpaid – a total repudiation of the needs which caution money had been devised to meet in the 1750s.[22]

In these circumstances artists could no longer stand for the system of payment that had grown up piecemeal through the seventeenth and eighteenth centuries. This went with regular seasons of known length (carnival, spring, autumn) and provided payment in instalments, generally four (*quartali*) – one as singers arrived for rehearsals, one after the last night, and the other two in between. Impresarios who defaulted on one or more *quartali* can be traced as far back as 1687; singers had to be particularly wary of minor impresarios who ran comic opera seasons in eighteenth-century theatres.[23] In the first half of the nineteenth century, however, a handful of leading impresarios – backed by enhanced subsidies – won a reputation for prompt payment.

Now, in a changed environment, nobody could be relied upon. Leading singers took to demanding payment by the performance rather than by the season or the month – an arrangement that had already begun to come in with the spread of repertory opera and the breakdown of the old seasonal calendar. Even then Lilli Lehmann – not yet a big star – could get paid by the dodgy impresario 'Colonel' J. H. Mapleson only by waiting for a lucrative Patti night and then sitting tight in his room until the money had been taken in at the box-office; this was a more comfortable version of the measure resorted to by a desperate Italian chorus in Odessa in 1881 – they tramped the streets around the theatre in the vain hope of catching the impresario. On another occasion singers got their fees only when they 'energetically demanded' them between acts 2 and 3, with the bass flourishing his cane – it was, he said, his 'guarantee'.[24]

As a result of such experiences the best soloists now wanted to be paid before, not after, each performance; an extra precaution, insisted upon by the famous tenors Alessandro Bonci and Giuseppe Borgatti, was payment in advance, ahead of the season, for the last two performances (when the impresario might be worst tempted to pocket the box-office takings and flee from his creditors).[25]

Much less is known of any difficulties singers may have had in getting paid since the First World War. In leading Italian opera houses, gradually taken under the wing of the state from 1920, they have had fewer and fewer dealings with impresarios. Italy's creaking bureaucracy has now and then given opera houses serious trouble by failing to pay subsidies on time. Minor creditors have therefore faced long delays; since the 1950s leading singers and unionized choruses have probably done better.

Early contracts with singers occasionally required payment in 'ringing' (*sonante*) coin. Down to 1789 money for everyday purposes meant coin; to people like singers who hoped to live well above subsistence level it meant gold or silver. Paper money, introduced during revolutions and wars, earned a bad name for losing value: well into the nineteenth century coin remained the preferred medium.

It none the less had problems of its own. In the old disunited Italy and surrounding areas there circulated the coins of more than a dozen Italian and German states, as well as those of Spain and France, some a century or two old. A prima donna at Vicenza in 1806 was paid in a mixture of Austrian, Bavarian, North German, French, and Tuscan coin; when the Duchy of Modena issued an official tariff in 1823 it listed seven pre-1796 coins of its own and seventy-nine foreign ones, all liable to be met with.[26] There were also currencies of account – not minted, but used for bookkeeping or, like the guineas charged by British doctors long after the coin had vanished, to distinguish professional fees from wages. Unless singers' contracts specified payment in the actual (*effettivo*) coin named – which might cause difficulties if it happened not to be obtainable on the spot – they were likely in practice to stand a loss of a few percentage points by the time their fee was translated into ringing coin. Even in the late nineteenth century, when European currencies had been simplified, leading artists often demanded gold francs, which might give them a 9 per cent edge on the same sum in ordinary francs.[27]

This complexity, typical of the *ancien régime*, was better understood at the time than it is now. Though people sometimes differed over rates of exchange, they knew which lira or scudo or ducat they meant out of the several varieties available; they did not, however, always make it clear to the later historian. Besides picking our way through such uncertainties, we have to bear in mind the effects of inflation, slow through much of the eighteenth century, headlong in the mid 1790s and the latter stages of the Napoleonic wars as well as in the two twentieth-century world wars. As a general rule, we can only compare money payments: rewards in kind, common down to the 1730s at least (both in courts and in public theatres), are incalculable and must be left out; the same is true of most benefit performances, and of travelling and lodging allowances. For this reason, and because the evidence is fragmentary, little can usefully be said about the period down to about 1680. After that, we may hope to reach tentative answers to some questions: fees are a guide even though a rough one.

What were the comparative rewards of 'service' at court and of freelance singing in public theatres? Of serious and comic opera? Of different vocal types? Of different seasons and theatres? Did rewards grow or fall in the course of the eighteenth century? Of the nineteenth?

From about 1680 until the second quarter of the eighteenth century, good singers had a choice between taking long-term service with a court and hazarding a career in public theatres. The former was described in 1729 as 'certain and continuous though middling in its rewards', the latter as 'uncertain but more lucrative'.[28] The contrast was overstated: courts had their discontinuities; and a long-term engagement in a royal chapel need not prevent singers from being granted occasional leave to sing in Venice, Bologna, or Milan. Still, there was a choice. What was the price of choosing service?

Cavagnino in 1666–7 could earn in one Venice carnival season 150 doubloons – roughly equivalent to his annual salary of 2,250 Piedmontese lire from the Turin ducal chapel, the highest amount paid to any singer on that establishment between 1661 and 1725; when the Turin court started its own carnival seasons of opera, the castrato Domenico Cecchi earned, in 1689, nearly twice this maximum (L. piem. 4,132–10–0), an amount itself more than doubled for Senesino in 1730. Giulia Masotti in those same Venice seasons of 1666–7 commanded 400 doubloons; in 1674, when she engaged herself to the Vienna court as chamber singer, she earned an annual salary roughly three-fifths of that, shortly raised (and kept) to three-quarters. Her Venice fee had been exceptionally high, the result no doubt of her erotic as well as vocal appeal – something that could not have lasted. Her Vienna salary lasted a quarter-century.[29]

Turin and Vienna were among the grandest of courts, best able to afford a steady patronage (except in wartime). Other court and church establishments underwent marked ups and downs. From the late seventeenth century the pay of church choirs unattached to courts seems to have moved down more often than up; examples are San Petronio, Bologna, where the salaries paid in 1670–80 fell by more than half when the choir was restarted in 1701, and the cathedral choir at Bergamo, which suffered a one-third pay cut in 1724.[30] At St Mark's, Venice, where salaries by 1725 were already doubtfully competitive with opera, a good tenor entering the choir in 1765 had to spend six years on a salary of 300 ducats a year, with no more than 'the usual reasonable leaves' to sing in opera (compare the 258 ducats paid to a comic bass for a Venice carnival season at the second-rank Teatro San Samuele in 1786).[31]

The balance of advantage had shifted since the 1670s. Till then, service in a leading church choir or a royal establishment (which could include opera performances) had been the most financially rewarding work open to singers, but for the odd carnival season in a Venice public theatre. By the latter half of the eighteenth century it was, for good singers, at best a useful sideline and an insurance against old age, for the mediocre, a bread and butter job. Even in the Naples royal chapel the salaries in the years 1752–68, for which we have complete records, did not exceed thirty Neapolitan ducats a month (save for Caffarelli, who got thirty-five); this was one-tenth the monthly salary paid to the best singers at the Teatro San Carlo (Senesino in 1739–40 and Caterina Gabrielli in 1763–4). But the career rate earned by the mediocre was a mere six ducats a month: the tenor Tommaso Scarlatti, brother of the great Alessandro, never rose above this in at least thirty-eight years' service, and neither did many others. A few got rises just after they had sung in opera elsewhere, no doubt successfully: it made them worth hanging on to. Caffarelli held on to his post through at least forty-five years, and thought the salary worth angling for even when it should have been suspended while he earned large sums in opera abroad; but although it represented security for his old age, he did not depend on it.[32]

The court at Dresden illustrates the ups and downs of establishments less firmly based than those of Vienna or Madrid. An Elector of Saxony coming to the throne in 1680 found an Italian choir, paid between 600 and 1,000 thalers a year each, and a German choir paid between 100 and 350; but he also found deficit and plague. As a temporary expedient he made do with a cheap German choir, largely confined to church music, while he planned to gratify his passion for opera by bringing in a separate Italian company headed by the prima donna Margherita Salicola. She arrived in 1685, and by 1687 an Italian group was in place, at salaries ranging from Th. 600 to Salicola's Th. 1,500 (over £300). War, however, meant that salaries were unpaid for years; when Salicola left in 1693 she collected almost three years' arrears. The next Elector was so hard pressed by war that in 1707 he dismissed all his singers; they too had been long unpaid.

After the wars had ended, the Dresden court was able in 1717–20 to splurge on extravagant opera seasons, with Italian companies engaged by the year at unheard of fees: Th. 7,000 (well over £1,000) for Senesino; Th. 10,500 shared between the composer Antonio Lotti and his wife, the prima donna Santa Stella; and from Th. 2,000 to Th. 3,500 paid to each of the other serious singers; only a local woman and an Italian pair engaged for comic intermezzi got less. No wonder this was the company from which Handel recruited artists for some of his best financed London seasons. But the standard could not be kept up: in 1725, after a gap, Dresden reverted to building up a permanent Italian establishment that was to perform in church, chamber, and opera alike. Its members were, to begin with, little-known singers who were paid from Th. 433 to 567, but in time some famous singers were appointed and others won reputation as well as salary increases: by 1756, after a quarter-century's service, the castrato Ventura Rocchetti was earning Th. 2,400, other salaries ran from Th. 1,400 to 4,000 (for the leading castrato Angelo M. Monticelli), while another composer and prima donna pair – J. A. Hasse and his wife, the famously agile Faustina Bordoni – between them drew Th. 6,000. Yet war, siege, and fire were shortly to disperse the music establishment all over again.[33] Near the turn of the century, in 1794 and 1803,

Dresden salaries ranged from Th. 283 to 2,833, with most clustered between Th. 600 and 1,700; the impression is of Italian companies of modest level, headed by one or two starrier singers.[34]

What this story suggests – it could be matched, with variations, elsewhere in Northern Europe – is that before the opera market was fully in place a court could be a singer's Klondike. The 1717–20 seasons, with fees close to those available in London, must have struck the artists engaged for them as little short of miraculous, and although the 1687 and later seasons meant waiting years for one's pay the chaos of European war at that time probably made them too seem worth while. Like the Klondike, however, these court bonanzas were apt to dry up suddenly; Dresden then offered at best a steady job at moderate pay. Only in 1730–56, a creative period presided over by Hasse, did it manage a regular establishment on which star singers as well as more routine performers were content to serve, with opportunities now and then to sing in Venice or Rome.

Comic intermezzo singers in the lavish 1717 Dresden season were relatively low paid – even though the female singer, Livia Costantini (la Polacchina), was a well-known specialist. The celebrated pair of intermezzo singers Rosa Ungarelli and Antonio Ristorini did somewhat better at the Teatro San Samuele, Venice, in 1730: their joint fee for the Ascension Fair season valued them individually well ahead of the seconda donna Anna Girò and the young tenor Angelo Amorevoli, but well behind the castrato Antonio Pasi and at a mere third of the prima donna Faustina Bordoni.[35] This may none the less have been a high water mark: when comic opera shortly afterwards split off as a distinct genre, performed in theatres or seasons less exalted than those reserved for opera seria, the leading Naples buffa Marianna Monti earned less than half the second woman's fee at the San Carlo.[36] Scattered accounts of opera buffa seasons at Florence in the 1750s and Venice in 1785–6 show equally modest levels of reward. In the latter season, differentials were as flat as in mid seventeenth-century Venetian opera: the lowest-paid singer earned (over five months) Fcs 605, just over a third of the Fcs 1,760 that went to the comic baritone, his highest-paid colleague.[37]

Such modest rewards followed logically from the assumption that comic opera must be cheaper to put on than serious. By the Napoleonic period, however, the genres converged more and more in their musical character, and singers specialized less: this may explain why a prima donna and tenor at La Fenice, Venice, in 1805–6 earned exactly the same fees for a spring season of comic opera and a carnival season of serious opera,[38] and why the fees paid to the Almaviva and Figaro in the original 1816 production of Rossini's *Il barbiere di Siviglia* (Manuel García and Luigi Zamboni) were in line with what had recently been paid in the same theatre to performers of opera seria, the usual fare at that address.[39] Comic opera went on being treated as a cheap genre at least until 1838 (when La Scala equalized prices of admission), but in leading theatres the management now had to economize on scenery, costumes, and chorus rather than on the principals' fees.

Because opera seria was the genre eighteenth-century officials thought most important, we are better informed about the pay of singers who specialized in it. Tables 2 and 3 give different insights into the period before the steep inflation of the revolutionary and Napoleonic years.

Table 2 sets out the fees paid to singers (and to the leading dancer or pair of dancers) at the court theatre in Turin. This theatre kept up an unvarying policy of putting on two serious operas each carnival season, with some ups and downs in what the noble managers could afford to spend, but with no fundamental change (one season, 1748, has been left out because it was a scratch affair, put on cheaply at the end of a damaging war; so have a few non-carnival seasons that marked a special occasion). Opera seria was itself a largely unvarying genre, with a standard cast of first and second men (both castrati, though the second man's part might go to a woman), first and second women, tenor, a small *ultima parte* of either sex, and, as a rule, no bass; it was normally interleaved with a ballet. Carnival seasons did vary in length with the date of Easter – something people remembered when they bargained over fees – but not very widely. Table 2 therefore allows us to compare like with like – so long as we bear in mind that figures for the earlier years leave out a good deal of payment in kind; those for 1689 should be rounded up by an unknown amount, perhaps by as much as half.

The figures are all documented in Piedmontese lire, a currency of account; this makes them comparable over a century, but does not as a rule tell us what equivalent sum artists were paid in coin. The Piedmontese lira, like other such currencies, gradually lost value in this period against gold and silver. Between 1700 and 1785 it was legally devalued by a total of 17 per cent against gold coins and 13 per cent against silver; its actual loss of value was probably somewhat greater.[40] This corresponded roughly to a slow increase in most prices of goods from about 1730, not just in Piedmont but in Europe. The prices of different articles, however, moved at different rates: we cannot hope to devise a 'singer's cost of living index' as we work out the real income of labourers whose wages went to buy a few basic necessities. All the same, a fee of 1,000 Piedmontese lire in 1788 was clearly worth less than the same fee in 1730 – possibly 10 or 20 per cent less.[41]

For these reasons the highest fee recorded, Marchesi's in 1788 (itself exceptional at the time), was only a little higher in real terms than the highest

Table 2. Fees for carnival seasons at the Turin Royal Theatre in Lire piemontesi (L.piem.1 = francs 1.18 (1801))

	1.o uomo	1.a donna	2.o uomo	2.a donna	tenor	ult. parte	leading dancer
1689	4,133 Cecchi	4,713 Riccioni	3,263 Pistocchi		1,813 Mozzi	500 Aureli	
1730	8,731 Senesino	9,978 Faustina		900 Lancetta			
1737	9,975 Senesino	5,403 Visconti					2,993[a] Campanini
1739	7,149 Gizziello	8,000 Cuzzoni	1,829 Veroni		2,660 Tolve		
1741	8,645 Carestini	6,650 Visconti	2,827 Chimenti	2,494 Gallo	3,824 Amorevoli	780 Gioanetti	2,328 Aquilanti
1742	7,481 Salimbeni	3,200 Barlocci	2,560 Albuzio	2,560 Venturini	2,880 Barbieri	1,121 Valvasoni	4,400[a] Le Febure
1743	7,980 Salimbeni	3,957 T. Baratti	3,200 Tozzi	1,760 Ronchetti	5,600 Babbi	634 Buini	
1744	8,313 Gizziello	4,800 Turcotti	2,194 Ricciarelli	2,400 Elmi	5,600 Babbi	780 Buini	3,325 Aquilanti
1745	4,988 Nicolini	4,800[b] Paghetti		2,240 Casarini	2,145 Bonifacci	878 Gallieni	2,560 Collucci
1749	3,900 Triulzi	3,413 Stabili	1,950 Ciardini	1,560 Vestri	2,243 Carlani	878 Castelli	2,500
1750	4,838 Morigi	3,413 Stabili	1,853 Poma		1,950 Ottani	975 Peretti	
1751	7,313 Elisi	3,120 Casarini	2,097 Cornaggia	1,463 Colizzi	3,120 Panzacchi	1,170 Peretti	5,363[a] Sabatini
1752	8,313 Monticelli	7,313 Aschieri	1,463 Ghiringhelli	1,950 Conti	2,145 Pignotti	1,170 Peretti	3,218 Alovar

1753	3,900 Luini	6,650 Sanni-Grandi	2,438 Tagliavini	2,096 Strambi	2,145 Francesconi	926 Peretti	3,218 Alovar
1754	6,630 Mazzanti	6,650 Pompeati-Imer	3,071 Masi-Giura	2,438 Montelati	3,559 Ottani	780 Porta	3,413 Alovar
1756	6,825 Potenza	3,900 Masi-Giura	1,755 Ghiringhelli	780 Bonanni	3,413 Ottani	331 Costa	
1757	11,733 Gallieni	7,800 Mattei	2,367 Rolfi	1,041 Monari	3,413 Ottani	1,041 Suardi	6,627[a] Angiolini
1760	9,467 Elisi	8,520 C. Gabrielli	1,200 Calcina	1,420 Baglioni	3,413 Ottani	426 Pesci	3,297 Salomone
1761	7,573 Guadagni	5,207 Parigi	1,515 Demezzo	1,420 Mazzola	1,799 Nicolini	473 Gotti	5,491[a] Saunier
1762	7,573 Aprile	9,467 C. Gabrielli	1,893 Martinengo	1,609 F. Gabrielli	2,840 Ottani	426 L'Eglise	5,000[a] Devise
1763	7,573 Potenza	5,207 Tartaglini	1,609 Priori	1,420 Romani	2,840 Ottani	426 Re	3,787 Favier
1765	7,573 Aprile	7,573 Pilaja	1,893 Cicognani	1,704 Lampugnani	2,509 Ettore	473 Lorenzini	3,124 Salomone
1766	10,867 Manzoli	3,408 Maccherini	1,515 Priori	1,515 Degrandis	2,600 Ottani	600 Calcina	3,787
1767	5,860 Reina	6,153 Girelli	800 Cerri	1,893 Giacomazzi	2,700 Ettore		4,260 Viganò
1768	7,573 Fabris	8,500 C. Gabrielli	1,609 Emiliani	947 F. Gabrielli	2,600 Ottani	473 Lorenzini	4,733 Pirrot
1769	6,627 Mazzanti	3,597 Spagnuoli	1,231 Paduli	1,136 Gherri	1,420 Pini	473 Polidori	4,733 Pirrot
1770	4,733 Benedetti	7,573 Girelli	1,420 Bedini	1,420 Boselli	1,893 Pini	473 Polidori	3,769 Campioni
1771	5,680 Tonarelli	8,520 Girelli	1,420 Schiroli	1,136 Nicolini	1,704 Fobicaldi	473 Polidori	6,833 D'Aubreval

Table 2. (cont.)

	1.o uomo	1.a donna	2.o uomo	2.a donna	tenor	ult. parte	leading dancer
1772	7,573 Aprile	7,573 Agujari	1,420 Casatiello	947 Zibetti	1,609 Ciprandi	473 Giordani	6,627[a] Favier
1773	4,733 Luini	11,360 Agujari	1,704 Santi	1,325 Varesi	1,893 Ciprandi	473 Polidori	14,400[a] Lany/Mme Pitrot
1774	7,032 Rauzzini	9,940 Teiber	1,041 Piatti	1,420 Varesi	1,893 Afferri	426 Silvani	6,608 Vallay
1775	5,207 Compagnucci	5,207 Bonafini	1,893 Santi	1,515 Bonanni	1,515 David	473 Borelli-David	7,573[a] Campioni
1776	6,627 Aprile	10,413 Teiber	1,515 Catena	1,325 G. Gardi	1,897 Panzacchi	379 M. Gardi	8,520[a] Canziani
1777	6,627 Aprile	9,940 De Amicis	1,425 Coppola	1,325 Lorenzini	1,420 Pulini	426 Granatelli	5,207 Franchi
1778	8,993 Pacchierotti	4,260 Carrara	1,515 Camilli	1,420 Baglioni	1,893 Scovelli	378 Dorelli	
1779	3,550 Bedini	9,940 De Amicis	1,136 Benigni	1,420 C. Lorenzini	2,035 Scovelli	379 G. Lorenzini	
1780	6,153 Rubinelli	4,923 Balducci	1,136 Muschietti	1,325 Raineri	2,083 Limperani	379 Sanviti	5,207 Gallet
1781	5,680 Bedini	6,627 Todi	1,136 Benigni	1,420 Baglioni	1,893 Prati	379 Marzorati	
1783	6,627 Consoli	8,520 Todi	1,420 Gherardi	1,420 Lorenzini	1,515 Simon	379 Rossi	3,313 Fabiani
1784	4,923 Neri	6,153 Banti	1,825 Casatiello	1,420 Lorenzini	2,844 David	379 Pallavicini	
1785	10,413 Marchesi	3,787 Serra	1,136 Benigni	1,231 Cloche	2,121 Scovelli	379 Pallavicini	5,207 Franchi

1786	2,272 Tajana	6,627 Pozzi	947 Gilardone	947 Sansoni	3,313 David	379 Pastorelli	4,260 Clerico
1787	6,627 Crescentini	5,680 Morichelli	1,192 Benigni	1,291 Benvenuti	3,787 Babbini	397 Pallavicini	5,207 Gallet
1788	13,253 Marchesi	3,976 Marchetti-Fantozzi	1,042 Savoi	1,213 Onorati	2,200 Carri	380 Monti	3,325 Beretti

Notes:

From 1741 performances are at the new Teatro Regio; before then at the old Teatro Ducale (later Regio).
After 1730, some years are left out of the table either because there was no season (on account of war) or because precise figures are unavailable. Fees are given to the nearest lira.

[a] fee paid to a pair of dancers

[b] singer fell ill after first opera; replaced in second opera by Visconti (fee L.piem. 8,312)

Sources: S. Cordero di Pamparato, 'Un duca di Savoia impresario teatrale', RMI 45, 1941; A. Basso, ed., *Storia del Teatro Regio di Torino*, Turin, 1976–88, I.

fees paid in the 1730s to the equally famous Senesino and Faustina. From 1745 these was if anything a fall in the general level of singers' fees. This may well reflect the slackening of interest in opera seria in the latter half of the century.

From 1750 we can also observe a widening of differentials between the fees paid to stars (the first man or first woman or both) and those paid to the other singers, the second man, second woman, and *ultima parte* in particular. These secondary parts may in some years have been growing thinner (not that this was as yet a general change: witness Annio and Servilia in Mozart's *La clemenza di Tito* of 1791, both substantial parts). More likely, audiences bored with opera seria tended to concentrate on a few star performers, so the management could get away with cheaper casting of the other parts.

Tenors, though valued less as a rule than the first man and woman, nearly always maintained some differential over the *secondi*. By 1786 the celebrated Giacomo David was getting more than the *primo uomo* – the first tenor to do so in this theatre. Here was a sign that, with the castrati in decline, the tenor voice was beginning to engage the audience's interest as more than the stereotype utterance of kings and old men; a few years beyond the end of our table, in 1796, Cimarosa would entrust to a tenor the powerful tragic role of Orazio in *Gli Orazi e i Curiazi*. (In 1743–4 Gregorio Babbi, another famous tenor, had been paid more than the first woman, but, in terms of eighteenth-century vocal hierarchy, to beat the leading castrato was a more notable achievement.)

Audiences' new interest in ballet at the expense of opera seria is shown by the fee paid in 1769 to an individual dancer, markedly higher than the prima donna's; in 1771 a dancer was paid more than the first man. Pairs of dancers had in some earlier years been paid more than one of the two leading singers, but this was a breakthrough. In 1773 a ballet pair were paid not only three times more than the first man but a good deal more than Lucrezia Agujari, famous for her agility and her stratospheric high notes – and she was, at least nominally, the highest paid prima donna in eighteenth-century Turin. Ballet dancers' fees remained high; it would take the craze for Rossinian opera in the 1820s to boost leading singers' fees decisively past them.

For the rest, Table 2 shows us not unexpected patterns in a few singers' careers. The fees paid to the tenor Ottani between 1750 and 1768 suggest a rapid ascent, a plateau of earning power and probably of quality, followed by a marked though still respectable decline. Such patterns, however, are better observed in Table 3, which compares the fees paid to singers between 1730 and 1788 in six leading Italian cities.

This table compares like with like by restricting itself to opera seria given in the fashionable season and in the leading theatre of each city. The Turin and

Table 3. *Comparative fees paid in leading eighteenth-century theatres (in franc equivalents)*

			1.o uomo	1.a donna	2.o uomo	2.a donna	tenor	ult. parte	leading dancer
1730	TO	C	10,303 Senesino	11,774		1,062			
1730	VE	C	9,300 Farinelli	11,000 Cuzzoni	6,200	2,170	2,200		
1733	BO	P	2,825 Farinelli	2,825 Tesi	2,260 Caffarelli	1,356		678	
1737	TO	C	11,771 Senesino	6,376 Visconti					2,993[a]
1738	MI	C	4,813 Salimbeni	2,195	1,540	1,925	1,925		
1738–9	NA	A–C	10,049 Caffarelli	15,834 Tesi					
1739	MI	C	4,813 Appiani	7,700 Visconti	2,406 T. Baratti		4,620[b]	770	
1739	TO	C	8,436	9,440 Cuzzoni	2,158 Veroni		3,139 Tolve		
1739	Rome	C		1,338 Manzoli					
1739	BO	P	3,254 Carestini	2,644	2,034 Salimbeni	1,074	1,695 Amorevoli	565	2,034
1739–40	NA	A–C	16,066 Senesino	12,058	2,667 Manzoli	4,368 T. Baratti	4,582 Amorevoli		
1740	MI	C	7,123 Salimbeni	7,700 Visconti	2,310	1,925 Aschieri		886	
1741	TO	C	10,201 Carestini	7,847 Visconti					
1742	TO	C	8,828 Salimbeni	3,776	3,021	3,021	3,398	1,323	5,192[a]
1742	BO	P	3,842 Appiani	2,034 Turcotti	2,237	1,187 T. Baratti	1,695 Babbi	415 Veroni	
1743	TO	C	9,416 Salimbeni	4,669 T. Baratti	3,776	2,077	6,608 Babbi	748	
1744	TO	C	9,809	5,664 Turcotti	2,589	2,832	6,608 Babbi	920	3,924
1745	TO	C	5,886	5,664		2,643 Casarini	2,531	1,036	3,021
1749	MI	C	8,663 Manzoli	6,738 Casarini	1,540	1,925	5,968 Amorevoli	520	
1751	TO	C	8,629 Elisi	3,682 Casarini	2,474	1,726	3,682	1,381	6,328[a]
1752	TO	C	9,809	8,629 Aschieri	1,726	2,301	2,531	1,381	3,797
1758	Rome	C	6,581	2,408 Priori	1,605	803	2,408 Ciprandi	535	4,013
1760	TO	C	11,171 Elisi	10,054 Gabrielli	1,416	1,676	4,027	503	3,890

Table 3. (*cont.*)

			1.o uomo	1.a donna	2.o uomo	2.a donna	tenor	ult. parte	leading dancer
1762	TO	C	8,936	11,171 Gabrielli	2,234	1,899	3,351	503	5,900^d
1763	BO^c	P	5,791 Manzoli	4,633	1,858		3,475 Tibaldi	869	2,610
1763–4	NA	yr		17,400 Gabrielli					
1766	TO	C	12,823 Manzoli	4,201	1,788 Priori	1,788	3,068	708	4,469
1768	TO	C	8,936	10,030 Gabrielli	1,899	1,117	3,068	558	5,585
1769	TO	C	7,820	4,244	1,453	1,340	1,676 Pini	558	5,585
1770	TO	C	5,585	8,936	1,676	1,676	2,234 Pini	558	4,447
1772	TO	C	8,936	8,936	1,676	1,117	1,899 Ciprandi	558	7,820^d
1772	Rome	C	6,955 Elisi						
1773	TO	C	5,585	13,405	2,011	1,564	2,234 Ciprandi	558	16,992^d
1773–4	NA	yr					6,960 Tibaldi		
1777	TO	C	7,820	11,729 De Amicis	1,682	1,564	1,676	503	6,144
1778	TO	C	10,612	5,027 Carrara	1,788	1,676	2,234	446	
1778	BO^d	P		6,313 De Amicis		695	3,475 Tibaldi	522	2,606
1779	TO	C	4,189	11,729 De Amicis	1,340	1,676	2,401	447	
1780	TO	C	7,261	5,809 Balducci	1,340	1,564	2,458	447	6,144
1780–1	NA	yr	10,701 Marchesi	11,310 Balducci	870	1,305	5,090 Pini	435	
1781	TO	C	6,702	7,820	1,340	1,676	2,234 Prati	447	
1781–2	NA	yr	10,179 Consoli	11,310 Carrara	2,262	1,305	6,786 Prati	435	12,441
1783	TO	C	7,820 Consoli	10,054	1,340	1,676	1,788	447	3,909
1785	TO	C	12,235 Marchesi						
1785–6	NA^e	yr	12,554	10,179		2,175	7,125		12,441
1788	TO	C	15,573 Marchesi	4,692	1,230	1,453	2,596	448	3,925

Naples court theatres were of equal pretensions, those of Milan and Venice close behind. The Rome theatre, though almost as large, enjoyed little court favour and no subsidy, while the Bologna theatres were markedly smaller than the rest – and Bologna was the only city in the table to have a fashionable season other than carnival. To establish the pay structure in each season, the table shows all the fees known to have been paid, but for purposes of comparison it names only those singers whose fees were recorded in more than one city.

If we are to compare fees we need to express them in a single currency. The only currency for which I have found exchange rates against all the currencies artists were paid in is the French franc, which did not exist before 1795, but which afterwards was a standard means of payment. To translate 1730 fees at a rate of exchange that prevailed after 1795 (even then with fluctuations) is obviously arbitrary. On the other hand it need be no more misleading than a table of fees in a currency of account like the Piedmontese lira, so long as we keep in mind that an equivalent Fcs 1,000 in earlier years is worth somewhat more in real terms than the same sum paid in later years.

Patterns of fees in the table show a pleasing rationality. Already in the late 1730s what singers could earn was neither a grotesque nor an arbitrary sum; it was a market quotation. Look at the fees paid between 1739 and 1743 to the

Notes to Table 3

[a] fee for a pair of dancers
[b] joint fee for a tenor and his wife, who sang 2.a donna
[c] inaugural season at new Teatro Comunale; cast also included a bass (Fcs 1,158)
[d] Gluck's *Alceste* at Teatro Comunale; no 1.0 uomo; cast also included a bass (Fcs 1,158)
[e] season included for general comparative purposes (1.0 uomo Roncaglia, 1.a donna Morichelli, tenor Mombelli)

C = carnival; P = primavera (spring); A = autumn
TO = Turin, old Teatro Ducale, then Regio (before 1741), new Teatro Regio (from 1741);
MI = Milan, Teatro Regio-Ducale; VE = Venice, Teatro S. Giovanni Grisostomo; BO = Bologna, Teatro Malvezzi (before 1763), then Teatro Comunale; Rome = Teatro Argentina; NA = Naples, Teatro San Carlo
Fees computed @ Lira piemontese 1 = Fcs 1.18; Lira milanese 1 = Fcs 0.77; Lira veneta 1 = Fcs 0.50; Lira bolognese 1 = Fcs 1.13; Roman scudo 1 = Fcs 5.35; Neapolitan ducat 1 = Fcs 4.35
Sources: A. Basso, ed., *Storia del Teatro Regio di Torino*, I, *passim*; C. A. Vianello, *Teatri spettacoli musiche a Milano*, pp. 338–42; A. Paglicci-Brozzi, *Il Teatro Regio-Ducale di Milano nel secolo XVIII*, pp. 64–5; N. Mangini, *I teatri di Venezia*, p. 143 (whose sums given in ducats are here assumed to be in lire venete); C. Ricci, *I teatri di Bologna*, pp. 535–56, 645–62; Pierleone Ghezzi, caricature caption, BAV Cod. Ottob. Lat. 3117 c. 110; E. Celani, 'Musica e musicisti in Roma 1750–1850', *RMI* 18, 1911, pp. 46–54; M. G. Pastura Ruggiero, 'Fonti per la storia del teatro romano nel Settecento conservate nell'Archivio di Stato di Roma', in *Il teatro a Roma nel Settecento*, II, p. 578; B. Croce, *I teatri di Napoli*, 1st version, *passim*; ASN Casa Reale Antica 965–6, 970, contracts and receipts.

contralto Teresa Baratti. In four cities they establish a pattern: her earning power was middling; she could command a respectable sum in a *seconda* part, but the one time we see her as prima donna (Turin, 1743) she was engaged at a relatively low fee to offset an expensive first man and tenor. Again, the fees paid to Caterina Visconti (in 1737–41), Caterina Gabrielli (1760–8), and the tenor Giuseppe Tibaldi (1763–78) are consistent at different levels.

The sums paid to Felice Salimbeni (1738–43), Giacomo Manzoli (1739–66), and the tenor Angelo Amorevoli (1739–49) all show a young singer rapidly increasing his earning power; these were indeed among the most highly regarded singers of their day. On the other hand Antonio Priori, a castrato whom we see in 1758 at an early stage in his career, singing a first woman's part in Rome (as Manzoli had in 1739), by 1766 is found singing a second man's part for less money. Once at least, in 1770, he was to appear as first man (at Bologna, in the locally unfashionable carnival season).[42] We do not know what he was then paid, but it looks as though Priori, like Teresa Baratti, had to settle for a middling career and moderate rewards. Alessandro Veroni (Turin 1739, Bologna 1742) seems to have done worse still; possibly he was at the end of an undistinguished career. The drop in Domenica Casarini's fee between 1749 (Milan) and 1751 (Turin) is at first sight puzzling; she went on to sing as prima donna at the San Carlo, Naples, in 1751–2, so she can hardly have lost reputation between the two dates. Her Turin fee was probably docked because she spent some weeks in gaol for having had a fellow-singer beaten up by thugs.[43]

The table shows another consistent relationship – that between fees paid to a singer in comparable theatres. The Milan, Naples, and Turin theatres in particular, allowing for the longer Naples engagements, paid at about the same standard. Evidence for Rome is too scattered to show anything. At Bologna, however, singers consistently accepted fees half or two-thirds lower than they could get in the big royal theatres. This is not to be accounted for by any decline in the singers' standing. The explanation is in part the smaller size of the Bologna theatres and the absence of a court (perhaps also the convenience of living at the hub of the opera market), but more particularly the season, which was not carnival.

'The fee you have asked for', an impresario was to tell a baritone in 1861, 'is fit only for a carnival season'. From the beginnings of opera to the break-up of the seasonal system in the late nineteenth century, singers expected to earn their highest fees in carnival, and were willing to take less at other times. In 1822–3 the last of the great castrati, G. B. Velluti, appeared at Trieste in the autumn for half his Venice carnival fee – though the autumn season (like the spring) was as a rule longer than any carnival; some other early nineteenth-century singers did much the same.[44]

Before 1770 or therabouts, carnival paid specially well: in many towns it was the only opera season allowed, so demand was at its peak. To judge from scattered evidence, singers took, in spring, autumn, and the seasons attached to trade fairs held at various times between April and October, as little as one-third their carnival fee. With heightened activity from 1770, the ratio flattened out: in less fashionable seasons singers could now hope to earn, performance for performance, between half and four-fifths of their carnival fee – if they found an engagement.[45]

In the nineteenth century, evidence of what singers were paid multiplies but, paradoxically, becomes harder to use – because the policies and fortunes of opera houses now changed more often, so that it is less easy to compare like with like. One main point has already been demonstrated elsewhere.[46] The fees paid to leading singers in Italian opera houses went up steeply in the late 1820s, so that in the 1830s they were two or three times what anyone had been paid in the eighteenth century. There were two intertwined causes – enhanced demand both in Italy and abroad, and the renewed fashion for serious opera that set in with Rossini. The new standard was kept up until 1848; after a slump due to revolution, war, and economic crisis, when singers either had to take pay cuts of up to a third or seek better terms in the Americas, it seems to have been largely restored in the latter 1850s and 1860s.

Evidence from the last third of the century shows a wide range of payments: while a few singers could command unprecedented fees in Cairo or New York – and even in Italy Patti's fee of Fcs 10,000 per performance was ten times what Pasta and Malibran had made in the 1830s – run-of-the-mill artists earned between 500 and 1,000 francs a month, not just at home but in the less glamorous foreign engagements that had multiplied in places like Athens, Malta, and the Azores.

Had the rise in leading singers' fees in fact done anything to draw minor singers' reward along with it? Table 4 seeks to establish how the pay structure moved over a long period.

The Naples royal theatres lend themselves to such an inquiry: they changed little (the San Carlo was rebuilt after a fire in 1816, but to much the same capacity) and their pretensions were high throughout – though under increasing strain from the 1840s. The nineteenth-century seasons shown in the table were all run by impresarios (five out of eight by Domenico Barbaja).[47] We need to allow for some financial ups and downs. High Napoleonic inflation explains the fee paid in 1811 to the leading buffa Elisabetta Gafforini.[48] This and the 1819–21 seasons were run on the

Table 4. *Salary structure at Naples Royal Theatres, 1780–1867 (San Carlo and Fondo; singers' monthly salaries in franc equivalents)*

	1.o uomo	1.a donna	contralto	tenor	bass or baritone[a]	2nd bass	other
1780–1	1,070 Marchesi	1,131 Balducci		509 Pini			44/87/131
1785–6	1,255 Roncaglia	1,018 Morichelli		713 Mombelli			218
1811		4,766 Gafforini					
1819–21		3,954 Colbran	1,088 Pisaroni	1,460/1,349 Nozzari	2,610 Galli		
		1,054/1,235 Dardanelli		1,324 David			
1826–7		7,200 Pasta					
1829		3,000 Tosi	705 De Vecchi	4,550[b] Rubini	2,135[b] Lablache	214 Benedetti	39 to 229[c]
		790 Sedlacek					
		512[b] Manzocchi					
1836		2,616[b] Manzocchi		? Basadonna	1,962 Barroilhet	523 Antoldi	39 to 166
		654 Barilli Patti		1,439 S. Ronzi		86 Benedetti	
		392 Franceschini		1,308 S. Patti			
1842–3		? G. Ronzi	301 Taglioni	? Basadonna	3,010 Coletti	430 Arati	73 to 430
		4,300 Loewe		2,795 Fraschini			
		3,440 Tadolini		387 Tamberlick			
		2,924 Derancourt					
		430 Gruitz					
1850–1		6,160 Tadolini		3,080 Cuzzani	3,080 De Bassini	440 Arati	?
		2,640 Evers		1,760 Miraglia			
		1,760 Gabussi		1,584 Baldanza			
		1,305 Bendazzi		1,320 Fedor			
		528 Zecchini					

Table 4. (cont.)

	1.o uomo	1.a donna	contralto	tenor	bass or baritone[a]	2nd bass	other
1866–7		7,000 Bendazzi	2,800 G. Tati	6,582 Stigelli	4,000[d] Pandolfini	425[e] Arati	
		5,000 M. Palmieri		2,800 Bertolini	3,200 Colonnese		
		900 Montebello		2,571 T. Palmieri			
		300 De Angelis					

Notes to Table 4:

[a] Includes basso cantante and baritono.
[b] Fee paid jointly to leading singer and his/her spouse/sibling.
[c] Basso buffo Giuseppe Fioravanti was also engaged at Fcs 555 a month.
[d] Singer also earned extra flat fee of Fcs 2,160 for performing Mephistophélès in *Faust*, not foreseen in contract.
[e] Singer now billed as '1.o basso' but still singing minor parts.

All sums except those for 1826–7 and 1866–7 originally in ducats; those for 1829–51 rendered at known contemporary exchange rate, earlier sums at standard rate of Duc. 1 = Fcs 4.35.

Sources: ASN Casa Reale Antica f. 965, 970 (contracts and receipts), Min. Interno II inv. f. 706 ('Stato dell'importo delle compagnie di canto e ballo'), Teatri f. 68 ('Conto delle ritenute . . . da passarsi alla Cassa dei Professori Giubilati'), f. 98 (Barbaja to Lonchamp, 11 April 1811); M. Ferranti Giulini, *Giuditta Pasta e i suoi tempi*, Milan, 1935, pp. 89–90.

expectation of high profits and high government subsidies, the product of Barbaja's gambling monopoly; later seasons were somewhat more modestly financed, though the San Carlo was still the second most lavishly subsidized Italian theatre. That apart, the seasons are broadly comparable.

The table on the whole confirms the notion of a plateau reached in the late 1820s and maintained (after the shock of 1848) until the economic crisis of the 1870s. It shows that down to 1867 a leading prima donna could out-earn everyone else, tenors included. Early in the century, baritones and 'singing' (coloratura) basses – those shown included some of the very best, such as Galli and Lablache – could do as well as or better than at least some of the tenors they sang alongside, even the celebrated Nozzari and David, who created most of the tenor roles in Rossini's serious works.

The table also brings out how the San Carlo, grand monarchical house though it was, persistently employed some low-paid singers in leading parts. Of these, two had just embarked on successful careers (Manzocchi, 1829, and Tamberlick, 1842–3) and would shortly command much higher sums. But Carlotta Gruitz sang parts like Lucia di Lammermoor and Adalgisa in *Norma* for several years (1840–4, 1846–7) without leaving any mark or apparently rising above the basic salary paid to the utility bass Marco Arati (a local legend who served with scarcely a break from 1841 to 1878). Franceschini (1836), Zecchini (1850–1), and Montebello (1866–7) sang comparable leading parts. Some of these may have been debutantes who sank without trace. Others, though technically prima donnas, may well have been utility singers only a little better off than the ten or twelve minor singers most of whom in 1829–43 were paid under Fcs 200 a month, a few under 100.

Such pay was still well ahead of labourers' or seamstresses' wages (at Fcs 26 a month or less). Though Marco Arati's unchanging salary worked out at about Fcs 14 a day, it was very much better than getting Fcs 14 per performance in a leading part at some third-rank or small-town theatre: it came in every day, and it offered security – at the cost of singing minor parts year in year out.

An opera company that gives nearly 200 performances a year (as the Naples company did at its two theatres)[49] is bound to use in leading parts an array of singers only some of whom are stars and are paid accordingly, while others are near beginners and others yet are workhorses: an all-star policy – as a San Carlo management made up of hopeful amateurs demonstrated in 1834–5 – is ruinous. Similar patterns can be found in other large companies, in Italy and elsewhere. The paybooks of the Metropolitan Opera in New York from the 1890s to the 1920s show some singers of leading roles making vast amounts while others earned far more modest sums: in 1896–7, for instance, Melba made $1,600 per performance while the forgotten contralto Eugenia Mantelli sang leading Verdi and Wagner parts four times a week for the equivalent of $48 per performance; comprimari made from $8 to $125 a week, singing five times. The long-serving Marco Arati was matched at La Scala in our own century by the contralto Ebe Ticozzi: after modest engagements in second- or third-rank theatres, occasionally in leading parts, she served the Milan house off and on from 1933 to 1956 as a comprimaria, at an unchanging (and by then equally modest) Lire 3,600 a month for the first ten years; in real terms her pay remained much the same through the inflationary years that followed.[50]

Even in opera houses of the highest pretensions, then, some singers earned a middling income. Many others did far worse, not just in semi-improvised stagings put on for a night or two: a full spring season of thirty performances (in the small Piedmontese town of Voghera in 1839) earned the prima donna Fcs 11 per performance, the comprimari Fcs 3.[51]

What determined the level of fees? To say that Melba was worth thirty-three Mantellis is an abstraction. There was a level of transcendent

Table 5. *Fees earned by Luigia Bendazzi, 1850–75*

City	Theatre	Season and dates	Fee	Franc equivalent (per month)
Bologna	unspecified	E–A1850 (10.06–5.12)	Austrian L.600 per mo.	522
Trieste	Grande	CQ1851 (to 23.3)	Aus.L.4,500	1,120
Naples	S. Carlo	P–E1851	Duc.300 per mo.	1,305
Naples	S. Carlo	A–C1851–2	Duc.550 per mo.	2,393
Florence	La Pergola	A1852 (20.8–30.11)	Francesconi 500	841
Parma	Regio	C1854 (to 3.3)	Aus.L.12,000	3,480
Genoa	Carlo Felice	A–C1855–6 (15.9–12.3)	Aus.L.23,500	3,408
Bologna	Comunale	A1856 (15.9–30.11)	Fcs 12,000	4,800
Venice	La Fenice	CQ1857 (to 26.3)	Aus.L.30,000	6,960
Reggio E.	Municipale	F1857[a] (2.4–20.6)	Aus.L.15,000	4,745
Venice	La Fenice	CQ1858 (to 7.4)	Aus.L.30,000	6,525
Naples	S. Carlo	1866–7	Fcs 7,000 per mo.	7,000
Milan	Castelli	P1875 (20.4–30.6)	Fcs 4,600	1,974

Notes:
[a] opening season of new theatre
Fees are for the season unless otherwise stated.
C = carnival; Q = quaresima (Lent); P = primavera (spring); E = estate (summer);
A = autumn; F = fiera (trade fair season)
Sources: Contracts, Piancastelli 43.105–16; ASN Teatri f. 68

quality which all recognized but few could attain: a singer could hold out for *hors concours* terms, literally beyond competition; Giuditta Pasta did so almost from the start.[52] That was what the manager of the Met, Giulio Gatti-Casazza, had in mind when (according to report) he declared that no singer as such was worth more than $500 a performance: the rest was drawing power, and Caruso, who was content with $2,500 a performance, was accordingly his cheapest artist.[53] Below this level, the market prevailed: close continual measurement of one artist's standing against another's, both by managements and by the artists themselves.

Standing, however, changed over time. We are seldom able to measure a singer's earning power over her whole career. Table 5 does this.

The series of payments is incomplete, but it covers all the main stages of Luigia Bendazzi's career as a successful dramatic soprano, from her second (or third) engagement to one of her last. The engagements listed, other than the first and last, were all in front-rank theatres; in all of them Bendazzi contracted to sing four times a week, so they are comparable.[54]

The figures in the last column tell a clear story, not unlike that of the tenor Ottani in Table 1 (if we allow for the greater number and commercialization of nineteenth-century theatres). Bendazzi almost at once established herself as a singer out of the common run. But it was her success in Naples in 1851, marked by a near doubling of her fee, that launched her. (The modest fee at Florence in autumn 1852 had almost certainly been agreed before her Naples success; if so it stood in a normal relation to her 1851 carnival fee). Further success confirmed her as a leading singer; her 1856–8 fees show her on a high plateau, with Bologna and Reggio understandably paying somewhat less than La Fenice and the San Carlo, two of the three foremost and best-subsidized Italian theatres. Though we next have a gap in the evidence, her 1866–7 Naples fee suggests that she was maintaining her position. Not for much longer: the last entry shows her singing at a large third-rank Milan theatre for a fee lower than any she had accepted since her earliest days in the profession.

The explanation was almost certainly vocal decline, perhaps coming together (though we know nothing about this) with financial problems. Improvidence was the reason why another famous Verdian singer, Erminia Frezzolini, kept making comebacks in which her surviving musical and dramatic skills contended with her wrecked voice. In 1874 she agreed to sing for Fcs 250 a performance at another large third-rank theatre, this time in Bologna. She was to have a benefit after the third performance; whether the season would get that far was – we may guess – uncertain. At least Frezzolini was able to stipulate that she would have new costumes and the ballet would be performed after the opera rather than between the acts: she presumably looked well, and, whether with applause or hisses ringing in her ears, she got home early.[55]

From the 1860s to the 1920s we have less reliable evidence about Italian fees than for the earlier period: in a more liberal regime it seldom found its way into government archives, and with the break-up of the old seasons a singer's income now came in irregular packets.

Though the range of possible payment was now wider than ever – from the ultra lavish to the miserly – at the top of the profession there may have been a further general rise. In the 1830s Pasta and Malibran had set an Italian record of Fcs 1,000 a performance; the first to match it was (so far as we know) the tenor Pietro Mongini, at La Scala in 1860; others followed, all, like Mongini, front-rank singers, but not *hors concours*.[56]

That a tenor should have made the breakthrough was symptomatic. The powerful dramatic tenor had emerged in the late 1830s. From about 1860 he became a mainstay. A set of model accounts for a carnival-Lent season at a front-rank theatre, drawn up in 1879 by an experienced man, assumed that a good tenor would cost Fcs 40,000 or 50,000 and a good prima donna Fcs 25,000 or 30,000 – early nineteenth-century practice turned upside down. The model also assumed a mere Fcs 10,000 or 15,000 each for the contralto and the baritone.[57] All this is borne out by what we know of actual fees paid. The internationally renowned tenor Roberto Stagno was paid Fcs 5,000 a performance for a short Turin season in 1885; in a regular season at the San Carlo in 1898 his disciple Fernando De Lucia, already at the height of his fame, was getting Fcs 2,100 a performance.[58] Both the prima donna (unless exceptional) and the baritone (though of high quality) were now paid less than the tenor. This was demonstrated by a season at the Teatro Argentina, Rome, in 1874–5: two sets of tenor, soprano, and baritone, all leading singers, were ranked by their fees in that order.[59]

'You will in any case be able to earn more [here in Spain] than you are now earning at home.' So an agent wrote to an Italian baritone in 1868.[60] This was one reason for travelling once the possibility of long service in a foreign court had vanished. The Wagnerian tenor Giuseppe Borgatti thought it natural that he should get more for singing abroad than his standard Italian fee, which in 1896 stood at Fcs 1,100 per performance; he settled in the end for just Fcs 100 more (at Alexandria), but still, some differential there must be if he was to put up with foreign ways.[61] The other great reason for crossing the Alps or braving the seas, accepted by singers far less exalted than Borgatti, was fear of unemployment in an overcrowded home market. This seems to explain why fees at the lower end of the trade, in places like Oporto or Athens, were much the same as middling or poor singers could get at home, while in foreign cities with a rich élite or a developed industrial and commercial middle class leading singers did better than they could anywhere in Italy.

Madrid from about 1730 to 1860 consistently paid about half again as much as the best Italian opera houses.[62] It and St Petersburg were the two European examples of lavish funding by an élite able to draw on the resources of a backward but centralized country. Even so St Petersburg – with Moscow, it had begun in 1730 by importing comic opera – did not at once compete at the highest level. Regulations of 1766, which codified the practice of years, laid down a maximum fee for a primo uomo of Roubles 3,500 a year (under Fcs 15,000): when the very best singers could get almost as much in an Italian carnival season, they were unlikely to be tempted into the snows, and indeed they left Russia to more workaday artists. Not until 1799 did a prima donna attain the Fcs 25,000 a year or thereabouts which at least six Italians had enjoyed at Madrid before 1759.[63]

Sparse nineteenth-century evidence suggests that this level was kept up in the two main cities, with more modest fees at Odessa. Arriving in St Petersburg in the midst of the 1905 revolution, the blacksmith's son Titta Ruffo, an extraordinary singer but, at twenty-eight, not yet established, was able to notch up sixty-six performances at Fcs 1,500 each; on getting home to his brother and sisters' Milanese walk-up flat he pulled Fcs 100,000 in notes from under his shirt and threw them into the air so that they covered the floor.[64]

London and Paris, up to about 1870 the capitals of the two most advanced economies in the world, were the most lucrative – more than Vienna, where from 1740 Maria Theresa could no longer afford large-scale productions: opera, run by impresarios, settled down to forming part of the ordinary Italian network and paying accordingly.

London paid very high fees right from the start of Italian opera in 1708–9; both early and late in the eighteenth century it paid a few singers in the region of £1,200–£1,500 a year (Fcs 30,000–37,500) – somewhat above Madrid, – with lesser artists paid in proportion.[65] The town was, however, so expensive for visitors that – according to the writer Giuseppe Baretti, who lived there – most Italian musicians left no better off than they came, some minor ones after a spell in a debtor's prison.[66] There may be some truth in this, with a touch of exaggeration: if things were so bad, why did Italians keep coming? In the early nineteenth century, fees were raised in practice by cutting down the Italian opera season to coincide with the 'London season', a mere four months from April to July; this left artists free to sing elsewhere the rest of the year. The great baritone Antonio Tamburini was able to earn at least £1,460 in 1834 and £2,000 in 1835 between fees and guaranteed benefits – only a little less than the most exalted prima donnas, Ronzi and Pasta, had made a few years earlier.[67]

Benefit nights were an important part of singers' earnings, particularly abroad. In Italy they were not insignificant, but the country was too poor to yield more than Fcs 1,000 to 3,000 per benefit even in leading theatres, whereas in Paris, London, or, later, in Buenos Aires they could bring in amounts far larger though seldom documented. Benefits enacted a personal relationship, ostensibly between the artist as humble servant and members of the public as appreciative and bountiful patrons. There was some financial risk where the singer agreed to pay the notional running costs of the theatre (as much as £130 at the King's Theatre in the Haymarket in 1717, nearly £50 more than the actual costs) while pocketing the night's takings; only the most famous singers could get a benefit clear of expenses. At other times the artist and the manager shared the profits, or staged a fake benefit with the manager collecting all the proceeds.[68]

On occasion a singer was given cash in lieu of a benefit, or contracted for a guaranteed minimum beyond which any profits would be shared. These are surer guides to what could be earned than the fabulous sums promised or rumoured. Mrs Billington at the height of her fame in 1802 was given £500 in lieu (twice over, at both Covent Garden and Drury Lane); Tamburini in 1835, also in London, was guaranteed £400, one-quarter of his fee for the season.[69] This was clearly worth having, and so were the smaller amounts earned by lesser singers' benefits. Nor were the accompanying gifts in kind to be ignored. As late as 1911 in Buenos Aires – where, as we have seen, old ways were kept up – singers as famous as the baritone Giuseppe De Luca lent their names to fake benefits on condition that they kept the gifts.[70]

Altogether the singing profession, if you did well, brought a number of fringe benefits away from the opera house. Italy offered the possibility of singing in church; for some who could play an instrument eighteenth-century Bologna had places in an ancient municipal band;[71] early in that century the Roman prince who was Handel's patron not only had singers in his household to perform oratorios and cantatas but employed casuals, some of them well known in opera.[72] Down to the early twentieth century rich people in places like Naples and Rome gave concerts in their drawing rooms: the tenor Fernando De Lucia began by appearing in such concerts, while the student Gigli – forbidden to take private engagements – eked out his income by singing, under an assumed name, as many as three in one day; they brought in some Fcs 100 each.[73]

All these resources (save the town band) were to be had abroad, for much higher rewards. So at least singers hoped; there was ample precedent, like the two grand concerts given about 1712–13 by the Lord Chamberlain of England and his wife, for which several women singers were paid £20 or £40 each but the castrato Nicola Grimaldi – clearly the great draw – got £200, nearly a quarter of his annual salary.[74] You could also give lessons to rich people, chiefly women: according to the tenor Giulio Marco Bordogni, who in 1830 had settled down to teaching in Paris, you could make more in this way than in a middling opera season in Italy.[75]

But although leading singers appearing in London, Paris, St Petersburg, or New York did well by working on the fringes of the opera season, it could mean less of a gold mine than they had expected. Tamburini thought he could get £60 a concert, but in fact sang for the Concert of Ancient Music for 12 guineas, near the top fee for such high-minded London concerts in the 1820s and 1830s.[76] A little earlier, Violante Camporesi had sung in concerts at Preston, Derby, and Norwich for something like £25 a time.[77] This kind of concert tour through the English provinces earned the leading baritone Antonio Cotogni, in 1870, Fcs 18,000 – as much as a colleague of equal eminence would presently make in a season of the same length at La Fenice, Venice: well worth having, but Venice was perhaps more fun than Preston.[78]

Nor were the great capitals less hard work than Italy. The London season would shortly end, Giuditta Pasta wrote to her mother in 1833: 'Thank heaven I'll have a bit of a rest, yesterday I worked off two more free concerts . . .'. Though she made money from private engagements, an implicit tit-for-tat exchange had her giving free charity concerts, some (for 'orphans' and the like) no doubt arranged by the nobility and gentry who invited her into their drawing rooms, others given on behalf of individual musicians. During the 1831 season she sang in thirty-one paid concerts, twenty-five free concerts, and seven benefits for her colleagues. This puts a gloss on her contractual limit of two opera performances a week.[79]

The singer's Eldorado was – like everyone else's – the New World. Few things are easier than to put down a string of huge fees earned by Tetrazzini or Caruso. It is easier still to repeat figures that were bandied about but that may have been inflated. A better course is to ask a few questions.

When did the Americas start paying well enough to attract leading singers in their prime? Maurice Strakosch, an impresario who knew a lot (even though his memoirs may not be fully reliable) blamed the rise in New World fees on that most colonial economy, Cuba, with a wealthy élite based on slavery and, from 1838, an opera house as capacious as La Scala.[80] By 1849, when revolution and war were driving some of the best singers out of Europe, the baritone Cesare Badiali claimed (in a private letter to an experienced agent) to have a seventeen-month contract for Havana worth some Fcs 7,500 a month – a few hundred more than the equally famous Paul Barroilhet was then getting in Madrid (another refuge from the troubles), and more than twice the salary of yet another front-rank baritone, Achille De Bassini, at the San Carlo in depressed Naples.[81] It seems plausible: the differential paid for the hazards of the voyage – still long and uncomfortable – and the risk of yellow fever.

Havana was an important opera date because it easily linked up by water with New York and with the Mississippi valley. A further influence was the highly successful North American concert tour which P. T. Barnum organized in 1851 for the soprano Jenny Lind: 100 concerts at $1,000 a concert and a share of the profits.[82] After the break of the Civil War, improved railways and steamships greatly eased travel.

What was the range of reward on offer? Even at the Met, as we have seen, it could be wide. A middling Italian baritone, continuously active but not in the Badiali class, was offered in 1863 Fcs 1,100 a month to appear for six months in Guatemala, Salvador, and Costa Rica; the cost of living, the agent assured him, was low. He seems not to have gone, even though he was then earning only Fcs 500 a month at Lille; yellow fever may have outweighed other considerations.[83]

New World largess came from a curious mixture of sources, industrial and commercial on the one hand, agrarian and colonial on the other. During Patti's six-month concert and opera tour of North America in 1886–7, the highest opera takings were in Mexico City, where for a week every performance brought in over $10,000; only New York was in this class.[84] The resources of capital cities that concentrated the wealth of an agrarian hinterland help to explain why leading Italian singers now flocked to South America in particular – that, and the convenient fit between the cold-weather season in the southern hemisphere and the slack summer season in Europe.

Even when this had been going on for twenty years the soprano Romilda Pantaleoni, soon to create Verdi's Desdemona, stated in 1885 that she would go only for '*grosso lucro*' ('big money': Fcs 25,000 a month and a benefit guaranteed at Fcs 15,000).[85] She still had yellow fever in mind. Where, unusually, we have reliable figures of earnings – at the huge, luxurious Teatro Colón, Buenos Aires, in 1910–11 on the crest of the opera boom – the foremost singers were indeed making *grosso lucro*: Fcs 40,000 a month (5,000 a performance) for the tenor Florencio Constantino; 8,000 a performance for another tenor, Giuseppe Anselmi; 70,000 a month (7,000 a performance) for Titta Ruffo, then at his peak; between 6,250 and 25,000 a month for other well-known artists, with the contralto as usual the worst paid.[86] There were undoubtedly comprimari who got much less, and Italian singers in popular theatres who operated in a different world, minnow to the Colón's whale; but we do not know what they earned.

These Buenos Aires fees are close to those paid early this century in leading North American houses, where Italian artists were less dominant – not only the Met but the Manhattan Opera and the Chicago Grand Opera.[87] For the best-known singers Eldorado went on until the great crash of 1929 stopped it, both north and south. The Met for the next two decades kept to a maximum of $1,000 a performance, a third of what Gigli had been getting. In real terms, theatre fees have never fully recovered. The reasons are looked at in chapter 9.

In 1918, after Rosa Ponselle, the young Neapolitan woman from Meriden, Connecticut, had made a sensational debut at the Met, the opera house's chief backer Otto Kahn came into her dressing-room. '"A little memento for you," he said, handing me a plain white envelope; in it was crisp new thousand-dollar bill.'[88] It valued her in a way many generations of Italian singers, not a few of whom had sung on empty stomachs, would have understood.

16 The Guerra children's company in *Crispino e la comare*.
(Museo Teatrale alla Scala, Milan)

17 The Guerra children's company in De Ferrari's *Pipelet*, *c.* 1904.
(Dr Guido A. Tedeschi)

18 The Guerra children's company with their teacher-impresario, Ernesto Guerra. (Museo Teatrale alla Scala, Milan)

19 Arnaldo Tedeschi, star of the Guerra children's company.
(Dr Guido A. Tedeschi)

20 Arnaldo Tedeschi as the officer in *Il barbiere di Siviglia*.
(Dr Guido A. Tedeschi)

7

CAREERS

'The children's [opera] company is a great hit, the theatre is packed out every night, they're so sweet, poor little things . . .' So a noblewoman reported from Venice in 1842.[1] For some, the singer's life began well before puberty. This was true not just of the children of operatic families, like Adelina Patti, who helped her parents out of a tight corner by singing in concert at the age of seven. From 1783 to 1910 (in South America down to 1920) companies of pre-pubertal Italian children sang complete operas.

One or two seem to have been family groups; most, however, were run by an impresario who recruited the children of needy families, trained them, and toured them. They sang comic operas – not too difficult for light voices – until in 1903 a teacher-impresario had his lead singer, Arnaldo Tedeschi (billed as aged six, in reality nine), sing 'Di quella pira' from *Il trovatore* between the acts; his company of forty-eight children later performed *Lucia di Lammermoor* and *Rigoletto*, all singing treble. They earned more than they could have done in other jobs, though less than minor adult singers; Arnaldo remembered his teacher-impresario with affection, so that company at least was not a sweatshop.

If any of these child singers made an adult career in opera we do not know of it. Such troupes seem to have been a closed corner of the profession. As part of the vast market for child labour they were, by 1910, under attack; that, together with the rise of the cinema, accounts for their disappearance.

Why did none of the children go on singing for a living? Possibly because the man who trained them had by definition no interest in them as adults.

It is easy to paint a dark picture of an Italian singer's debut at most times from the eighteenth century to the twentieth. Low pay, factional jealousies, storms of boos and hisses – all were risks. But the debutant seldom faced them alone. He had as a rule the support of a teacher, a family, a patron, childhood friends, some of whom would be present. As we know from the story of Luigia Bendazzi and Federico Dallara, such ties were not always benign, but they fended off the impersonality of the modern job market. On occasion a young singer could feel she had an entire town behind her, like Nina Pedamonti, from Voghera: as an amateur she sang in the witches' chorus when *Macbeth* was given there in 1868; a group of subscribers paid (a not uncommon device) for her to study at the Turin conservatory; halfway through her four-year course she gave a concert, again in the town theatre, to raise more money; she then won a second prize, launched out in opera, but, on marrying a successful conductor, limited herself to concert appearances.[2]

Some of these early associates might follow a singer throughout her career. By hostile onlookers they were known as *procoli*, hangers on; one critic alleged in 1879 that, battened on as they were by parasites, Italian singers could hope to save real money only by taking engagements abroad.[3] This was overstated. Well-off Europeans down to 1914 or 1939 had retainers as well as servants; Italians had extended families. *Procoli* attracted notice because successful singers were the new rich.

Not everyone's debut was traumatic. Some young people almost slipped into opera through singing in church and studying with the director of the choir (who might double as chief répétiteur of the opera house). As an adolescent the baritone Antonio Tamburini, the son of a carpenter cum horn player, sang in church choirs, on occasion in the opera chorus in and around his home town of Faenza; at eighteen he began to appear as a soloist in minor opera seasons nearby; the rest was a series of ever more rewarding engagements, accompanied by further study and culminating in a great career, chiefly in London and Paris.[4] Entry by way of the church choir was still available in the 1850s to a young Roman ceramics worker who became as famous as Tamburini, Antonio Cotogni,[5] and to a third, more average baritone, Giovanni Marchetti: after training with a member of one Central Italian choir (Loreto) he joined another (at Orvieto Cathedral); for modest fees he sang solo in lesser churches and, probably, in minor opera performances before making his debut in a leading theatre at Florence, aged (it seems) thirty-seven – a late start.[6]

There were also amateurs who turned professional only when they were thoroughly grounded, among them people as far apart as the soprano Bicchelli, a miniature painter whom Burney heard and admired in 1770; Eugenia Tadolini, daughter of an upper civil servant, who at eighteen was admitted to her local musical academy, three years before her brilliant stage debut at Parma in 1830; and the tenor Mirto Picchi, a bank employee until 1946, when he launched out as Radames in a 5,000-seat theatre.[7]

For many young singers from about 1750, the first step once they were trained was to get themselves to market. This meant at first going to Bologna.

When the centre shifted to Milan everyone met at a café near La Scala; there you could observe – except in carnival when nearly everyone was away working –

the celebrity, in solemn dignified repose . . . the young impetuous debutant, fresh from the scene of his first great triumph; the blatant, swaggering nincompoop, boasting of victories he had not won; and the modest, earnest youth, overshadowed with doubt about his success, and fears for the future. . . . at times . . . the eye rested in some retired corner on a haggard, careworn face, watching with avidity to lay hold on a few crumbs of comfort in the encouraging glance of agent or comrade.[8]

With the opening in 1877 of the glass-roofed Galleria the market set up there – in its cafés and its cubbyhole offices high up, but especially on its floor. It was still the place for job-hunters in the late 1940s, before the telephone took over.

An engagement once secured, a debut for most meant facing the public in a strange town as a member of a company none of whom, perhaps, they had met before. This was already true in 1776, when the thirteen-year-old Crescentini appeared at the small town of Fano. We hear chiefly about the late nineteenth century, when beginners had many – often risky – opportunities.

Some crumpled up, like two young women pupils of reputable teachers. One failed twice over after virtually losing her voice; her family were left in 'dismal poverty'. The other was so agitated as to show little of her true quality; at the Bilbao opera house in northern Spain she was reduced to 'mental prostration'; the second-night audience, it seemed, would have to be told that she would do her best. A third was hissed at Rimini but managed to carry on: 'She really' – the impresario reported to the agent who had placed her – 'sings as far out of tune as it's possible for a singer to do. . . . A fine present you've made me . . . ! Still, she is a very nice girl, so we'd better let her down gently in what's reported in the papers.'[9]

The hazards of a debut might be nothing to do with the singer's own failings. A young tenor, at Ancona in 1872, could not be heard because the audience was shouting and demonstrating against the supervisory board, which had ruled out the engagement of another tenor; the performance was stopped.[10] A soprano who was to have appeared in *Don Pasquale*, a light lyric part, suddenly found that her debut had been switched to *Beatrice di Tenda*, a dramatic one steeped in pathos.[11]

The worst hazard was the right of the management or the supervisory board to cancel a new singer's contract by issuing a legal *protesta* or repudiation. It grew out of a long-standing custom that beginners' contracts were not final till they had opened their mouths in public. Before records and broadcasting, no one could be sure of what a new voice would sound like.

Even singers who had been negotiated for and awaited through more than a year could prove disappointing, as three Italians did at Würzburg in 1721; the prince-bishop sent one of them back.[12] In the old Italian states, the supervisory board might dismiss a beginner to forestall disturbances in the theatre; the beginner would then be left unpaid – an arrangement that was eventually built into contracts, and upheld by the courts in 1861.

In united Italy two circumstances could give rise to a *protesta*. One was the debutant's 'inadequacy', observed in rehearsal and notified in writing, generally by the conductor. The other was 'public disapproval' in perform- ance. The former was hard to take but clear. The latter was readily contested. The courts upheld a further custom – that a beginner had a right to be heard in three performances before being dismissed on grounds of 'public disapproval', though one court in 1907 raised doubts by finding that a singer who was 'loudly and unanimously hissed' could be got rid of after one go.[13] In practice, such total failure led most beginners to give up.

Experienced singers could be *protestati* if the supervisory board demanded it or if their contracts allowed for it; but under a court ruling of 1859 they normally had to be paid the first quarter of their fee.

As repertory opera spread, and with it helter-skelter conditions of performance, *proteste* became more frequent. In a Milan *Faust* of 1872 three tenors, two prima donnas, and a contralto were dismissed in rehearsal; so, at Casale in the following year, were seven tenors in a row. Not all those dismissed took it lying down. A small-part singer – the Savona impresario had picked him up in a tavern where he was entertaining the customers – was dismissed in rehearsal by the conductor; he lurked behind a pillar and hit the conductor a mighty blow on the head with a stick; luckily a bowler hat muffled the impact.[14]

Even well-known singers could be dismissed, as the tenor Ottavio Nouvelli was from La Fenice, Venice, in 1891 after the local first performance of *Cavalleria rusticana*; the executive committee that acted for the proprietors thought he might have been unwell, but, urged on by the conductor and by Mascagni's publisher, agreed to a *protesta* on the grounds that the audience had rejected him.[15] Nouvelli's only resource would then be to sue. Such methods were at least direct, unlike those of the New York impresario Oscar Hammerstein, who got rid of the failing and expensive Nordica by an organized campaign of cigar-smoking (something she particularly disliked) and by offering to downgrade her to cheap matinées – hints of a kind later dropped by Hollywood producers.[16]

Most singers, however, were not dismissed. Young ones then had to make the most of a career that might be short and that already in the first quarter of the eighteenth century was highly competitive: of 287 singers known to have appeared in Venice between 1701 and 1725 (still at that time the headquarters of opera production), 122 lasted one season and another 141 sang in two to five; part of the explanation was rapid turnover in middling and poor singers.[17]

What became of those who did not make it to the top? The evidence does not allow of a precise answer. For men in 1701 the best hope was a place in a church choir. For both sexes in 1801 and especially in 1901 there were possible engagements in opera at many levels of quality, followed by teaching. As in all modern theatrical professions, some disappeared into jobs unconnected with opera, some women into marriage.

As the La Scala company in 1865 were rehearsing a new opera, with the composer in attendance, the impresario burst in, stopped the orchestra, and said he wanted to rehearse a different opera with a tenor who was making an emergency debut the next day. The composer shouted, wept, and stamped his feet at this 'murder of Art'; the baritone shouted that he would not rehearse two operas in one evening; the impresario shouted back in dialect 'I'm paying and I give the orders'. After an exchange of insults the impresario slapped the baritone; in the resulting scrum the conductor fell down, a drunken inspector from the supervisory board fell on top of him, the chorus intervened, and the baritone and the bass came to blows over the soprano, with the one grabbing the other in the 'reproductive region'. The impresario ran off.[18] On other occasions a comic bass beat up an impresario[19] and a diminutive impresario who had endured three months' continual difficulties from the baritone Victor Maurel, the original Iago, at the end of the season called him in, sat him down, rained blows on him, showed him out, and called after him 'Now, dear Maurel, we are even'.[20]

Such rough and ready encounters between singers and impresarios did not happen every day. They none the less marked an important difference between Italian opera management as singers experienced it – hurried, generally plebeian, even crude, dealing with people face to face – and the more impersonal, bureaucratic management sometimes found abroad. It is doubtful whether any singer in an Italian theatre before 1920 (when modern bureaucracy began to come in) ever met with anything like the three-page letter of advice addressed to the contralto Rosa Morandi in 1817 by an official of the Paris Opera. 'Your taste is appreciated, as is your method, which is well-judged; but it is thought that you do not control your intonation sufficiently, which sometimes makes your voice a little sharp.' She ought not to touch the male singer on the shoulder, still less on the knee: 'These familiarities are not permitted in good French society.' And so on.[21] An

Italian impresario might have said all this (in less buttoned-up language); he would scarcely write it, short of a breakdown in relations and an impending lawsuit.

Before singer and impresario came face to face, they would normally have corresponded to agree terms. Both moved about; season followed on season with hardly a break; to miss one, especially carnival, was thought the worst possible advertisement.[22] This made for a crisscross of negotiations by letter, with everyone anxious to secure the best possible engagement, often in more than one season or town.

The business was complicated by agents. Nowdays a musical agency is a business firm, powerful, often international. In the late eighteenth and nineteenth centuries agents were creatures of the operatic bazaar, men (and a few women) of little or no substance, who competed to be first with an artist's acceptance of a contract and so win a percentage of the fee – to begin with as low as 5 per cent.

Back in 1665, when Venice was almost the only place to offer 'mercenary' engagements at high fees, the agent working in Rome for a Venetian impresario had thought it best not to approach a young singer until he was sure his principal wanted her: if he allowed her time to gossip about it 'she could get up on her high horse and make large demands'.[23] A century and a half later, there was no time for such caution. An agent might speculate on trying to bring together a singer and a management neither of whom had commissioned him – and, when caught out, might fake a reply;[24] managements got several agents to approach a singer in the hope that one might undercut the others; agents at times colluded with an impresario to jockey a singer into accepting a lower fee; in the end more than one might try to claim a percentage. Singers for their part might try to evade paying it. Negotiations could be so complex as to obscure the rights and wrongs of the matter.

At times a singer not in the top flight offered to bribe an agent with an extra percentage or sweetener in exchange for a good part or an engagement abroad. Some named terms ('business is business', one soprano commented unnecessarily as she offered 10 per cent instead of the then usual 8), others hinted 'You will not find me ungrateful'.[25]

In such circumstances there could be no steady relationship between artist and agent. A baritone whose operatic career lasted from the 1850s to the 1880s dealt with at least forty-four agents.[26] Agents made for much bad blood; singers often denounced them as 'a lot of swine'[27] and so on; the hurried rhythm of the opera business made them indispensable. Printed contract forms of the late nineteenth century included the agent's commission as a matter of course. The leading tenor Mario Tiberini, who claimed never to have written a word to a single agent, spoilt the effect by adding 'and most of the time I don't even reply to their offers'.[28] Some of the time, clearly, he did.

The only steady relationship was that between a few leading or highly promising singers and a yet smaller number of impresario-managers. The manager paid a singer or dancer a monthly salary over one, two, or three years, and hoped to profit by exploiting the artist's services. A few leading Italian impresarios of the first half of the nineteenth century pioneered the system, notably Alessandro Lanari; it meant taking on seasons in many towns so as to send artists round a circuit without leaving expensive gaps in their schedules. When Lanari and his fellows had no convenient season of their own they would 'market' their 'stock' by selling their artists to other managers for a time.

To a beginner, such a contract offered rates that increased year by year but that still allowed the agent a huge profit if the singer broke through. Antonio Selva, the eighteen-year-old whom Verdi in an emergency plucked from the chorus to sing the bass part in *Ernani* (1844), was under three-year contract to a manager who paid him Fcs 3.48 a day; on this he supported his brother, and was so poor that after his success a nobleman offered to have a suit made for him.[29]

By the late 1850s the three years in such contracts had grown to five: Charles Santley, hard up after his Italian debut, narrowly escaped signing one that would have committed him to singing anywhere in Italy, first at Selva's rate, ultimately for a maximum of Fcs 435 a month less all expenses – and, he later felt, would probably have wrecked his voice if it had not first starved him to death.[30] The young Barbara Marchisio got out of a lifelong tie to an agent when the Italian courts threw it out in 1859 as an unlawful interference with freedom of contract; indeed they ruled against all such exclusive arrangements, even those limited in time.[31] But by the 1880s, under an eight-year contract probably made in Paris, the conductor Emanuele Muzio was still maintaining his pupil the tenor Eugène Durot and successfully placing him in the Italian provinces.[32]

For the singer the worst of such contracts was not necessarily the loss of potential earnings. To those who made an overwhelming success a wise manager offered a better contract or a bonus. Giulia Grisi, who fled to Paris, supposedly from a contract that had over three years to run, had been given a fresh contract with an option to cancel or alter the terms again every eighteen months; she almost certainly went because Paris offered more than she could ever make in Italy.[33] The real trouble was being at someone else's disposal: one minor singer still did not know on September 2 where her manager intended to place her for the autumn season, which normally started about that date.[34] Giuseppina Strepponi's experience of the system led her to reject it: she need then no longer endure 'continual reproofs like an unwilling schoolgirl'.[35]

On the other hand the tenors Moriani and Duprez thought their long-term contracts – which included skilled instruction by Lanari's musical director Pietro Romani – had served to launch them. The system, Duprez recorded much later, when he had no need to flatter, 'preserved me for a fixed term from all business worries, and handed me over to a man capable of directing and supporting a young artist with all the resources at his command'.[36] To cope with the system, a young singer – like a star tennis player today – needed above all a good deal of self-possession.

Most singers were not bound to an impresario-agent; they carried on their own negotiations. This, for many years and down almost to our own day, meant bazaar bargaining.

The unspoken rule was that no one began by naming a true price. The singer would start from a figure higher than anyone was likely to pay; the impresario would name a fee lower than he expected to provide. This gambit (often alleged by each of the players to be all they could concede) would be decried by the other side as a *sparata* (opening shot) or *cannonata*. Ritual then demanded that the two parties should approach, by a series of steps, terms acceptable to both. Many bargains were sealed in this way, though in most negotiations time pressed and there was not leisure for the utmost refinements of bazaar haggling.

How things might go wrong was shown in 1874 by an otherwise ordinary transaction between the prima donna Isabella Galletti Gianoli and the veteran Roman impresario Vincenzo Jacovacci. He wished her to sing Amneris, a part new to her; by this date the practice had grown up of paying leading singers by the performance rather than by the season, and of guaranteeing them a number of performances.

Jacovacci began by offering Fcs 1,000 per performance, payable after each performance, and a guaranteed twenty performances starting on December 26. Galletti countered with a demand for Fcs 1,200, payable part on arrival, the rest before each performance (this was during the depressed 1870s, when impresarios' finances were specially rocky); she also wanted a guaranteed twenty-six performances and a later opening date, as she needed more time to learn the part. Jacovacci came back with Fcs 1,100, a guaranteed twenty-two performances, and an opening on December 30. Galletti lost patience; she declared his terms unacceptable, and signed a contract with another impresario who offered her the chance of singing an opera specially written for her. At that point Jacovacci accepted all her demands and urged her to break the new contract (on payment of a penalty). She commented to a third party that if Jacovacci had agreed earlier to some of her demands she 'might have come to an accommodation'; his meanness was at fault. Jacovacci was notoriously mean (he had to be, for he ran a theatre with high pretensions on an inadequate subsidy); all the same, he probably was following the habits of a lifetime, and expected Galletti to go one more round. There were still ten weeks to go to the season: why hurry?[37]

In such negotiations, leading singers' chief concern was not to lose status by accepting less than their direct competitors were known to have had in similar circumstances: 'The price', as was said in 1849 of a young tenor – good but not comparable to the very best – 'must be the thermometer.'[38] This was true all the way from 1665, when two Roman sisters known as the Flower Girls (Fiorare) held out for 300 scudi each rather than the 250 offered by a Venice impresario – it was 'what has habitually been paid even to ordinary singers, and . . . they feel they are no less good than the rest' – to 1871, when Victor Maurel declared that the impresario of the San Carlo was free to value another baritone more highly, but he, Maurel, could not accept that.[39]

This need not surprise us. Singers had to manage careers, likely to be short, in a poor society where failure meant starvation, and where every penny must be haggled for; they made all they could. Once cash became the 'thermometer' – as it already was in seventeenth-century Venice – keeping one's place in the ranking order demanded eternal vigilance. Only one singer is known to have avoided bargaining altogether. Bianca Donadio, who flourished about 1880, fixed a fee (Fcs 2,500 per performance) and sang only when someone was prepared to pay it and she felt like it; she was a pious Frenchwoman (Blanche Dieudonné) who ended by retiring to a convent.[40]

Like other members of the opera world, singers engaged in negotiation deployed a language of 'friendship' and 'esteem', stressed their own 'honesty' and 'disinterestedness', and brought out all the 'sacrifices' they had made for the other party's benefit, which they expected to see returned. As early as 1654 a singer annoyed at the slowness of negotiations with a Venice impresario protested his 'affection' and complained of 'the scant esteem shown for my person'.[41] Two hundred years later his successors were using virtually the same words.

A 'friend' to them could be a person one had yet to meet, who had shown his 'friendship' by doing one a favour. There is a curious parallel with the world of the Andalusian village studied by the anthropologist Julian Pitt-Rivers:

A friend is . . . someone whom one likes and admires and wishes to be associated with for that reason. The association is established through a favour which expresses one's *simpatía*. If the favour is accepted, then the bond of friendship is established. Mutual confidence supposedly comes into existence. One is then entitled to expect a return of favour. For favour is at the same time both personal esteem and also service.

The emotional attitude of friendship can be proved only by a material gesture. This makes friendship unstable: 'The friend who fails one ceases to be a friend.' Pitt-Rivers sees it all as arising from the egalitarianism of the hill village, where relationships are based on contract rather than status.[42]

The opera business, once freed from dependence on the great, was an egalitarian village of a sort. No one, however well paid, was really a lady or a gentleman; most relationships were based on contract; all had to face together the test of success or failure in the theatre. But the strains of multiple seasons and engagements made for a more than peasant acrimony.

Agreement, once secured by the crossfire of letters, had to be embodied in a *scrittura*, literally 'writing'. This was normally a private contract rather than a more elaborate notarial document. An initial step, common in Italy, was the *compromesso*, a pre-contract binding the parties for a stated period (which might be a few days) but allowing either to back out at the end of it on certain conditions. There were also oral agreements, statements on one's word of honour, and letters of acceptance that fell short of a contract.

On the whole, the readiness of most singers and most impresarios to abide by these arrangements strikes one more than the clamant examples of bad faith. There was genuine indignation in the reproof sent by an agent (more solid than most) to the tenor Enrico Giordani, who had agreed by letter to sing in a small town but now declined to sign the contract: 'This is a dastardly act unbefitting the honest man that Giordani has always been, and therefore I must believe that you will come to your senses, and will go to Medicina as agreed.'[43]

This whole area of preliminary undertakings was uncertain in law; what you could get away with depended on the logic of the market. A noble impresario (who was also a powerful official in the papal government) threatened to sue a prima donna's father for having set aside a pre-contract on the grounds that some trifling reservations had not been met by the expiry date; but when Alessandro Lanari cancelled a minor woman singer's pre-contract for a season at La Fenice, Venice, she only 'railed, complained bitterly, and wept'.[44]

So too the duties imposed by contracts varied with the singer's bargaining power. They grew more detailed from the mid eighteenth century, as enforcement gradually switched from arbitrary rule to the courts and what had earlier been left to custom came to be spelt out. But only minor singers had to pay a heavy fine if they failed to turn up – amounting to double the agreed salary plus the extra cost of hiring a replacement; only they could have their contracts revoked at any time (with their wages paid only to the end of the month) because they had performed 'imperfectly' just once – indeed no grounds need be stated; only they could be made to sing twice a day in any part the management chose, or be sent to perform in other theatres and other towns.[45] More important singers crossed out such clauses in printed contracts and wrote others in; if they then skipped because they had got a more appetizing contract elsewhere the impresario might threaten to charge them the cost of a substitute[46] but in practice could only sue for damages; the usual outcome was some kind of agreed compensation.[47]

Singers' first duty was to reach the *piazza* (the town where the season was to take place) by a certain date. While fixed seasons prevailed, and with them the need to learn new operas, this was about three weeks before the first night – typically December 6 for a carnival season opening on December 26, though by custom it was all right to arrive up to December 10 if no date had been set.[48] In the season just ended, all members of the company had had to make sure that they did not appear within a set distance of the theatre, codified by about 1820 as sixty miles (thirty for minor parts). Until recording and broadcasting came in, an important part of a singer's appeal was novelty; one who appeared in Venice in 1760–1 was threatened by the impresario with legal action for having taken off the bloom by singing in private houses and in a church.[49]

A few of the company travelled by post (a relatively fast conveyance), more by a lumbering coach; along rugged Mediterranean coasts (from Leghorn to Genoa, for instance) Tosca's proposed flight by boat was a singer's normal route before railways were fully in place in the 1880s.

The conveyance would be full of singers' trunks. Though singing depends on the human body alone, singers had to take with them heavy impedimenta – the 'trunk arias' (*arie di baule*) they would interpolate or substitute for any that did not suit them, and a variety of costume items.

'Trunk arias' were not just a matter of whim: a contract of 1754 required a singer to bring them.[50] Operas were written 'on' the singers who were to launch them, but not everyone might be suited. Costume items (*piccolo vestiario*) included almost everything other than a dress or suit: shirts, tights, stockings, footwear, hats, plumes, gloves, crowns, diadems, turbans, wigs; leading singers at times made sure that they were required to bring only basic items (*alla francese*) and not the more historical or exotic items (*di carattere*).[51] From about 1850, with repertory opera and enforceable copyright, singers no longer needed 'trunk arias', but many now had to bring whole costumes; some were still being trundled about to minor engagements in the jet age.[52]

As soon as the company arrived, rehearsals would start. From the mid seventeenth century to the 1870s, about twenty days was reckoned in Italy to be the time needed to learn and rehearse an unfamiliar opera. Around 1650–60, when operas contained long recitatives, a few leading performers were studying their parts in the summer preceding the Venice carnival, but they did not come together before the three-week rehearsal period.[53]

That was the ideal. In practice, singers of mid eighteenth-century opera seria might rehearse for as little as a week, though they took a little longer to study their parts: their solo arias needed little coordination, and the chief librettist of the genre, Metastasio, complimented a prima donna on taking the trouble to rehearse with the other principals.[54] Even when the chorus came back and opera seria had more ensembles, an 1823 manual named fifteen days as the time allowed by custom; for comic or sentimental opera, ten would do.[55] In 1853 *Il trovatore*, then new, was rehearsed from scratch at Reggio Emilia in seventeen days, the immense *Prophète*, at Bologna (1860), in sixteen.[56]

Accidents could still happen. If the first of the two scheduled operas failed, the company might have to throw together in four days a 'fall-back opera' which they either knew or could piece out with trunk arias – and this while they were learning the second scheduled opera. When nearly everyone and everything travelled, a lot could go wrong. The composer might arrive late from the town where he had been working, as Galuppi did in Venice in 1762: twelve days before the opening night, he had not yet turned up; though he had sent some music ahead, nineteen arias were still missing. Two years later, much the same happened with Sacchini. New arias for a comic opera in 1759 were being fed to the singers a day or two before the first performance, and the finale was ready only after the third.[57]

The libretto, again, might have arrived late, or the whole season have been planned late: Donizetti's singers had the former trouble over *Lucrezia Borgia* and *Parisina*, Rossini's the latter over *Il barbiere*. Even without an unexpected hitch, the composer of an Italian opera down to about 1850 might well be writing the last act while the cast were learning the first. Opera in this worked like modern musical comedy.

'Poor things, they rehearse from 10 to 3 or 3.30, go off and grab a bite, and then sing in the evening': that was at the Italian opera in Paris in 1813.[58] On other occasions singers went through the dress rehearsal on the day of the first performance. No wonder some first nights of what were to become standard works – *La Cenerentola, Norma* – were virtual failures: everyone was tired out.[59]

How, then, could an experienced British manager talk about 'the careful and gradual getting up of the operas' in Italy compared with the accustomed London rush? Or the sober New England woman who was Nordica's mother report from Milan and Brescia in 1879 that 'the Italians give plenty of rehearsals', 'nothing is done in this country, as a rule, without thorough preparation'? (For a modest production of *Don Giovanni* her daughter had had twenty twice-daily rehearsals, fifteen with piano and five with orchestra).[60]

Faced, from early days, with the demand for one new work after another, singers had devised a fast, well-schooled routine. But it was exposed to the hazards of a tight schedule, made worse by distances and slow communications; above all, it was hard work. The great French tenor Adolphe Nourrit, used to the leisurely methods of the Paris Opera, was devastated by it when he tried himself out in Naples in 1838. True, he had other problems, vocal and personal, to drive him to suicide.[61] Other foreigners who worked with Italian companies grumbled: 'Never in my life have I studied so much,' the German Marianne Pyrker wrote in 1749 after learning six operas in three months; 'a career as a singer in Italy', the Frenchwoman Anna de la Grange wrote in 1846, 'is really too tiring'. Yet, like most Italians, they coped.[62]

When repertory opera meant that a singer could be expected to appear at little or no notice, the rehearsal period came down with a bump. Already in 1828 the tenor Giovanni David was allowed in an emergency to sing one of 'his' parts with only one week's rehearsal. This – or at least four or five days – seems to have been the norm down to mid century.[63] A lavish season at Bologna in 1852 demonstrated it. Four repertory operas went on at intervals of ten to twenty days, each with an orchestral rehearsal, a dress rehearsal, and a first performance on successive days.[64] Far worse was to follow.

To cope with so unrelenting a schedule, singers needed above all robust health. It has always been easy to make fun of them as valetudinarians. Here is Fanny Burney observing the great coloratura specialist Lucrezia Agujari:

This singer is really a *slave* to her voice; she fears the least breath of air. She is equally apprehensive of any heat. She seems to have a perpetual anxiety lest she should take cold; and I do believe that she neither eats, drinks, sleeps, nor talks without considering in what manner she may perform those vulgar duties of life so as to be most beneficial to her voice.[65]

Imagination might have told Fanny that Agujari's body and mind, not just her voice, made up her professional equipment. Here and there a singer can be found who treated his voice as an independent entity, like the tenor Pasquale Brignoli: he once fell off a train in an American railway station; people rushed to help, fearing broken bones; he merely sat up and 'solemnly sang a bar or two. Finding his voice uninjured, he burst into heartfelt prayers of thanksgiving, and climbed back into the car.'[66] The voice, however, remains bound up with the whole of a singer's physical and emotional responses.

Agujari might well worry about draughts, then and now a backstage hazard. Heat could affect voices and instruments alike, as in a sticky London July. Cold threatened in Italian theatres and lodgings: before central heating came in, they were inadequately warmed (if at all) by wood-burning stoves and charcoal braziers; young American sopranos who experienced them between 1860 and 1914 ended by huddling in overcoats, warming their feet on a hot brick between rehearsals, being nearly asphyxiated by fumes.[67] Eating, drinking, and sleeping could be affected by continual moves from one town or one set of lodgings to another; the fuss that singers made about their lodgings was not all self-importance. Moving about could also mean catching cold: even a short trip to see her daughter – Giuditta Pasta was told – might jeopardize her performance next day; she acquiesced, but felt it 'slavery'.[68]

When singers did fall ill it was even more unwelcome than it is today: only the best-subsidized companies had understudies (who in any case would harm the box-office takings); in an age of slow communications, replacements were hard to get. Even when Venetian commercial opera had been going for well over a century, a minor singer's illness could bring about a legal dispute over the unpaid half of her salary, without either side even mentioning medical certificates or permissible sick leave; the management did invoke a rudimentary notion of payment pro rata for those performances the artist had managed to sing.[69] Medical certificates came in by the early nineteenth century, at least in Italy; in Bohemia as late as 1838 a court threw out the certificate put in by an Italian singer on the grounds that her birth and profession were alike low; instead it took the word of the theatre director, a nobleman.[70] Sick leave was codified as eight days for leading singers, four for minor ones, during regular seasons; repertory opera brought more varied arrangements.

This still did not solve the problem of the singer who felt off colour without being clinically ill. Even a medical certificate might be suspect – impresarios were not above faking one when it helped them (easy enough in an age of imprecise medicine), and were correspondingly suspicious when it did not. Occasions when singers agreed to perform below their best probably outnumbered those when they declined on a whim. Their motive was not just pressure from a beleaguered management. Adelaide Corbini, who was to have sung Norma in a minor Naples theatre, already felt that 'they [the audience] are against me'; on waking up hoarse she begged the supervisory board to order a change in that night's bill and avoid 'disturbance in the theatre' – riot directed against her.[71]

One reason for feeling not at one's best was left out of Fanny Burney's catalogue. The voice is a secondary sexual characteristic, and responds to events in sex life. An experienced leading bass told me that 70 per cent vocal fitness required one to abstain from sex for four or five days before the performance; 100 per cent required ten days – 'who'd want to put up with that?' Such rules are arbitrary; but in spite of reticence on the subject (varied by nineteenth-century fads like the belief that masturbation caused loss of voice) it is clear that a 'temperate' sex life was thought best; 'amours' were blamed in 1836 for one woman's vocal shortcomings.[72]

Women singers were at risk from the effects of menstruation or pregnancy. The former risk was known, but for lack of acceptable understudies women often had to perform below their best, or else incurred blame for missing a performance through 'caprice'.

At a time when contraceptive methods were primitive or unknown, pregnancy was a constant hazard. Quite apart from its possible ill effects, physical and emotional – deepened when a singer like Giuseppina Strepponi had to conceal it or explain it away for fear of scandal, – pregnancy exposed a woman to having her contract cancelled unless she had declared it at the time of signing; the more strait-laced legal commentators and at least one surly impresario tried to invoke (as part of a common Napoleonic inheritance) French court rulings that in an unmarried or separated woman it justified damages as well. In practice, only the Rome and Naples authorities – as usual the most obscurantist – seem to have imposed cancellation whether or not pregnancy was visible or otherwise likely to harm a singer's performance. Francesca Festa Maffei thus lost her contract for Rome in 1807; soon afterwards she miscarried, but she still could not get her engagement back; after prolonged bargaining she settled for less than half her fee as compensation. Not even Rome or Naples applied French law on damages (though one Naples official invoked a woman's unmarried state as extra grounds for cancellation); under united Italy, a court in 1879 ruled it invalid.[73]

Even short of pregnancy, singing – dependent on an organ never wholly under control – can mean extraordinary stress. After twenty years' hard work Lilli Lehmann endured what sounds like a depressive breakdown, though it was diagnosed as 'anaemia of the brain due to a lifelong mental strain'; she got over it through a mixture of vegetarianism and exercise.[74] A man who had been in the First World War once saw Rosa Ponselle waiting to go on, pale and trembling, her hand shaking and cold; he was reminded of his fellow-soldiers waiting to go over the top.[75] Much the same has been reported of Callas.

These were all heroines of the profession. Others seemed more complacent. Singers' letters rarely tell one much about their feelings: most have not been good at expressing themselves on paper (if they had been, they might not have become singers); many seem content to dwell on two things – their own triumphs, and the terms of contracts. 'Your humble servant . . . scored a tremendous success. The others did their best'[76] – this kind of statement is common.

Yet inarticulacy and even crassness are no guide to singers' inner experience. Here is a rare glimpse: 'The minute I hear my own high note, I want to burst on it and break my throat and body on it, and almost succeed; then I find myself in the next phrase (which is a quick one) singing like a runner that has just breasted the tape, if he had to go on running.' [77] The writer is untypical – the actress daughter of Sir Herbert Beerbohm Tree, who early this century tried to launch herself as a singer in Italy; but in her self-consciousness she perhaps brings out what many have felt. The mark of the good singer as of the Wimbledon competitor is commitment of the whole person, moral as well as physical.

Next, from the heart of the Italian profession, is Augusta Boccabadati; early in her career she writes to her sister – likewise a singer, daughter of a singer, and married to a singer, not, therefore, a correspondent one could show off to. Augusta has triumphed in her first opera at Genoa, but she worries about the next, with a part for her undoubtedly worse than the other principals'. 'Never mind', she concludes, 'we'll make sure to *maintain ourselves* always in the foremost place, even at the cost of *life itself*'.[78]

In its youthful excess this matches the determination of one of the last great castrati, Gasparo Pacchierotti: awkwardly tall and thin, and with a voice 'often undependable and nasal', in his early years he would practise at night in the attic so as not to disturb the neighbours; by hard work he got voice and person under control and broke through to 'the foremost place' at the late age of twenty-nine. Even then he needed time to settle into a part: he would tell friends 'Come and hear me after the third performance'. Yet the intense pathos of his singing was said to have reduced an orchestra to tears, no mean feat.[79]

This, the high artistic commitment that makes the profession at its best a noble one, should be kept in mind when we consider its more mundane side, in particular the complex of vocal requirements, customary precedence, and status-seeking untranslatably known as *convenienze*. Anxiety about this took up a good deal of singers' time and thought.

The root cause was that a market in singers had to work in a society still profoundly hierarchical. Opera was less the cause than the occasion. Church music gave trouble over *convenienze* when singers had to be got together for a special occasion; but that was rather seldom.[80] In opera, nearly every season meant a new combination of singers and, down to the late nineteenth century, new parts for them to sing – hence fresh uncertainties about where they would stand in the company hierarchy and how well they would be suited.

The purpose of *convenienze* was defined by a lawyer acting for a prima donna. They were directed wholly 'to acquiring and maintaining a singer's *reputation* in the art he practises, and since on the greater or less esteem a singer enjoys depends the greater or less price he can exact for his labours, in acquiring or maintaining his reputation or *convenienza* he does no more than safeguard and preserve his property . . .'.[81]

In the early days of opera, before singers had been fully classified into types, the question was whether the part you were offered was a *prima parte*. Was it the title part? The longest part? The highest? Was the character represented of princely status? These tests were all applied. Though the last two may seem to us absurd (and were already made fun of in the commercial-minded England of Handel's day), they made sense in the ultra-hierarchical society of continental Europe, where the right of one dignitary to walk ahead of another was of utmost concern: Metastasio was still discussing in 1748, for the benefit of Italian singers at Dresden, just how imperatives of the characters' rank and of dramatic effect should be balanced in placing them on stage.[82]

In Venice, another commercial-minded place, at least one singer in 1665 thought to profit by requesting more arias; those were years when the number of arias per opera reached an all-time high.[83] Opera seria, when it emerged as a genre with, as a rule, six or seven characters each allocated to a singer of distinct rank (first woman, second woman, and so on), had fewer and longer arias; these had to be carefully dosed not only throughout the opera but within each act. As fashion changed again from the late eighteenth century and more concerted pieces came in – together with fewer characters and more rapid, often more violent action dominated by the leading lady – one soprano asked for 'not many numbers', so long as her part was 'very tragic' and gave plenty of opportunities for vocal acting: there was a risk of overtiring oneself.[84]

But although it might now be wise to concentrate on a few demanding numbers, the aria was still what mattered most to singers: did it bring out their best points? Was it suitably placed within the opera? In the early nineteenth century the prima donna by custom needed a big entrance aria (*di sortita*) and a culminating display piece (*rondò*) often placed to bring down the final curtain. Even Giuditta Pasta, whose strong suit was tragic grandeur rather than coloratura fireworks, made up for Rossini's having neglected to give his Desdemona an *aria di sortita* by interpolating one from another opera.[85] Three prima donnas objected vehemently to the placing of other matter just before their *rondò*: the trouble could be that the prima donna was given too much tiring ensemble singing to do beforehand (she did not mind doing it afterwards), or that a big aria for the tenor was being inserted distractingly ahead of hers, or, on the contrary, that the suppression of a previous bass aria was making the *rondò* come on too soon, almost like a 'sherbet aria' for a minor singer during which the audience looked for refreshment.[86]

Before we decide that all this was grotesque vanity or whim, we should recall that operas were written 'on' individual singers: not only should the music fit their voices, so that composers often waited to write the arias until they had heard the voices that were to deliver them; the libretto too should ideally make the most of their strong points.[87] Lucrezia Agujari, demanding lines that would enable her to sing the syllables *ombra* in her low register,[88] was like a Hollywood star seeing to it that the camera shot her good profile: the fuss about *convenienze* had much in common with the trouble taken to ensure that every detail of a Garbo or Gable part lived up to the required image. And if Handel made to throw Cuzzoni out of the window because she refused to sing a particular aria, it was after all a matter of her *convenienze* against his: nor was it then clear that his ought to prevail.[89]

Unlike Hollywood, the opera business of the period up to 1850 worked in a society that understood itself by classifying. Hence the proliferation and inflation of titles: by the 1800s a *seconda donna* had to be known as *altra* (other) *prima donna*; *assoluto*, originally applied to one person only, came to be demanded by all leading performers; those billed as 'co-equal' (*a vicenda*) might, at worst, have to have their parts assigned by lot and their names printed diagonally across each other.

Some labels marked vocal resources rather than status. It was generally agreed that no one should be made to sing outside his comfortable range. Extraordinary refinements might go well beyond such simplicities, as when a court – giving judgment in a dispute between the bass Domenico Cosselli and an impresario, already arbitrated by Donizetti and another composer – ruled that a *primo basso cantante assoluto* engaged for a season of comic and sentimental opera could not be made to sing a part suited to a *basso serio*, even though it lay well within Cosselli's means; the real trouble was that the part had no arias, but that was not what the judgment turned on.[90]

One of the ambivalent prizes such labels held out was the custom of holding early rehearsals at the prima donna's lodging; it went on into the first half of the nineteenth century. A woman who received so many men was held by some to be immoral; yet it made her central and unique. For the composer to visit her and go over her arias was deemed a privilege; a Zerlina in *Don Giovanni*, at Milan in 1814, bitterly resented it when the composer of the next opera visited the Donna Anna but did not come to her.[91]

That singers spend much of their time consumed with jealousy of each other is a cliché; there is something in it. At the disreputable end of the profession, two Neapolitan women who in 1729 sang comic opera at the same theatre were such rivals both in song and in love that Francesca Grieco tried to have Rosa Albertini disfigured; when Albertini escaped with light scratches the Viceroy gave her an armed guard, but one night at her house door she was shot dead through the partition of her sedan chair. Grieco was packed off to a convent; the murderer – well connected – in the end got off with a fine.[92]

That was an extreme version of a feud common among pairs of singers. The most notorious example is that between Faustina and Cuzzoni, which probably did not (as alleged) culminate in their pulling each other's hair on stage; it can be matched at most times.[93] Between men, a feud could lead a tenor as late as 1782 to stab a comic bass (ineffectually); by 1873 a jealous tenor merely sabotaged a property throne so that the baritone fell through it.[94]

'Singers of nearly equal abilities, though of different kinds', Burney explained, 'regard one another with horror; reciprocally imagining that all the applause gained by their colleague is at their own expense.'[95] Though Burney spoke from experience, there was more to it than that. Hierarchy abhors parity. Where the point of your existence is your superiority to others, an equal is hard to place, let alone bear. When there was only one big opera season in each town and one prima donna in each season, Lucrezia Agujari never heard Caterina Gabrielli sing: as she pointed out, 'They two could never be in the same place together.'[96] If equals were brought together, factions readily developed among their admirers: when Faustina and Cuzzoni each had to cope for weeks with catcalls from the other's fans, the wonder is that they got through two seasons.

Professional solidarity, one must admit, has not been marked among singers of Italian opera, except at times in the chorus. Even in recent times the tenor Galliano Masini's refusal of an encore – he harangued the audience, pointing out that earlier in the performance the soprano had been denied one by the conductor – may have sprung from his early experience as a docker and trade unionist.[97] The castrati Gaetano Guadagni and Ferdinando Mazzanti did take trouble to bring out the best in fellow-members of the company with whom they were on friendly terms; the young Giuditta Pasta was helped by two older prima donnas (Violante Camporesi and Giuseppina Grassini) who might have felt threatened, and she in turn helped younger singers; Marietta Piccolomini, whose acting ability helped out her small voice ('homeopathic', she called it), was extravagantly modest, attributing all success to the composer and to her 'excellent colleagues'.[98] These were no doubt matched by others unrecorded. But the prevailing tone was susceptibility.

Nordica put it well. People, she said, did not realize 'what it is to come out before the public and in its presence then and there compete for one's position' (the Wimbledon contender again). Unlike writers or painters, singers knew at once what the audience thought:

With singers, side by side, there is applause or silence. . . . The singer is obliged to prove her art on sight. . . . She receives the verdict of the public in the very moment of production. It is exactly like any other trial of skill, and with the vanquished the situation is a hard one to sustain stoically. Consequently, singers are keenly sensitive to their position.[99]

This showed itself in a compulsive need for praise. Few artists in his experience, Gounod wrote, could 'admit the good faith of those who do not admire them unreservedly, or who prefer a conscientious silence to insincere praise'. He was right about singers. It made for relations at best wary with most colleagues, and with composers and impresarios too.[100]

One way to secure praise was to pay for it by subscribing to the many journals run by theatrical agents, and then by paying again for 'insertions' (reproductions of favourable notices). These journals were the curse of the profession from 1820 to 1919, when the manager of the Met, Giulio Gatti-Casazza, urged the leading Milan agent to give up 'the old, rancid, hateful system of praising artists who subscribe even if they're bad and of running down those who don't subscribe even if they're good'.[101]

In the early years, down to 1848, journals met a real thirst for news of opera, and they always had some use as bulletin boards and casting directories. But the men who ran them were too often petty blackmailers who sent unsolicited copies and then dunned singers for 'arrears' at the substantial rate of Fcs 30 a year, at times threatening legal action. A novice singer, Adelina Mosconi, in 1880 found herself dunned in this way by a minor agent – she had sent his paper back, explaining that she could afford no more, but he had persisted, saying she might pay when she 'could and would'; as soon as she got a modest engagement he wrote demanding his 'arrears', heavily underlined. The telling thing is that though upset, and insistent that he should stop sending the paper, Mosconi undertook to subscribe 'the moment I get a decent contract' – and even to pay the 'arrears'.[102] In this market as in others glutted with labour, the weak preyed on the weak.

If agents were to be feared and distrusted, impresarios were not much better. True, there were exceptions. The agent Camillo Cirelli seems to have been the only one of Giuseppina Strepponi's early lovers who behaved decently (he was the father of her first child and tried to help her through her later pregnancies). The impresario Domenico Barbaja, though a blusterer, showed real sympathy with the depressed Adolphe Nourrit – 'a good chap',

Nourrit wrote, '[he] made me be sensible in spite of myself'; but Nourrit was too far gone for help.[103] A few impresarios were married to prima donnas whose seasons they managed, and one third-rank bass was married to an equally third-rank woman impresario.[104]

On the whole, however, the relation between singer and impresario was as wary as that between one singer and another. The shifting pattern of seasons hardly allowed it to grow beyond the rushed business of first negotiating for and then getting through two or three months' hectic work; the few singers who pursued a routine in one place, like Felicita Suardi, thirty-six years an understudy at the Turin royal theatre,[105] were attached to an institution rather than to a person. Wariness was reinforced if the impresario failed; when, in 1755, a planned Venice season fell through at the last moment the artists did not even know where to seek compensation: two men each claimed that the other had been the impresario responsible.[106]

It was not a simple exploitative relationship. Just as impresarios were go-betweens rather than employers, so singers colluded in exploiting themselves, above all by agreeing to sing four, five, or even six times a week – far more often than anyone would think of doing today.

This became a problem early in the nineteenth century, as vocal writing grew more relentless, with shorter recitatives, and instrumental accompaniments grew heavier: the eighteenth-century norm of five performances a week at the Turin opera house, one of the grandest, seems not to have caused complaint. By 1820–40 the best singers wished to sing no more than three or at most four times a week, and often stipulated that there must be no more than two performances on consecutive days.

Even then there were reasons for taking on more. While the fixed calendar of opera seasons lasted, a few performances lost – typically because of illness – out of the number contracted for had to be made up in a hurry by a set date: the tenor Duprez thus found himself singing *Lucia di Lammermoor* six times in the last week of carnival at Parma in 1837, while another tenor, Gaetano Fraschini, sang heavy Verdi parts four nights in a row at the end of the 1860 Lisbon season: he was, he said, 'prostrated from the exertion'.[107]

These singers were helping out the management. Sometimes, however, leading singers were just making money: why else was Carolina Unger willing in 1837 to give extra performances (above four a week) at Fcs 500 each? Why was Eugenia Tadolini singing five times a week in Vienna in 1844, in operas 'very awkward for her'? Or, at the San Carlo, Naples (1884), the bass Ormondo Maini as Boito's Mefistofele, a part he found 'exceedingly tiring'? When La Scala in 1902 offered the baritone Maurice Renaud something like a present-day work rate – ten performances of one opera over six weeks or so –

he found it 'wholly unacceptable', particularly as he was taking less than his usual fee per performance for the sake of Art (in the shape of Berlioz's *La Damnation de Faust*); and even in the 1950s Giulietta Simionato is said to have performed thirteen times in thirteen days by shuttling between Milan and Rome – not the only one to put sleeping cars or, later, jets to that use.[108]

These were all established singers who could have done otherwise. Young or moderately successful artists had as a matter of course to sing leading parts five nights a week, all the way down to the 1920s, in theatres that might be minor in prestige but large in size. Even then the management might on occasion push them further: if Titta Ruffo is to be believed, his youthful tour of Sicily and Calabria in 1898–9 at one point had him singing eleven nights out of twelve.[109]

These conditions recurred briefly in wartime Naples in 1944–6, when the San Carlo gave, on average, eight performances a week to houses packed with Allied soldiers. We do not know how often individual singers performed, but many are said to have burnt themselves out.[110]

The worst excesses took place in the New World down to the 1920s, at the hands of Italian singers in South America and of singers of all kinds in the United States. Not content with performing in Santiago every other day, Hariclea Darclée (the original Tosca, then in decline) sang three times a day on two successive days – presumably in one-act operas, but one cannot be sure, when Mary Garden in New York sang two full-length works in one day, and the tenor Manuel Salazar sang *Lucia* in the afternoon and *Carmen* that same evening (thrown in with three other heavy assignments that week in Asheville, North Carolina). There was much more of this – the result of unsubsidized, profit-driven management, but also of singers' low regard for the discrimination of New World audiences, mixed with a high regard for their purse.[111]

Many singers' careers, it has been said, were cut short by this self-exploitation, or else by making too early a start.[112] Overwork as part of a reckless mismanagement of her life did for Giuseppina Strepponi's; by and large, however, we do well to be sceptical. To say that x's voice was wrecked is to make a judgment not everyone might share: there were, for instance, discordant opinions about the state of Isabella Colbran's voice while she was creating one heroic Rossini part after another. To describe a career as too short assumes, first, that there was a right length, and secondly that singers wished to go the distance.

At all times – so far as we know – some singers appeared for a few years only, while others went on for thirty years or more, typically but not exclusively those who were singing actors rather than pure vocalists, like

Caterina Gabrielli, famed for declamation, or the comic bass who appeared in Rome at the age of eighty.[113] We lack statistics such as could prove that the average length of careers went down at any time – say in the first half of the nineteenth century. Nor is it clear that most singers wished to go on as long as possible.

'The theatre needs youth', the experienced composer Hasse wrote in 1769. True, some went on past fifty, but an early start was the norm, and so was a career weighted towards the early part of life.[114] The conditions of singing down to about 1870 made it a strenuous routine even for the best paid. Nor was it pleasant to struggle on with declining vocal resources, like the tenor Raffaele Mirate, the original Duke in *Rigoletto*: when over fifty he was held to his engagement at the San Carlo, Naples, though three doctors certified his voice to be 'so disordered as suddenly to fail him altogether when he least expects it'.[115]

Women may have felt a particular spur to make money as fast as possible and retire, so as to look after their children or to lead a respectable life away from strange men's eyes, or both. Giuditta Pasta at twenty-nine thought of retiring in three years' time: she was making a lot of money in London and Paris, she felt keenly the separation from her daughter, and she looked forward to becoming a 'peasant' at the villa she had just bought on Lake Como. She was sincere: when she did retire, tourists on the lake would see her driving a flock of turkeys to their roost. Her friend Violante Camporesi likewise talked at thirty-four of going back to her family for good, and was still talking about it eight years later. In putting off retirement these two were not necessarily indulging their vanity. Their investments might have gone wrong, as Pasta's did in 1833; this probably accounted for her staying on past her best and, later still, attempting unfortunate comebacks.[116] More ordinary singers likewise hung on because they had inadequate savings and no pensions.

The few leading singers whose investments we know about placed most of their savings in land, houses, mortgages, and bonds issued by governments or by old trading corporations; Erminia Frezzolini played the Paris stock market and lost half her fortune, but she was known to be reckless.[117] Even 'safe' investments such as government bonds could fluctuate badly or, at the extreme, lose all their value through revolution; loans or mortgages could remain unpaid; banks could fail. This probably explains why some leading singers fell on hard times, like the baritone Achille De Bassini, who had to sell his villa near Naples, and Francesca Festa Maffei, who at one point pledged her knives, forks, and spoons; both took to giving lessons, and Festa, after several months' desperate search, found engagements for herself and her daughter and opened a theatrical agency: at fifty, she hoped within two years to pay all her debts.[118] Others lost everything: Andrea Castellan, who created the second tenor part in Mercadante's *Il bravo* in 1839, died fifty years later in a small Piedmontese town where he had long been a tobacconist; in our own century, the ex-docker Galliano Masini ended among his former workmates.[119]

The popular myth that such reverses were due to high living is hard to credit: before 1914 at least, it took a great deal of splurging to get through the amounts leading singers were paid. Gambling, however – whether at the card table or on the stock exchange, – could be a short-cut to ruin. Again we know little about singers' gambling habits, but the chances are that others besides Isabella Colbran, Rossini's separated wife, lost heavily at cards. In her retirement at Bologna she was bored, childless, with few interests to fill the void left by the end of a busy career. The retirement pleasures a later Neapolitan singer looked forward to were 'much *tresette* and *scopone* [Italian card games, not necessarily played for high stakes] and a few macaroni with pumpkin and meat sauce'[120] – no doubt representative of many who were unlikely to settle down with a good book.

Singers who did find an occupation rarely strayed far from the crafts they knew. The leading tenor Nicola Tacchinardi, trained in boyhood as a painter, on his retirement in 1830 built a small theatre in his country house where he was 'director, singer, painter, and chief stagehand'; he also set about collecting Old Masters. Half a century later and on a grander scale, Adelina Patti at her Welsh castle enacted mimed plays, some of them based on operas.[121]

A rare intellectual singer married a Baltic German noble who worked in the Russian civil service. On his neglected estates Alice Barbi studied agronomy, drainage, cattle raising: 'I went about the vast heaths and marvellous huge forests, with my head still full of song, my thoughts often turning to my own beloved, beautiful country, firmly determined to improve the lives of so many human beings, to succeed in what seemed to me a worthwhile mission . . .'. In the intervals of this Tolstoyan endeavour she spent much time with a cultivated Viennese woman; the two of them would undertake a course of reading, for instance of Italian Renaissance authors, and, in their solitude, felt it to be an intense experience. Alice's retirement bore fruit in one of her daughters, who married the Prince of Lampedusa (author of *The Leopard*) and became a leading psychoanalyst.[122]

A more characteristic ending was that of Eugenia Tadolini. She came of a solid bourgeois family in Forlì, an equally solid town in Romagna, and was thought one of the finest vocalists of the 1830–50 period, though on the cool side as an actress; her Lady Macbeth was the occasion of Verdi's trying to stir her into life with his famous letter asking for the 'voice of a she-devil', an injunction taken too literally in our own day. Long separated from her husband and teacher – a composer over twenty years older, – she retired at the height of her powers, when she was forty-three, and settled down in Naples with her surviving child, one of two she had had by a noble lover. But the boy died in the cholera epidemic of 1855–6, to her deep grief. After a while she tried to take her mind off things by driving about behind two magnificent English horses she had bought – 'It was high time I went in a carriage, not as all the women of the chorus do'; but this too palled. When Garibaldi took Naples in 1860 Eugenia and her current lover, a young Neapolitan prince, fled to Paris; there they stayed.

'Long live Garibaldi for getting me here!' she later wrote. She adored Paris – 'After my terrible misfortune this is the first time I feel alive. What *life*!' To her brother's later suggestion that she might come back to live in Forlì she replied that every day in Paris was like a public holiday in Italy; at Forlì she would have to exchange visits for fear of being buried alive, whereas in Paris she could drive out (now in a hansom), look at the crowds, go window shopping, and then receive a few friends in the evening. They may have been Italians, for she still did not know French well.

She worried about money: she had earned large sums only late in her career, and then had lived rather extravagantly in Naples; her income was down to Fcs 5,000 (£200) a year. So she cooked for herself once a day, with relish, sometimes Romagnolo pasta dishes; she moved to a cheaper flat, but as the move took her from the Champs-Elysées to the Rue du Faubourg Saint-Honoré it was hardly a descent into squalor. Whether she stayed on through the 1871 siege and the Commune we do not know; perhaps she did, for the following year she was writing that not even a revolution could dislodge her. She died that same year of typhoid after refusing at first to see a doctor: it reminded her of her children's deaths. In her letters from Paris she never mentioned music.[123]

8

THE AGE OF THE TENOR

When the tenor came forward – we are in a large, popular-priced Florence theatre in the early years of this century – 'it was as if the audience were all of one sex, or as if he belonged to a third sex able in equal measure to captivate the senses of both, such was his overwhelming dominance.' Soprano and baritone got 'even, temperate applause'; that for the tenor was 'superhuman'.[1]

Sex goes a long way to explaining the rise of the tenor. In Italian opera he was dominant from about 1840, certainly until the 1920s, arguably ever since; on the night before these lines were written, over 100,000 people sat in a London downpour to hear Pavarotti. Yet nothing of the kind could have been expected in the first two centuries of the genre.

High voices were then dominant. Many operas were composed for an array of sopranos and contraltos, with perhaps one normal male voice. The eighteenth-century love of coloratura brought a fashion for exploiting an ever higher range; by 1770 – so an experienced man wrote – Venice could show scarcely one good contralto: all, castrati and women, wanted to be sopranos, 'even though they should burst'.[2] Between 1800 and 1830, when castrati were fast vanishing, the female contralto in breeches took over many parts of tragic heroes and lovers.

Tenors in opera seria had been relegated to the parts of kings and old men; their typical range was low, verging on the baritonal; the lovers' parts they sang in comic opera were mellifluous rather than ardent. Basses were so neglected (save as comic performers) that in 1765 Padre Martini could decry a general shortage:[3] the trouble was scarcity not of these, the commonest male voices, but of openings for them. It all points to a long entanglement between the sensibilities of audiences and high voices, felt as still more entrancing if sexual ambiguity could work its way in – through a male lover singing soprano, or a woman playing the part of a man (better still, of a man disguised as a woman, or a woman disguised as a man).

The highest range of the voice does seem to exert a permanent appeal. Even between 1830 and 1914, when attitudes had changed, the finest contraltos and baritones drew smaller crowds than equivalent sopranos and tenors; with one exception – the contralto Marietta Alboni – they were paid less. (The one operatic bass to have out-earned all contemporaries was Fyodor Chaliapin, and his strength lay as much in acting as in voice).[4]

Between 1830 and 1850 the tenor joined the soprano in passionate expression. First he took over from the female contralto the role of lover; then he became a *tenore di forza*, uttering in his chest voice sentiments of adoration or defiance. This meant bringing into Italian opera a newly masculine sexuality.

Duprez, according to legend, started it all in his Italian period by finding the 'chest high C'. Some tenors, however, had already been working towards it. A report that two tenors of the mid eighteenth century could go up to high C or even D 'in full voice' is contradicted by another; 'full voice' may have meant no more than the bright resonance a few can achieve with the head voice most eighteenth-century tenors moved into above G.[5] In 1814 Giovanni David – a specialist in high-lying coloratura – was said to have acquired more power in his voice as he got over smallpox, 'and now . . . he will have still more success because he has almost completely forgotten his head notes [*falsetti*]'.[6] This suggests both that David was pushing his chest voice upwards and that audiences were hankering after that effect. Three tenors were known for heroic energy and power, displayed in the parts for which they were remembered: Matteo Babbini for Cimarosa's Orazio (1796), Andrea Nozzari as Rossini's Otello (1816), and Domenico Donzelli as the Roman proconsul in *Norma* (1831). Whether they sought to carry their chest register up towards high C we do not know; if David, a more decorative singer, was heading that way, the chances are that others were too.

The parts just mentioned suggest how the opportunities for tenors had widened since the late eighteenth century. By the 1830s they were the lovers; the contralto in breeches began to seem old-fashioned. The mature works of Bellini and Donizetti established other normal male singers as the pillars of romantic opera: the baritone (known till about 1840 as the *basso cantante*, a bass able to sing coloratura) in the parts of villains or men of power; the true bass, already familiar from some of Rossini's works, as priest or noble father.

Only for a few years were composers in doubt over this new array of vocal types. Bellini in 1828 considered making the *basso cantante* (the supremely elegant Antonio Tamburini) the hero of *La straniera*, but in the end decided that 'the bass can never play a lover'; ten years later Mercadante consented to make the baritone the lover in *Elena da Feltre* only because the expected tenor was unsuitable.[7] From his debut in 1839 Verdi was clear about the new heterosexual casting. When a contralto was proposed as the hero of *Ernani* (1844) he scouted the notion. In Verdi's works the tenor was always the voice for love or sentiment, though not always the chief or the most admirable character; neither he nor any other male singer was asked to sing coloratura.

As is the way when vocal writing changes, many singers and critics accused Verdi of ruining voices with his demands for a line at once fast, energetic, and sustained. The new manner might be called declamatory or dramatic, Anna de la Grange wrote in 1846, 'but I call it simply the *shrieking* manner' (requiring, her mother added, lungs like a bull's): '. . . an artist cuts at least ten years off her life.'[8] Yet singers came forward like Gaetano Fraschini, the archetypical powerful dramatic tenor or *tenore di forza*, who created five Verdi parts; he was known as 'the tenor of the curse' from the high spot of his performance as Edgardo in *Lucia di Lammermoor*, a part itself the archetype of the tenor as a lover perpetually about to burst into flame. By 1877 the *tenore di forza* was so much the norm that an agent was asked to supply one 'who can shout well' to sing all the tenor parts in a season at Bilbao; the repertory was to include *La sonnambula* and *I puritani*, works that demand refined lyrical singing.[9] The 'shrieking manner' had carried everything before it.

In that same year, 1877, the Spanish tenor Julian Gayarre first displayed at Covent Garden his 'quasi-nasal' emission – what Bernard Shaw was to call his 'goat-bleat'.[10] There was a flock of such goats; Gayarre had been preceded by Francesco Tamagno, who would later create Verdi's Otello. Both were marvels even if their sound was unpleasing by the lights of the pre-Verdi period. Tamagno, the poor trattoria keeper's son, had first made a mark by interpolating a sensational high B in a Donizetti part he had been called upon to sing at short notice.[11] The key to 'superhuman' applause was now the high note shot fortissimo from the chest.

This was true wherever in the world opera had a popular following. At the New York Academy of Music in 1865 an emergency announcement that the tenor Maccaferri would sing in *Il trovatore* led most of the audience to walk out: Maccaferri, a resident Italian, was known for a 'strong but coarse voice' and 'ludicrously awkward' acting. Yet he suddenly 'threw out from his broad chest the C in alt, as clear and strong as a trumpet call': at this the astonished orchestra clapped, many of the audience flocked back from the bars, the cry went up for an encore. Maccaferri did it again: amid bravos and flowers he 'stalk[ed] forward, with an air of gloomy contempt for those who had just discovered his greatness'. But after a few nights he cracked on the C and was heard no more.[12]

Only a few specialist tenors still cultivated the graces needed for operas earlier than Verdi's – themselves cut down to a mere handful: Alessandro

Bonci, who flourished about 1900, had a core repertoire of five parts, in *Il barbiere di Siviglia*, *La sonnambula*, *I puritani*, *L'elisir d'amore*, and *Don Pasquale*. By a shift of emphasis, these and one or two other antiques – *Lucia di Lammermoor* in particular – were now vehicles for a new kind of prima donna, one who specialized in light coloratura and was more easily found than the right kind of tenor. The Italian-trained British tenor Sims Reeves complained in 1888 that the prima donna was taking over everything; what he meant was that in *Lucia*, a work once thought to be dominated by the tenor – he had sung it in his youth, over forty years earlier – the audience now left in droves after Lucia's death scene, without waiting for Edgardo's.[13]

Once power and ability to 'shout' were the requisites, tenors were born as much as made. This, together with the rapid expansion of the opera network between 1850 and 1914, meant that raw hopefuls could get an innings, like the four tenors who succeeded each other at Voghera in 1875 (the first three were hissed off the stage almost as soon as they opened their mouths), the one who came on drunk in 1885 (bringing such a storm of hisses that not even ballet would placate the audience and the performance had to be stopped), and the five in a row who tried themselves out in 1895.[14]

Even a leading tenor could be denounced by Verdi as a 'blockhead', like Giuseppe Fancelli: after patiently trying to rehearse him Verdi lost his temper, seized him by the scruff of the neck, pounded his forehead on the keyboard, shouting 'Will anything ever get into your head? Never!', and left the room. Fancelli took it meekly but complained to those present that Verdi wanted the impossible: a singer was to read his music accurately, sing on pitch and in time, and pronounce the words – 'How can you get through all that lot at one go?'[15]

This story may have gained in the telling, but crassness was undoubtedly the mark of some famous tenors. Tamagno, at least in South America, would chat during the performance with fellow-singers, orchestra players, and acquaintances in the stage boxes; he said he loved Russia in spite of the cold because no one there understood anything but the singer's voice and what he did with it, so that all attention was centred on him.[16] Tamagno was naively engaging, but Mario Tiberini and Roberto Stagno were pompous. Tiberini, denying that he had intrigued to impose his wife, a soprano, on La Scala (pretty well what he had done), wrote 'I am proud to hold up as a model for past, present, and future my life as an artist, which, with head held high, I can proclaim to be *stainless*.' Stagno, reporting his latest triumph, went on at length about the 'delirious frenzy' caused among the audience by 'their never having heard anyone sing with such sweet tone, such elevated and generous style, and such correct diction'; much more followed in the same vein.[17]

Bernard Shaw wrote in 1892 of the awful results of 'picking up any Italian

porter, or trooper, or gondolier, or ice-barrow costermonger who can shout a
high C; thrusting him into heroic roles; and sending him roaring round the
world to pass in every capital over the prostrate body of lyric drama like a
steam roller with a powerful whistle . . .'.[18] The low social origins of Italian
male singers, tenors in particular, were canvassed not because earlier singers
had been more genteel but because they stood out at a time when the
theatrical and musical professions, women singers among them, were hauling
themselves up into respectability.

Though touched with snobbery, Shaw's remark was accurate enough.
Earlier singers of Italian opera had shared in the freemasonry of a
long-standing profession into which many had been born. The new male
singers of the tenor age often came of poor artisan families that had nothing
to do with music.

Tamagno's father, the trattoria keeper who lost ten of his fifteen children,
is matched by Caruso's, a mechanic who drank; Enrico was one of seven
children (four died in infancy). Giuseppe Borgatti, the great Wagnerian
tenor, grew up illiterate; his mother died in giving birth to him in the open
countryside; the noble household where he had his first music lessons
employed him as a scullery boy, and when he got an introduction to a teacher
at the Bologna conservatory he walked there barefoot, sleeping in haylofts.
Alessandro Bonci, too poor to afford lodgings near the Pesaro conservatory,
in his first year regularly walked the twelve kilometres from his home to reach
the classroom by 9 a.m. Pietro Gubellini, successful just before the First
World War, was a carpenter's apprentice who, like Francesco Marconi
before him, was overheard as he sang for pleasure; the large amounts he
earned in a rackety career that took him over much of Europe and the
Americas were, as he claimed, spent largely on women. In the next generation
Beniamino Gigli was the son of a shoemaker who had fallen on hard times
and become a hawker. Among baritones there were the apprentice blacksmith Titta Ruffo (with some amateur musical talent in his mother's family)
and Carlo Galeffi, a non-commissioned officer's son who left school at eleven
and worked as an apprentice at cleaning weapons in the barracks armoury.[19]

How typical were these of the many dozens of contemporary male singers?
We have no statistical means of judging; exceptions there were, like the tenor
Emilio De Marchi, a career army officer. But Shaw with his porters and
ice-cream vendors was probably exaggerating only a little. How then did such
men find their way into opera?

Church choirs, though enfeebled, could still be a prop – to Bonci, Gigli, and
to yet another tenor, Giacomo Lauri-Volpi, an orphan who grew up in a
seminary. The newly expanded network of state music schools also helped

most of these men. But the best help was the omnipresence of teachers willing to gamble on a student who could not pay, and of interested listeners; several biographies include an account of how an aspiring young singer was helped during his military service by an officer with a love of opera.

That the singers who roused the greatest enthusiasm should many of them have started close to the gutter was the more notable because many of their women colleagues were becoming pillars of the community.

All Western theatrical and musical professions began in the early nineteenth century a long climb into respectability – in England marked by the knighthood conferred on Henry Irving in 1895, in the Italian straight theatre by the marriage of the great tragedienne Adelaide Ristori to a leading Roman aristocrat (1847) and, much later, by her appointment as lady-in-waiting to Queen Margherita. Because women on the stage had been thought worst 'tainted' they were at the head of the climb.[20] By 1848 – we have seen – Italian women singers could be described as wanting only marriage and fidelity. From then on, a number married into the aristocracy without, it seems, having to overcome the resistance that had met their forerunners.

Early women singers had, some of them, origins as humble as any 1900 tenor's. You could not get much humbler than Maria Maddalena and Teresa Pieri, sisters who flourished in the 1720s; they were known as the Polpette ('Rissoles') from their early trade of picking up horse-dung in the streets and making it into cakes.[21] At the same time, the whiff of the courtesan that for many years clung to women singers held out the chance of becoming a great man's mistress. This could lead to the secret marriage of Chiara Marini to Duke Ercole III of Modena, after the death of his estranged wife in 1791, or to the position of her Modenese contemporary Caterina Bonafini: after having been the mistress of the opera-mad Duke of Württemberg, she made money in Russia, went home, married a rich man, and received the best society of the town; even then an observer remarked that thanks to her personal qualities 'one forgets what she has been'.[22]

Openly marrying a nobleman with the agreement of his family was something else. Three women singers of the late seventeenth century married nobles before they could be stopped; the husbands, though, were ostracized by their families, barred from office, and driven into at least temporary exile.[23] The first and for many years the only singer to marry a patrician without trouble was Maria Maddalena Musi in 1703 – and she brought it off because, as the highest paid singer of the time, she could mend the dilapidated fortune of a widower with three children. Her only child by him died at six months; when her husband in turn died she made over the house and part of her fortune to her stepsons, lived quietly with her aunts in another part of Bologna, and died at eighty-two, leaving charitable bequests. The stepsons were duly grateful. While her husband was alive Musi had to put up with mild lampoons on her new gentility. She did not put up with a notary's wife who publicly and repeatedly called her 'a bit of stage rubbish'; on meeting the woman in church Musi insulted and struck her.[24]

A condition of the marriage was that she gave up her career. It was still the condition imposed on most of the nineteenth-century singers who married Italian nobles – over a dozen of them, including such stars as Henriette Sontag and Marietta Alboni.[25] The money was welcome; the profession that had earned it was not. Yet a prima donna in Italy, according to a visitor who sang there in 1789 after much experience of Germany, Paris, and London, was treated by the upper classes with unexampled deference.[26] No doubt the prima donna was made much of because opera lay at the heart of social life; it was quite another thing to take a working theatrical performer into the family. The French nobles who married Giulia Grisi and Adelina Patti (and then lived off alimony) were less fussy. Even Italian aristocratic families reconciled themselves to a wife's going back on stage (as Sontag, Alboni, and Clara Novello did) when financial disaster struck.

Such ennobled prima donnas were few, even if we count those married to non-Italian aristocrats; but they showed an opportunity and set a tone. The opportunity was closed to men singers: marrying into a higher class was for those who could bring a male heir a dowry. Nor was the tone much helped by successful male singers, who tended, like Bonci, to build themselves villas prophetic of sets for Hollywood musicals (a 1970s television film of Pavarotti's home life showed the model still going strong). Women, here as elsewhere in late nineteenth-century society, were the instillers of genteel manners.

Sometime after the 1850s the red cord came down that till then had run across London drawing-rooms where a concert was to take place, separating the artists' corner from the guests and making them feel like zoo exhibits.[27] Singers, women in particular, could now themselves be honoured guests. They still had to perform: hence Patti's enjoyment of an unusual visit to the King and Queen of Spain – 'just fancy . . . a soirée without music[,] what a blessing!'[28]

Plenty of women singers went on in the line of Angiolina Bosio, who looked elegant on stage but at dinner took snuff out of a 'huge – not particularly clean – bandanna handkerchief', or E. M. Forster's 'hot lady' (modelled on Tetrazzini) who told the British tourists in the first-class carriage 'that never, never before had she sweated so profusely'.[29] But just as late nineteenth-century 'Society' grew opulent and a trifle fast, some women singers cultivated an aura at once graceful and dashing. This may be seen in their embossed letterheads – Hariclea Darclée's surname in large gilt trellis work, Teresina Singer's first name on a curlicue ribbon held by a flying swallow, Lina Cavalieri's atop the menu of a dinner-party she gave with her Russian prince – and sometimes in their large upwardly sloping signatures, quite unlike the neat Victorian script of their predecessors.[30] Cavalieri – a beautiful ex-café singer with a limited voice, who went on to make silent films – was a portent of the star as a subject for women's magazines; her ghosted memoirs, which tell, among other things, how she escaped being kidnapped for a maharaja's harem by jumping out of a carriage, were dedicated to her women readers.

From about 1860, singers worked a system of repertory opera. This meant that the old seasonal arrangement with its ideal of two new and well-rehearsed operas was at an end; theatres now put on a rising proportion of familiar works, often for a few performances at a time; thanks to newly-built railways and telegraphs, singers could be brought in to fill a part at short notice.

For singers to have 'their' parts which they performed in one theatre after another was not new. An eighteenth-century singer could be identified with a part in a libretto which she sang again and again, as Marianna Benti Bulgarelli was with her friend Metastasio's Dido; but each time the music was tailored for her by a fresh composer. About 1800–25 Girolamo Crescentini and Giuditta Pasta tended to repeat a few parts, now with (more or less) the same music each time; this was exceptional – a tribute to their pre-eminence.[31] With repertory opera, a singer as famous as they, Titta Ruffo, might wish he had been able to 'restrict himself to five or six parts, study and polish them in every vocal and dramatic detail, and sleep happily without fear of competition':[32] in practice the system demanded that he and nearly everyone else should be ready to perform many parts. Where in 1866 a baritone was shocked to find that the Constantinople management expected him to sing any of eighteen parts, by the 1900s this had become the norm; a bass contracted for South America had to perform any of thirty-nine.[33]

It was now routine for a singer to take the stage after one piano and one orchestral rehearsal; often the piano rehearsal would do – or none. Even a gifted conductor of the new, dominant sort, Franco Faccio, was content with two piano rehearsals for the artists who were to sing at the Brescia fair, a short season apt to be got together in a hurry; he did show a new sense of priorities by demanding 'many' rehearsals with the orchestra alone, since the opera – Meyerbeer's *Dinorah* – depended on getting the instrumental colouring right.[34]

Far worse went on at major houses like the Liceu in Barcelona, where a leading singer in a new opera was allowed no more than ten days between receiving his part and performing it, or the Costanzi in Rome: there, a few hours before a Sunday matinée of *La Gioconda*, the prima donna went off to Naples to see a consultant about her sore throat, while the baritone (Titta Ruffo) had not yet arrived; *Pelléas et Mélisande* (then in rehearsal) was rushed on instead, to the disgust of an audience of shopkeepers and minor civil servants, who all but stopped it with a barrage of coughs and hostile comments. The San Carlo, Naples, lacked even that resource: when the tenor failed to turn up on the day *Andrea Chénier* was to have its first performance, posters cancelling it went up at 6 p.m.; in rehearsals – a local journal commented – the title part must have been shared between the prompter and a chair.[35]

Established singers were now better able to run their own careers – so it appeared: their contracts often entitled them to choose the opera they would sing first, and in some leading theatres – La Scala where we can observe it in 1866, the Metropolitan down to 1908 – they virtually made up the programme from week to week.[36] But there were drawbacks.

The opera one singer wished to appear in might not suit another: hence many disputes. A hangover from the old seasonal system was the identification of a singer billed as *assoluta* with her part: if somebody else had appeared as Lucia in the same theatre a few weeks earlier, if another, perhaps more popular artist was due to take it over later on, if a fellow-member of the company was known to have refused it – these were all grounds for arguing that your 'delicacy as an artist' forbade you to sing it.[37]

Insidiously, the artist's new freedom to sing one of 'his' parts almost at will encouraged sloppiness. Many leading singers would not rehearse in full voice or wear costume even at the dress rehearsal: their performance was complete, a known quantity; why bother? This was the kind of thing Arturo Toscanini fought against at La Scala from 1898. Many years later, some famous artists still could not see the point of his having made them behave like full members of a company.[38]

Managements riposted with clauses in printed contracts waiving 'exclusive' rights to a part and undertaking to sing in full voice and wear costume at dress rehearsals; leading singers crossed them out or bargained over them.[39] The clauses were at length imposed by Fascist decree in 1932. By then the whole thing had become a nuisance: witness an outburst at Covent Garden in 1929. At the dress rehearsal of *Norma* Rosa Ponselle, by agreement with the manager, Colonel Blois, sang the title part in street clothes because her costume was delicate. The Adalgisa, Irene Minghini Cattaneo, made a scene: the prima donna and the manager, she exclaimed, must be having an affair.[40]

English gentleman that he was, Blois may not have realized how much history underlay this bit of *convenienze*.

Leading singers could have their way because impresarios, at least in Italy, had grown feebler and more anonymous: a well-informed lawyer could argue in 1872 that it made little difference to artists whether one man rather than another ran a season.[41] The cause was the arrival of music publishers, armed with copyright, as the dominant figures in opera production; impresarios were now mere executants. To singers what mattered about publishers was their control of casting.

As there were only three important firms, reduced to two in 1888, a few people had even more power to advance or thwart a singer's career than Hollywood studio heads in the 1930s were to have over actors; and as the whole business was carried on in Milan, where most singers now lived, a lot was done in offices under continual siege from aspirants, through face-to-face dealings that largely escape us. These – the evidence we have suggests – were not on the whole corrupt, perhaps because publishers were in headlong competition with one another, perhaps too because several heads of firms (Giovannina Lucca, Giulio Ricordi, and Giulio's son Tito) knew a great deal about opera from the inside; they were not 'front office' people.

True, singers as a matter of routine asked publishers to back them or impose them on a management for a part in an opera; they did not always avoid sycophancy, as when a minor singer accepted a part in an unfamiliar work sight unseen: given 'the immense intelligence' of Giulio Ricordi, it was bound to suit her.[42] Even a leading prima donna, Maddalena Mariani Masi (who was keen to push her less successful sister), wrote to Giulio 'I depend on you ... and I will do nothing without your approval'; she would be 'desolate' at the mere thought of displeasing him or his firm; all his advice was 'sacred' – ought she to sing in a concert in Turin? Or show her bare midriff in *Le Roi de Lahore*?[43] Against this, the equally famous Gaetano Fraschini refused to deal with an impresario commended by Ricordi because he had pledged himself to a rival; and the tone of other singers' letters is genuinely friendly.[44] There was no doubt less humbug than in singers' dealings two centuries earlier with a more remote patron like the Duke of Mantua, but there was some.

A few leading singers acted for Ricordi as its local agents in the theatres where they were appearing: they kept and gave out parts, received hiring fees, supervised properties, and warned Signor Giulio when the impresario understated the takings. Whether they got any reward is unclear; the firm's goodwill may have been enough.[45]

In Italy there was now a wide array of opportunities, from a couple of performances in a minuscule hill town to a season under Toscanini at La

Scala, by way of engagements in the new popular-priced theatres called *politeama*, some of them open-air structures of cast iron and wood. There were also more chances abroad for Italian singers than ever before, as trains and steamships opened up the Americas, Australia, and south-east Asia. At the same time a new wave of foreign aspirants, many of them British and American, came to Italy to study and make a debut, sometimes, it appeared, squeezing out the natives.

All opera was becoming internationalized: much the same core repertoire – French and German as well as Italian – was given in London, Paris, Vienna, New York, St Petersburg, and Milan, by much the same group of artists. Sometime between the 1880s and the 1910s singers of Italian opera came no longer to be a distinct professional group outside Italy and the 'little Italies' of America north and south. Within these Italies, the profession kept its identity until about 1960, when television and modern air travel dispersed that too.

Opening up other continents was at first a bold extension of an established traffic: singers started going to Rio de Janeiro, Montevideo, and Buenos Aires about 1810, forty years before large-scale Italian emigration to those parts got under way; they were soon going to New York, the Ohio-Mississippi valley, Havana, and Mexico. For the next half-century or so this meant travelling mostly by water, under sail or in primitive steamers, to places some of them notorious for disease, yellow fever in particular: Erminia Frezzolini, who worked the New York–Havana–St Louis circuit in 1857, avoided the smallpox that killed her colleague Marietta Gazzaniga's husband, and got through a violent storm at sea, but was alarmed to hear that two or three Mississippi steamboats burnt up each week; a defaulting manager and bad hotels where you could not get served if you had no English completed her picture of the New World.[46] The reason she and others put up with it was that – so they trusted – El Dorado would pay.

The singers who crossed the Atlantic at this early stage were like those who in the previous century had gone to German-speaking towns and perhaps ventured on to the snows of Russia, Poland, or Scandinavia: minor or young artists, often in little family groups. In the Americas these were to be joined by a sprinkling of leading singers who (like Frezzolini) were down on their luck, or in decline, or, in 1848–9, were looking for work denied them in a Europe torn by revolution.

What they performed were not as a rule complete operas in well-rehearsed productions. Almost everywhere to begin with, and in small or remote towns well past 1900, a few Italians would perform arias or scenes, helped out by local singers and musicians and relieved by instrumental pieces: a nineteenth-century form of programme common in Europe and the Americas, now exported to Australia – where the successful formula in 1885 was said to be a 'combination' of two male singers, two women violinists who could also sing, and a woman pianist – and to Bombay and Calcutta; there, the five members of the Ida Poli Rosa Opera Concert Company performed in 1891 not only the usual excerpts but *Don Pasquale*, a work with a small cast that lent itself to this kind of touring. The prima donna's husband conducted a local orchestra said to have perpetrated 'horrors'; the troupe was no doubt hardened.[47]

How far Italian singers could roam may be seen from the careers of three women. Teresa Schieroni had appeared only in minor Italian seasons when in 1829 she turned up in Buenos Aires with her inseparable colleague, the still more obscure Margherita Garavaglia; an Englishman in the audience described Schieroni's acting as 'redundant, and at times rather violent'. The two women then went round the Horn to Valparaiso and Santiago, where they were not much liked, sailed to Lima, and, after an interval probably spent there and in Central America, were next heard of in 1833 at Macao, on the China coast, where they were giving versions of Rossini operas; they then repeated them in Calcutta.[48] All this they did under sail, but Rosina Aimo, a soprano who made her debut in 1874, was a child of the steam age. Her many Italian engagements never took her to a front-rank theatre; she was a 'tireless' workhorse who at the large Genoa *politeama* was said to 'sing night after night for weeks on end'. She also appeared in Spain (several times, in provincial towns as well as in Madrid), Portugal, France, Greece, Egypt, the Ukraine, Cuba, Mexico, San Salvador, Colombia (where she sang twenty-five operas), Australia, and New Zealand; she is last heard of in 1897 singing Norma, first in the small town of Viadana, near Mantua, and then among the currant warehouses at Smyrna.[49]

How did Italian singers adapt themselves to the far-off places they worked in? The short answer is: not at all. Until the break came, about 1880–1900, they were the purveyors of opera, which over much of the world was by definition Italian. Why should they learn other languages or other styles?

That two pairs of Italians sang English-language operas in the 1760s was a freak; that Teresa Strinasacchi twice sang in Czech in 1795, and Maria Bolla once in English a few years later, came of accidents of upbringing that had kept them in Prague and London long enough to know the languages.[50] Many Germans turned themselves into Italian singers, but no Italian seems ever to have returned the compliment.[51] Singers' rare comments on foreign towns (other than the most brilliant – Paris and St Petersburg) were negative. Constantinople was boring, Lisbon musically disappointing.[52] Their attitude, still common among Italian short-term migrants in the 1960s, was summed up very early by a member of Handel's company, Francesca Bertolli: London was good for 'guineas' and 'reputation'; no more need be said.[53]

These attitudes did not endear Italian singers abroad, especially when they were earning more than most natives. Some of the earliest migrants were mocked in France and stoned in Sweden.[54] That was in part resistance to novelty. Later on, Italians abroad themselves resisted inroads into the monopoly they had won. Clara Louise Kellogg, one of the earliest American opera singers, found that her New York stage debut in 1861 in an otherwise Italian company made her 'a foreigner in her own country'; the chorus in particular 'could sometimes hardly contain themselves. "Who is she", they would demand indignantly, "to come and take the bread out of our mouths?"'[55] Later still, in 1922, the first attempt to bring German opera with German singers to Buenos Aires – a stronghold where until 1961 the chorus sang all operas in Italian, whatever language the principals were using – ran into 'chauvinism' such that the conductor Felix Weingartner would not come again unless with his own Vienna Philharmonic for a quite separate season.[56]

Self-sufficiency could be kept up even through a long stay. Francesca Bertolli pursued guineas and reputation for eight years. Many eighteenth-century Italians stayed much longer, particularly in the more favourable parts of Central Europe; some settled down as state pensioners or as teachers of music or languages. Venanzio Rauzzini, a leading castrato, retired to Bath in 1780 as a teacher and concert-giver; contemporaries of his did the same in Dublin. There and in most European capitals small groups of Italian musicians could spend most of their lives in each other's pockets.[57] Once Italian immigration had built up in the New World there was a further inducement to stay, especially for middling singers: they now had not only Italian colleagues but an Italian audience, in a country far richer than theirs, and with far less competition.

In the Americas two main kinds of experience awaited singers. The famous and successful could appear before audiences dominated by the elite – largely white Anglo-Saxon Protestant in North America, of Iberian descent in Latin America – of big cities such as New York, Chicago, Rio de Janeiro, and Buenos Aires; Havana with its slave-based wealth ranked with these (from the 1830s to the 1880s), as did San Francisco in the decade and a half that followed the 1849 gold rush, and again from the 1880s. At this level, Italians kept their monopoly in South America from the 1860s (when front-rank singers started arriving in numbers) to 1914, but in North America they soon had to share it with artists from other traditions, especially German and French.

Middling or untried singers, on the other hand, could work in popular opera companies that depended almost wholly on audiences of Italian immigrants.

These, in Argentina, Brazil, Uruguay, and Chile, grew up together with the immigrant communities themselves: by 1879 there were enough Italians in Buenos Aires to support a *politeama* holding 4,000 and an intense theatrical traffic in plays and 'grand panoramic exhibitions' of recent events as well as opera; soon afterwards opera performances at a large theatre in a market area, originally a 'filthy wooden barn', were 'full of butchers in shirtsleeves smoking tremendous Tuscan cigars and spitting right and left';[58] at Rosario, an Argentine city peopled almost wholly by Italians, there were by 1907 three opera houses. In the United States, where Italian immigrants arrived later (in numbers from about 1890) and needed two or three generations to climb out of the ghetto, popular opera developed in our own century. It had audiences not only in New York and San Francisco but in smaller north-eastern towns with strong Italian communities: Hartford, Providence, Syracuse among others. The scale was more modest than in Argentina but the saturation no less: in the inner room of a Chicago restaurant in the 1940s you could hear complete Italian operas mimed by puppets to gramophone records.[59]

The two groups overlapped, a little – rather as opera seria stars and comic opera troupers had in eighteenth-century Italy. A few resident singers sang minor parts in seasons dominated by visiting stars; two well-known prima donnas, Elvira Colonnese and Hélène Theodorini, settled in Buenos Aires and taught local young women some of whom made their debuts in popular theatres. In New York, a few blocks of Broadway between 70th and 74th Streets held three hotels patronized by Italian singers and musicians (with Verdi's statue outside and an express subway to 42nd Street and the Met): the Ansonia, a château-like fantasy with thick soundproof walls, was where successful artists stayed, rehearsals were held, costumes measured, business transacted; another housed members of the claque, some of whom probably coached singers; more singers lived in the third; the hotels together made up a New World version of the Milan Galleria.[60] There was further overlap when a singer with a great name, perhaps fading, toured with a group of minor artists termed his 'company'.

Criss-crossing the vast American spaces was something nearly everyone did. We know most about North American conditions. These varied greatly, not just between high-class and cheap tours, but within a tour: a baritone in 1875 went from marvelling at his luxurious Washington hotel, at sleeping-cars and centrally heated dressing rooms with bath, to a theatre without water and a bug-ridden hotel at Raleigh, North Carolina. There was none the less a difference between Patti's tour of 1889–90 – her personal railway coach, at one point stopped overnight in the Texas desert amid Indian huts, had a saloon furnished in monogrammed blue plush, a satinwood bedroom, a bath, a piano, her own chef – and the 1905–6 tour of a desperate *Don Pasquale* troupe, hurrying through one-night stands in places like Meridian, Kansas, often 'without sleeping in a bed for six or seven nights. . . . after a performance we would hurry off to a railway station in a broken-down carriage drawn by two wretched horses that continually slipped on the ice-covered roads, only to find that a snowstorm had delayed our train for several hours.' Being called dagoes by the locals was an extra.[61]

Popular opera for immigrant audiences was even more freely improvised than its equivalent in Italy. An 1898 *Gioconda* – a sprawling work that has everything, from galleys to ballet – was put on at the Buenos Aires Politeama in three days because a tenor from Montevideo was passing through; it was a great success. An advertised 'season' could come to an end after three or four performances for lack of adequate box-office returns. Dates and titles of operas were announced only a few days ahead and not always kept to; in New York, the manager Alfredo Salmaggi would ask the audience at the close of one opera what they wished to hear next. Performances on Saturdays, Sundays, and holidays mattered most, for that was when the bulk of the audience was free; many brought packed meals. Membership of a Buenos Aires 'company' could change kaleidoscopically, with one or two singers staying on, others moving off to other theatres (in town or up country), yet others coming back from similar forays, and young aspirants taking turns to make their debut, as a rule in an exacting part like Aida. Now and then an Italian troupe stranded by failure or yellow fever would give a benefit performance to raise the fare home.[62]

We may get an idea of singers' experience from the doings of two workhorses, the tenor Antonio Imbimbo and his wife Elvira Ferri Imbimbo, an ample contralto who, like others in the New World, sang both opera and operetta, going straight from Amneris to Suppé's *Boccaccio*. In 1898 the couple took part in at least four 'seasons' at the Buenos Aires Politeama; these varied from a single performance to over four months, and included fourteen leading parts for him, nine for her. Antonio (perhaps flanked by Elvira) also co-managed and appeared in a 'season' at a new theatre in the harbour area which foundered after nine operas had been given in twenty days. Even this may not account for all they got through in that year; they were plainly set to go on till they were sung out.

In New York, the best-known popular seasons were run from 1918 (chiefly at the Brooklyn Academy of Music) by Alfredo Salmaggi, a tenor with Italian provincial experience; after an engagement cut short by a Boston-based company's failure he worked the vaudeville circuit, eking out 'La donna è mobile' with ocarina and mandolin solos, and taught in several cities; in New York he would play cards with Caruso and other famous Italian singers. His own singers included a black Aida, Caterina Yarboro, well before Marian Anderson broke the colour bar at the Met, but for the rest were nearly all Italians on the way up or out; the tenor Mario Pasquetta had a fine voice unhampered by stage sense – in *La forza del destino* he moved a tree stump downstage to sit on during his aria. Salmaggi would sit in the box-office to collect the takings night after night; this did not stop him from mounting large-scale performances, like a Chicago *Aida* given before an audience of 35,000.

His long hennaed hair and broad-brimmed hat were part of an outfit worn with variations by the musicians who ran Italian popular opera, whether in Brooklyn, San Francisco, or Buenos Aires; other distinguishing marks were the flowing black silk tie, the cape, and the Tuscan cigar. These men and their audiences carried on into the 1930s, at the extreme into the early 1950s, the ways of the profession as they had been in Italy about 1890: when union minimum rates for singers came to New York, Salmaggi at first contented himself with 'verbal agreements', then negotiated a special reduced rate.[63]

New World cities encapsulated those old ways all the better because they held a compendium of Italian trades: besides singers, maestros, impresarios, would-be critics, resting members of the chorus, the district round the Buenos Aires Politeama was full of Italian 'players, property men, painters . . . . sellers of artists' trifles, [and] waterfront carters'.[64] Picturesque though it sounds, we are hearing about a casual trade, subject to the anxieties, the scamped last-minute rush, and the low pay characteristic of such trades in late nineteenth-century cities.

Foreigners who wished to turn themselves into Italian singers were in large part products of the Italian musical diaspora. Their ambitions were roused by the spread of Italian opera and the omnipresence of Italian teachers.

Music, according to Charles Burney, was 'a manufacture of Italy'; it was natural for a trading country like Britain to import it as it did wine or tea.[65] He liked best Italian voices singing in their own language. But plenty of foreigners were ready to assimilate their voices if they could to those of Italians. As early as the 1650s a shadowy Englishman, Thomas Stafford, studied in Rome and sang Italian opera in Paris with a visiting troupe.[66] His many successors down to about 1850 were non-controversial because they and most people (outside France) accepted, like Burney, Italian hegemony over the art they wished to excel in: they asked nothing better than to become Italian singers.

The London-born Nancy Storace may have met with some prejudice from the Italian company at the King's Theatre,[67] but her career in Italy and Vienna (where she created Mozart's Susanna) was not seriously hampered, any more than was that of the Irishman Michael Kelly, the original Basilio. At most, Italians grumbled about the poor pronunciation of the Scotsman John Sinclair (who created the florid tenor part in Rossini's *Semiramide* in 1823) or the German Amalia Schütz. Yet Schütz was only one of several German and French artists who won great acclaim in Italy, singing and often creating the leads in early nineteenth-century operas.[68] They followed on the eighteenth-century Germans some of whom had done well both in Italy and at home, such as the great tenor Anton Raaff (the first Idomeneo), Johann Wallishauer (Valesi), who taught Weber, and the sopranos Mara and Teiber. There was even a Ukrainian peasant, sent to Italy for training, who sang Italian opera back home in the 1750s and became the leading Russian singer.[69] As late as the 1840s and 1850s two men who were to be the finest British singers of their day, Sims Reeves and Charles Santley, trained with Milan teachers in the old way, as honorary Italians; Santley won his early engagement at Pavia (under the name Carlo Santilli) by competing on equal terms with fellow-members of the profession.[70]

By the 1860s, however, British and American singers – especially women – were beginning to pay for Italian debuts or at least to sing for free. Greater ease of travel brought them to Italy, as it took Italians all over the world. Their motive was stated by Mrs Norton, the New England housewife who was Nordica's mother: 'Sure as you live, there is nothing better than Italian prestige.'[71] In this they were encouraged by Italian teachers abroad; as early as the 1820s the two leading teachers in Paris started sending to Milan a stream of women aspirants, few of whom made a success, though there is no evidence before 1860 that any of them were unpaid.[72]

Even in the 1870s, Lillian Nordica and the Canadian soprano Emma Albani (Marie Lajeunesse) quickly got paid engagements in Italy after a debut which for Nordica was unpaid. Both women later thought their Italian experience had been well worth while.[73] But it was one thing to be Nordica or Albani, already promising to rank among the finest singers of their day, another to be Maria Brennan, who had minor unpaid engagements in the 1860s and seems not to have been heard of again.[74] By 1910 Viola Tree, in her ill-judged attempt to make herself into a prima donna virtually overnight, found that she would have to pay for her small-town debut (with a top-up for the extra violinists she had insisted on), and then pay the publisher, the agents, the journals, for her proposed big-city launch as Salome. It was the cost of making people listen to high notes which, according to Tito Ricordi, a harshly honest counsellor, were like 'a train whistle'.[75]

In these conditions mediocre Italians too were now made to pay for a debut. According to a newspaper report, a woman whose husband could not afford it killed herself.[76] There were protests against the 'barbarian invasion', and hisses when Emma Abbott, from Peoria, interpolated 'Nearer, my God, to Thee' into a Milan *Sonnambula*; she made it up with the audience by singing old Italian songs. Abbott went on to run her own company in the United States; it performed Italian opera but was made up of non-Italians, and exploited the leading lady's Paris gowns and 'Abbott Kiss' more than her voice.[77] Meta Reddish, a businessman's daughter from upstate New York, was greeted with a cry of 'Down with Americans!' when she made a single unpaid appearance at the San Carlo, Naples, in 1911. For this *Sonnambula* she had been made to wait months and had then been summoned that very morning to an offstage piano rehearsal, all she got. She had not paid, other than 50 lire to the representative of the *camorra* or mafia – a specially arranged minimum rate.[78]

The artless memoir that tells of Reddish's career brings out (without intending it) how this slumming encouraged amateurish behaviour.

There was already something suspect about the reports sent back to their home towns in the Americas, north and south, of the Italian triumphs scored by young women aspirants. Hattie Louise Sims, for instance, had begun about 1880 in the opera house just built in the boom town of Central City, Colorado, and then – as Luisa Simi – was said to have had many Italian engagements until a breakdown 'due to overwork' ended her 'brilliant career' and sent her back to Denver to teach. Those engagements cannot be traced; nor can the equally brilliant ones reported of a number of Argentine contemporaries.[79] Simi and the rest no doubt did appear – in theatres too modest to have had their histories written. What was reported about them at home suggests that an Italian career was now a publicity tag rather than a genuine endeavour.

Meta Reddish, it is clear, did become a tolerable singer though never of the first quality; she was unlucky in being suited to coloratura parts when these were few and regarded as canary fanciers' pleasure. She soon got paid engagements in Italy, Spain, and the Americas, modest ones to begin with and then good ones. But she kept hankering after parts clearly unsuited to her, like Mignon, and using her social connections (such as Mrs Theodore Roosevelt, wife of the former president of the United States) to secure engagements; at least once she insisted on wearing her own wholly inappropriate costume instead of that provided by the management. Eight years after her debut she married a rich Englishman, gave a few concerts, and retired.

The search for 'prestige' rather than for self-identification comes out in the blossoming of semi-Italian stage names about the turn of the century. Many were thought up by Mathilde Marchesi. For early pupils who made genuine careers in Italy she had devised Italian-sounding names – Antonietta Fricci (Fritzsche) and Anna D'Angeri (von Angermeier). But for her late pupils she worked out names based on the places they had come from, like Oselio (from Oslo), Toronta, Nevada, Vilna, and Melba, that could sound Italian only to non-Italians, and the same was true of Nuovina and Parkina (a Miss Parkinson from Kansas City).[80] They all appeared (those that did) in an international repertoire, mainly outside Italy. Pseudo-Italian names kept cropping up in the United States, for instance the powerful tenor Aroldo Lindi (a Swedish-American called Harold Lindau), who flourished between the wars; the last may have been Arturo Sergi (Arthur Kagan), active in the 1960s – chiefly in German opera.

It took longer for Italian-born singers to stop assuming that all opera was their province. By 1914 there was still a powerful demand abroad for the best male singers to perform an Italian repertoire – Verdi, Puccini, *Il barbiere di Siviglia*, *Cavalleria rusticana* and *Pagliacci*, plus certain French operas (*L'Africaine*, *Les Pêcheurs de perles*, *Hamlet*) that were still annexed thanks to great tenors (Caruso, De Lucia) and baritones (Titta Ruffo, De Luca). The well-informed agent Franco Fano, however, pointed out that on the international market the profession was in decline, women in particular.

Foreign singers, he wrote, besides learning to sing in Italian had become more versatile and more cultured; Austrian and Russian opera houses now used the native language, with visiting Italians awkwardly keeping to their own; London and North America depended heavily on non-Italians; only in Spain and Latin America was opera in Italian still the rule.[81]

The overthrow of the Italian language as the natural medium of all opera, and of Italian-trained singers as its exponents, can be dated precisely in London and Vienna. At Covent Garden a new management in 1887 broke with the long-standing policy of giving everything in Italian. At the Vienna State Opera only scattered performances in Italian took place after 1881; among the staple works the last Italian-language *Mignon* was given in 1876, the last *Faust* in 1878, the last *Huguenots* in 1884. Even Italian operas were given far more often in German than in Italian; Verdi's *Otello*, performed within a year of its creation, went straight into German – with great success.[82] Italian singers were now in the position of those British engineers who, after setting up railways all over the world, found themselves superseded by natives.

In North America the First World War gave Italian male singers scope because most other Europeans went off to fight, and the effect wore on even after Italy's late entry.[83] But Fano's analysis was to be confirmed by time – and Latin America too would soon fall away. In the years since 1945 it has been possible for a singer to keep a personal identity as an Italian-American while cultivating an international repertoire, and without at any point needing to identify himself with the Italian operatic tradition.[84]

In Italy the turning-point came as late as the 1940s with the retreat from Wagner. The composer had wanted Italian voices to sing his works; all through the Wagner craze (at its height about 1900–14) they did so, in their own language, and through the between-the-wars afterglow. From 1940, however, first *Der Ring des Nibelungen* and then the other operas were put on in German with German-speaking artists. The change antedated the jet plane and the long-playing record, which between them have imposed original-language productions on most leading opera houses. Its immediate causes are unclear. But it was a tacit admission that even at home the Italian hegemony was over.

21 Annibale Pio Fabri (1697–1760), famous tenor. (Civico Museo
Bibliografico, Bologna)

22 Bust of the tenor Francesco Tamagno. The coat with fur collar was a token of success. (Museo Teatrale alla Scala, Milan)

23 Postcard showing the two tenors born in Montagnana, near Padua, Aureliano Pertile and Giovanni Martinelli. (Mr Paul Morby)

24 A rare portrait of a singer smoking: the baritone Eugenio Giraldoni, who
flourished about 1900. Early this century, surprising numbers of singers smoked.
The tenor Gigli occasionally smoked over forty a day. (Museo Teatrale alla
Scala, Milan)

25 What singers saw in a virtually all-Italian city overseas: the Teatro Colón at Rosario, Argentina. (Archivo General de la Nación, Buenos Aires)

26 President Marcelo T. de Alvear of Argentina (centre) and his wife, the former light soprano Regina Pacini (to his left). (Archivo General de la Nación, Buenos Aires)

9

THE COMING OF MASS SOCIETY

Loveliest of Italian opera houses, La Fenice was in a bad way. By November 1891 its boxholder-proprietors, like Venice itself, had seen their income hit by a prolonged slump; over the previous decade they had, on average, been able to mount the traditional carnival season only every other year. The city council had withdrawn its subsidy twenty years earlier; it had relented briefly in 1889–90, but had once again cut off funds. The boxholders' own contribution was about half what they had been paying just before the onset of depression in 1873. Their executive committee none the less planned a full season in carnival 1892, with three large-scale operas – *L'Africaine*, *Otello*, and a recent work, Franchetti's *Asrael*. They farmed it out, as usual, to leading impresarios – Luigi Piontelli the active partner – whose artistic choices were made for them by the publisher Ricordi. Trouble struck when the impresarios decided to cut wages.

Piontelli had previously paid the chorus – sixty-six singers and their chorus master – a total of Fcs 1,975 a week; he now proposed to pay them only Fcs 1,300, nor would he pay the agent's commission which – it seems – had traditionally been shared out among them. He made a like offer to the orchestra.

In the late nineteenth century chorus singers and players (together with the corps de ballet if there was one) were called *masse*. The response of the Venice lot befitted the new age of mass society. They insisted on getting the commission: the impresarios had cut pay 'to the bone', and it was only right that they should get any extra that was going. They threatened to go off to the Teatro Rossini, where the rival publisher Sonzogno was mounting a season; the students at the conservatory, who had been hired as an extra chorus, backed them by refusing to appear. The La Fenice executives took the side of the chorus – a gesture that cost them nothing, for they did not offer to raise the boxholders' stake. In the end Piontelli brought in strikebreakers, as he had done at Genoa a year earlier; his new chorus was recruited from as far away as Trieste, Milan, Bologna, and Rome. The chorus master – member of a family that had held the post almost continuously since 1815 – took his forces off to the Rossini. The following year La Fenice once again skipped carnival; the publisher Sonzogno ran a six-week Lent season there; this time the proprietors let him cut the stagehands' and ushers' wages as well.[1]

Soloists – our inquiry has shown – were creatures of the market who acted as competitive individuals. Chorus singers were always a group apart, imbued with a rough and ready solidarity that found expression in collective bargaining when it was at all possible, though most of them were also too poor to refuse enlistment as strikebreakers.

Little is known about choruses in the early days of semi-commercial Italian opera. In the late eighteenth century they began to play a part in opera seria; in comic opera the demands on them were modest and, in small troupes, could be met by members of the company who did other jobs. In both genres they were often, at this stage, choruses of men only. Even in mixed choruses the ratio, well into the nineteenth century, was typically two men to one woman; down to 1830 we hear of performances of operas requiring mixed choruses in which the women were simply left out,[2] and as late as the 1892 season just mentioned Venice was so short of sopranos that ten extra women (strikebreakers apart) had to be imported. The reason was almost certainly that choruses remained for many years the disreputable end of the profession: adequate singers for them were hard to find, adequate women singers particularly so.

Did anyone move up from the chorus to become a leading or comprimario singer? Even in the past forty years or so examples are rare: the soprano Giovanna Casolla, the bass Ivo Vinco, perhaps a few more. In earlier years it is hard to be sure because the names of the chorus were seldom listed; but we virtually never hear of such a step up. There is a little more evidence of soloists ending their careers in the chorus, like Natale Dutto (1891–1959), a Fiat car worker, son of a glover who sang first tenor in a cathedral choir, and himself a tenor: he made his debut in 1923 at a popular theatre, had a ten-year career, and then spent eighteen more as a member of the chorus and small-part singer, mainly for the Italian radio.[3] By and large, however, solo and chorus work were distinct. Hard up as Francesco Tamagno was, the disappointment of being told by his teacher at the conservatory that he could hope only to become a good chorus singer made him drop out – even though, the teacher added, he could earn good money in England.[4]

'The *pariahs* of art' – so the official supervisor of Rome theatres called chorus singers in 1872.[5] They were, he wrote, casually employed, ill paid artisans who worked at other trades for a living, by and large unfit for a leading opera house.

Their occupations were nothing new. Most Italian chorus singers had always been market women, cobblers, fishermen, cooks, and the like, who sang in their spare time. Few could read music; exceptional groups that could (at Bergamo and Trieste) may have been recruited from church choirs.[6] As long as audiences kept up the cult of the solo voice, they tolerated a chorus fit only for simple music; when the nineteenth-century interest in collectivity began to influence even Italian opera, the state of the chorus by and large disabled it from attempting more. Verdi, whose late operas did require more, insisted – when he was in charge – on *masse* that were carefully chosen and rehearsed; like the Rome official just quoted, he urged that in a few leading opera houses they should be permanent, salaried groups.[7] But in the 1870s, when the Italian state had just withdrawn from subsidizing opera, this was an idea whose time was still far off.

Choruses had always been regarded as the working class of the opera world. By their superiors they were thought of as rough, insubordinate, apt to drink, smoke, and gamble in their collective dressing room; on one occasion at least they were drunk on the first night (of *L'Africaine* at Turin, in 1875, which went badly).[8] The chorus master was part labour contractor, part shop steward: at the Teatro Comunale, Bologna, in 1852 it was found that since 1848 he and his flock had colluded in a private arrangement whereby members paid a sum for each rehearsal they had missed, and at the end of the season the money went on a slap-up binge for all; meanwhile the supervisory board's inspectors could never find out who was absent.[9]

The date 1848, year of revolutions, is significant: we know of strikes in each of the preceding three decades, leading (at Parma, Piacenza, and Lucca) to arrests, sometimes of the entire chorus; but only at times of upheaval did strikes succeed – in 1848–9, and again at Italian unification in 1859–60. In the latter period the Bologna chorus won, in two stages, a wage increase of something like a third; they referred to themselves as 'this corps which has given honourable service for twenty-eight years', and put forward demands (eventually dropped) for permanent salaried status, to which they believed they had a right in law. The impresario offered to deal with this 'mutiny' by bringing in strikebreakers, but the supervisory board chose compromise: it was a time of democratic agitation when, as the equivalent Naples official said of a simultaneous chorus dispute, 'the less educated class believes it can demand anything it wishes'.[10]

Once united Italy had settled down, strikebreaking worked well enough. A mutual aid society for chorus singers was founded in Milan in 1885, but there is no sign that it could do much for its members beyond paying their funeral expenses.[11] The *masse*, however, could draw comfort here and there from the municipalities some of which now subsidized opera. As elected bodies – though on a narrow franchise – they heeded sentiment in the town; few councillors wanted the opprobrium of sacking poor people with children to feed, less than ever if they worked in something as newsworthy as the opera season. The old despotic governments had had similar concerns, but – faced with the rising costs of opera since the 1820s – had experimented with economic liberalism: this meant letting the impresario get rid of old or weak chorus singers, especially if they refused to take a wage cut.

Chorus members at the Regio, Turin, in the 1870s (the group who were drunk on the first night) resisted the entry of graduates from the new conservatory, where singing had been introduced specifically to provide the opera house with an 'intelligent and educated' chorus; the earliest graduates, once on the establishment, joined in trying to keep out their successors.[12] In defending their jobs even when they had held them for nearly forty years, sang out of tune, sent substitutes to rehearsals, or just missed a few so as to work at other theatres, chorus singers were defending their livelihood; but they were also defending all that made Italian choruses inadequate to the new grand opera summed up by *Aida*. The problems thrown up can be followed in detail at the San Carlo, Naples, where all these ills were reported of the chorus in the quarter-century after unification.[13]

The root causes of trouble were two. First, the San Carlo, which until 1844 had kept up the highest artistic pretensions and had been open the year round (with breaks for religious festivals), was now in decline; its season was shrinking and would shrink further from 1878, to a mere four months. Secondly, unification in 1860 had brought a cockaigne period when people got themselves enrolled in the San Carlo *masse* irregularly: numbers almost doubled. The old Bourbon government had tried to deal with the first problem by giving part of the *masse* a 'subvention' – a proportion of their pay ranging from one to two thirds – while the theatre was closed. The new Italian government, followed by the municipality, tried to deal with the second by purging the chorus of the old and incapable. It bought out part of the surplus in 1864 with pensions chargeable to the state treasury. This and every further attempt, however, brought a rain of petitions from singers who denied all allegations, or else claimed that they and their families would be reduced to 'begging for a piece of bread'.

Lack of an effective pension scheme (such as existed in the richest church choirs) gave them every inducement. The old Bourbon scheme based on members' contributions lived from hand to mouth; even after the courts in 1876 ruled that the state had a duty to pay all pensions, whether the fund could meet them or not, most retired musicians received Fcs 19.12 a month, well below a labourer's wage. No wonder even a chorus singer with forty-eight years' service resisted being pensioned off. She could do so because the regulations were vague: the test was 'incapacity' through age or chronic illness. If she avoided being declared incapable she could at least draw her 'subvention', which was much higher than a pension – about three to four times as much. In 1876–80 this woman and three other ancients stayed at home during the season – the management would not let them perform, – but they still drew their part-pay out of the municipal subsidy.

Resistance took many forms. Singers withheld birth certificates or gave false information; some refused to be medically examined. Leading musicians connected with the theatre – the conductors Nicola De Giosa and Giuseppe Puzone and the chorus master Giuseppe Nicoli – again and again certified that a singer was not incapacitated; so on occasion did teachers from the conservatory. When they had to admit that a singer's voice was in poor shape they opined that she could still be an experienced guide for the new entrants among the second sopranos. De Giosa's and Puzone's approach can be gauged by their having also upheld orchestral players' right to send in substitutes – with their leave. In 1885, when all this had been going on for twenty-two years, Nicoli – still chorus master – acknowledged in a general way the need for a 'radical measure affecting the whole of the choral *massa*, which because of its age shows a deplorable weakness'. A year later, however, leading doctors and musicians on a committee set up to examine singers the impresario wished to have pensioned off turned out, all but one, to be ill or about to leave Naples.

In some ways this was a characteristic display of mutual aid among southerners anxious to keep what was left of the privileges formerly handed out by the Bourbons. Yet in the north too people were reluctant to sack incapables among the *masse*. At Bologna in 1855 the chorus master declined to name the worst women singers; he pointed out four as equally bad; the impresario was then told by the supervisory board to pick two of them for dismissal by lot. A *Lohengrin* at Parma in 1888 was said to be disastrous because voiceless chorus singers had been kept on 'out of a spirit of philanthropy'.[14] Some of this was indeed human compassion; rather more flowed from the multiple system of control and the smallness of Italian communities. If you were not unambiguously in charge, why take on the odium of sacking people you would go on meeting day after day? It took a Toscanini ruthlessly to uphold the demands of art.

San Carlo singers' privilege came of their having been on an official establishment. Under united Italy such groups – orchestras as well as choruses – were often disbanded; not all resisted as long as the Naples *masse.*[15] The nub of privilege was a regular salary. Chorus singers' median pay in 1840–60 was about Fcs 40 to 50 a month at La Scala and the San Carlo; other leading theatres showed a rate of Fcs 2 per performance, as a median in the fashionable Bologna season, a maximum in Rome and (in 1870) at Parma. Here as elsewhere in the profession, women earned as much as men; if anything the best women got slightly more thanks to their rarity. While the season was on, the best daily rates roughly equalled the La Scala and San Carlo monthly rates, but it made a big difference if the monthly rate (or even a lower 'subvention') went on being paid at other times. By 1891 the average at La Scala – then the premier opera house – was Fcs 90 a month; though the chorus was unestablished it was the only one, the San Carlo apart, to get rehearsal pay.[16]

An unestablished chorus singer in a good season made about as much as a skilled building worker – but except in times of slump the builder could work the year round. No wonder choruses went on being recruited from people with other trades to fall back on. Among those who at length won permanent jobs from 1950 were many people like the forty-seven-year-old upholsterer who for years had 'given up his evenings to learn his part, skipped a meal when an onstage rehearsal was called between 12 and 2, gone to bed late on performance nights, and got up next morning, dead on his feet, to open his workshop'.[17]

True, with the spread of Italian opera over much of the world fresh opportunities opened up. The New York Metropolitan, for instance, in 1896–7 had an Italian chorus, fifty strong, who were paid $15 (Fcs 75) a week ($10 a week during rehearsals), alongside an American chorus of equal size and pay. A generation later, in 1924–5, sixty-eight out of the 105–strong Met chorus had Italian names; by then they were earning $49 a week over twenty weeks. These were probably the best American rates: at the new San Francisco Opera in the 1920s chorus singers got under $10 a week, without rehearsal pay.[18] By posting from Russia to Chile, with other stops in between, Italy included, 'suitcase professionals' could hope to make a living from chorus singing alone; a Milan agent in 1907 specialized in placing them. Even then they ran into dead months when they might have to pawn their possessions; while on tour they would make a bit more by selling parmesan cheese on the side.[19] They too found their way into the permanent choruses set up after the Second World War.

Early this century, with the profession in retreat outside Italy, chorus singers may have been among its more successful exports. Even then there were warning signs, as when the Manhattan Opera House, set up in 1906 as an advanced competitor of the Met, recruited a chorus among New York voice students, with a last-minute stiffening of expert Italians: though the chorus master was a young Italian, the founder of the Manhattan promised that the result would be 'wholly different from an Italian chorus, in which every woman looks the same and every man seems to be built on the same lines and both men and women appear never to have learned more than four gestures'; the reviewers praised the chorus for its youth and vigour.[20] Such criticisms of Italian choruses were to go on for many years.

Soloists, meanwhile, were undergoing – most of them unawares – a slow change in their status. This has been put by J. B. Steane (who dates it between 1920 and 1970, and applies it to all opera singers) as a change from 'star' to 'musician': 'The balance of power has shifted, managers, producers, and conductors have occupied the ground which the singer has lost,' but now that the singer is 'just' a musician he has acquired new responsibilities, a new dignity, and greater professional respect.[21] Further happenings since Steane wrote may make us wonder whether television and arena staging have not after all brought back the star tenor. But the change he sets out was already descried in 1914 by an Italian observer, the composer Giacomo Orefice.

Italy, Orefice wrote, had virtually lost its most famous singers to the Americas; but it had acquired 'a considerable nucleus of good and intelligent artists' with whom a genuine ensemble could be built up. Though the audience still demanded good voices, the value now placed on the orchestra, on the conductor, and on staging made it easier to do without 'great' singers.[22]

The story of the profession in Italy since Orefice wrote forms a postlude to its three centuries of European and then world-wide domination of opera.

Its themes are three. First, as Orefice perceived, singers have grown musically more literate thanks to the spread of conservatory education. Secondly, the opera houses they have worked in – far fewer than before – have been increasingly subsidized and controlled by the state. Thirdly, the age of mass society has brought deep changes in the running of opera and in singers' place within it, in part through the advent of effective trade unions and of social legislation, in part through new means of communication. Because these changes overlapped with the twenty-year rule of fascism, they have been shaped by fascist measures, themselves a portent of the new mass age.

Singers' new status as musicians rather than stars is hardest to pin down. 'Good and intelligent artists' did come forward; between the two world wars they enabled the conductor Vittorio Gui to bring back into the Italian repertory, through special seasons in Turin and Florence, several forgotten comic operas of Rossini as well as those of Mozart; others sang in difficult new works, or took part in the 1942 Rome performance of Berg's *Wozzeck*, at that time banned as 'degenerate' by Italy's ally Nazi Germany. Yet how new was this? There were always Italian singers, especially comic ones, of whom the following could have been written:

he is the soul of the opera; no one could perform the comic part better; he understands the stage; vigorous; an actor all over; quick-witted; clever; knows how to draw comedy out of nothing. His voice is not large or of the first quality, but it can be heard, and it is so well managed that compared with him in an ordinary man's or servant's part no one else is worth a straw.[23]

We might be hearing about Sesto Bruscantini or Claudio Desderi, baritones happily still with us. It is in fact a description of Carlo Righenzi, written in 1665.

Against Orefice's judgment, one might argue that Italian singers have missed some chances open to 'good and intelligent artists'. They have scarcely figured in the international revival of Monteverdi's operas that has gone on for over sixty years; and yet those great works cry out for Italian voices. When asked to account for this, musicians and teachers reply that the singing classes in the conservatories are still obsessed with nineteenth-century Italian opera.

It has no doubt been hard for them to shake off the inheritance of the last splurging expansion of Italian opera on the tide of *verismo*, the violently naturalistic school launched in 1890 by *Cavalleria rusticana*. If a 'shouting' tenor was already wanted in 1877, how much more were audiences in the *verismo* period disposed to stake all on a passion torn to tatters and a loud high note. There were artists – Claudia Muzio and Fernando De Lucia – who united the searing intensity called for by *verismo* parts with deeply schooled control. There were also a few classicists who went on putting musicality first; the great mezzo Ebe Stignani – a dignified presence on stage rather than an actress, – reported many disputes with conductors who wanted her to prolong high notes for effect.[24] But there were also, down to the 1950s, many for whom *verismo* licensed shrieking, staggering, and playing to the gallery. Not by chance, this coarsening of musical sensibilities went together with the introduction to Italy of the professional claque; it flourished in Rome, where an audience of bureaucrats with few musical interests needed to be stirred up.[25]

By the 1920s a perhaps unprecedented gulf divided the best of Italian opera singing from the worst. At one end was La Scala, with Toscanini infusing life and warmth into the young Mariano Stabile's Falstaff and trying – with thirteen onstage rehearsals of the sextet – to jolly them into the Lucia of Toti Dal Monte, a pure-toned but cool singer, besides launching Puccini's

Turandot and Boito's *Nerone* and running seasons of all-round high distinction.[26] At the other end was a small-theatre *Puritani* that joined equally unlimited enthusiasm and incapacity:

all were attempting things beyond their powers: the twelve players holding on to the liferaft of the piano continuo; the old, decayed conductor . . . the singers, who climbed up to the top of their range, tearing from their innards inchoate and desperate shrieks and, as though singing wasn't enough to think about, also had to take care not to let the patches on the costumes show too obviously.

At one point a flat crashed to the ground, putting the chorus to flight in a cloud of dust just as they were defying the enemy in 'Suoni la tromba'. But at the end the tenor was applauded by his friends, the soprano by hers. They could be applauded in part because a small town had as yet no clear standard of comparison, such as radio and filmed opera were shortly to provide.[27]

Again, how new was this? It was new in that there were – down to 1918, with some carry-over into the next twenty years – far more minor seasons than before where inadequate performers could wreck themselves on serious works like *I puritani*. But as far back as 1752 Farinelli was said to earn more applause for 'a big trill and a blast through the nose' than for his finest pathetic aria: the blame was put on 'gondoliers and artisans' who liked only the showiest display, and who by sheer volume of applause could often sway an audience.[28] Even if we discount a touch of snobbery in this report, some hearers at all times have probably been more stirred by athletic vocal display, some by expressive musical art. All one can say is that *verismo* made it easy for some audiences to prefer raw power. The end of its sway coincided with the virtual merging of the Italian into the international opera singing profession. What has gone on, whether on stage or in the auditorium, over the past thirty years or so has been much the same in Italy as in Paris, London, and New York.

The reorganization of opera with state subsidy and a form of state control was not unique to Italy; it has happened all over Europe, essentially because in advanced economies the costs of opera rise faster than either the possible takings or the general price index.[29] In Italy it was hastened by discontent at boxholders who blocked financial reform, and by the tensions of the First World War; publishers could no longer control the market. La Scala became a public institution (*ente autonomo*) in 1920; so, between 1926 and 1936, did the main – soon to be the only – opera houses in ten other cities; from the latter year, municipalities in smaller towns with opera seasons of more than a month also had to set up a public body to run them. Impresarios were left to run minor seasons, chiefly in the south. Some years went by before the government accepted the need for subsidy out of the public purse (fed by the radio licence fee), but by the 1930s the essentials were in place – not only subsidy but, in each of the main opera houses, an administration responsible to a ministry in Rome and headed by a superintendent who was a government appointee.[30]

The fascist dictatorship, fully imposed at the start of 1925, coloured by its ideology and tone changes that had much in common with what was happening elsewhere. Planning, rationalization, and the ordering of workers and management into unions and cartels were everywhere fashionable. In the United States an opera director wrote in 1938: 'Like every collective activity of modern life our art urges towards centralization. The individualistic shoestring is as outmoded as the plutocratic trust.'[31] This was a plea, put forward in a trade union journal, for a central casting bureau – something fascist Italy had already launched.

Though the reforms now enacted within the profession had been called for by Italian trade unions before fascism was heard of, they took their shape from the authoritarianism in which the regime gloried. Fascist methods also brought back, along with subsidy and government control, habits of dependence typical of the old pre-unification Italian states.

The main fascist measures came in 1931–2, as part of the much-touted reordering of the whole of Italy into a 'corporate state'. A 1931 law brought police control of stage censorship and, amid a welter of prohibitions, forbade the wearing of masks; police chiefs were to attend dress rehearsals. All were reversions to the ways of the pre-1860 states. (These controls were later vested in a new body ultimately called the Ministry of Popular Culture). Decrees of 1932 forbade the use of theatrical agents; instead, all theatres were to use a national casting bureau under the control of the Fascist Party and of the fascist 'federations' (cartels or unions) that grouped theatre employers and workers: the bureau was usually known by its abbreviation Collospett. An attempt was later made – it soon failed – to coordinate all opera seasons and repertoire. Under a 1934 decree all singing teachers had to be conservatory graduates and to qualify for a professional register; a register of singers was planned in 1943, but lost sight of in the fall of the regime. From 1932, therefore, singers had to belong to the fascist trade union and party – a condition not particularly meaningful when it was shared with millions of fellow-citizens who likewise had to join if they were to get work.[32]

More was to come. A 1935 decree set out to regulate singers' pay. It laid down maxima of Lire 6,000 (about £66) per performance for sopranos and tenors, L.5,000 for lower voices. An escape clause let an official committee authorize higher fees for 'exceptional' singers; a confidential list was presently drawn up of those allowed to go up to L.20,000 per performance (the sopranos Gina Cigna, Maria Caniglia, and Toti Dal Monte, the tenors Gigli, Lauri-Volpi, and Tito Schipa, the bass Ezio Pinza), while two other tenors could go up to L.10,000 and a few named mezzos and baritones could better the maximum by L.1,000 or 2,000.[33]

Like some other fascist measures, these made less practical difference than one might think. Agents (already fewer than they had been before 1914) went right on working: some openly wrote and even signed contracts on singers' behalf; but they were now known as 'secretaries' or 'accountants'.[34]

The attempt to centralize all contractual bargaining began with wholesale muddle such that the Teatro Reale in Rome (the former Costanzi) briefly 'resumed its independence'.[35] By 1938, when its work can be observed, Collospett had settled down to behaving like any agency: it reported the fees singers wanted, adding now and then that they might be open to further negotiation. It did not after all deal with everything: Schipa, it wrote, might not be available if he had personally committed himself abroad, and when singers dealt direct with the superintendent of La Fenice, Venice – as Magda Olivero did, demanding L.1,800 rather than L.1,500 per performance – Collospett merely underwrote the resulting bargain. There was also an information network among superintendents and artists, separate and busy. All engagements, however, had to be confirmed by Collospett, and all contracts had to go through its office; this made a lot of paperwork, which seems to have been dealt with efficiently. The novelty was that its letters sometimes ended 'Fascist greetings' – just as under the Napoleonic republics of 1797–1804 the letters of impresarios and supervisory boards had ended 'Liberty – Equality'.[36]

Maximum fees had in effect been set by the great depression of 1929–33. In the Americas it meant cuts in fees steeper than the contemporary fall in prices; the Met's new $1,000 top – accepted by all but Gigli – was slightly above the L.20,000 Italian maximum for 'exceptional' singers.[37] In practice, most Italian fees were well below the official maxima. At La Fenice, the only opera house for which evidence is to hand, Iva Pacetti and Margherita Carosio, two of the leading sopranos of the period, in 1938 got L.4,000 per performance, raised to L.4,500 for Carosio a year later; everyone else got much less.[38] By this time La Fenice was no longer on a par with La Scala, which may have been able to pay more. Carosio, however, demanded L.4,500 on the grounds that she was paid that by other government-subsidized houses. The maxima may have done something to establish a framework. But the depression, and the accompanying triumph of the cinema, had a far greater effect.

Carosio's argument for her extra L.500 – she was moved by 'reasons of principle' – was only one of a number of signs that the old bargaining habits were little changed. Olivero and the mezzo Gilda Alfano ended by 'making an exception' and agreeing fees which, as they wrote, were below their usual standard, though somewhat more than La Fenice had at first proposed. Alfano's request to the superintendent (the advanced composer Goffredo Petrassi) to show 'friendship' and give her 'the pleasure of working in your theatre' could have been written 100 years earlier to any impresario; it yielded L.200 on top of the L.1,000 offered. Other fees were agreed after a little bargaining, somewhat brisker than the nineteenth-century norm.

Singers who ingratiated themselves with the regime did so as their forerunners had buttered up the old pre-1860 governments, with an extra dose of abjection from the language of propaganda in a mass society. Mussolini himself dealt with opera like one of the old monarchs: he liked to be present at important first nights, to give his opinion (not always favourable), and to be appealed to personally; he stage-managed a visit from Lauri-Volpi so that a high honour for the singer (the decree for which he had signed that morning) should appear to come as a surprise.[39]

The Duce's 'infinite goodness', his 'unerring judgment', his 'enlightened understanding' – here was the language of petition from chorus singers and impresarios.[40] His signed photograph was 'the most longed-for prize' of Toti Dal Monte's career (it was one of a batch of seven sent to artists appearing at La Scala).[41] He was 'the *messenger* of God to our Italy and to the world, sent to defend all that is beautiful, noble, and great': this from Gemma Bellincioni, a famous ex-singer, ageing, in financial trouble, who wheedled large sums from the Duce for her old-fashioned singing school by adulatory letters, flowers for his daughter, and personal interviews, until Mussolini scrawled across one of her requests 'Enough!'.[42] Though Bellincioni was a sincere fascist, it is in a way reassuring that these people all wanted something: Dal Monte asked indirectly in 1942 for help in securing a part at La Scala, a traditional request from a singer to a despot, just as the superintendent of La Fenice, who hoped that 'pressure' from the Ministry of Popular Culture would induce a leading tenor to appear at his theatre, might have been addressing a late seventeenth-century Duke of Modena.[43]

A nastier figure was cut by the tenor Muzio Giovagnoli, who not only used Mussolini's personal secretary to win parts at the Rome Opera and La Scala but denounced as anti-fascists conductors who did not appreciate him at his true worth,[44] and by the soprano Maria Labia: a child of a Venetian noble family, she had an unusual career, much of it spent in Germany and Poland; that may explain how she could publish, five years after everyone had got to know the fate of the Warsaw Ghetto, an account of a 1930s Warsaw in which 'the oily, obliging, ferocious ghetto Jew was preparing to devour the country'.[45]

Labia was a rare example of a singer moved by ideology. Among the silent opposition was Titta Ruffo, who would have been a convinced socialist even if his brother-in-law the deputy Giacomo Matteotti had not been murdered by fascists. The vast majority of singers, however, did not write to the Duce (though anxious groups among the *masse* did), did not denounce their fellows (though there were some anonymous denunciations, as in most walks of Italian life), were no more political than they ever had been, and got on with the job.

For the rest, fascism made little difference to the running of opera. The fascist official in charge, Nicola De Pirro, was on the populist wing of the movement and wished to bring the theatre to the people. He set up the Carro di Tespi (Cart of Thespis), touring companies that performed in a marquee to audiences of up to 5,000; the opera companies in 1937 gave seventy-five performances in forty-two provinces. De Pirro also backed opera in other open-air settings.[46] Whatever the quality of these ventures (opinions differ), they were not as new as was made out: with government subsidy they replaced or revived the open-air theatres many of which had fallen victim to the cinema craze. For singers they meant extra employment at a bad time.

What singers did not get from fascism was security against unemployment or old age. By the turn of the century the old musical establishments, like the San Carlo, had lost most of their privileges. There was then talk of a modern social security scheme, but it looked like costing too much. In those opera houses that became public institutions, the *masse* got contributory health insurance; at the San Carlo they were again on a salary from 1927 (though in 1932 it was left unpaid for months and then cut); nowhere had they a pension or anything to fall back on if, as happened in 1943 to three members of the Rome chorus, they were sacked after thirty years. Freelance musicians had a sketchy kind of health insurance or none. Mussolini, when appealed to by the *masse*, gave some money out of discretionary funds, but that was all.[47]

The coming of effective social security in post-war Italy has made a big difference to the economic life of the profession. A 1947 law set up a fund (its acronym is Enpals) to provide workers in the theatre, opera included, with health insurance and retirement pensions. True, by 1987 Enpals was in crisis and was even later than Italian funds usually are in starting to pay out pensions – three or four years instead of one or two. On the other hand, its pension taken together with the occupational pension paid to singers on an establishment made up a proportion of final salary far higher than most retired people enjoy in Britain or the United States – up to 100 per cent or more. Italy's embracing of the welfare state has not been half-hearted.[48]

The *masse* won established jobs in all the main opera houses at various times in the 1950s; so did stagehands and all other theatre workers. Chorus singers since then have been engaged by a committee on which the trade unions are represented, and are officially known as 'chorus artists'. Besides a regular salary and an occupational pension, they have elaborate arrangements governing workload (122 hours a month, divisible according to specific rules), overtime, length and times of rehearsals, paid holidays (thirty working days), and maternity leave. A former deputy manager of the Turin opera has complained that because of the power and susceptibility of trade unions within this system the chief conductor or musical director can do little about the quality of chorus singers' performance: the only sanction, dismissal on the grounds that they no longer fulfil the conditions of their appointment, is virtually useless. Candidates are also said to be poor: anybody can sign on as a singer at the labour exchange, which opera houses must still resort to by law in the absence of a Collospett (theoretically revived by post-war legislation, but never set up). As a result, places are often left unfilled; in the 1980s, Bulgarian choruses were imported to sing Wagner and, nearer the bone, a Czech chorus to sing Rossini at the festival named after him.[49]

Such complaints imply that Italian chorus singers were at one time more biddable and better qualified. This seems unlikely. Choruses have had their ups and downs and have at times given strong performances; but the solo voice has always been at the heart of Italian opera.

Putting the *masse* on decent all-year-round wages has made opera houses very expensive to run, in Italy even more than in most other countries. It has also, for the first time, cut down the relative cost of soloists.

From the seventeenth century to the late nineteenth century, soloists' fees made up about half the total cost of a season. In 1985–6 at La Scala their share was under one-fifth; the salaries of 666 staff accounted for three-fifths. Total costs were about L.70 billion (just under £32 million).[50] In the words of a *Financial Times* writer, 'it is an under-trumpeted fact' that over the past century 'the comparative fees of leading opera singers have fallen steadily'.[51] The best singers still earn well, but the greater economic and social equality of our time is incompatible with fees at Patti level.

In the opera houses of post-war Italy soloists found conditions formally little changed, but for the ending of police control and of maximum fees. The ban on agents was still in force; it was kept on in a law of 1967, though agents worked openly and the most important one, Liduino Bonardi, ran an agency so identified in its letterhead. The unlooked-for arrest of several opera house superintendents in 1978 for having used agents was to bring about a change in the law the following year.[52] More subtle, uncodified changes, however, had crept in.

The old bazaar culture had almost vanished. In preparing the 1951 season the superintendent of La Fenice had to do virtually none of the bargaining his predecessor had faced in 1938. Letters to and from singers were direct, most of them brief, and supplemented with telegrams and telephone calls. One or two declined parts which they thought beneath them, but without fuss. Some were auditioned by the conductor; the baritone Gianfranco Malaspina objected (it meant travelling) but, after some correspondence, acquiesced. Most signed letters of intent (now legally binding); some had contracts. Only another baritone, Afro Poli, tried to raise his fee by altering his contract to read L.80,000 instead of 70,000 (£40) per performance, but the management firmly brought back the original figure.[53]

The old fascist maxima implied a schedule of fees; by 1950, experience of a network of subsidized opera houses over the previous two decades may have led singers tacitly to accept it – indexed for inflation. There may be a wider explanation: although the 'economic miracle' – the heyday of Italian industrialization – was to come only eight years later, changes may already have been under way that led people to embrace a faster, less niggling mode of doing business.

It is hard to say: reliable evidence dries up after 1950. Stories of bazaar bargaining to drive up fees – told of Callas and her husband in 1952, and of the wife of the tenor Franco Corelli in 1963 – have to do with the record industry.[54] Rapid post-war expansion thanks to the long-playing record perhaps suggested to some people a Klondike to be made the most of.

Italian singers were among the best-sellers of the industry from 1902; they not only made money from royalties – Caruso is said to have earned over £400,000 – but became famous in places where they would never appear.[55] The primacy of the new medium was symbolized in 1920 by the young Lauri-Volpi's decision to break his contract with an impresario, at what turned out to be vast cost, rather than forgo recording.[56] But Italian singers could never make a fortune from sales in their own country – a mere 10,458 in 1924.[57] To make a world-wide reputation through the gramophone, it has been suggested, they needed first to establish themselves in the opera houses of the English-speaking countries, the headquarters of the industry: the baritone Carlo Galeffi never caught on there, though he was admired at home; on the international recording scene he made little mark.[58]

For many Italian singers, especially in the 1930s and 1940s, film mattered more than recording. A few had appeared in silent films: this was not as odd as it sounds, for the acting style and conventions of early silents had much in common with those of opera; though Caruso's two films were disastrous, beautiful women singers – Bellincioni and Cavalieri – did well for a time. The sound film was the real opportunity. Gigli made sixteen films from 1935: all were said to be bad, but, as he pointed out, they brought lots of money and a large public following.[59] There were many other Italian opera films, ephemeral and more cheaply made than the recent *Traviata* and *Otello* directed by Franco Zeffirelli; a few now turn up on video. In Hollywood the Italian-American tenor Mario Lanza had a brief post-war success.

The Italian radio (EIAR, later RAI) was another important source of work. In the early 1930s, group listening made up for the small number of licence fee payers (less than one-tenth those in Britain). Broadcast opera suited the fascist policy of 'going to the people'; for singers it made up part of the loss of custom to the cinema. EIAR set up its own choruses, three of them by the 1950s totalling about 200. In 1931 it put out sixty-nine broadcasts of fifty-four complete operas, and this rate was kept up in later years; performances under fascism were confined almost wholly to Italian works, with *verismo* dominant, but the post-war repertoire was international and lively. A number of singers made careers at least as much on the air as in the theatre; some performed in as many as seventeen consecutive years. The soprano Adriana Guerrini won engagements in major opera houses only after she had done well in broadcasts; the lyric tenor Emilio Renzi, on the other hand, had a successful ten-year career on the air and then failed in the theatre. Radio also helped the stylist Gabriella Gatti, whose distinction in parts like the Countess in *Le nozze di Figaro* meant little to the bulk of the Italian theatre audience.[60]

These singers flourished during and just after the Second World War; hence they are little remembered outside Italy. Slightly later singers like Renata Tebaldi (debut 1944) and Giuseppe Di Stefano (debut 1946), to mention only the most famous, had international careers and became known throughout the Western world on long-playing records. From then on, singers of Italian opera no longer made up a distinct profession even in Italy.

There as everywhere else, casts are now international; opera has joined the global village. According to a former superintendent, a few multinational record companies and agents so dominate the market for singers that Italian opera houses other than La Scala are now in effect their concessionaires.[61] In the English-speaking countries and Japan, the big audience experiences opera through television and video; CD video discs with high-quality sound started in earnest in 1988. Video opera is so far based on theatre productions filmed on the spot. The reason is cost: even taking a Covent Garden production into a studio would, in 1988, have added £175,000 to initial costs that were already high, in part because of leading singers' demands for a hefty advance on royalties. Working in a studio from the beginning would have been prohibitive.[62]

Video opera, then, looks like requiring singers to go on working in the theatre; but it may also require them more and more to fit the expectations of a world-wide audience. This already means that they need to sound like their records. Will it also mean their becoming more like film stars in looks and ability? At least one filmed opera has shown us actors who mime to a pre-existing recording. That may point to the future. Opera was from the start an expensive invention; in a mass society its cost may drive it into such contrivances, or sink it altogether. All we can be sure of is that men and women will want to go on hearing their fellow-creatures enact a story in song.

NOTES

INTRODUCTION: A LIVING TRADITION

Page references are not given to (a) certain theatre histories arranged as annals, where the year referred to is clear from the text; (b) very short pamphlets. First references to journal articles cite total pages followed by the specific pages referred to, e.g. pp. 233–69:251–2.

Italian theatre seasons are referred to as follows. A = autumn; C = carnival; E = summer (estate); F = fair; P = spring (primavera); Q = Lent (quaresima).

1 V. Bellini, *Epistolario*, ed. L. Cambi, Milan, 1943, p. 38.
2 A. Ademollo, *I teatri di Roma nel secolo XVII*, Rome, 1888, p. 105; C. A. Vianello, *Teatri, spettacoli, musiche a Milano nei secoli scorsi*, Milan, 1941, p. 210.
3 Obituary of Erminia Frezzolini, cutting from unidentified newspaper, 9 Nov. 1884, Piancastelli Autog.
4 Works Progress Administration, *The History of Opera in San Francisco (San Francisco Theater Research*, VIII), San Francisco, 1938, pp. 8–9.
5 Pierleone Ghezzi, caricature of Gioseppino, BAV Cod. Ottob. Lat. 3117 c. 181. See P. Petrobelli, 'I musicisti di teatro settecentesco nelle caricature di Pierleone Ghezzi', in L. Bianconi and G. Morelli, eds., *Antonio Vivaldi. Teatro musicale, cultura e società*, Florence, 1982, II, pp. 415–26.
6 Gioanni Tacconi to Count Francesco Conti, 5 April 1788, Piancastelli 130.13.
7 Giuseppe Verdi to Eugenio Toccagni, 14 July 1843, ISVP xerox 33/12; Giuseppina Strepponi to Mauro Corticelli, 15 Jan. 1859, in F. Walker, *The Man Verdi*, London, 1962, p. 230; Augusto Pecori to Alessandro Lanari, 26 Dec. 1848, BNF CV 400/159.
8 R. A. Mooser, 'Un musicista veneziano in Russia: Catterino Cavos', *NRMI* 3, 1969, pp. 13–23.
9 See N. Pirrotta, *Li due Orfei*, Turin, 1969; Eng. transl. as *Music and Culture in Italy from the Middle Ages to the Baroque*, Cambridge, Mass., 1984.
10 The organization and finance of opera are studied in three essays by F. Piperno (down to 1780), J. Rosselli (1780–1880), and F. Nicolodi (1860–present), all in L. Bianconi and G. Pestelli, eds., *Storia dell'opera italiana*, Turin, 1987– , IV, pp. 1–229, which also includes an excellent essay by S. Durante on singers: IV, pp. 347–415. See also Rosselli, *The Opera Industry in Italy from Cimarosa to Verdi*.

The Role of the Impresario, Cambridge, 1984; L. Bianconi and T. Walker, 'Production, consumption and political function of seventeenth-century opera', *Early Music History* 4, 1984, pp. 209–96.

11 *Corriere della Sera* (Milan), 13 June 1987, p. 27.

I MUSICIANS ATTENDING

1 E. Rosand, 'Barbara Strozzi, virtuosissima cantatrice. The composer's voice', *JAMS* 31, 1978, pp. 241–81, and 'The voice of Barbara Strozzi', in J. Bowers and J. Tick, eds., *Women Making Music*, Urbana, Ill., 1986, pp. 168–90; H. Prunières, *L'Opéra italien en France avant Lulli*, Paris, 1913, pp. xxxvii–xxxviii. This chapter is a shorter, rewritten version of the first two parts of my article 'From princely service to the open market: singers of Italian opera and their patrons, 1600–1850', *Cambridge Opera Journal* 1, 1989, pp. 1–32.

2 Bianconi and Walker, 'Production, consumption', p. 260.

3 A. Newcomb, *The madrigal at Ferrara 1579–1597*, Princeton, 1980, I, pp. 7, 47, 269.

4 Newcomb, *Madrigal at Ferrara*, I, pp. 12–13, 101–3, 183–90; W. Kirkendale, 'Zum Biographie des ersten Orfeos, Francesco Rasi', in L. Finscher, ed., *Claudio Monteverdi. Festschrift Reinhold Hammerstein zum 70. Geburtstag*, Laaber, 1986, pp. 297–329.

5 Newcomb, *Madrigal at Ferrara*, p. 200; S. Reiner, 'La vag'Angioletta (and others)', *AnMu* 14, 1974, pp. 26–88.

6 Antonio Gianettini to Duke of Modena's secretary, 13 Aug. 1689, ASMO Mus b. 1/B; C. Timms, 'Bontempi, Giovanni Andrea Angelini', *TNG*; M. von Fürstenau, *Zur Geschichte der Musik und des Theaters am Hofe der Kurfürsten von Sachsen*, Dresden, 1861–2, I, pp. 11–16, 260–2, 295–7.

7 A. Ademollo, *La bell'Adriana e altre virtuose del suo tipo alla corte di Mantova*, Città di Castello, 1888, pp. 89–119, 123.

8 A. Ademollo, *La Leonora di Milton e di Clemente IX*, Milan, 1885.

9 Ademollo, *Bell'Adriana*, pp. 303–4.

10 Ademollo, *Leonora*.

11 John Evelyn, diary for 19 April 1687, quoted in *The Diary of Samuel Pepys*, ed. R. C. Latham and W. Matthews, London, 1970–83, X, pp. 281–2; C. Ricci, *Figure e figuri del mondo teatrale*, Milan, 1920, pp. 281–2.

12 H. Mayer Brown, 'The geography of Florentine monody. Caccini at home and abroad', *EaMu* 9, 1981, pp. 147–68:158–62; Prunières, *Opéra italien en France*, pp. 25, 89–90.

13 J. Milhous and R. D. Hume, eds., *Vice-Chamberlain Coke's Theatrical Papers 1706–15*, Carbondale, Ill., 1982, p. 245.

14 P. Petrobelli, 'Francesco Manelli – documenti e osservazioni', *Chigiana*, n. s. 24, 1962, pp. 43–66; J. Whenham, 'Manelli, Francesco', *TNG*.

15 E. Wellesz, 'Einige handschriftliche Libretti aus der Frühzeit der Wiener Oper', *Zeitschrift für Musikwissenschaft* 1, 1918–19, p. 281; H. Knaus, *Die Musiker im Archivbestand des Kaiserlichen Obersthofmeisteramtes (1637–1705)*, Vienna,

1967–9, I, pp. 23, 33, II, p. 77; L. von Köchel, *Die Kaiserliche Hofmusikkapelle in Wien von 1543 bis 1867*, Vienna, 1869, pp. 58–60.

16 Bianconi and Walker, 'Production, Consumption', pp. 234–43.

17 Claudio Monteverdi to Alessandro Striggio, 24 July 1627, in *Monteverdi. Lettere, dediche e prefazioni*, ed. D. de' Paoli, Rome, 1973, p. 267.

18 See note 7.

19 M. Viale Ferrero, 'Repliche a Torino di melodrammi veneziani', in M. T. Muraro, ed., *Venezia e il melodramma nel Seicento*, Florence, 1976, pp. 148, 159–64.

20 Queen Christina to Giacomo d'Alibert, 7 March 1668, in A. Ademollo, 'Le avventure di una cantante al tempo di Innocenzo XI', *L'Opinione* (Rome), 28 July 1880.

21 Nicola Paris to the Margrave of Brandenburg-Ansbach, 1 Feb. 1697, in H. Mersmann, *Beiträge zur Ansbacher Musikgeschichte*, Leipzig, 1916, p. 28. The rival singer was Carlo Landriani.

22 Giuseppe Chiarini to the Duke of Savoy, 26 Nov. 1666, in M.-T. Bouquet, *Musique et musiciens à Turin de 1648 à 1775*, Turin, 1968, pp. 168–9.

23 O. Termini, 'Singers at San Marco in Venice: the competition between Church and theatre (*c.* 1675–*c.* 1725)', *RMA Research Chronicle* 17, 1981, pp. 65–96:67, 69–71.

24 I. Fenlon, *Music and Patronage in Sixteenth-Century Mantua*, Cambridge, 1980, I, pp. 110, 190.

25 Prunières, *Opéra italien en France*, pp. 86–94.

26 L. Bianconi and T. Walker, 'Dalla *Finta Pazza* alla *Veremonda*. Storie di Febiarmonici', *RIDM* 10, 1975, pp. 379–454:444.

27 A. Ademollo, 'Le cantanti italiane celebri del secolo decimottavo: Margherita Salicola', *Nuova Antologia*, 1 Oct. 1889, pp. 524–33.

28 Cardinal Grimani to Duke of Modena, 1708–9, ASMO Mus b. 2. The soprano was Francesco De Grandis.

29 Giovanni Antonio Cavagna to Marco Faustini, 3 April, 16 May, 27 July, 20 Oct. 1665, ASV Scuola Grande di S. Marco b. 188 c. 85, 98, 125, 208; cf. Vincenzo Dini to Faustini, 1665, *ibid.* b. 188 c. 52, 218, b. 194 c. 137.

30 Bouquet, *Musique et musiciens à Turin*, pp. 81–2, 176–9. Bouquet's 'Veneria' for Cavagnino's location in carnival 1667 should be read 'Venetia.'

31 Prunières, *Opéra italien en France*, pp. 152–5, 172–3; Francesco Folchi to Duke of Modena's secretary, no date [late seventeenth century], G. B. Nini to Padre Livrani, 7 Jan. 1690, ASMO Mus b. 1/B, 2.

32 Carlo Righenti [Righenzi] to M. Faustini, 7 Oct. 1665, ASV Scuola Grande di S. Marco b. 188 c. 53–4.

33 To the Duke of Modena's secretary from Carlo Antonio Riccardi, 23 June 1674, from Pietro Benigni, May 1691, ASMO Mus b. 2; Roberto Papafava to the Grand Prince Ferdinand of Tuscany, 30 May 1693, in L. Puliti, 'Cenni storici della vita del serenissimo Ferdinando dei Medici, Gran Principe di Toscana', *Atti dell'Accademia del R. Istituto Musicale di Firenze*, Florence, 1874, pp. 50–1; Niccolò Donnamaria to [?], 21 April 1748, BE MO MSS Campori App. 2447 (soliciting a request from the authorities at Mantua to safeguard Caffarelli's salary from the Naples royal chapel).

34 Francesco Zanchi to Faustini, 23 Aug. 1654, ASV Scuola Grande di S. Marco b. 188 c. 14.

35 B. Brunelli, 'L'impresario in angustie', *Rivista italiana del dramma* 5, 1941, pp. 311–41: 331–3; Knaus, *Musiker im Archivbestand*, II, pp. 9, 10, 23, 27, 42–3, III, pp. 45, 140–1.

36 Brunelli, 'Impresario in angustie', pp. 319–28.

37 Antonio Alamanni to Duke of Modena, 3 Feb. 1690, ASMO Mus b. 2; more generally, M. Fabbri, *Alessandro Scarlatti e il Principe Ferdinando de Medici*, Florence, 1961.

38 R. L. and N. Weaver, *A Chronology of Music in the Florentine Theater 1590–1750*, Detroit, 1978, pp. 41, 62–9, 71; S. Durante, 'Cantanti per Reggio 1696–1717', in S. Davoli, ed., *Civiltà teatrale e settecento emiliano*, Bologna, 1985, pp. 301–7; Durante, 'Cantante', pp. 364–7.

39 Faustino Donalli to the Duke of Modena's secretary, 6 Oct. 1683, ASMO Mus. b. 1/B.

40 S. Cordero di Pamparato, 'Un duca di Savoia impresario teatrale e i casi della musica Diana', *RMI* 45, 1941, pp. 240–60.

41 G. Cosentino, *La Mignatta: Maria Maddalena Musi, cantatrice bolognese famosa*, Bologna, 1930, pp. 25–6, 112–13, 115–19, 122–4, 127–8.

42 Bianconi and Walker, 'Production, consumption', pp. 274–82; C. Sartori, 'Profilo di una cantante della fine del secolo XVII: Barbara Riccioni', in *Festschrift K. G. Fellerer zum 60. Geburtstag*, Regensburg, 1962, pp. 454–60; P. Besutti, *La corte musicale di Ferdinando Carlo Gonzaga ultimo duca di Mantova*, Mantua, 1989.

43 Patent issued to Maria Maddalena Pieri, 13 May 1721, and later patents, ASMO Mus b. 1/B.

44 Minutes of letters from the Duke's secretary to Siface, 24 June 1686, to A. Alamanni, 7 July 1689, to the Duke, no date, from Origoni, 6 Sept. 1690, ASMO Mus b. 2.

45 Extract of letter from Milan, 22 Nov. 1713, ASMO Mus b. 2; U. Kirkendale, 'Antonio Caldara – la vita', *Chigiana*, n.s. 6–7, 1969–70, pp. 223–346:248–9, 254, 255–6, 265; W. Dean, 'Scarabelli, Diamante', *TNG*.

46 Durante, 'Cantanti per Reggio' (in 1696–1701 nearly all those who sang in opera at Reggio were billed as dependants of rulers, in 1710–17 only about a third); Weaver and Weaver, *Chronology of Music in the Florentine Theater*, p. 266. Cf. F. Walker, 'A chronology of the life and works of Nicola Porpora', *Italian Studies* 6, 1951, pp. 29–62:34; L. Lindgren, 'La carriera di Gaetano Berenstadt, contralto evirato, ca. 1690–1735', *RIDM* 19, 1984, pp. 36–112:47.

47 Francesco Guicciardi to the Duke of Modena's secretary, 17 May 1729, ASMO Mus b. 1/B.

48 Teresa Bolognini Fontana to Padre G. B. Martini, 17 Sept. 1752, in Durante, 'Cantante', pp. 379–80.

49 Bartolomeo Nucci to Padre Martini, 20 May 1774, CMBM BO 1.3.165.

50 G. M. Ortes to J. A. Hasse, 30 Jan. 1768, MCCV Cod. Cicogna 2658 no. 146 (about Traetta's *Amor in trappola*, at the Teatro San Moisè).

51 To Padre Martini from Giuseppe M. Giardini, 8 Feb. 1751, from Gaetano Guadagni, 7 Feb. 17[?], CMBM BO 1.23.76, 1.4.65.

52 F. Della Seta, 'I Borghese (1691–1731). La musica di una generazione', *Note d'archivio* n.s. 1, 1983, pp. 139–208: 193–6, 200 (the owners of the Teatro Capranica did acknowledge some responsibility: when Ossi's claims on the Borghese remained unpaid they granted him 4 per cent interest); B. Croce, *I teatri di Napoli*, 1st version, Naples, 1891, p. 321.

53 Croce, *Teatri di Napoli*, p. 215.

54 L. Frati, 'Antonio Bernacchi e la sua scuola di canto', *RMI* 29, 1922, pp. 473–91, esp. pp. 478–9.

55 Deputazione dei Pubblici Spettacoli to King of Naples, 22 March, 3, 6 Nov. 1802, ASN Casa Reale Antica, Teatri e Feste Pubbliche f. 1269 fasc. 17, 27, 65, 82, 86, 110.

56 For a fuller account: Rosselli, *Opera Industry*, pp. 96–9.

57 'Eine Selbstbiographie von Gertrud Elisabeth Mara', *AMZ* 10, 1875, cols 545–7, 549–50, 561, 565, 577: H. C. Robbins Landon, *Haydn: Chronicle and Works*, London, 1976–80, II: *Haydn at Eszterháza*, p. 55 (note). The events referred to occurred in 1771 and 1776.

58 Figures worked out from the data in Robbins Landon, *Haydn at Eszterháza*, pp. 70–82, show the median length of stay for men singers between 1768 and 1790 as two years ten and a half months, for women singers as two years two months. Italian or Italianized singers generally contracted for two or three years, often left or were dismissed within a few months or a year or so, but sometimes stayed on for four or five years. Some, mainly German, singers stayed on much longer. Among the few long-serving Italians (over eleven years each) were Haydn's mistress Luigia Polzelli and the tenor Benedetto Bianchi, the one Prince Esterhazy had flogged early in his engagement.

59 P. Metastasio to L. Trapassi, 9 Feb. 1767, in Metastasio, *Tutte le opere*, ed. B. Brunelli, Milan, 1953, IV, p. 527.

60 R. Strohm, 'Aspetti sociali dell'opera italiana del primo Settecento', *Musica/Realtà* 2, 1981, pp. 117–41.

2 CASTRATI

1 This chapter is a version, shorter and much rewritten, of my article 'The castrati as a professional group and a social phenomenon, 1550–1850', *AcMu* 60, 1988, pp. 143–79.

2 As when Haböck (a doctor) in 1914 interviewed Alessandro Moreschi, the last notable castrato to sing in St Peter's: F. Haböck, *Die Kastraten und ihre Gesangskunst*, Stuttgart, 1927, pp. 126–7.

3 C. Burney, *Music, Men, and Manners in France and Italy*, ed. H. E. Poole, London, 1969, pp. 128, 63–4. Cf. [J.-J. Le François de Lalande], *Voyage d'un François en Italie*, Venice-Paris, 1769, VI, pp. 345–9, and similar reports by other travel writers (1764–87) summarized in Haböck, *Kastraten*, pp. 233–47.

4 F. D'A[mico], 'Evirato', *ES*. See also P. Browe, *Zur Geschichte der Entmannung*, Breslau, 1936; A. Heriot, *The Castrati in Opera*, London, 1956; H. Hucke, 'Die Besetzung von Sopran und Alt in der Sixtinischen Kapelle', *Miscelánea en homenaje a Monseñor Higinio Anglés*, Barcelona, 1958–61, I, pp. 379–96.

5 J. P. L. Withof, *De castratis commentationes quatuor*, Lausanne, 1762, pp. 30–41. For ancient views on castration, Browe, *Entmannung*, pp. 53–8.

6 C. Burney, *A General History of Music*, ed. F. Mercer, London, 1935, II, pp. 528–30.

7 C. d'Ollincan [pseud. of C. d'Ancillon], *Traité des eunuques*, Berlin, [1707], esp. pp. 115–21, 158–64. Like Withof (see note 5), this erudite historian depended heavily on ancient and humanistic sources; he nowhere states how he came by his alleged knowledge of castration practice in his own day.

8 Browe, *Entmannung*, pp. 7–8, 10–11.

9 I. Fenlon, 'Monteverdi's Mantuan "Orfeo": some new documentation', *EaMu* 12, 1984, pp. 163–72, and 'The Mantuan "Orfeo"', in J. Whenham, ed., *Claudio Monteverdi. Orfeo*, Cambridge, 1986, pp. 1–19.

10 A. Milner, 'The Sacred Capons', *Musical Times* 114, 1973, pp. 250–3; T. Walker, 'Castrato', *TNG*; Haböck, *Kastraten*, p. 428; Browe, *Entmannung*, pp. 86–91.

11 Hucke, 'Besetzung von Sopran und Alt', p. 388 (note).

12 Francesco Poncini to Padre Martini, 10 July 1778, CMBM BO 1.1.158.

13 Knaus, *Musiker im Archivbestand*, I, p. 65; series of individual payments to members of church choirs in R. Bowman, 'Musical information in the archives of the Church of Santa Maria Maggiore, Bergamo, 1649–1720', in I. Bent, ed., *Source Materials and the Interpretation of Music*, London, 1981, pp. 332–5; O. Gambassi, *La cappella musicale di San Petronio. Musici, organisti, cantori e strumentisti dal 1436 al 1920*, Florence, 1987, part 2; ASN Scrivania di Ragione, reg. 38 (payments to musicians of the Naples royal chapel).

14 D'Amico, 'Evirato'; A. Maugars, *Réponse faite à un curieux sur le sentiment de la musique en Italie*, ed. J. Lionnet, *NRMI* 19, 1985, pp. 686, 694; Strohm, 'Aspetti sociali', pp. 117–41 (identifying castrati as bearers of increasing musical professionalism but about 100 years on; there may have been repeated waves of specialization).

15 General studies are T. H. Aston, ed., *Crisis in Europe 1560–1660*, London, 1965; G. Quazza, *La decadenza italiana nella storia europea*, Turin, 1971; O. Chadwick, *The Popes and European Revolution*, Oxford, 1981, esp. pp. 212–13, 246; the revisionist R. T. Rapp, *Industry and Economic Decline in Seventeenth-Century Venice*, Cambridge, Mass., 1976; and esp. P. Stella, 'Strategie familiari e celibato sacro tra '600 e '700', *Salesianum* (Turin) 41, 1979, pp. 73–109. Statistics of monks and nuns as a proportion of population in E. Boaga, 'Il seicento', *Dizionario degli istituti di perfezione*, ed. G. Pelliccia and G. Rocca, Turin, 1974– , s.v. 'Italia', and esp. in C. J. Beloch, *Bevölkerungsgeschichte Italiens*, Berlin-Leipzig, 1937–61, I, pp. 73–86, 187, II, p. 19 (sets out contemporary statistics and the considerable problems they raise).

16 W. L. Weckhrlin, *Chronologen*, Frankfurt, 1779–81, I, p. 174, quoted in Haböck, *Kastraten*, p. 148.

17 For Padre Don Filippo Melani, see Prunières, *Opéra italien en France*, pp. 16 (note), 174–7.

18 G. Delille, *Famille et propriété dans le Royaume de Naples (XVe–XIXe siècles)* Paris, 1985; Stella, 'Strategie familiari e celibato sacro'.

19 Lalande, *Voyage d'un François*, VI, p. 348.

20 Browe, *Entmannung*, pp. 99–117.

21 'Nota della spesa che andarà per far castrare il N.', ASMO Mus b. 2.

22 Padre Girolamo Chiti to Padre Martini, 6 Feb., Martini to Chiti, 18 Feb. 1750, CMBM BO 1.12.106–7.

23 Contract of 3 Aug. 1671 between Salvatore and Olimpia Nannini, represented by Sante Nannini, and the teacher Antonio Masini, in G. L. Masetti Zannini, 'Virtù e crudezza. Scolari di canto e famiglie tra rinascimento e barocco', *Strenna dei romanisti* 41, 1980, p. 338.

24 Contract of 30 Nov. 1697 between Giovanni Donato Rizzo, of Castellana, and Nicola or Niccolò Tricarico, of Gallipoli, in G. A. Pastore, 'Un raro documento su l'evirazione dei cantanti nel secolo XVII', *Letture dell'Accademia Salentina di Lettere Scienze ed Arti* 1, No. 2, April 1955.

25 N. Lucarelli, *Domenico Bruni*, Umbertide, 1990, pp. 16–19.

26 C. Pampaloni, 'Giovani castrati nell'Assisi del Settecento', *Musica/Realtà* 8, 1987, pp. 133–54: 142.

27 E. Faustini-Fasini, 'Gli astri maggiori del bel canto napoletano', *Note d'archivio* 12, 1935, pp. 297–316, 15, 1938, pp. 121–8, 157–70, 258–70: 124; F. Balatri, *Frutti del mondo*, ed. K. Vossler, Milan, 1924, p. 12.

28 R. L. Weaver, 'Materiali per le biografie dei fratelli Melani', *RIDM* 12, 1977, pp. 252–95, and 'Melani', *TNG*.

29 Bowman, 'Musical Information', p. 323.

30 To the Dukes of Mantua from their Rome agents Paolo Facconi, 9 Feb. 1613, and Anna Vittoria Ubaldini, 27 Oct. 1661, in A. Bertolotti, *Musici alla corte dei Gonzaga in Mantova dal secolo XV al XVIII*, Milan, 1890, pp. 90, 109.

31 Petitions of Rinaldo Gherardini [probably 1670s] and of Silvestro Prittoni (accepted 11 May 1687), ASMO Mus b. 2 (and see note 21).

32 Pampaloni, 'Giovani castrati', p. 140; Lucarelli, *Bruni*, p. 16; B. Marcello, *Il teatro alla moda*, ed. A. D'Angeli, Milan, 1956 (original edn 1720), p. 32; G. Sacchi to Padre Martini, 11 Dec. 1782, CMBM BO I.10.45; G. Sacchi, *Vita del cavaliere Don Carlo Broschi*, Venice, 1784, pp. 7–8; Haböck, *Kastraten*, pp. 197, 202–3.

33 Vianello, *Teatri a Milano*, pp. 211–12.

34 These are Giovanni Andrea Angelini Bontempi, Girolamo Crescentini, Cristoforo Arnaboldi (*fl.* late eighteenth century), Gioseppino (sang women's parts in Rome, 1742), Gaetano Berenstadt, Giovanni Antonio Predieri: C. Mutini, 'Angelini Bontempi', *DBI*; C. Timms, 'Bontempi', *TNG*; 'Girolamo Crescentini (Aus seiner brieflichen Mittheilung; Neapel 24 April 1837, übers.)', *AMZ* 39, 1837, cols 614–17; Vianello, *Teatri a Milano*, pp. 283–4; Ghezzi caricature of Gioseppino, BAV Cod. Ottob. Lat. 3117 c. 160; Lindgren, 'Gaetano Berenstadt'; L. Busi, *Il Padre G. B. Martini*, Bologna, 1891, pp. 31–62.

35 Durante, 'Cantante', pp. 376–83; T. Culley, 'The influence of the German College in Rome on music in German-speaking countries during the 16th and 17th centuries', *AnMu* 8, 1969, pp. 1–35, *ibid.* 9, 1970, pp. 20–63; Gambassi, *Cappella di San Petronio*; M. F. Robinson, 'The governors' minutes of the Conservatorio S. Maria di Loreto, Naples', *RMA Research Chronicle* 10, 1972, pp. 1–97, fuller and more precise (though dealing with one conservatory only) than S. Di Giacomo, *I quattro antichi conservatori musicali di Napoli*, Milan, 1924–8.

36 O. Mischiati, 'Una statistica della musica a Roma nel 1694', *Note d'Archivio* n.s. 1, 1983, pp. 209–27; G. Rostirolla, 'Maestri di cappella, organisti, cantanti e strumentisti attivi in Roma nella metà del Settecento' , *ibid.* 2, 1984, pp. 195–268.
37 Gambassi, *Cappella di San Petronio*, pp. 32–3, 298–306.
38 *Diary of Samuel Pepys*, VIII, p. 155 (7 April 1667).
39 Application by Agostino Di Secresca, orphan, for admission to Conservatorio di S. Maria di Loreto, Feb. 1751, BSPM NA XIII.7.18 fol. 27[13].
40 Di Giacomo, *Quattro conservatori*, I, pp. 88–90; Robinson, 'Governors' minutes', pp. 56, 67–8; BSPM NA xx[A]/1.45 (candidate admitted to S. Maria di Loreto, 1755, at half the usual fee 'on account of being a eunuch') and XIII.7.18 fol. 27[25] (Governors of Pietà dei Turchini to the Minister Bernardo Tanucci, 25 Sept. 1763, tacitly equating castrati with orphans as candidates for admission).
41 J. W. Hill, 'Oratory music in Florence', *AcMu* 51, 1979, pp. 108–36, 246–67: 249–50, *ibid.* 58, 1986, pp. 127–77.
42 Padre Martini to [?] at Assisi, minute, no date, to Martini from Fra Francesco Maria Benedetti, 24 Nov. 1736, from Fra Paolo Serafino Facconi, 22 Aug. 1755, CMBM BO Cod. 80 P.123.18a, I.9.102, I.7.62.
43 Ademollo, *Teatri di Roma*, pp. 99, 106, 149; M. Murata, *Operas for the Papal Court (1631–1668)*, Ann Arbor, 1981, pp. 7–9, and 'Further remarks on Pasqualini and the music of MAP', *AnMu* 19, 1979, p. 125–45:126–8; B. M. Antolini, 'La carriera di cantante e di compositore di Loreto Vittori', *Studi Musicali* 7, 1978, pp. 141–88; E. Celani, 'I cantori della Cappella Pontificia', *RMI* 14, 1907, pp. 83–104, 752–90: 779, *ibid.* 16, 1909, pp. 55–102.
44 Culley, 'Influence of the German College' (and see note 34).
45 U. Prota-Giurleo, *I teatri di Napoli nel Seicento*, Naples, 1962, p. 298.
46 M. Murata, 'Il carnevale a Roma sotto Clemente IX', *RIDM* 12, 1977, pp. 83–99: 93–4.
47 U. Prota-Giurleo, 'Matteo Sassani detto Matteuccio', *RIDM* 1, 1966, pp. 97–119.
48 Pistocchi to G. A. Perti, 8 March 1702, CMBM BO P.143.71.
49 Faustini-Fasini, 'Astri maggiori', part 2, pp. 299–310.
50 P. Cattelan, 'La musica della "omnigena religio"', *AcMu* 59, 1987, pp. 152–86.
51 Lucarelli, *Bruni*, pp. 53–5, 65–71.
52 Termini, 'Singers at San Marco', pp. 55–96:69–74.
53 F. Piperno, 'Francesco Gasparini, le sue abitazioni romane, i suoi allievi coabitanti (1717–1727)', *Esercizi. Arte Musica Spettacolo* (Università di Perugia, Facoltà di Lettere e Filosofia) 4, 1981, pp. 104–15; E. Celani, 'Musica e musicisti in Roma 1750–1850', *RMI* 18, 1911, p. 1–63:16–17, *ibid.* 20, 1913, pp. 33–88, *ibid.* 22, 1915, pp. 1–56.
54 G. Rostirolla, 'Gli "ordinari" della cappella musicale di San Pietro in Vaticano', *Note d'archivio* n.s. 4, 1986, p. 229.
55 Celani, 'Cantori della Cappella Pontificia', pt 2, p. 779.
56 Grimaldi, *Cappella musicale di Loreto*.
57 Bowman, 'Musical information', pp. 342–3; Carlo Lenzi to Padre Martini, 22 Feb. 1779, CMBM BO I.9.66.
58 L. Ayestarán, *La música en el Uruguay*, Montevideo, 1953, I, pp. 230, 303ff.

59 Timms, 'Bontempi'; Sacchi, *Vita di Carlo Broschi*, pp. 17–27.

60 Prunières, *Opéra italien en France*, pp. 187–90; Weaver, 'Materiali per le biografie dei fratelli Melani', pp. 271–4; F. Ravagli, *Il Cortona*, Città di Castello, 1896.

61 Burney, *Music in France and Italy*, pp. 92–3; D. Heartz, 'Farinelli and Metastasio: rival twins of public favour', *EaMu* 12, 1984, pp. 358–66; correspondence between Cardinal Lorenzo Ganganelli and Padre Martini, 1760–1, CMBM BO 1.15.110, 115–15a.

62 M. Benoit, *Versailles et les musiciens du Roi*, Paris, 1971, pp. 269–70, 324–9, 348–50, 362; L. Sawkins, 'For and against the Order of Nature: Who Sang the Soprano?', *EaMu* 15, 1987, pp. 315–24.

63 Chiti to Martini, 9 Sept. 1752, CMBM BO 1.6.31. Pasqualino was probably Pasqualino Betti.

64 Ghezzi, caricature of Cavaliere Valeriani [Valeriano Pellegrini], BAV Cod. Ottob. Lat. 3116 c. 162.

65 ASBO Ufficio del Registro, vol. 29 fol. 151^r–153^v (*notaio* Roffeni Gioacchino, *dimissione*, 2 Aug. 1732, and inventory at death).

66 Heriot, *Castrati in opera*, pp. 153–4, 156, 198–9; Lucarelli, *Bruni*, pp. 68–9; Vianello, *Teatri a Milano*, pp. 283–4.

67 ASBO Ufficio del Registro, vol. 200 fol. 176^r–183^v (*notaio* Pedretti Agostino Ignazio, will opened 13 May 1726).

68 Lucarelli, *Bruni*, p. 73.

69 Bernacchi to Padre Martini, CMBM BO 1.18.152–67, and in G. B. Martini, *Carteggio inedito*, ed. F. Parisini, Bologna, 1888, pp. 321–3; Lindgren, 'Gaetano Berenstadt'; Ghezzi, caricature of Andrea Adami, BAV Cod. Ottob. Lat. 3114 c. 120.

70 To Padre Martini from Chiti, 18 Feb. 1751, 8 Feb. 1752, from Ignazio Balbi, 27 Dec. 1758, from Elisi, 23 Jan. 1760, CMBM BO 1.6.1, 13, 1.9.50, 1.1.173.

71 L. Frati, 'Antonio Bernacchi e la sua scuola di canto', *RMI* 29, 1922, pp. 473–91; C. S[artori], 'Crescentini, Girolamo', *ES*; N. Lucarelli, 'Girolamo Crescentini: la vita, la tecnica vocale analizzata attraverso alcune sue arie tipiche' (tesi di laurea, University of Perugia, 1983–4).

72 G. Roncaglia, *La Cappella del Duomo di Modena*, Florence, 1957, pp. 197–204; A. Gandini, *Cronistoria dei teatri di Modena dal 1539 al 1871*, Modena, 1873, I, pp. 134–5; Giuliani's contracts, BE Mo MSS Campori App. 2447.

73 Faustini-Fasini, 'Astri maggiori', part 1, pp. 310–16; Balatri, *Frutti del mondo*; Busi, *Padre Martini*, pp. 31–62, 140–86.

74 Gasparo Pacchierotti to Giuseppe Micali, 19 Feb. 1819, BN NA MSS x.AA.27(161).

75 Ricci, *Figure e figuri*, pp. 73–87; M. F. Robinson, *Naples and Neapolitan Opera*, Oxford, 1972, pp. 61–2; Heriot, *Castrati in Opera*, pp. 143–51.

76 G. A. Angelini Bontempi, *Historia musica*, Perugia, 1695, pp. 239–40.

77 Words anonymous [?by Francesco Melosio], music by Fabrizio Fontana; performed by the Ensemble Sergio Vartolo at 14th Congress of the International Musicological Society, Bologna 28 Aug. 1987.

78 S. Rosa, 'Satira I: la musica', quoted in Celani, 'Musica e musicisti in Roma', pt 1, p. 13; G. Parini, 'Il teatro', in his *Poesie e prose*, ed. L. Caretti, Milan-Rome, no date, pp. 331–7, lines 70–2.

79 Quoted in MS of speech by a late nineteenth-century director of the Conservatorio [?Pietro Platania], BSPM NA 5.5.6[31].

80 'La musica', Parini, *Poesie e prose*, pp. 202–5, lines 1–6, 85–90.

81 Baldasare Angelini to Padre Martini, 1741–3, CMBM BO I.4.135, 146, 154.

82 Letters of 1746 and 1749, in Martini, *Carteggio inedito*, pp. 194, 208, and G. Rostirolla, 'La corrispondenza fra Martini e Chiti', in *Padre Martini: Musica e cultura nel Settecento europeo*, Florence, 1987, pp. 211–75: 232–3. For Martini's cordial relations with castrati, P. Petrobelli, 'The Italian years of Anton Raaff', *Mozart-Jahrbuch* 1973–4, pp. 233–73:271–2.

83 Balatri, *Frutti del mondo*; A. G. Bragaglia, 'Degli "evirati cantori"', *Amor di libro* 5–7, 1957–9:7, pp. 79–81 (prints in full Rolli's and Senesino's letters in BCI SI Autog. Porri fasc. XXXVI no. 4).

84 Metastasio, *Tutte le opere*, III, pp. 313–4, 565, 878, IV, pp. 725–6 (letters of 26 Aug. 1747, 15 Sept. 1750, 15 Dec. 1753, 1 May 1769).

85 *Ibid.* III, pp. 313–4, IV, p. 315 (letters of 26 Aug. 1747, 10 Oct. 1763).

86 Heriot, *Castrati in Opera*, pp. 27, 51–7; Haböck, *Kastraten*, pp. 302–11.

87 Croce, *Teatri di Napoli*, p. 205.

88 A. Ademollo, *La più famosa delle cantanti italiane della seconda metà del secolo XVIII (Caterina Gabrielli)*, Milan, 1890, pp. 10, 27.

89 Haböck, *Kastraten*, pp. 435–6.

90 Stendhal, *Rome, Naples et Florence*, 1826 version, ed. V. Del Litto, Lausanne, 1960, p. 294; for Farinelli's discreet 'courting' of the prima donnas he sang with, Sacchi, *Vita di Carlo Broschi*, p. 16.

91 Balatri, *Frutti del mondo*, pp. 156–65.

92 Pistocchi to G. A. Perti, 5 May 1700, 21 Dec. 1701, 8 March, 7 June 1702, CMBM BO P.143.1, 2, 23, 71; Busi, *Padre Martini*, pp. 140–86.

93 Contract, 21 Jan. 1704, ASBO Archivio Notarile 5–1–1 (*notaio* Benazzi Filippo, no. 7); Pistocchi to Perti, 8 March, 3 May 1702, CMBM BO P.143.57, 71; S. Mazzetti, *Repertorio di tutti i professori antichi, e moderni della famosa Università e del celebre Istituto delle Scienze di Bologna*, Bologna, 1847, p. 227.

94 See notes 68, 70.

95 Marcello, *Teatro alla moda*, p. 32.

96 Delille, *Famille et propriété*, pp. 355–60.

3 WOMEN

1 The subject has been little investigated but for some facetious anecdotal accounts by late nineteenth-century historians. A rare modern treatment (of the decades on either side of 1600) is A. Newcomb, 'Courtesans, muses, or musicians?', in Bowers and Tick, eds., *Women Making Music*, pp. 90–115.

2 Croce, *Teatri di Napoli*, pp. 368–73.

3 Filippo Livigni, *I due castellani burlati*, Bologna, 1785, quoted in Cosentino, *La Mignatta*, pp. 21–2 (where misattributed to Goldoni).

4 Pietro Aretino, *Lettere*, I, p. 105, quoted in A. Einstein, *The Italian Madrigal*, Princeton, 1949, I, pp. 94–5.

5 Zaccaria Tevo, *Il musico testore*, Venice, 1706, p. 22.

6 Benoit, *Versailles et les musiciens du Roi*, pp. 44, 252–3, 257.

7 Notes by Giustino Martinoni on singers at Teatro ss. Giovanni e Paolo, Venice, 1663, in S. Mamy, introduction to A. Zeno, D. Lolli, and G. Giacomelli, *La Merope* (*Drammaturgia musicale veneta* XVIII), Milan, 1984, p. xv.

8 Luisa Sanches's note, forwarded to Mazarin 7 Aug. 1644, in Prunières, *Opéra italien en France*, p. 57 (note).

9 Bragaglia, 'Degli "evirati cantori"' 5, pp. 74–6.

10 Croce, *Teatri di Napoli*, pp. 341–2.

11 *Gaceta Musical* (Buenos Aires), 15 May 1875.

12 G. Ward and R. Whiteing, *Both Sides of the Curtain*, London, 1918, pp. 29–33.

13 Count Alessandro Zambeccari to his brother Francesco, 30 June 1728, 24 Oct. 1731, BU BO MSS 92/II/18.

14 Croce, *Teatri di Napoli*, p. 437.

15 *Ibid.*, pp. 384–5, 446.

16 Metastasio, *Tutte le opere*, IV, p. 601 (letter of 24 Feb. 1768); Hasse to Ortes, 31 Oct. 1767 (and similar commendations of Caterina Flavis and Anna De Amicis as 'good girls', 15 June 1768, 24 Dec. 1770), MCCV Cod. Cicogna 3197–8*bis*; Donizetti to Alessandro Gandini, 7 Oct. 1841, in L. F. Valdrighi, *Musurgiana*, Bologna, 1970, p. 452.

17 Petition of Agostino Del Bene, [1787], ASV Inquisitori di Stato b. 914, documenti vari.

18 Croce, *Teatri di Napoli*, p. 168.

19 *Ibid.*, pp. 175, 178, 180; Prota-Giurleo, *Teatri di Napoli*, pp. 293–303.

20 Kirkendale, 'Francesco Rasi', pp. 298–300.

21 Bianconi and Walker, 'Dalla *Finta Pazza*', pp. 440–4.

22 P. M. Capponi, 'L'educazione di una virtuosa nel secolo XVII', *Spettatore musicale* 3, 1968, pp. 12–15.

23 To Padre Martini from Pierantonio Tinelli, 1770, from Fra Nicol'Antonio Natalini, 1754, from Cristoforo Pritelli, 1775–6, CMBM BO I.10.83, I.9.1, 39, 55.

24 C. Sartori, 'La prima diva della lirica italiana: Anna Renzi', *NMRI* 2, 1968, pp. 430–52:450–1.

25 Prunières, *Opéra italien en France*, p. 139 (and see note 21).

26 Sir Bernard Gascoigne [Guasconi] to Henry Benett (First Secretary to Charles II), Castello [Venice] 7 June 1664, in M. Mabbett, 'Italian musicians in Restoration England (1660–1690)', *M&L* 67, 1986, pp. 237–47: 245.

27 A. Ademollo, 'La Giorgina', in *Fanfulla della domenica*, 1881, no. 49; Croce, *Teatri di Napoli*, pp. 201–3, 222 (note), 207–8, 210, 218.

28 F. Valesio, *Diario di Roma 1700–1742*, ed. G. Scano, Milan, 1977–9, I, pp. 14, 72, 93, 341, 385, II, p. 21.

29 F. Walker, 'Some notes on the Scarlattis', *Music Review* 12, 1951, pp. 185–203: 190–1.

30 Prota-Giurleo, *Teatri di Napoli*, pp. 307–13.

31 Scarabelli's 'conversion' by the saintly musician Paris Algisi is reported in a letter to Padre Martini from Fra Paolo Serafino Facconi, 8 July 1779, CMBM BO I.7.77 (i.e. long after the supposed event, which is not listed among Algisi's feats in the 'Catalogo degli aggregati' of the Accademia Filarmonica of Bologna, no. 249).

32 Croce, *Teatri di Napoli*, pp. 373–85, 445–8, 517, 564, 602–4, 701–2.

33 Count Francesco Zambeccari to his brother, 4 Sept. 1708, in L. Frati, 'Un impresario teatrale del Settecento e la sua biblioteca', *RMI* 18, 1911, pp. 64–84:68.

34 Strohm, 'Aspetti sociali', pp. 126–7; Petrobelli, 'Teatro settecentesco', p. 423.

35 B. Croce, *Un prelato e una cantante nel secolo XVIII*, Bari, 1946, p. 41–3, 52–3; K. von Dittersdorf, *Autobiography*, New York, 1970, pp. 16–25.

36 *DNB*; *The Complete Peerage*, ed. G. E. C[okayne] and V. Gibbs, s. v. Peterborough; L. Lindgren, 'Parisian patronage of performers from the Royal Academy of Musick (1719–1728)', *M&L* 68, 1977, pp. 4–28:15–16.

37 Diary of Giovanni Cosimo Rossi-Melocchi, quoted in C. E. Troy, *The Comic Intermezzo*, Ann Arbor, 1979, pp. 49–54, 188–90 (where translated somewhat differently).

38 Frati, 'Un impresario teatrale', p. 78.

39 Croce, *Teatri di Napoli*, p. 327; 'Selbstbiographie von Gertrud Elisabeth Mara', cols 596, 609.

40 Ademollo, *Caterina Gabrielli*; Vianello, *Teatri a Milano*, pp. 193–5.

41 Metastasio, *Tutte le opere*, IV, pp. 68–9 (letter of 23 Sept. 1758).

42 Burney, *General History*, II, pp. 881–2; *The Early Diary of Fanny Burney 1768–1778*, ed. A. R. Ellis, London, 1907, II, p. 115.

43 E. Salucci, *Manuale della giurisprudenza dei teatri*, Florence, 1858, pp. 39–42; P. Ascoli, *Della giurisprudenza teatrale*, Florence, 1871, pp. 89–100; N. Tabanelli, *Il codice del teatro*, Milan, 1901, pp. 25–7.

44 E. Rosmini, *La legislazione e la giurisprudenza dei teatri*, Milan, 1872, I, pp. 361–7.

45 A. Ghislanzoni, *Gli artisti da teatro*, Milan, 1865, book VI, ch. 4.

46 *Il Palcoscenico* (Naples), 30 Sept. 1848, in *100 anni di vita del Teatro San Carlo 1848–1948*, Naples, 1948, pp. 184–5.

47 Celani, 'Musica e musicisti in Roma', pt 2, pp. 86–8.

48 *Ibid.* pt 3, pp. 26–9; G. Radiciotti, *Gioacchino Rossini: vita documentata*, Tivoli, 1927–29, I, p. 23.

49 Walker, *Man Verdi*, pp. 48–95; M. De Angelis, *Le carte dell'impresario*, Florence, 1982, pp. 135–90; J. Budden, *Verdi*, London, 1985, pp. 46–7.

50 Giovanni Migliavacca, 'Alla cantante Vittoria Tesi, per un fatto occorsole alla villa del Principe Hilburgausen di Vienna a Hoffen', BU BO MSS 3855 (S).

51 Lady Granville to her sister Lady Carlisle, 28 May 1827, in *Letters of Harriet Countess Granville*, ed. F. Leveson Gower, London, 1894, I, p. 410.

52 These paragraphs are based on Giuditta Pasta's and her family's extensive correspondence in LPA NY. See also K. A. Stern, 'A documentary study of Giuditta Pasta on the opera stage', PhD thesis, City University of New York, 1984; M. Ferranti Giulini, *Giuditta Pasta e i suoi tempi*, Milan, 1935; J. Rosselli, 'Vita e morte di Bellini a Parigi', *RIDM* 19, 1984, pp. 261–76: 270; P. Maes, *Un ami de Stendhal: Victor Jacquemont*, Paris, 1934.

53 Luigia Boccabadati to Carlo Del Chiaro, 1832–3, Piancastelli Autog. and BE MO MSS Campori App. 2447; Virginia Boccabadati to Luigi Ronzi, 23 Dec. 1854, Piancastelli Autog.

54 D. Concordia to Giovanni Marchetti, 14 Aug. 1870, Piancastelli Autog. s.v. Marchetti.

55 Erminia Frezzolini to her sister Amalia Marchetti, St Louis, no date but 1857–8, *ibid.*

56 B. de la Grange (Anna de la Grange's mother) to [?], no date, MTS Coll. Casati 340.

57 Mercadante to Francesco Florimo, 2, 30 Nov., 10 Dec. 1830, 12 Dec. 1831, in S. Palermo, ed., *Saverio Mercadante: biografia, epistolario*, Fasano, 1985, pp. 88–100, 119–22.

4 THE COMING OF A MARKET

1 Domenico Rodomonti to Giacomo Carissimi, 19 March 1639, in Culley, 'Influence of the German College', pt 2, pp. 46–7. This chapter is based partly on the last section of my article 'From princely service to the open market'.

2 P. Fabbri and R. Verti, *Due secoli di teatro per musica a Reggio Emilia*, Reggio Emilia, 1987.

3 B. Brumana and M. Pascale, 'Il teatro musicale a Perugia nel Settecento', Università di Perugia, Facoltà di Lettere e Filosofia, *Esercizi. Arte-musica-spettacolo* 6, 1983, pp. 71–134.

4 C. Ricci, *I teatri di Bologna*, Bologna, 1888, pp. 95–7.

5 C. Sartori, 'Profilo di una cantante', p. 459.

6 Antonio Vandini to Padre Martini, 21 Jan. 1738, CMBM BO I.23.111.

7 Antolini, 'Carriera di Loreto Vittori', p. 149; Bianconi and Walker, 'Dalla *Finta Pazza*', pp. 417–18.

8 Murata, 'Carnevale a Roma', pp. 91–2; Bouquet, *Musique et musiciens à Turin*, pp. 71–3.

9 Metastasio, *Tutte le opere*, III, pp. 932, 980, 1070–1; cf. C. Morales Borrero, *Fiestas reales en el reinado de Fernando VI*, Madrid, 1972, pp. 41, 43.

10 Ricci, *Teatri di Bologna*, p. 123.

11 N. Mangini, *I teatri di Venezia*, Milan, 1974, p. 107; G. Radiciotti, *Contributi alla storia del teatro e della musica in Urbino*, Pesaro, 1899, p. 10; *Gaceta Musical* (Buenos Aires), 25 July 1875.

12 Ortes to Hasse, 23 Jan. 1768, MCCV Cod. Cicogna 2658 no. 145.

13 Printed invitation to Pisaroni's benefit at Teatro del Corso, Bologna, 8 Aug. 1818, BARCH BO Avvisi di teatro.

14 Saliceti (Minister of Police at Naples) to Soprintendente dei Teatri, 18 Dec. 1809, ASN Teatri f. 146; poster advertising Maria Marcolini's benefit in Rome, 9 Nov. 1808, Biblioteca di Storia dell'Arte e Archeologia, Rome, Manifesti teatrali. See G. Valle, *Cenni teorico-pratici sulle aziende teatrali*, Milan, 1823, pp. 63–73; Rosselli, *Opera Industry*, p. 183.

15 Bagnacavallo leaflets, 1900, Piancastelli 30.50.

16 Francesco Belisani to Ubaldo Zanetti, 7 Feb. 1722, BU BO MSS 3917.

17 *Gaceta Musical* (Buenos Aires), 4, 25 July 1875 (benefit of Maddalena Mariani Masi); *El Derecho* (Carácas), quoted in *Annuario dell'arte lirica e coreografica italiana*, Milan, 1897–8, p. 183 (benefit of Maria De Nunzio).

18 Contract with Signora Girolama, ASV Scuola Grande di S. Marco b. 188 c. 22; cf. Mangini, *Teatri di Venezia*, p. 60.

19 Paolo Rolli to Francesco Bernardi (Senesino), 23 Jan. 1729, BCI SI Autog. Porri f. XXVI no. 4.

20 'Nota di spese fatte dall'impresario Antonio Mango per servizio del Teatro Capranica nell'anno 1732', ASCR FC 538/a; Croce, *Teatri di Napoli*, p. 493.

21 Weaver and Weaver, *Chronology of Music in the Florentine Theater*, pp. 76–81.

22 Valle, *Cenni teorico-pratici*, pp. 76–81.

23 G. B. Bonola to Lanari, 10 Feb. 1848, BNF CV 349/106.

24 Pacifico Balducci to Lanari, 1833, *ibid.* 346/36.

25 R. Verti, 'The *Indice de' teatrali spettacoli*, Milan, Venice, Rome 1764–1823: preliminary research on a source for the history of Italian opera', *Periodica Musica* 3, 1985, pp. 1–7.

26 Abate Vincenzo Grimani to Polo Michiel, 23 March, 27 April, 6, 17 July 1675, MCCV MSS PD C1062 c. 348, 394, 475, 481.

27 Carlo Mazzini to Faustini, 12 Dec. 1665, ASV Scuola Grande di S. Marco b. 188 c. 373; figures for 1840s derived from post times in correspondence of Alessandro Lanari, BNF CV.

28 Faustini's contracts with singers, 1650s–60s, ASV Scuola Grande di S. Marco b. 188 c. 22, 204, b. 194 c. 12, 28, 29, 32, 40; Mangini, *Teatri di Venezia*, p. 60.

29 Contracts between Faustini and Lucietta Gomba detta Vidmana, 18 July 1659, in Brunelli, 'Impresario in angustie', p. 314; Milhous and Hume, eds., *Vice-Chamberlain Coke's Theatrical Papers*, pp. 120–1; Lucrezia Baldini's contracts with Vivaldi for Teatro S. Angelo, Venice, C1727, in F. Degrada and M. T. Muraro, eds., *Antonio Vivaldi. Da Venezia all'Europa*, Milan, 1978, p. 82, and with P. Navaglia for Brescia, C1730, ASV Avogaria di Comun Misc. Civile 4099/352/13; Rome contracts between the impresario Carlo Buttelli and the singer Mario Bondichi for puppet opera at Teatro dei Granari di S. Agnese, C1732, and between the impresarios Giuseppe Polvini Faliconti and Scipione Coccetti for lease of Teatro Pace, 8 April 1732, ASR Tribunale Civile del Governatore b. 265, cedulae et iura diversa, Notai del Tribunale del Governatore (notaio Giuseppe M. Grilli) b. 15 c.163^r–165^v, 192^r–193^r.

30 Causa De Santis-Gabrielli, 1769, ASCR FC f. 451.

31 Contracts for seasons in 1754 and 1755 between the owners of the Teatro del Cocomero, Florence, and Domenico and Anna De Amicis, ASCF Accademia degli Infuocati f. 8371; printed contract forms of 1767, BE MO MSS Campori App. 2447, of 1780 in ASV Inquisitori di Stato b. 914, ASN Casa Reale Antica f. 965–71.

32 Brunelli, 'Impresario in angustie', p. 331.

33 Carlo Mazza to Padre Martini, 16 Feb. 1738, CMBM BO I.23.99.

34 Rosselli, *Opera Industry*, p. 126.

35 Roberto Stagno to Carlo D'Ormeville, 27 Jan. 1888, MTS Coll. Casati 1087.

36 R. Giazotto, 'La guerra dei palchi', *NRMI* 1, 1967, pp. 245–86, 465–508, *ibid.* 3, 1969, pp. 906–33: 929–32; accounts of failed Venetian season, 1760s, ASV Inquisitori di Stato b. 914, untitled fasc.

37 Metastasio, *Tutte le opere*, III, pp. 6–7 (letter of 24 April 1757); O. E. Deutsch, ed., *Handel, a Documentary Biography*, London, 1955, p. 237.

38 To Padre Martini from Gaetano Guadagni, 23 Jan. 1774, from Placido Mazzafera, 17 Sept. 1779, CMBM BO I.4.62, I.14.172.

39 G. Roncaglia, 'La musica alla Corte Estense dal 1707 alla costituzione del Regno d'Italia', *Atti e memorie della Deputazione di Storia Patria per le antiche province modenesi*, ser. 10, 1, 1966, pp. 259–77: 275–6; V. Tardini, *I teatri di Modena*, 1898–1902, III, s.v. Federico Fedi, Lodovico Verri, Alfonso Pareschi, Paolo Borgetti.

40 Giuseppina Strepponi to Avvocato Maestri, 3 Jan. 1843, BE MO MSS Campori App. 2447.

41 ASV Scuola Grande di S. Marco b. 194 c. 24 (contract, 5 May 1652, between the impresario M. Faustini, two other partners, and the singer Polifillo Zancardi to put on five seasons at Teatro S. Cassiano, Venice), Avogaria di Comun Misc. Civile 4099/352/13 (contract, 6 Oct. 1726, between the singer Lucrezia Baldini and the impresario Pietro Navaglia for a season at Brescia; payment in boxes to a value of 100 zecchini); L. Moretti, 'Documenti e appunti su Sebastiano Ricci', *Saggi e memorie di storia dell'arte*, Florence, 1976, pp. 97–125:115–16 (Faustina Bordoni's investment of 3,000 ducats in her own season at Teatro S. Cassiano, Venice, c1729).

42 Contracts and other documents concerning Venice *imprese a carato*, ASV Capi del Consiglio dei X, Mazzetti, b. 2, 19 April 1757 (F1757, Teatro S. Salvador), Notarile Atti reg. 4288 c. 170^v–173^v (F1757, theatre to be determined), 4289 c. 253^v–256^r, 261^r–266^r, 294^r–295^r, 300^r–304^v, *passim*, 322^r–329^v, *passim*, 343^{rv}, 353^r–356^v, *passim*, 358^v–362^r, 369^v–370^v (F1758, S. Salvador and S. Samuele), 4290 c. 431^r–433^v (A–C1758–9, S. Moisè), 492^r–498^v (F1759, S. Salvador and S. Angelo), 4291 c. 618^v–630^v, *passim* (F1760, S. Salvador), 735^v–736^v, 749^r–750^r (F1761, S. Angelo), 4292 c. 909^r–911^v, 923^r, 929^r–932^v, *passim* (F1762, S. Angelo). See also Mangini, *Teatri di Venezia*, p. 119 (F1765, theatre to be determined).

43 G. Morelli and T. Walker, 'Tre controversie intorno al S. Cassiano', in Muraro, ed., *Venezia e il melodramma del Seicento*, pp. 97–120.

44 Pietro Camuri to Lanari, 29 Nov. 1823, BNF CV 352/106 (reporting answer of Isabella Fabbrica's father to offer for Teatro La Pergola, Florence).

45 Francesco Piccoli to Padre Martini, 29 April 1766, CMBM BO I.9.7.

46 C. Ehrlich, *The music profession in Britain since the eighteenth century*, Oxford, 1987, pp. 76–9; F. Degrada, 'L'opera napoletana', in *Storia dell'opera*, ed. A. Basso and G. Barblan, Turin, 1977, I, p. 260.

5 TRAINING

1 This was noticed by F. Chrysander, 'Lodovico Zacconi als Lehrer des Kunstgesanges', *Vierteljahrschrifte für Musikwissenschaft* 7, 1891, pp. 337–96, 9, 1893, pp. 249–310: 277.

2 Outdated but still useful: N. Tamassia, *La famiglia italiana nei secoli decimoquinto e decimosesto*, Milan, 1910. P. Ginsborg, *A History of Contemporary Italy. Society and Politics 1943–1988*, Harmondsworth, 1990, gives the family unusual and welcome importance.

3 Contract between the tenor Giuseppe Tibaldi and his father, June 1771, CMBM BO H.63 c.1^{r-v}. I owe this reference to Sergio Durante.

4 A. De Angelis, 'Erminia e Giuseppe Frezzolini', *RMI* 32, 1925, pp. 438–54; obituary of Erminia from unidentified newspaper, 9 Nov. 1884, Piancastelli Autog.

5 To Giovanni Morandi from Natale Costantini, no date but 1845, from Carolina Cuzzani Costantini, 11, 15 Sept. 1846, Piancastelli 407.133–6.

6 M. J. Phillips Matz, 'Generations: a work in progress', *Opera News* (New York), 30 Jan. 1988, pp. 26–9, 46.

7 Ghezzi, caricature of Giacomo Vitale singing at the Teatro Pace, Rome, and his uncle Antonio Amaducci, BAV Cod. Ottob. Lat. 3115 c. 144; see Petrobelli, 'Musicisti di teatro settecentesco', p. 419.

8 'Selbstbiographie von Gertrud Elisabeth Mara', cols 500–1, 513–14; E. Gorin Marchisio, *Le sorelle Marchisio*, Milan, 1930, pp. 17–26; R. Ponselle and J. A. Drake, *Ponselle*, New York, 1982, pp. 12–13.

9 Antonio Gianettini to the Duke of Modena's secretary, Venice 29 Jan. 1689/90, ASMO Mus b. 1/B.

10 C. Burney, *The Present State of Music in France and Italy*, London, 1771, p. 71; H. Taine, *Voyage en Italie*, Paris, 1884⁵, I, p. 100; F. Walker, *Letters of a Baritone*, London, 1895, pp. 224–5.

11 V. Manfredini, *Regole armoniche o sieno precetti ragionati per apprendere la musica*, Venice, 1775, p. 10 (note); Domenico Dragonetti's comments on Brigida Banti, quoted in Robbins Landon, *Haydn: Chronicle and Works*, III: *Haydn in England*, pp. 277–8; for the persistence in present-day Italy of singers unable to read music, P. Rattalino, *L'ente lirico va in trasferta*, Milan, 1983, p. 142.

12 R. Allegri, *Il prezzo del loro successo*, Milan, 1983, pp. 147–51.

13 E. Gara, *Caruso, storia di un emigrante*, Milan, 1947, pp. 15–21; ASV Capi del Consiglio dei Dieci, Mazzetti b. 1 (26 May 1751), and Notatorio Filze b. 49 (25 Sept. 1751); Vianello, *Teatri a Milano*, pp. 211–12.

14 Tamassia, *Famiglia italiana*, p. 257.

15 Rossini's letters to Nicola Ivanoff, 1840–53, Piancastelli 405.267–325, partly printed in G. Rossini, *Lettere*, ed. G. Mazzatinti and G. Manis, Florence, 1902, pp. 96–9, 101–2, 109–11, 134–52 *passim*.

16 Luigia Bendazzi to Federico Dallara, 1856–9, *passim*, Piancastelli 43.1–152; Angiolina Tiberini to [?], 18 March 1863, MTS Coll. Casati 1167. 'Figlio[lo]/a[la]' (son or daughter) was often applied to pupils in eighteenth-century conservatories and orphanages. The composer Quirino Gasparini's private pupils were referred to as his 'little conservatory': Gaspare Gasparini to Padre Martini, 21 Oct. 1778, CMBM BO L.117.63.

17 F. Walker, 'A chronology of the life and works of Nicola Porpora', *Italian Studies* 6, 1951, pp. 29–62; A. Salvagnini, *Il R. Conservatorio di S. Pietro a Majella in Napoli. Relazione*, Naples, 1914, pp. 93–4.

18 Walker, *Letters of a Baritone*, pp. 105–19.

19 This and the following paragraphs are based in part on my article 'L'apprendistato del cantante italiano: rapporti contrattuali fra allievi e insegnanti dal Cinquecento al Novecento', *RIDM* 23, 1988, pp. 157–81.

20 The teacher was Giacomo Guglielmi, son of the composer Pietro Guglielmi the elder: *Catalogo della collezione d'autografi lasciata alla R. Accademia Filar-*

monica di Bologna dall'abate . . . Masseangeli . . ., ed. E. Colombani, Bologna, 1881, s. v. Guglielmi.

21 Lucarelli, *Bruni*, pp. 28–9; Gara, *Caruso*, pp. 15–21.

22 Contract, 9 Nov. 1665, between Canon Bastian Enno and the impresario Marco Faustini, ASV Scuola Grande di S. Marco b. 188 c. 64.

23 Antonio Gianettini to the Duke of Modena, Venice 6 Feb. 1705/6, ASMO Mus b. 1/B.

24 A. Basso, *Il Conservatorio di musica 'Giuseppe Verdi' di Torino*, Turin, 1971, pp. 27–37, 227–9; G. Pannain, *Il R. Conservatorio di musica 'S. Pietro a Majella' di Napoli*, Florence, 1942, pp. 26, 29, 32–3; T. Chirico, 'La scuola di musica del R. Orfanotrofio Provinciale di Reggio Calabria e le istituzioni musicali napoletane', *NRMI* 21, 1988, pp. 462–91.

25 Edict of Innocent XI, 4 May 1686, in J. Bowers, 'Women composers in Italy 1566–1700', in Bowers and Tick, eds., *Women Making Music*, pp. 139–40.

26 L. M. Kantner, *Aurea Luce. Musik an St Peter in Rom 1790–1850*, Vienna, 1979, p. 142.

27 G. Vio, 'Precisazioni sui documenti della Pietà in relazione alle "Figlie del coro"', in F. Degrada, ed., *Vivaldi veneziano europeo*, Florence, 1980, pp. 101–22:118–20; *Il Conservatorio 'Benedetto Marcello' di Venezia 1876–1976*, ed. P. Verardo, Venice, 1977, pp. 152–3, and *ibid.*, pp. 189–95, P. Pancino, 'Il problema dei rapporti tra insegnamento e vita musicale a Venezia . . . i quattro conservatori'; M. V. Constable, 'The Venetian "Figlie del Coro": their environment and achievement', *M&L* 63, 1982, pp. 181–212; W. Osthoff, 'Pasquale Anfossi maestro d'oratorio', in M. T. Muraro, ed., *Metastasio e il mondo musicale*, Florence, 1986, pp. 275–313: 293; J. L. Berdes, 'Maddalena Lombardini-Sirmen virtuosa veneziana e la storia delle istituzioni concertistiche a Torino', in *Culture et pouvoir dans les Etats de Savoie du XVIIe siècle à la Révolution*, Paris, 1987, pp. 177–96.

28 Cordero di Pamparato, 'Un duca di Savoia impresario teatrale', pp. 238–9.

29 [J. E. Cox], *Musical Recollections of the Last Half-Century*, London, 1872, I, pp. 52–6; W. T. Parke, *Musical Memoirs*, London, 1830, II, p. 214; *Private Correspondence of Lord Granville Leveson Gower*, ed. Castalia Lady Granville, London, 1916, II, p. 311.

30 Kirkendale, 'Francesco Rasi', pp. 298, 302–3.

31 Busi, *Padre Martini*, pp. 26–30; S. Durante, 'Alcune considerazioni sui cantanti di teatro del primo Settecento e la loro formazione', in Bianconi and Morelli, eds., *Antonio Vivaldi*, II, pp. 427–81: 449–53; Pierleone Ghezzi, caricature of Paolo Boi, BAV Cod. Ottob. Lat. 3115 c. 137; Francesco Andrea Barbieri to Padre Martini, 5 Aug. 1768, CMBM BO 1.7.210.

32 Case of *Antonio Palella* v. *Flavia Muzzillo*, 1737, ASN Processi antichi, Tribunale dell'Uditore di Guerra e Casa Reale (no class mark at the time of consultation).

33 G. A. Ricieri to Padre Martini, 24 April 1733, in Martini, *Carteggi inediti*, p. 52; Pierleone Ghezzi, caricature of Francesco Maggiore, BAV Cod. Ottob. Lat. 3117 c. 36.

34 Correspondence between Padre Martini and A. Bernacchi, Nov. 1753, CMBM BO 1.18.161–2, 164.

35 The paragraphs dealing with Luigia Bendazzi (1826/7–1901) are based on Piancastelli 43.1–152, mainly correspondence addressed to Federico Dallara.

36 Heriot, *Castrati in Opera*, pp. 96, 111, 115, 121, 142, 162; Lucarelli, 'Girolamo Crescentini', p. 13.

37 Francesco Belisani to Ubaldo Zanetti, 4 Dec. 1720, in L. Frati, 'Musicisti e cantanti bolognesi del Settecento', *RMI* 21, 1914, pp. 189–202: 200; M. A. Pastura Ruggiero, 'Fonti per la storia del teatro romano nel Settecento', in *Il teatro a Roma nel Settecento*, Rome, 1989, II, pp. 505–87: 541, 548.

38 A. Lancellotti, *Le voci d'oro*, Rome, 1953, pp. 155–9.

39 Titta Ruffo, *La mia parabola*, Milan, 1937, pp. 51–6, 77–106, 111–19.

40 Stern, 'A documentary study of Giuditta Pasta', ch. 2 and pp. 1–7, 43–4, 71.

41 V. Carpi, *Al di qua e al di là dell'Atlantico*, Florence, 1909, pp. 1–4.

42 Stern, 'A documentary study of Giuditta Pasta', pp. 250–1. Similar emphasis on *perfezionamento* in Domenico Mombelli to Antonio Gandini, 10 June 1823, BE MO MSS Campori App. 2447. For Malibran, G. Cottrau, *Lettres d'un mélomane*, Naples, 1885, p. 18.

43 Interview with Nino Meneghetti, 21 June 1988.

44 M. Del Monaco, *La mia vita e i miei successi*, Milan, 1982, pp. 7–32, 36–7.

45 Angelini Bontempi, *Historia musica*, quoted in L. Bianconi, *Il Seicento* (*Storia della musica*, IV), Turin, 1982, p. 63; similar timetables at Versailles, Benoit, *Versailles et les musiciens du Roi*, pp. 250–2, and at the Naples conservatory in 1819, F. Pastura, *Bellini secondo la storia*, Parma, 1959, p. 47.

46 Walker, *Letters of a Baritone*, p. 118; 'Lucius', *American and Italian Cantatrici; or, a Year in the Singing Schools of Milan*, London, 1867.

47 P. F. Tosi, *Opinioni de' cantori antichi e moderni*, ed. A. Della Corte as *Canto e bel canto*, Turin, 1933 (1st edn Bologna, 1723), pp. 41–2.

48 D. Bispham, *A Quaker Singer's Recollections*, New York, 1920, pp. 88–9; similar account in F. Litvinne, *Ma vie et mon art*, Paris, 1933, p. 16.

49 C. Pancaldi, *Vita di Lorenzo Gibelli*, Bologna, 1830, pp. 34–5.

50 Sample complaints: F. Taglioni, *Progetto di riforme musicali didattiche, chiesastiche, teatrali*, Naples, 1861 (in ASN Teatri b. 53); V. Ricci, 'La cultura del cantante italiano', *La critica musicale* 1, 1918, pp. 93–8; V. Buonassisi, *Il musicista, il cantante*, Florence, 1960, pp. 14–22.

51 Letters of Adelaide Borghi-Mamo, 1838–83, MTS Coll. Casati 132–7; of Adelina Patti, 1864–1913, MOA NY, LPA NY; of Tancredi Pasero and Afro Poli, Carla Magda Fulli's printed repertoire, ATLaF Spettacoli 1938, Lettere 1950–1.

52 R. Donington, *The Interpretation of Early Music*, new version, London, 1974, p. 516.

53 E. V. Foreman, 'A comparison of selected Italian vocal tutors of the period circa 1550 to 1800', DMA dissertation, University of Illinois, 1969, p. 5.

54 S. Durante, 'Theorie und Praxis der Gesangsschulen zur Zeit Händels: Bemerkungen zu Tosis *Opinioni de' cantori antichi e moderni*', *Veröffentlichungen der Händel-Akademie* (Karlsruhe) 1, 1988, pp. 59–72: 60–5.

55 Elizabeth Grant of Rothiemurchus, *Memoirs of a Highland Lady*, ed. A. Tod, Edinburgh, 1988, II, pp. 84–6.

56 H. Goldschmidt, *Die italienische Gesangsmethode des XVII. Jahrhunderts und ihre Bedeutung für die Gegenwart*, Breslau, 1890, pp. 14–22, 28–38, 44–62, 63–78; Chrysander, 'Lodovico Zacconi', pt 1; Foreman, 'Selected Italian vocal tutors', pp. 99, 102; Claudio Monteverdi to Alessandro Striggio, 24 July 1627, in Monteverdi, *Lettere, dediche e prefazioni*, p. 267.

57 G. B. Mancini, *Pensieri, e riflessioni pratiche sopra il canto figurato'* in Della Corte, *Canto e bel canto* (1st edn Vienna, 1774); Manfredini, *Regole armoniche*, p. 5 (note); P. Petrobelli, 'Un cantante fischiato e le appoggiature di mezza battuta: cronaca teatrale e prassi esecutive alla metà del '700', *Studies in Renaissance and Baroque Music in Honor of Arthur Mendel*, Kassel, 1974, pp. 363–76; Robinson, *Naples and Neapolitan Opera*, pp. 100–5, 143–9.

58 G. Crescentini, 'Raccolta di esercizj per il canto all'uso del vocalizzo, con discorso preliminare', [*c.* 1810], BASCR A. Ms. 133; M. Perrino, *Osservazioni sul canto*, Naples, 1810; A. M. Pellegrini Celoni, *Metodo breve, e facile per conoscere il piantato della musica e sue diramazioni*, Rome, 1823, p. 16.

59 F. Lamperti, *Guida teorico-pratica-elementare per lo studio del canto*, Milan, [*c.* 1864], and *L'arte del canto in ordine alle tradizioni classiche ed a particolare esperienza*, Milan, [1883]; L. Giraldoni, *Guida teorico-pratica ad uso dell'artista cantante*, Bologna, 1864, and *Compendium. Metodo analitico, filosofico e fisiologico per la educazione della voce*, Milan, 1889; E. Panofka, *Voci e cantanti*, Sala Bolognese, 1984 (1st edn 1866); E. Delle Sedie, *Arte e fisiologia del canto*, Milan, 1876; M. García, *Traité complet de l'art du chant*, Paris-London, 1851³ (1st edn 1840). On García, see B. Marchesi, *Singer's Pilgrimage*, London, 1923, p. 17. Tevo, *Musico testore*, pp. 31–40, as early as 1706 dealt at length with the physiology of the throat, but in a spirit of Aristotelian classification, not as a guide to vocal practice.

60 Delle Sedie, *Arte e fisiologia del canto*, pp. 98–119; N. Mari, *Canto e voce. Difetti causati da un errato studio del canto*, Milan, 1970² (1st edn 1959).

61 E. Imbimbo, *Observations sur l'enseignement mutuel appliqué à la musique*, Paris, 1821, pp. 35–44; Lamperti, *Guida teorico-pratico-elementare*, pp. vii–viii; Panofka, *Voci e cantanti*, pp. 77–9, 84–6.

62 Replies from Antonio Cotogni, Adelaide Borghi-Mamo, Antonietta Fricci, Enrico Delle Sedie, Giulia Grisi, Antonio Poggi to inquiry from the Bologna writer Ferdinando Guidicini, 1869, Piancastelli 407.245, 258, 276, 284, 307. In 1847 and 1863 the sopranos Erminia Frezzolini and Angiolina Tiberini asked their teachers for ornaments they could use in revivals of early nineteenth-century operas: MTS Coll. Casati 457, 1167.

63 M. E. Henstock, *Fernando De Lucia*, London, 1990, pp. 338–45.

64 C. Dalmas, *Guida pratica teatrale d'Italia*, Villafranca, 1907, pp. 15–17; *Guida Monaci*, Rome, 1909, pp. 986–8.

65 Walker, *Letters of a Baritone*, pp. 277–83.

66 E. Eames, *Some Memories and Reflections*, New York, 1927, pp. 50–6; M. Marchesi, *Aus meinem Leben*, Düsseldorf, 1888.

67 List of Marchesi's pupils, LPA NY Marchesi Coll. c/15. Caroline Smeroschi, described by Marchesi, *Aus meinem Leben*, pp. 142–3, as an Italian (and so spelt

by her), seems to have been Italian only by marriage: she appeared at the Teatro San Carlo, Naples, in 1881–2 under the name Smeroski Carbone. For the true extent of Melba's training by Marchesi (nine months, after seven years in Australia with the Italian Pietro Cecchi), W. R. Moran, ed., *Nellie Melba: a Contemporary Review*, London, 1986, pp. 41–58.

68 Marchesi, *Aus meinem Leben*, pp. 143, 238; Walker, *Letters of a Baritone*, p. 177.

69 L. Lehmann, *My Path through Life*, New York, 1914, p. 253.

70 G. B. Shaw, *Music in London 1890–94*, London, 1932, III, p. 241; Eames, *Some Memories*, pp. 50–6.

71 This and the following paragraphs are based on [L. Melzi], *Cenni storici sul R. Conservatorio di Musica in Milano*, Milan, 1873, 1878; L. Corio, *Ricerche storiche sul R. Conservatorio di Musica di Milano*, Milan, 1908; Basso, *Conservatorio di Torino*; Pannain, *Conservatorio di Napoli*; C. Sartori, *Il R. Conservatorio di Musica 'G. B. Martini' di Bologna*, Florence, 1942; *Parma. Conservatorio di Musica – studi e ricerche*, Parma, 1973; *Il Conservatorio 'Benedetto Marcello' di Venezia*.

72 A. Ghislanzoni, 'Del canto corale', *Gazzetta musicale di Milano* 22, 12 May 1867, pp. 145–7; M. Ruta, *Storia critica delle condizioni della musica in Italia e del Conservatorio di S. Pietro a Majella*, Naples, 1877, pp. 20–8.

73 E. De Amicis, *Francesco Tamagno: ricordi della sua vita e aneddoti inediti*, Palermo, 1902.

74 M. Calvetti, *Galliano Masini*, Leghorn, 1979.

75 Ruta, *Storia critica*, pp. 115–22.

76 The figures in *Conservatorio 'Benedetto Marcello' di Venezia*, pp. 282–92, leave out some external diplomas in singing, often taken by people who were internal students in another subject.

77 Titta Ruffo, *Mia parabola*; G. Borgatti, *La mia vita d'artista*, Bologna, 1927; B. Gigli, *Memorie*, Milan, 1957; G. Lauri-Volpi, *L'equivoco*, Milan, 1939; Del Monaco, *La mia vita*.

78 Sartori, *Conservatorio di Bologna*, pp. 16–22, 35–6, 48–52, 67, 90–100; royal decree no. 1945 of 11 Dec. 1930 in Buonassisi, *Musicista*, pp. 151–8.

79 Walker, *Letters of a Baritone*, pp. 27–30, 76–7, 96–8, 105–10, 132–4.

80 Interview with Eléna Arizmendi, Buenos Aires, 23 June 1988.

81 Mari, *Canto e voce*, p. 59.

6 PAY

1 Metastasio, *Tutte le opere*, III, p. 516 (letter of 2 May 1750).

2 A. J. Bloomfield, *The San Francisco Opera 1922–1978*, Sausalito, Calif., 1978, p. 76 (note).

3 Palermo, ed., *Mercadante*, p. 108.

4 BTBR DC cart. 3b (A, B) (lawsuit between Luigia Boccabadati and the heirs of the impresario Aniceto Pistoni; the case turned on whether payment was due for performances missed through illness). See Rosmini, *Legislazione dei teatri*, I, pp. 468–70, 509, II, p. 27.

5 Adam Smith, *The Wealth of Nations*, quoted in Ehrlich, *Music Profession in England*, p. 76; J. Ebers, *Seven Years of the King's Theatre*, London, 1828, pp. 48–9.

6 Giuseppe Giusti, 'Per il reuma d'un cantante', 1841.

7 A. Basso, ed., *Storia del Teatro Regio di Torino*, Turin, 1976–82, I, p. 267 (note).

8 Duca di Corleto, preface to libretto of Gluck's *Paride ed Elena*, Naples, 1777, quoted in Degrada, 'L'opera napoletana', in *Storia dell'opera*, ed. Basso and Barblan, I/I, p. 260.

9 Accounts in U. Prota-Giurleo, 'Breve storia del teatro di corte e della musica a Napoli nei secoli XVII–XVIII', in *Il Teatro di Corte del Palazzo Reale di Napoli*, Naples, 1952, pp. 3, 42.

10 Lanari to Donizetti, 25 Feb. 1837, *Studi Donizettiani* 3, 1978, p. 42.

11 G. Depanis, *I concerti popolari e il Teatro Regio di Torino*, Turin, 1914–15, II, pp. 40–1; Henry Abbey's Day Book, MOA NY (detailed accounts of Patti's and other US tours); Patti to Edward Hall, 23 Dec. 1893, LPA NY.

12 A. Scalaberni to G. Marchetti, Nov. 1889, Piancastelli Autog. s.v. Marchetti.

13 Contract with Elisa Polli for Teatro Castelli, Milan, P1875, MTS contratti Canedi.

14 Accounts of season at Teatro Apollo, Rome, 1874–5, ASCR tit. xv (*cause eredi Jacovacci*, 1881) (the leading singers were Ernesto Nicolini and Emma Wiziak); A. De Maddalena, *Prezzi e mercedi a Milano dal 1701 al 1860*, Milan, 1974, II, p. 420.

15 *Annuario dell'arte lirica italiana*, 1940, quoted in G. Feliciotti, *Adriana Guerrini, una voce che ritorna*, Bologna, 1980, p. 15.

16 *Il teatro italiano. Anno 1913*, Milan, 1914, pp. 226–32, 296–7.

17 C. Santley, *Student and Singer*, London, 1892, pp. 89–90.

18 Contract with Michele Trojani, of L'Aquila, for Teatro Pallacorda, Rome, C1758, ASR Notai della Curia del Governatore uff. 35 vol. 122 c. 594ʳ; A. Gazzuoli to Lanari, 1837, BNF CV 364/144.

19 Giazotto, 'Guerra dei palchi', pt 1, pp. 494–7; further evidence of difficulty in getting payment from the Grimani theatres in Venice in Antonio Cottini to Duke of Modena, March 1691, to Duke's secretary, 26 July 1691, minute of secretary's letter, [1692] (summaries by nineteenth-century archivist), ASMO Mus b. 2. See Marcello, *Teatro alla moda*, p. 29; M. A. Pastura Ruggiero, 'Per una storia del teatro pubblico in Roma nel secolo XVIII. I protagonisti', and 'Fonti per la storia del teatro romano del Settecento nell'Archivio di Stato di Roma', in *Il teatro a Roma nel Settecento*, Rome, 1989, I, pp. 453–86:477, II, pp. 505–87:560–1, 576; A. Cametti, *Il Teatro di Tordinona poi di Apollo*, Tivoli, 1938, II, pp. 389–94; Rosselli, *Opera Industry*, pp. 101–3.

20 A. Colombati to G. Marchetti, 6 Feb. 1885, Piancastelli Autog. s. v. Marchetti.

21 Contracts, 1840, with Nina Silvestri and Leopoldo Massa, petition by Gaetano De Felice to Minister of the Interior, 27 Aug. 1834, and other papers concerning Teatro La Fenice, Naples, ASN Teatri f. 146.

22 The Rome Court of Appeal ruled in 1903 that, on a literal reading of the contract, the Rome city council as landlord of the Teatro Argentina was entitled to withhold the whole of the caution money deposited by the impresario Guglielmo Canori for the CQ1899 season (cut short by his failure). Lawyers for the council argued that

the money was intended to secure the performance of the impresario's obligations as tenant, and that artists were aware of the risks they ran and must look out for themselves: sentence, 9 July 1903, ASCR tit. XV (*causa* Canori; refers to similar sentence, 1899, in *causa* Monaldi). Cf. Rosselli, *Opera Industry*, p. 113.

23 P. F. Tosi to Duke of Modena, 1687, ASMO Mus b. 1/B; Valle, *Cenni teorico-pratici*, pp. 51–8.

24 Lehmann, *My Path through Life*, pp. 275, 320; G. Nicolesco to [?], Odessa 27 Oct. 1881, MTS Coll. Casati 877.

25 Bonci and Borgatti contracts for Barcelona and Alexandria, 1897–8, Valentino Fioravanti's contracts of 1873 and 1875, MTS Coll. Casati 111, 121–4, 494–5; Isabella Galletti Gianoli to Tito Ricordi, 19 Oct. 1874, AR MI.

26 Account of payment to Camilla Balsamini, MTS; G. Boccolari and A. Selmi, 'Monete e cambi nel Ducato di Modena dal 1819 al 1859', *Archivio economico del Risorgimento italiano* III–IV, f. 3; Valle, *Cenni teorico-pratici*, pp. 51–8.

27 The tenor Enrico Barbacini stated in 1878 that 40,000 gold francs were equivalent to 44,000 paper francs: to Giulio Ricordi, 21 Nov. 1878, AR MI. More generally, see E. L. Dulles, *The French Franc 1914–1928*, New York, 1929. The calculations in the following pages are based on the exchanges in the essays on the pre-unification states in *Archivio economico del Risorgimento italiano*, on E. Martinori, *La moneta*, Rome, 1915, and on actual exchange rates named in contemporary documents.

28 Paolo Rolli to Francesco Bernardi, 23 Jan., 4 Feb. 1729, BCI SI Autog. Porri f. XXVI no. 4. See Deutsch, ed., *Handel, a Documentary Biography*, p. 237.

29 Masotti's 400 doppie = L.ven. 10,800. Her Vienna salary was Florins 1,500 (L.ven. 6,255 at a hypothetical rate, worked out from later exchanges, of Fl.1 = L.ven. 4.17), then, from 1677, Fl. 1,860 (L.ven. 7,756).

30 Gambassi, *Cappella musicale di San Petronio*, pp. 24–32, and part 2; Colombani, ed., *Catalogo della collezione Masseangeli*, s.v. Goccini.

31 Termini, 'Singers at San Marco', *passim*; Gaetano Latilla to Padre Martini, 2, 9 Nov. 1765, CMBM BO 1.22.178–9; ASV Inquisitori di Stato b. 914, Teatro S. Samuele (payment of L. ven. 1,650 (= just over 266 ducats) to each of the two bassi buffi Domenico Poggi and Giovanni D'Antoni, one for A1785, the other C1786).

32 Salary payments, 1752–68, ASN Scrivania di Ragione reg. 38; monthly returns by Maestro di Cappella or Governatore, 1737–65, *ibid*. Casa Reale Amministrativa 343 IIb, III; Prota-Giurleo, 'Teatro di Corte', pp. 92–3; Croce, *Teatri di Napoli*, pp. 348, 507.

33 Fürstenau, *Musik und Theater am Hofe von Sachsen*, I, pp. 254–67, 279–80, 291, 297, 306, 309–10, II, pp. 12–19, 50–3, 105–6, 111, 132–6, 142–3, 160–1, 165–6, 172, 204, 239, 272–5. (The salaries quoted for Senesino and the Lottis are for 1717–18. They received slightly less for 1719–20).

34 R. Engländer, 'Zur Musikgeschichte Dresden gegen 1800', *Zeitschrift für Musikwissenschaft* 4, 1922, pp. 199–241: 221–31.

35 Mangini, *Teatri di Venezia*, p. 124. (See Table 4.)

36 Croce, *Teatri di Napoli*, pp. 348, 445 (Duc. 1,004–2–5 to Teresa Baratti, contralto, Teatro S. Carlo, 1739–40; estimated Duc. 400 to 500 (about Fcs 1,740 to 2,175) a year to Monti).

37 Accounts for Teatro del Cocomero, Florence, seasons A1754–5, P1757–8–9, ASCF Accademia degli Infuocati f. 8371 (maximum fees of 120 zecchini paid jointly to the young prima buffa Anna De Amicis and to her father the primo buffo Domenico De Amicis, 1754 (= 120 francesconi or 672 francs each); of 60 zecchini to the prima donna Maria Ranaldi, 1757; other fees ranging from 25 francesconi for the *ultima parte* (utility) to 110 francesconi; in 1758–9, Francesco Baglioni and his three daughters collectively were paid 300, then 360 francesconi); accounts of two seasons at Teatro S. Samuele, Venice, A1785–C1786, ASV Inquisitori di Stato b. 914 (fees ranging between L. ven. 1,210 and 3,520 for the two seasons together; a second woman appeared in A1785 only for L. ven. 550).

38 Fees paid to Rosa Pinotti (L. ven. 11,000 for each season) and Girolamo Marzocchi (L. ven. 10,000), P1805, C1806, ATLaF Consuntivi, Atti anteriori al 1818. (These, held in times of war and defeat, were poor seasons.)

39 García was paid Scudi 1,000, Zamboni Sc. 700, and the prima donna Geltrude Righetti-Giorgi Sc. 650; cf. fees of Sc. 1,100 and 900 paid to the prima donna Haeser and the tenor Tacchinardi in 1808, of Sc. 900 to the prima donna Ester Mombelli in 1822: M. Rinaldi, *Due secoli di musica al Teatro Argentina*, Florence, 1978, I.

40 G. Felloni, *Il mercato monetario in Piemonte nel secolo XVIII*, Milan, 1968, pp. 202–15. For the devaluation of currencies of account, see F. Braudel and F. Spooner, 'Prices in Europe from 1540 to 1750', *Cambridge Economic History of Europe*, IV, 1967, pp. 378–486.

41 Detailed price movements in De Maddalena, *Prezzi e mercedi*; R. Romano, *Prezzi, salari e servizi a Napoli nel secolo XVIII (1734–1806)*, Milan, 1965.

42 S. Paganelli, 'Repertorio critico degli spettacoli e delle esecuzioni musicali dal 1763 al 1966', in L. Trezzini, ed., *Due secoli di vita musicale*, Bologna, 1966, II, p. 5.

43 Croce, *Teatri di Napoli*, pp. 433–4.

44 Antonio Lanari to G. Marchetti, 3 Aug. 1861. Piancastelli Autog. s.v. Marchetti; Rosselli, *Opera Industry*, pp. 189–90.

45 Calculations of the fees per performance paid to leading singers, within six or eighteen months (i.e. while their standing was little changed), at the Teatro Regio, Turin, and at the Senigallia fair show ratios of 2.3:1 (Pasquale Potenza, Turin C1756, Senigallia F1757), 1.37:1 (Elizabeth Ferron, Turin C1822, Senigallia F1821), and 1.23:1 (Nicola Tacchinardi, Turin C1822, Senigallia F1822): Basso, ed., *Storia del Teatro Regio di Torino*, I, II; G. Radiciotti, *Teatro, musica e musicisti in Sinigaglia*, Milan, 1893; 'Attestato' by proxies for the associated impresarios of the Senigallia season, 3 May 1757, ASV Notarile Atti b. 4289 c. 201^r–202^v (*notaio* Marc'Antonio Cavagnis). These assume five performances a week in Turin and, at Senigallia, fifteen (eighteenth century) and twenty (nineteenth century) performances during the fair.

46 Rosselli, *Opera Industry*, pp. 59–65.

47 The table leaves out, as untypical, the 1834–6 seasons run by an ambitious joint-stock company with many noble shareholders; it employed Carolina Unger at Fcs 12,097 and Maria Malibran at Fcs 20,733 per month, though other salaries were on a more normal scale: Rosselli, *Opera Industry*, pp. 62, 106–7, and 'Artisti e impresari', in *Il Teatro di San Carlo*, Naples, 1987, I, pp. 27–60.

48 Habituation to inflated fees may explain why Gafforini five years later, during the post-war slump, turned down Fcs 6,000 to create Rosina in *Il barbiere di Siviglia*. Geltrude Righetti-Giorgi, who sang the part for just over half that, is remembered for it as the more successful Gafforini is not: Rinaldi, *Teatro Argentina*, I, pp. 492–9.

49 The average annual number of performances at the San Carlo in 1832–8 was 109 (of thirty-two different operas), at the Fondo seventy-nine (of twenty-four operas): J. Black, *Donizetti's Operas in Naples 1822–48*, London, 1982, p. 9–10.

50 Metropolitan Opera paybooks, MOA NY; contracts and other papers of Ebe Ticozzi, MTS CA 7454–80 (1923–4 engagements at L.1,000 a month, up to L.100 a day, or L.4,500 a season; maximum La Scala pay L.5,800 a day in 1956).

51 A. Maragliano, *I teatri di Voghera*, Casteggio, 1901, pp. 35–6.

52 Stern, 'A documentary study of Giuditta Pasta', p. 40.

53 E. C. Moore, *40 Years of Opera in Chicago*, New York, 1930, p. 253; G. Gatti-Casazza, *Memories of the Opera*, New York, 1941, pp. 302–3.

54 In Venice she agreed to sing five times a week in the last weeks of carnival.

55 Contract with the impresario Cesare Bellincioni for Teatro Brunetti, 13 March 1874, Piancastelli Autog. s.v. Frezzolini. Cf. Mark Twain's account of another Frezzolini comeback, *The Innocents Abroad*, New York, 1869, II, ch. 2.

56 Mongini contract, ASCM Sp. P. 112/1; cf. fee of Fcs 1,000 per performance paid to Teresa Stolz, Brescia, F1871: C. Sartori, *Franco Faccio e 20 anni di spettacoli di fiera al Teatro Grande di Brescia*, Milan, 1938, pp. 11–14. For Pasta and Malibran: Rosselli, *Opera Industry*, p. 65.

57 F. d'Arcais, 'L'industria musicale', *Nuova Antologia*, 1 May 1879.

58 MTS Coll. Casati 1082; Henstock, *De Lucia*, p. 255.

59 Fees for a season of sixty performances (ASCR tit. XV *causa eredi* Jacovacci, 1881):

		Fcs		Fcs
T	Nicolini	47,737	Anastasi	27,000
S	Wiziak	39,000	Pozzoni	26,000
Bar	Aldighieri	35,000	Lefranc	25,000

60 L. Feralli to G. Marchetti, Valladolid 28 March 1868, Piancastelli Autog. s.v. Marchetti.

61 Borgatti to D'Ormeville, 1896–7, MTS Coll. Casati 121–4.

62 Rosselli, *Opera Industry*, pp. 63–5; Morales Borrero, *Fiestas reales*, pp. 45–53.

63 This was Teresa Maciurletti: R. A. Mooser, *Annales de la musique et des musiciens en Russie au 18e siècle*, Geneva, 1951, I, pp. 97, 122, 142–5, 228–9, II, pp. 63–6, III, p. 774. Domenico Bruni had previously breached the R.3,500 maximum in 1787, when he was paid R.4,000 a year (about Fcs 17,000), but in 1791 the company was temporarily dissolved as too expensive: Lucarelli, *Bruni*, pp. 42–3.

64 Titta Ruffo, *Mia parabola*, pp. 268–70, 279–80.

65 Milhous and Hume, *Vice-Chamberlain Coke's Papers*, pp. 76–8, 120, 164, 179, 228–9; C. Price, 'Italian opera and arson in late eighteenth-century London', *JAMS* 42, 1989, pp. 55–107:76–7; E. Gibson, 'Earl Cowper in Florence and his correspondence with the Italian Opera in London', *M&L* 48, 1987, pp. 235–52:

244; F. C. Petty, *Italian Opera in London 1760–1800*, East Lansing, Mich., 1980, pp. 7–8.

66 G. Baretti, *Account of the Manners and Customs of Italy*, London, 1769, quoted in Petty, *Italian Opera in London*, pp. 9–10.

67 Tamburini's contract with the impresario Laporte, 4 April 1833, Piancastelli 638.73. For London fees in the 1820s, Ebers, *Seven Years of the King's Theatre*, pp. 12–13, 387ff.

68 St V. Troubridge, *The Benefit System in the British Theatre*, London, 1967, pp. 11–14 and *passim*; for the 1717 London opera season, Lindgren, 'Carriera di Gaetano Berenstadt', p. 45.

69 Troubridge, *Benefit System*, p. 20; Tamburini contract (see note 67).

70 Contracts with De Luca, Florencio Constantino, and Graziella Pareto for 1911 season at Teatro Colón, BMTC BA.

71 Members of the Musici Palatini (originally thirteenth-century town criers) included the well-known comic bass Pellegrino Gagiotti (trombone, 1719–22 or later) and the leading teacher of singing Antonio Mazzoni (1785): ASBO Archivio degli Anziani b. XXV. See O. Gambassi, 'Origine, statuti, ordinamenti del Concerto Palatino della Signoria di Bologna', *NRMI* 18, 1984, pp. 261–82, 469–502, 631–42.

72 U. Kirkendale, 'The Ruspoli Documents on Handel', *JAMS* 20, 1967, pp. 222–73: 255.

73 Henstock, *De Lucia*, pp. 11–14; B. Gigli, *Confidenze*, Rome, 1942, pp. 36–8. Rossini held out the possibility of lucrative Naples concerts to the tenor Pietro Cazzioletti: undated letter [*c.* 1816–21], Piancastelli 406.32.

74 Milhous and Hume, *Vice-Chamberlain Coke's Papers*, pp. 191–3.

75 Bordogni to G. B. Benelli, 14 Feb. 1830, in B. Cagli, 'Rossini a Londra e al Théâtre-Italien di Parigi', *Bollettino del Centro Rossiniano di Studi*, 1981, pp. 7–53: 52–3.

76 Tamburini to Laporte, 7 May 18[34 or 35], receipt, 24 July 1838, for Concert of Ancient Music appearance, Piancastelli 638.68, 72. See Ehrlich, *Music Profession in Britain*, pp. 40–1, 49.

77 She refused 20 guineas for Norwich, but in the end sang two concerts there: to Louisa Bacon, 10 Sept., to Mr Pettet, 7 Oct. 1822, Piancastelli Autog. s.v. Camporesi.

78 Cotogni to Ferdinando Guidicini, 27 Feb. 1870, Piancastelli 407.260; Francesco Graziani's contract for La Fenice, Venice, CQ1877, MTS Coll. Casati 647.

79 Pasta to her mother Rachele Negri, 9 July 1833, Pasta's list of her 1831 London engagements, LPA NY.

80 M. Strakosch, *Souvenirs d'un imprésario*, Paris, 1887, pp. 79–98. For Cuba: S. Ramírez, *La Habana artística: apuntos históricos*, Havana, 1891.

81 Badiali to Lanari, 28 June 1849, BNF CV 343/88 (fee of 24,000 Spanish colonnati (silver dollars) from Oct. 1849 to Feb. 1851); Rosselli, *Opera Industry*, p. 64; Table 4.

82 W. P. Ware and T. C. Lockard, *P. T. Barnum Presents Jenny Lind. The American Tour of the Swedish Nightingale*, Baton Rouge, La., 1980, pp. 14–15, 179–81.

83 G. B. Montrésor to G. Marchetti, 11 May 1863, Piancastelli Autog. s.v. Marchetti.
84 Henry Abbey's Day Book, MOA NY (but in 1894, ten opera performances in Mexico City with Tamagno brought in an average $2,214, probably because of the slump).
85 MTS Coll. Casati 922.
86 Monthly payments to Giuseppe De Luca (gold Fcs 22,000 rising to 25,000 over two seasons), the rising light soprano Graziella Pareto (12,500), the tenor Angiolo Pintucci (11,000 rising to 15,000), the bass Nazzareno De Angelis (11,000), the contralto Fanny Anitua (6,250), contracts for 1910/11 seasons, G. Lusardi's receipt for Anselmi's fee, Titta Ruffo to Consigli e C.ia, 12 Feb., 1 April 1910, BMTC BA.
87 Paybooks, MOA NY; I. Kolodin, *The Metropolitan Opera*, New York, 1966[4], pp. 163, 298, 369; Moore, *Opera in Chicago*, pp. 140–1; J. F. Cone, *Oscar Hammerstein's Manhattan Opera Company*, Norman, Okla., 1966, p. 199.
88 Ponselle and Drake, *Ponselle*, p. 56.

7 CAREERS

1 Faustina Capranica Guiccioli to Bartolomeo Capranica, Sept. 1842, in B. M. Antolini, 'Cronache teatrali veneziane: 1842–1849', *Musica senza aggettivi. Studi in memoria di Fedele d'Amico*, Florence, 1991, pp. 297–322:299. See J. Rosselli, 'Cuteness was all. Operatic Shirley Temples', *Opera* 40, 1989, pp. 30–4; Pastura Ruggiero, 'Fonti per la storia del teatro romano', pp. 565–6.
2 Maragliano, *Teatri di Voghera*, pp. 155, 168–9, 190–1, 196; G. Berutto, *I cantanti piemontesi*, Turin, 1972, p. 205. Pedamonti's stage name was Pedemonte.
3 D'Arcais, 'L'industria musicale'. Cf. C. de Boigne, *Petits Mémoires de l'Opéra*, Paris, 1857, p. 330.
4 G. Maccolini, *Della vita e dell'arte di Antonio Tamburini fino al giugno 1842*, Faenza, 1842 (in Piancastelli 638.100).
5 N. Angelucci, *Ricordi di un artista*, Rome-Milan, 1907, pp. 17–25.
6 Giovanni Marchetti's scrapbook, Piancastelli Autog.
7 Burney, *Music in France and Italy*, pp. 151–2; biography of Eugenia Tadolini in *Figaro* (Milan), 10 March 1847, and notice of her election to Accademia Filarmonica of Forlì, 25 June 1827, Piancastelli 434.3, 123; M. Picchi, *Un trono vicino al sol*, Ravenna, 1978, pp. 26–36.
8 Santley, *Student and Singer*, pp. 88–9.
9 To G. Marchetti from Signora Angiolini, 1883–5 (about Delfina Battaglia), from Lauro Rossi, 12 Oct. 186[?] (about la Zappa), Piancastelli Autog. s.v. Marchetti; Antonio Pieraccini to Antonio Alaimo, 9 Jan. 1857 (about la Francesconi), Piancastelli 391.90.
10 Luigia Morelli to Ippolito Canedi, 10 Jan. 1872 (about the tenor Bassini), Piancastelli 680.110.
11 Itala Florenza to Canedi, Savona 1 Feb. 1873, Piancastelli 672.151.
12 Johann Philipp Franz von Schönborn, Prince-Bishop of Würzburg, to Agostino Steffani, July 1720–March 1722, Fondo Spiga, vol. 29, Palazzo di Propaganda Fide, Rome (transcripts kindly communicated by Colin Timms).

13 Rosmini, *Legislazione dei teatri*, I, pp. 138–9, 140–2, 500–1, 519–20; II, pp. 11–18;
   Ebe Ticozzi's 1924 contract, MTS CA 7456; 1907 court ruling in *Rivista di diritto
   commerciale* (Milan) 7, 1909, pp. 338–44.
14 Carpi, *Al di qua e al di là*, pp. 14, 17 (Milan performance at Teatro Carcano); H.
   Panizza, *Medio siglo de vida musical*, Buenos Aires, 1952, pp. 36–7.
15 Correspondence between the impresario Achille Cicogna and Direzione of
   Teatro La Fenice, 25 Jan. 1891, ATLaF Spettacoli b. 72; M. Girardi and F. Rossi,
   eds., *Il Teatro La Fenice. Cronologia degli spettacoli 1792–1936*, Venice, 1989.
16 Cone, *Manhattan Opera Company*, p. 128–9.
17 Durante, 'Alcune considerazioni sui cantanti', pp. 431–3.
18 F. M. Piave to Verdi, 17 March 1865, *Studi Verdiani* 4, 1986–7, p. 165 (note).
19 P. E. Ferrari, *Spettacoli drammatico-musicali e coreografici in Parma*, Parma,
   1884, p. 175 (Teatro Ducale, C1833, impresario Claudio Musi, comic bass Guido
   Maggiorotti).
20 Gatti-Casazza, *Memories of the Opera*, pp. 192–3 (impresario Cesare Corti at La
   Scala, *c.* 1889).
21 Chevalier Fournel, régisseur of the Paris Opera, to Rosa Morandi, 18 Feb. 1817,
   Piancastelli 407.168. Morandi was singing at the Théâtre-Italien, which then
   came under the supervision of the Opera.
22 Rossini to N. Ivanoff, 30 July 1844, Piancastelli 405.297.
23 Arcangelo Cori ('Arcangelo del liuto') to M. Faustini, 8 Aug. 1665, ASV Scuola
   Grande di S. Marco b. 188 c. 91.
24 Amato Ricci to Napoleone Moriani, 21 July 1851, MTS CA 3670.
25 To I. Canedi from Virginia Pozzi Bramanti, Giuseppina Flori, Nicola Bellocchi,
   1869–74, Piancastelli 542.204, 672.153, 684.39; Margot Kaftal to D'Ormeville, 17
   June 19[?05], MTS Coll. Casati 684.
26 G. Marchetti's scrapbook, Piancastelli Autog. For relations between singers and
   agents: Rosselli, *Opera Industry*, pp. 135–52.
27 Settimio Malvezzi to G. Marchetti, 21 June 1866, Piancastelli Autog. s.v.
   Marchetti; similar sentiments in Nicola Tacchinardi to Lanari, 26 Feb. 1828, BNF
   CV 411/87.
28 Mario Tiberini to Giulio Ricordi, 17 Feb. 1871, AR MI.
29 F. Capranica Guiccioli to B. Capranica, 25 March 1844, in Antolini, 'Cronache
   teatrali veneziane', p. 308. The agent was Count Camillo Gritti, husband of the
   soprano Ester Mombelli.
30 Santley, *Student and Singer*, pp. 133–4, 136; similar contracts with Adelina Patti
   and Bianca Donadio in Strakosch, *Souvenirs d'un imprésario*, pp. 17, 182–3.
31 Rosmini, *Legislazione dei teatri*, II, ch. 10.
32 Muzio to Giulio Ricordi and Eugenio Tornaghi, 1882–5, AR MI (xeroxes in
   ISVP).
33 E. Forbes, *Mario and Grisi*, London, 1985, pp. 23–5; but cf. M. De Angelis, ed.,
   Le cifre del melodramma, Florence, 1982, I, p. 39. For partial renegotiation of the
   young Patti's five-year contract with Covent Garden, H. Klein, *The Reign of
   Patti*, New York, 1920, pp. 61, 77–8, 102–3.
34 Sisara Antonini to Lanari, 2 Sept. 1840, BNF CV 343/65.

35 G. Strepponi to Lanari, 23 June 1839, *Carteggi verdiani*, ed. A. Luzio, Rome, 1935–47, IV, pp. 275–6.

36 Moriani to Bartolomeo Merelli, 9 Jan. 1838, MTS CA 3645; G.-L. Duprez, *Souvenirs d'un chanteur*, Paris, 1883, p. 84.

37 I. Galletti Gianoli to T. Ricordi, 19 Oct. 1874, AR MI.

38 Lanari to Ercole Marzi, 15 April 1849, BNF CV 393/58 (about the tenor Achille Errani).

39 To M. Faustini from Carlo Vittorio Rotarii, 21 Aug., from C. Mazzini, 5 Dec. 1665, ASV Scuola Grande di S. Marco b. 188 c. 66–7, b. 194 c. 144, 157; V. Maurel to Canedi, 15 Aug. 1871, MTS Coll. Casati 835 (the other baritone was Gottardo Aldighieri).

40 Strakosch, *Mémoires d'un imprésario*, pp. 183–3.

41 Francesco Zanchi to M. Faustini, 23 Aug. 1654, ASV Scuola Grande di S. Marco b. 188 c. 14. Other examples: Brunelli, 'Impresario in angustie', pp. 317, 330; Rosselli, *Opera Industry*, pp. 132–4.

42 J. A. Pitt-Rivers, *The People of the Sierra*, Chicago, 1971[2], pp. 137, 139.

43 Alessandro Magotti to [Enrico] Giordani, 1880, BARCH BO Coll. Autog. xli 11.119.

44 A. Gazzuoli to Lanari, Dec. 1836, BNF CV 364/99.

45 Contracts for Malta, 1872–3, and for Teatro Regio, Turin, 1873, MTS Coll. Casati 1448, 1482; printed contract form used by impresa of Teatro S. Carlo, Naples, 1898, Piancastelli 548.17.

46 Pastura Ruggiero, 'Fonti per la storia del teatro romano del Settecento', p. 577.

47 Rosmini, *Legislazione dei teatri*, I, pp. 433–4, 436–44.

48 This and other customary practices in Valle, *Cenni teorico-pratici*, pp. 24–34, 85–8, 91, 107ff. A contract for Venice in c1667 proposed to the Roman Giulia Masotti required her to arrive in mid November, possibly because she would need to learn from scratch two leading parts with much recitative; but a contract with Giovanni Giacomo Biancucci for the same theatre in c1665 named 'the beginning of December': Brunelli, 'Impresario in angustie', p. 331; ASV Scuola Grande di S. Marco b. 194 c. 28.

49 *Protesta* by Prospero Olivieri (impresario of Teatro S. Angelo, Venice, AC1760–1) against Domenico Pacini, ASV Notarile Atti b. 4291 c. 699[rv]. Earliest known contractual clause (Rosa Morandi, 1822), Piancastelli 612.26.

50 Virginia Monticelli's contract for Teatro del Cocomero, Florence, A1754, ASCF Accademia degli Infuocati b. 8371.

51 Luigia Boccabadati's contracts for Teatro Valle, Rome, AC1828–9, and for La Scala, Milan, 1826, BTBR DC c. 3b (B); Lodovico Graziani's contract for Teatro Comunale, Bologna, A1860, ASC BO Dep. P. Sp. Tit. I rub. 1 (1860).

52 E.g. by the baritone Tito Gobbi: on show in the museum at Bassano del Grappa. Supplying one's own costumes was said to be normal for leading singers in a 1917 manual of theatrical practice, V. Soldani and P. Sibert, *Le imprese di teatro*, Turin, 1917, pp. 310–14. At the Teatro Colón, Buenos Aires, in 1910 Angiolo Pintucci had to provide his own costumes for five out of eighteen operas in his repertory, while the starrier Florencio Constantino had the option of doing so if he wished: contracts, BMTC BA.

53 To M. Faustini from Caterina Angiola Bottegli, Aug. 1667, from G. M. Donati, 23 July 1667, from Cavagnino, 20 Oct. 1665, ASV Scuola Grande di S. Marco b. 188 c. 170–1, 174, 208; Brunelli, 'Impresario in angustie', pp. 319–28, 336–8; Maria Lafon's contract for La Scala, CQ1860, ASCM Sp. P. b. 112/1.

54 Basso, ed., *Storia del Teatro Regio di Torino*, I, pp. 217–19; Metastasio to Anna De Amicis, 15 July 1765, *Tutte le opere*, IV, p. 397.

55 Valle, *Cenni teorico-pratici*, pp. 90–1.

56 S. Malvezzi to Giovanni Ricordi, 6, 10 May 1853, AR MI; 'Giornale delle prove e recite', Teatro Comunale, Bologna, ASBO Dep. P. Sp. Tit. I rub. 1 (1860) (the ballets in *Le Prophète*, including the skating ballet with its special technical requirements, had gone into rehearsal earlier).

57 *Proteste* by Count Francesco di Sarego [Serego] about Venice operas at Teatro S. Moisè, 24 Oct. 1759 (Giuseppe Scolari's *Il ciarlatano*), and at Teatro S. Salvador, 6 May 1762, 27 Jan. 1763/4, ASV Notarile Atti b. 4290 c. 549ᵛ–551ʳ, 4292 c. 919ʳ–920ʳ, 4293 c. 1110ⁱᵛ.

58 Luigi Barilli to Francesco Fiorini, 24 Feb. 1813, BASCR A. Ms. 3859 (about Théâtre-Italien, Paris).

59 See Rosselli, *Opera Industry*, pp. 6–9. Even in London, where she sang only two performances a week, Giuditta Pasta had to go through a dress rehearsal on the day of the first performance: to her mother, 4 June 1833, LPA NY.

60 Ebers, *Seven Years of the King's Theatre*, p. xxvii; *Lillian Nordica's Hints to Singers*, ed. W. Armstrong, New York, 1923, pp. 30–4.

61 L. Quicherat, *Adolphe Nourrit*, Paris, 1867, I, pp. 436–7.

62 E. H. Müller, *Angelo und Pietro Mingotti*, Dresden, 1917, p. 94; A. de la Grange to Mme Minelli, Bologna 29 Sept. 18[46], MTS Coll. Casati 338.

63 B. Capranica to D. Barbaja, 15 July 1828, BTBR DC; to Lanari from A. Gazzuoli, 11 Oct. 1838, from E. Marzi, 30 Dec. 1848, April 1849, BNF CV 365/49, 393/47–59.

64 'Promemoria serale per lo spettacolo autunnale 1852', ASC BO Dep. P. Sp. Tit. I rub. 1 (1853). One of the four operas had an extra rehearsal because the prima donna arrived late. There was also a week's gap in performances because of the sudden death of the impresario.

65 *Early Diary of Frances Burney*, II, p. 5. Cf. Henstock, *De Lucia*, pp. 103–4.

66 C. L. Kellogg, *Memoirs of an American Prima Donna*, New York, 1913, pp. 24–5.

67 *Lillian Nordica's Hints to Singers*, pp. 32–3, 50–1; C. Reddish, *A Chronicle of Memories*, Miami, 1950, p. 73.

68 Pasta to her daughter Clelia, 19 Jan. 1835, LPA NY.

69 Mutual *proteste* by Count F. [di] Serego and by Polonia Orlandi over non-payment of the second half of her salary at [?Teatro S. Salvador], Venice, F1762; she had fallen ill after the first five performances: ASV Notarile Atti b. 4292 c. 935ʳ–936ʳ.

70 Rosmini, *Legislazione dei teatri*, I, pp. 368–70; Rosselli, *Opera Industry*, pp. 128–9; contracts in MTS Coll. Casati 494–5, 647, and s.v. Canedi, ASN Teatri f. 68.

71 To Soprintendente dei Teatri, 17 July [?1837], ASN Teatri f. 146 (Teatro La Fenice, Naples).

72 Gaetano Giannini to Lanari, 21 June 1827 (about Adelaide Maldotti), BNF CV
400/45; Salucci, *Manuale della giurisprudenza dei teatri*, pp. 286–90.

73 Ascoli, *Della giurisprudenza teatrale*, pp. 117–18; Tabanelli, *Codice del teatro*,
pp. 134–8, 164–7; Pietro Romani to Lanari, [end 1836 or early 1837], BNF CV
405/171 (the impresario Andrea Bandini threatened to sue Eugenia Tadolini for
damages for being pregnant 'without a husband'); Celani, 'Musica e musicisti in
Roma', pt 2, pp. 43, 46–7; Commissioner of Police of S. Ferdinando, Naples, to
Soprintendente dei Teatri, 23 May 1835, ASN Teatri f. 146.

74 Lehmann, *My Path through Life*, pp. 397–401.

75 M. Labroca, *L'usignolo di Boboli*, Venice, 1959, pp. 191–5.

76 Teresa De' Giuli Borsi to Tommaso Gnoli, 5 May 1855, BE MO MSS Campori
App. 2447.

77 Letter of 1912 describing her *Traviata* at Cormons, Viola Tree, *Castles in the Air*,
London, 1926, p. 271.

78 Augusta Boccabadati to Cecilia Varesi, 28 March 1845, BE MO MSS Campori
App. 2447.

79 G. Cecchini Pacchierotti, *Ai cultori ed amatori della musica vocale: cenni
biografici intorno a Gaspare Pacchierotti*, Padua, 1844, pp. 4–6, 11.

80 Elaborate negotiations were needed before two leading basses from the Sistine
Chapel and Loreto could be got to appear together in a triduum at Osimo in 1754:
Fra Bonaventura Mancinelli to Padre Martini, 24 Nov. 1753, 9, 23 April 1754,
CMBM BO 1.10.152, 154, 155.

81 Plea on behalf of Luigia Boccabadati in suit against Pietro Cartoni and others
before Tribunale di Commercio, Rome, Sept. 1828, BTBR DC c. 3 b(B).

82 Adamo Francesco Ghinder, 'Relatione di quanto è avvenuto . . . doppo il mio
arrivo in Modena . . .', [?1699], ASMO Mus b. 2; Deutsch, ed., *Handel, a
Documentary Biography*, pp. 101, 248, 256; Metastasio to G. C. Pasquini and
Hasse, Feb. 1748, *Tutte le opere*, III, pp. 337–46 (Metastasio later suggested one
more possible test – whether the characters were the most virtuous: to A.
Bernacchi, 26 March 1753, *ibid*. pp. 805–6). In contrast with London satires,
Handel's librettist Paolo Rolli took seriously the notion that a king's part ought
to be important: to sig. Calebi [*c.* 1740], BCI SI Autog. Porri f. xxvi n. 4.

83 Cavagnino to M. Faustini, 10, 17 Oct. 1665, ASV Scuola Grande di S. Marco b.
188 c. 211–12. On number of arias per opera: J. Smith, 'Carlo Pallavicini', *PRMA*
96, 1969–70, pp. 57–71:66; J. Glover, 'The peak period of Venetian public opera:
the 1650s', *ibid*. III, 1975–6, pp. 67–82.

84 Virginia Blasis to Felice Romani, 26 April 1834, Biblioteca Civica, Turin, Fondo
Cossilla (the opera was to be written for the short fair season at Bergamo, where
singers performed six times a week). I owe this reference to Alessandro
Roccatagliati.

85 Stern, 'A documentary study of Giuditta Pasta', p. 171.

86 Genoveffa Canevassi Garnier to ex-Marquis Andreoli, [E1797], in Vianello,
Teatri a Milano, p. 219; Camilla Balsamini, drafts of letters concerning *Pizarro* at
Bologna, A1804, MTS CA 255; and see note 81.

87 F. Romani to Cavaliere di Lansfeld, 13 Nov. 1832, ASCM Sp. P. 6/4, to G. F.

Avesani, 22 Oct. 1833, ATLaF Librettisti b. 5 (demanding to know the singers for whom he was to write). I owe these references to Alessandro Roccatagliati.

88 Croce, *Teatri di Napoli*, pp. 535–6.

89 Deutsch, ed., *Handel, a Documentary Biography*, p. 227.

90 BTBR DC c. 3 b(A), *causa* Cosselli-Pistoni (the part offered was Elmiro in Rossini's *Otello*, put on as a 'fall-back opera' at Teatro Valle, Rome, C1827, when the expected second opera was not ready in time). For the classification of singers' titles, see Valle, *Cenni teorico-pratici*, pp. 35–45.

91 Lorenza Correa to F. Fiorini, 19 Oct., 8 Nov. 1814, BASCR A.Ms. 3860–1. The composer, J. S. Mayr, did in the end visit Correa, but she rejected the aria he had written for her. See J. Rosselli, *Music and Musicians in 19th-Century Italy*, London, 1991, p. 84.

92 Croce, *Teatri di Napoli*, pp. 301–2.

93 Deutsch, ed., *Handel, a Documentary Biography*, pp. 207–12, 216–18. Cf. similar episodes involving women in Rome in the 1670s, and Crescentini about 1800: Ademollo, *Teatri di Roma*, pp. 138–9; Lucarelli, 'Girolamo Crescentini', pp. 67, 72–8.

94 Padre Saverio Mattei to Padre Martini, 28 May 1782, CMBM BO I.24.42 (the comic bass was Giovanni Morelli, the tenor one Sciroli); Carpi, *Al di qua e al di là*, pp. 17–18 (season at Casale, 1873).

95 Burney, *General History*, II, p. 881.

96 *Early Diary of Fanny Burney*, II, p. 3.

97 Calvetti, *Galliano Masini*. This was in the 1930s; the soprano was Maria Caniglia.

98 Ortes to Hasse, 10 Jan. 1767, 23 Jan. 1768, MCCV Cod. Cicogna 2658 n. 131, 145; Camporesi and Grassini to Pasta, Pasta to Rossini, LPA NY; M. Piccolomini to T. Ricordi, 27 June, 9 Aug. 1855, 22 Jan. 1856, AR MI.

99 *Lillian Nordica's Hints to Singers*, pp. 163–5.

100 Charles Gounod to Mathilde Marchesi, 9 Jan. 1853, LPA NY, Marchesi Coll. A/2. Cf. the intellectual baritone Giuseppe Kaschmann, who got into trouble with fellow-singers for 'conscientious silence' (failure to applaud): to Giulio Ricordi, 1 March 1878, AR MI.

101 Giulio Gatti-Casazza to Giuseppe Lusardi, 30 Jan. 1919, MOA NY (Lusardi's paper had run down Rosa Ponselle and Geraldine Farrar, non-subscribers, even though he was the Met's official agent). For agents' journals, see Rosselli, *Opera Industry*, pp. 144–6.

102 Mosconi to the agent Pollazzi, of Florence, 10 April 1880, BE MO MSS Campori App. 2447.

103 Quicherat, *Nourrit*, I, pp. 405, 433–4, 502.

104 This was Giuseppe Marini, whose wife Carlotta Michelesi Marini ran seasons at Mantua, Lodi, and Crema in 1836–40: G. Rossi to B. Capranica, ASCR FC, *causa* Rossi-Gallieno e Scandaglia.

105 From 1750 to 1786: Basso, ed., *Storia del Teatro Regio*, I, pp. 227–9, 395.

106 ASV Notarile Atti 4287 c. 76^v–82^r, *passim* (season planned for Teatro S. Moisè, C1756).

107 Fraschini to T. Ricordi, 2 May 1860, AR MI; and see Rosselli, *Opera Industry*, pp. 126–8.

108 Carlo Balochino to Rossini, 31 May 1844, in F. Schlitzer, *Un piccolo carteggio inedito di Rossini con un impresario italiano a Vienna*, Florence, 1959, p. 84; O. Maini to Giulio Ricordi, 24 May 1884, AR MI; M. Renaud to D'Ormeville, 19 Aug. 1902, MTS Coll. Casati 978; Buonassisi, *Musicista*, pp. 93–4.

109 Valentino Fioravanti's contracts for Teatro Camploy, Venice, 1873, and Teatro Castelli, Milan, 1875, Ebe Ticozzi's contracts for Teatro Chiarella, Turin, and Teatro S. Carlos, Lisbon [both 1920s], MTS Coll. Casati 494–5, CA 7454, 7456.

110 Labroca, *Usignolo di Boboli*, p. 240.

111 J. Rosselli, 'The opera business and the Italian immigrant community in Latin America 1820–1930: the example of Buenos Aires', *Past and Present* no. 127, 1990, pp. 155–82: 173–5; Kolodin, *Metropolitan Opera*, pp. 92, 98, 135, 207, 217, 246, 435; C. Bishop, *The San Carlo Opera Company 1913–1955: Grand Opera for Profit*, Santa Monica, Calif., 1978, pp. 81–2.

112 D. Kimbell, *Italian Opera*, Cambridge, 1991, p. 421; J. Budden, *Verdi*, London, 1985, p. 46.

113 Ghezzi, caricature of sig. Mozzi (Anfronio), BAV Cod. Ottob. Lat, 3114 c. 121.

114 Hasse to Ortes, 7 May 1769, MCCV Cod. Cicogna 3197–8*bis*.

115 Correspondence between Mirate and the impresario Alfredo Prestreau, 19 Feb. 1866, ASN Teatri f. 67.

116 Stern, 'A documentary study of Giuditta Pasta', p. 165; V. Camporesi to Pasta, 16 July 1819, 4 April 1827, Pasta to her mother, 9 July 1833, LPA NY; Cox, *Musical Recollections*, I, p. 141. Later, Rosa Ponselle's 'early' retirement at forty probably owed much to a conservative investment policy that kept her fortune largely intact through the 1929–33 depression: Ponselle and Drake, *Ponselle*, pp. 159–77.

117 ASV Notarile Atti b. 4290 c. 427^{rv} (Ven. duc. 8,000 held by the long retired soprano Santa Stella Lotti in the Arte de' Pistori, the Venice bakers' corporation, 1758); Nancy Storace's will, 10 Aug. 1797, Sir John Soane's Museum, London (£5,000 East India Company stock); Cecchini Pacchierotti, *Cenni biografici intorno a Pacchierotti*, pp. 11–12; E. Tadolini's letters (see note 123); F. Festa Maffei to G. Calandrelli, 1827–8, MTS Coll. Casati 479, CA 2182, Piancastelli Autog.; E. Frezzolini to G. Marchetti, [late 1850s], Piancastelli Autog. s.v. Marchetti.

118 *Il Mondo Artistico*, 20 July 1881 (cutting in MTS Coll. Casati 321); and see note 117.

119 Berutto, *Cantanti piemontesi*, pp. 68–9; Calvetti, *Galliano Masini*.

120 Luigi Fioravanti to Giovannina Lucca, 15 Jan. 1876, MTS Coll. Casati 506. For Colbran, see R. Osborne, *Rossini*, London, 1986, pp. 83–4.

121 P. Ciarlantini, 'Una testimonianza sul teatro musicale degli inizi dell'Ottocento: il saggio "Dell'opera in musica" di Nicola Tacchinardi', *Bollettino del Centro Rossiniano di Studi* 19 (1989), pp. 65–135:74–9; Klein, *Reign of Patti*, pp. 276–7, 296–8, 302–5, 333–5.

122 Alice Barbi Wolff to [?], 10/23 Dec. 1907, MTS Coll. Casati 44.

123 Eugenia Tadolini's letters to her brothers, and other papers, Piancastelli 434; F. Battaglia, *L'arte del canto in Romagna. I cantanti lirici romagnoli dell'Ottocento e Novecento*, Bologna, 1979, pp. 151–63.

8 THE AGE OF THE TENOR

1 A. Palazzeschi, *Stampe dell'Ottocento*, Florence, 1938[2], pp. 152–3.

2 Ortes to Hasse, 22 Dec. 1770, MCCV Cod. Cicogna 2658 no. 193.

3 Fra G. M. Chiarenza to Padre Martini, 9 Dec. 1765, CMBM BO 1.3.178.

4 W. Ganz, *Memories of a Musician*, London, 1913, pp. 14, 287; Metropolitan Opera paybooks, MOA NY.

5 Lalande, *Voyage d'un François*, 1790 edn, quoted in Di Giacomo, *Quattro conservatori*, I, p. 235 (the two tenors were Gregorio Babbi and Angelo Amorevoli, but the passage – not in the original 1769 edition – is suspect); Petrobelli, 'Italian Years of Anton Raaff', p. 234.

6 Adelaide Carpano (David's mistress) to Duke Francesco Sforza-Cesarini, 28 May 1814, in Celani, 'Musica e musicisti in Roma', pt 3, pp. 28–9. For David: R. Celletti, *Storia del belcanto*, Fiesole, 1983, pp. 166–8.

7 Bellini, *Epistolario*, pp. 146, 160; Mercadante to F. Florimo, 26 Nov. 1838, in Palermo, ed., *Mercadante*, p. 189. The tenor originally proposed, Domenico Reina, did not in the event appear.

8 Anna de la Grange to Mme Minelli, 29 Sept. [1846], her mother to Mme Cambiag[g]i[o], no date, MTS Coll. Casati 337–8.

9 Italo Campanini to Canedi, 29 Aug. 1877, MTS Coll. Casati 233.

10 H. Klein, *Thirty Years of Musical Life in London*, London, 1903, pp. 99–100; G. B. Shaw, *London Music in 1888–89 as heard by Corno di Bassetto*, London, 1937, pp. 288–9.

11 De Amicis, *Francesco Tamagno*.

12 'Max Strakosch', cutting from unnamed New York newspaper, 27 Sept. 1879, Strakosch cuttings book, MOA NY.

13 *Sims Reeves. His Life and Recollections written by Himself*, London, 1888, pp. 33–5, 265–8.

14 Maragliano, *Teatri di Voghera*.

15 G. Adami, *Giulio Ricordi. L'amico dei musicisti italiani*, Milan, 1945, pp. 72–3.

16 *Gaceta Musical* (Buenos Aires), 6 July 1879; De Amicis, *Francesco Tamagno*.

17 Tiberini to Giulio Ricordi, 6 July 1870, AR MI; Stagno to Galiani, 15 May 1885, Piancastelli Autog.

18 Shaw, *Music in London 1890–94*, II, p. 145.

19 E. Caruso Jr and A. Farkas, *Enrico Caruso*, Portland, Ore., 1990, pp. 17–23. Borgatti, *Mia vita d'artista*, pp. 21–35; D. Bannenta, *Alessandro Bonci. Impressioni...*, Ferrara, 1901 (in Piancastelli 548.26), pp. 13–17; E. Biagi, *E' di scena Pietro Gubellini*, Bologna, 1939; Maragliano, *Teatri di Voghera*, p. 248 (note); A Marchetti, *Carlo Galeffi*, Rome, 1973, pp. 10–12; Lauri-Volpi, *Equivoco*.

20 See G. Ciotti Cavalletti, *Attrici e società nell'Ottocento italiano*, Milan, 1978.

21 Weaver and Weaver, *Chronology of Music in the Florentine Theater*, p. 339.

22 Gandini, *Cronistoria dei teatri di Modena*, I, pp. 99, 115; Mooser, *Annales de la musique en Russie*, II, pp. 137–9.

23 Cosentino, *La Mignatta*, pp. 32–3; Ricci, *Teatri di Bologna*, p. 96 (note). These were Teresa Rossi, Isabella Buffagnotti (both 1686), and Margherita Marchesini (1699), who married patricians of Bologna, Milan, and Modena.

24 Cosentino, *La Mignatta*, pp. 72–5, 77–80, 82, 90–100, 179–80; Ricci, *Teatri di Bologna*, p. 96 (note). Musi's husband was Pietro Berni degli Antoni.

25 Others were Adelaide Tosi, Clara Novello, Matilde Sessi, Marietta Piccolomini, Marietta Gazzaniga, Maria Waldmann, Carolina Alaimo, Sofia Scalchi.

26 'Selbstbiographie von Gertrud Elisabeth Mara', cols 595, 611.

27 Marchesi, *Singer's Pilgrimage*, pp. 103–5.

28 Patti to Edward Hall, 24 Dec. 1880, LPA NY.

29 L. Arditi, *My Reminiscences*, London, 1896, p. 37; E. M. Forster, *Where Angels Fear to Tread*, London, 1905, ch. 6.

30 MTS Coll. Casati 305, CA 5329; L. Cavalieri, *Le mie verità*, Rome, 1936, illustration. Signatures that fit the description are those of Darclée, Rosina Storchio, Gabriella Besanzoni, Gianna Pederzini, Leyla Gencer, and Renata Scotto. The unhappy Claudia Muzio's signature was large but steeply downward sloping, at least in a letter of 9 Aug. 1926; BMTC BA.

31 F. Piperno, 'Il sistema produttivo, fino al 1780', in Bianconi and Pestelli, eds., *Storia dell'opera italiana*, IV, pp. 3–75: 52–3; Lucarelli, 'Girolamo Crescentini'; Stern, 'A documentary study of Giuditta Pasta'.

32 E. Schwarzkopf, *On and Off the Record*, London, 1982, p. 142.

33 Luigi Parmeggiani to G. Marchetti, 1866, Piancastelli Autog. s.v. Marchetti; Vittorio Arimondi to D'Ormeville, 25 Dec. 1902, MTS Coll. Casati 34.

34 Faccio to A. Gerardi, 8 April 1870, in Sartori, *Franco Faccio e Brescia*, pp. 3–9. For similar arrangements at Teatro Regio, Turin, CQ1872, La Pergola, Florence, A1872, the Teatro Colón, Buenos Aires, 1909–10: MTS Coll. Casati 1498; L. Marzi to G. Marchetti, 10 Nov. 1872, Piancastelli Autog. s.v. Marchetti; contracts with G. De Luca, G. Pareto, A. Pintucci, F. Anitua, N. De Angelis, BMTC BA.

35 Printed contract form for Liceu, Barcelona, 1898, MTS Coll. Casati 111; V. Frajese, *Dal Costanzi all'Opera*, Rome, 1977–8, II, pp. 16–18 (performance of 28 March 1909); *La Maschera* (Naples), 13 March 1910.

36 Santley, *Student and Singer*, p. 234; Gatti-Casazza, *Memories of the Opera*, pp. 15–16. See also Rosmini, *Legislazione dei teatri*, I, p. 527.

37 Maddalena Mariani Masi to Giulio Ricordi, 26 Nov. 1875, AR MI. Similar statements from Maria Spezia, 31 May 1854, G. Kaschmann, 6 Nov. 1876, *ibid.*; from V. Arimondi, 1902, 1905, H. Darclée, 1891, Ninì Frascani, [*c.* 1910], Francesco Vignas, 1898, MTS Coll. Casati 34, 36, 305, 516, 1211.

38 Titta Ruffo, *Mia parabola*, p. 244; M. Labia, *Guardare indietro: che fatica!*, Verona, 1950, p. 116. See also Gara, *Caruso*, pp. 94–5.

39 Contracts with A. Bonci, Barcelona 1898, MTS Coll. Casati 111, with G. De Luca, Buenos Aires 1909, BMTC BA.

40 Ponselle and Drake, *Ponselle*, pp. 120–1.

41 Rosmini, *Legislazione dei teatri*, II, pp. 43–4, 364–5.

42 Medea Borelli-Angiolini to E. Tornaghi, 5 Dec. 1883, MTS Coll. Casati 142; petitions and thanks addressed to G. Lucca by G. Aldighieri, 16 Sept. 1872, V. Boccabadati, 4 July 1867, R. Stagno, 26 Oct. 1878, M. Mariani Masi, 7 Feb. 1875, A. De Bassini, 1879, MTS CA 34, 584, 1289, 5807, 6040; to Ricordi by Luigia Abbadia, 9 Sept. 1855, G. Kaschmann, 1 Oct. 1877, O. Maini, 16 Sept. 1872, 2 Oct. 1882, AR MI.

43 M. Mariani Masi to Giulio Ricordi, 1875–82, *passim*, AR MI. Similar letters from Maria Labia to Tito Ricordi II, 23 Jan. [1913], 6 April 1918, *ibid.*

44 Fraschini to Tito Ricordi I, 10 Feb. 1870, V. Boccabadati to [?], 18 Oct. 1858, AR MI; L. Fioravanti to G. Lucca, 15 Jan. 1876, MTS Coll. Casati 506.

45 From S. Malvezzi, 1853 (*Il trovatore* at Reggio Emilia), O. Maini (Viadana, Sept. 1862, Trieste, 14 Oct. 1875), G. Fraschini (Bergamo, 1850, Lisbon, 1960), M. Mariani Masi (*La Gioconda*, San Carlo, Naples, 20 March 1881, and in Spain, 18 Feb. 1883), AR MI.

46 E. Frezzolini to her sister Amalia Marchetti, St Louis, [no date, but 1857–8], Piancastelli Autog, s.v. Marchetti. For American touring circuits, Rosselli, 'Opera business', pp. 162–7.

47 Paolo Giorza to Leone Giraldoni, 5 April 1885, MTS CA 2924; *Statesman* (Calcutta), 25 Feb., 6 March 1891.

48 *British Packet* (Buenos Aires), 24 May, 21 June 1834; C. Pitt, 'India', *The New Grove Dictionary of Opera*, London, 1992.

49 Berutto, *Cantanti piemontesi*, pp. 9–11.

50 R. Fiske, *English Theatre Music in the Eighteenth Century*, Oxford, 1973, pp. 305–14; O. Teuber, *Geschichte des Prager Theaters*, Prague, 1883–8, II, p. 326; M. Kelly, *Reminiscences*, ed. R. Fiske, Oxford, 1975, pp. 258–9.

51 Berutto, *Cantanti piemontesi*, pp. 254–5, asserts that Emma Turolla, who flourished about 1880, 'made an intensive study of German in order to sing Wagner in the original', and implies that she did so as a regular member of the Vienna State Opera; but in Vienna in 1883–4 she was listed among the Italian guest singers, who normally sang in their own language: *Das Kaiserlich-Königliche Hof-Operntheater in Wien. Statistischer Rückblick*, ed. A. J. Weltner *et al.*, Vienna, 1894. Turolla may, however, have sung in German elsewhere. Her career ended in Budapest in 1890.

52 Angiolina Peracchi to Felice Romani, Constantinople 29 May 1836, Teresina Brambilla Ponchielli to A. Ponchielli, Lisbon 25 Nov. 1878, MTS Coll. Casati 934, CA 2474; similar complaints about lack of artistic satisfaction in Russia in Francesco Marconi to D'Ormeville, 3 Oct. 1894, Coll. Casati 798.

53 Francesca Bertolldi [*sic*] to G. M. Orlandini, 24 Oct. 1732, CMBM BO P.141.34.

54 Prunières, *Opéra italien en France*, pp. 146–50, 267–8.

55 Kellogg, *Memoirs of an American Prima Donna*, pp. 40–1.

56 Weingartner to Cirilo Grassi Díaz, 4 Oct. 1922, BMTC BA.

57 Mooser, *Annales de la musique en Russie*, I, pp. 284, 287–8 (careers of the comic singers Rosa Costa and Gabriele Messieri), III, p. 774 (prima donna Teresa Maciurletti); Robbins Landon, *Haydn: Chronicle and Works*, III: *Haydn in England*, pp. 266–8; Kelly, *Reminiscences*, pp. 2–3.

58 A. Taullard, *História de nuestros viejos teatros*, Buenos Aires, 1932, pp. 409–14 (Teatro Doria, later Marconi).

59 Information from Prof. Morris Vitalis.

60 Information from Mary Jane Phillips Matz. The other two hotels were the Sherman Square and the Alamac.

61 Carpi, *Al di qua e al di là*, pp. 77, 85, 93, 98; Arditi, *Reminiscences*, pp. 275–6; Henry Russell, *The Passing Show*, London, 1926, pp. 134–7. Cf. Henriette

Sontag's US travels – the most tiring she had ever experienced – on her 1852–4 tour: H. Stümcke, *Henriette Sontag: ein Lebens- und Zeitbild*, Berlin, 1913, pp. 238–9, 242–3.

62 This account of Buenos Aires seasons is based on many small items in local newspapers: *La Patria italiana* (later *La Patria degli Italiani*), 1882, 1898, *Giornale d'Italia*, 1911, *La Razón*, 1925, *Gaceta Musical*, *passim*. For New York I am indebted to Mary Jane Phillips Matz for her personal recollections; see also her 'Heap big man', *Opera News* (New York), 29 Dec. 1958.

63 Works Progress Administration, *History of Opera in San Francisco*, pp. 67–72; M. G. Bosch, *História del teatro en Buenos Aires*, Buenos Aires, 1910, p. 347; AGMA (New York) 3, May–June 1938, 4, Feb.–April 1939.

64 Bosch, *História*, p. 347.

65 Burney, *General History*, II, pp. 671–2.

66 Prunières, *Opéra italien en France*, p. 168.

67 R. Fiske, 'Storace', *TNG*.

68 F. Toye, *Rossini*, London, 1934, p. 107; A. Gazzuoli to Lanari, 21 April 1838, in J. Rosselli, *L'impresario d'opera*, Turin, 1985, pp. 247–8. Other foreigners important in Italian romantic opera were Carolina Unger, Henriette Méric-Lalande, Sophia Löwe, Gilbert-Louis Duprez, Joséphine Fodor-Mainvielle, Josephine Deméric, Paul Barroilhet, and Adelaide Comelli [Chaumel].

69 Mooser, *Annales de la musique en Russie*, I, p. 241.

70 Sims Reeves to A. Mazzucato, 3 July 1876, 5 Sept. 1877, MTS CA 6828–9; Santley, *Student and Singer*, pp. 117–18.

71 *Lillian Nordica's Hints to Singers*, p. 18.

72 Davide Banderali to Giovanni Ricordi, 1820s–40s, *passim*, AR MI; Giulio Marco Bordogni to G. B. Benelli, 21 Jan., 29 Nov. 1826, in Cagli, 'Rossini a Londra e al Théâtre-Italien di Parigi', pp. 49–50.

73 *Lillian Nordica's Hints to Singers*, pp. 29, 42–50, *passim*, 68–9, 80–2, 131–4; Emma Albani to Eva Gauthier, 30 Oct. 1905, 12 June 1909, LPA NY, Gauthier Collection. Nordica's second season, at Brescia, had a Fcs 1,000 subsidy from the rich young American tenor who sang with her.

74 Rosmini, *Legislazione dei teatri*, I, p. 528.

75 Tree, *Castles in the Air*, pp. 39, 272–4, 284–5, 296.

76 *Il Pungolo* (Milan), 22 Sept. 1883, quoted in *La Musica* (Naples), 1 Oct. 1883 (about Leonilda Diotti).

77 Sadie E. Martin, *The Life and Professional Career of Emma Abbott*, Minneapolis, 1891, p. 34 and *passim*.

78 Reddish, *A Chronicle of Memories*, pp. 33–56.

79 *The Glory that was Gold: The Central City Opera House*, Denver, 1936, pp. 7, 125, and 2nd supplement, p. 17; Rosselli, 'Opera business', p. 165.

80 List of Marchesi pupils, LPA NY Marchesi Collection C/15.

81 F. Fano, 'Opera italiana all'estero', in *Il teatro italiano. Anno 1913*, pp. 233–4.

82 H. Rosenthal, *Two Centuries of Opera at Covent Garden*, London, 1958, pp. 222–5; *K.-K. Hof-Operntheater. Statistischer Rückblick*, pp. 158–69.

83 C. Bishop, *The Boston National Opera Company and Boston Theater Opera Company*, Santa Monica, 1981, pp. 2–9.

84 The character tenor Luigi Vellucci, born and brought up in the Italian-American community of Providence, Rhode Island, was trained by a Polish-American teacher and, through a long freelance career, has sung such non-Italian parts as David, Valzacchi, and Shuisky: interview, 25 May 1988. A close contemporary, Tony Amato, an ex-comprimario tenor who since 1948 has run the small-scale Amato Opera Company in New York, in contrast had a strongly Italian musical grounding, but finds that two-thirds of his audience are Jewish and very few are Italian-American; though his repertoire includes Italian rarities, his company is American in its eclecticism: interview, 9 May 1988; G. Martin, 'New York's smaller opera companies', *Opera* 36 (1985), no. 9; *Il progresso* (New York), 14 Sept. 1986, Supplement B, p. 8.

9 THE COMING OF MASS SOCIETY

1 Correspondence between Count Alessandro Tornielli and Giuseppe Zoppetti (direttore agli spettacoli and secretary of the board of La Fenice) and Piontelli and Cesare Corti, Nov.–Dec. 1891, figures for municipal subsidy (Fcs 79,000 a year in 1869–71, 50,000 in 1889–90) and boxholders' contribution (Fcs 100,000 and 54,000), ATLaF Spettacoli b. 2, Sussidio comunale b. 3. For Piontelli's strikebreaking at Genoa: G. Monaldi, *Impresari celebri del secolo XIX*, Rocca S. Casciano, 1918, pp. 201–2.
2 *Teatri Arti e Letteratura* (Bologna), 23 July 1829 (*Le Comte Ory* at Teatro S. Benedetto, Venice, P1829); A. Bandini, 'Progetto per l'appalto del nuovo Ducal Teatro di Parma', 12 Oct. 1830, ATRP (alleges that women's chorus was left out of *Semiramide* and *Il crociato in Egitto* at La Fenice, Venice).
3 Berutto, *Cantanti piemontesi*, pp. 105–6.
4 De Amicis, *Francesco Tamagno*.
5 Alessandro Carcano, deputato ai pubblici spettacoli, 'Progetto d'ordinamento delle masse corali e d'orchestra del Teatro Comunale di Roma', 28 Nov. 1872, ASCR tit. XV.
6 G. Rossi-Gallieno, *Saggio di economia teatrale*, Milan, 1839, pp. 49–50.
7 G. Verdi, *I Copialettere*, ed. G. Cesari and A. Luzio, Milan, 1913, pp. 248–9 (note), 681–2 (letters of 1871–2). Faccio in 1871 requested a chorus 'with a fair musical background': Sartori, *Franco Faccio e Brescia*, p. 14.
8 Teresina Singer to G. Lucca, 31 Dec. 1875, MTS CA 5329.
9 'Promemoria serale, Autunno 1852', ASBO Dep. P. Sp. tit. I rub. 1 (1853). See Rosselli, *Opera Industry*, pp. 118–19.
10 Correspondence between the impresario Ercole Tinti and the supervisory board, ASBO Dep. P. Sp. tit. I rub. 1 (1860); Soprintendente (Duca di Donato) to direttore, Ministero della Istruzione Pubblica, 27 Oct. 1860, ASN Teatri f. 128.
11 *Annuario dell'arte lirica e coreografica italiana* (Milan) 1, 1897–8, pp. 280–1.
12 Basso, *Conservatorio di Torino*, p. 79.
13 The following paragraphs are based on many documents in ASN Teatri f. 67, 68, 74, 128. See Rosselli, 'Artisti e impresari', pp. 53–5, and, for similar, much earlier difficulties with the orchestra, U. Prota-Giurleo, *La grande orchestra del Teatro San Carlo nel Settecento*, Naples, 1927, pp. 11–14, 23–38.

14 Mauro Corticelli to Deputazione, 24 Oct. 1855, ASBO Dep. P. Sp. tit. I rub. 1
(1855); G. Marchesi, *Giuseppe Verdi e il Conservatorio di Parma (1836–1901)*,
Parma, 1976, p. 102.

15 *Orchestre in Emilia-Romagna nell'Ottocento e Novecento*, Parma, 1982, esp.
preface by L. Pestalozza.

16 La Scala salary roll, 1858–9, ASCM Sp. P. b. 112/2; figures for Teatro Comunale,
Bologna, CQ and A1850, Teatro del Corso, Bologna, P1855, ASBO Dep. P. Sp. tit.
I rub. 1 (1850), rub. 2 (1855); for Rome, 1840, BNF CV 353/85, 364/144; for Teatro
Ducale, Parma, 1870, ATRP; replies from Teatro Regio, Turin, Teatro Carlo
Felice, Genoa, and La Scala to inquiries from La Fenice, Venice, Nov. 1891,
ATLaF Spettacoli b. 72.

17 Rattalino, *Ente lirico*, pp. 13–14.

18 Metropolitan Opera paybooks, MOA NY; Bloomfield, *San Francisco Opera*, p. 14
(note).

19 Rattalino, *Ente lirico*, pp. 13–14, 28; Dalmas, *Guida pratica teatrale*, pp. 59–62.
The agent was Francesco Mozzi.

20 Cone, *Manhattan Opera Company*, pp. 46–7, 60. The chorus master, Gaetano
Merola, later founded the San Francisco Opera.

21 J. B. Steane, *The Grand Tradition*, London, 1974, p. 6.

22 G. Orefice, 'Il nostro teatro lirico', in *Il teatro italiano. Anno 1913*, pp. 185–7.

23 Marc'Antonio Correr to M. Faustini, 6 Nov. 1665, ASV Scuola Grande di S.
Marco b. 188 c. 207.

24 B. De Franceschi and P. F. Mondini, *Ebe Stignani: una voce e il suo mondo*, Imola,
1980, p. 22.

25 Labroca, *Usignolo di Boboli*, pp. 162–6; F. Possenti, 'La "claque" a teatro',
Strenna dei romanisti 37, 1976, pp. 453–6.

26 H. Sachs, *Toscanini*, London, 1978, pp. 142–3, 148–59, 166–7, 177–9.

27 Labroca, *Usignolo di Boboli*, pp. 149–50.

28 [?G. Cattaneo], *La libertà del cantare*, Lucca, 1752, p. 7.

29 See W. J. Baumol and W. G. Bowen, *Performing Arts – The Economic Dilemma*,
New York, 1966.

30 L. Trezzini and A. Curtolo, *Oltre le quinte. Idee, cultura e organizzazione del
teatro musicale in Italia*, Venice, 1979, pp. 31–41, 48–9; H. Sachs, *Music in Fascist
Italy*, London, 1987, pp. 55–73; F. Nicolodi, 'Il sistema produttivo, dall'Unità a
oggi', *Storia dell'opera italiana*, ed. Bianconi and Pestelli, IV, pp. 169–229:
195–201.

31 Ernst J. M. Lert, 'Taking a system or taking chances?', *AGMA* (New York) 3
(Jan.–Apr. 1938).

32 G. Azzaroni, *Tra riforme e compromessi. Il teatro musicale in Italia tra il 1920 e il
1980*, Bologna, 1981; Trezzini and Curtolo, *Oltre le quinte*, pp. 48–51; L.
Pestalozza, 'Lo stato dell' organizzazione musicale: la svolta del fascismo e la sua
lunga durata', *Musica/Realtà* 2, 1981, pp. 143–60; Labroca, *Usignolo di Boboli*,
pp. 135–9. For earlier trade union advocacy of some of these changes: E. Reina, *I
pubblici spettacoli e le provvidenze di legislazione sociale*, Rome, 1915, pp.
139–42. The planning of a professional register for singers is documented in a 1943
letter from Gigli to Mussolini, ACS SPD CO 545.962.

33 Information kindly communicated by Fiamma Nicolodi. The other singers allowed exceptional maxima were the tenors Giuseppe Lugo and Galliano Masini (L.10,000), the mezzos Gianna Pederzini (L.7,000) and Ebe Stignani, and the baritones Tancredi Pasero and Mariano Stabile (all L.6,000, Stignani and Stabile only for certain parts).

34 Correspondence between Goffredo Petrassi, superintendent of La Fenice, and 'secretaries' or 'accountants' acting for Lugo, Pacetti, and Cigna, ATLaF Spettacoli 1938.

35 Count Paolo d'Ancora, vice-governor of Rome and chairman of management committee of Teatro Reale dell Opera, to N. De Pirro, 29 July 1932, ACS SPD CO 509. 740/1.

36 Correspondence of G. Petrassi, 1937–8, passim, ATLaF Spettacoli 1938.

37 Kolodin, *Metropolitan Opera*, pp. 389–90; Gatti-Casazza, *Memories of the Opera*, pp. 303, 310–16; R. Christiansen, *Prima Donna*, Harmondsworth, 1986², pp. 207–9.

38 ATLaF Spettacoli 1938, *passim*.

39 Lauri-Volpi, *Equivoco*, pp. 204–5; F. Nicolodi, *Musica e musicisti nel ventennio fascista*, Fiesole, 1984, pp. 306–472; Sachs, *Music in Fascist Italy*, pp. 148–54.

40 To Mussolini from chorus members of Teatro Reale dell'Opera, Rome, 23 May 1942, from Ottavio Scotto, 4 May 1929, Carlo Gatti to N. De Cesare, 5 June 1943, ACS SPD CO 509.740/2, 555.902.

41 T. Dal Monte to Mussolini, 24 Nov. 1932, *ibid.* 126.563.

42 G. Bellincioni to Mussolini, 1929–39, and related papers, *ibid.* 509.455.

43 Petrassi to O. Tiby at Direzione Generale del Teatro, Ministero della Cultura Popolare, 30 Nov. 1937, ATLaF Spettacoli 1938. The tenor was Francesco Merli.

44 M. Giovagnoli to N. De Cesare, April–Sept. 1942, ACS SPD CO 532.557.

45 Labia, *Guardare indietro: che fatica!*, p. 95.

46 N. De Pirro, *Il teatro per il popolo*, Rome, 1938, pp. 5–10, 14–15; Labroca, *Usignolo di Boboli*, pp. 154–7; Trezzini and Curtolo, *Oltre le quinte*, pp. 42–44.

47 *Popolo d'Italia*, 21 Nov. 1929 (interview with Senator S. Borlotti, regio commissario straordinario in charge of La Scala), correspondence between Mussolini's secretariat and Giuseppe Baratono and Walter Mocchi regarding the S. Carlo, 1932–5, from members of Teatro Reale chorus and trade unions, 1942–3, Ministero delle Corporazioni circular, 3 April 1940, ACS SPD CO 555.902, 548.630, 509.740/2, MinCulPop b. 13 fasc. 175.

48 C. Cantarano, ed., *Codice della legislazione dello spettacolo*, Rome, 1968, pp. 806–36; *Corriere della Sera* (Milan), 24 April 1987, p. 23; interview with Prof. Umberto Bruno, Naples, 22 May 1987.

49 'Contratto collettivo di lavoro con i dipendenti del Teatro alla Scala' (local variation on the national contratto collettivo), 1985, kindly communicated by Dr C. M. Badini, then superintendent; Rattalino, *Ente lirico*, pp. 62–4, 97; Nicolodi, 'Sistema produttivo', pp. 221–2.

50 C. Testi, 'Fine del teatro-carrozzone: la Scala anni '90 un'azienda su cui investire', *Italia Oggi* (Milan), 6–7 Dec. 1986, p. 5. For soloists' fees as a proportion of total costs, Rosselli, *Opera Industry*, pp. 50–4, 58–9, Bianconi and Walker, 'Production, consumption', p. 230.

51 A. Thorncroft, 'Lessons to be learnt from the Met', *Weekend Financial Times*, 6 Jan. 1990, p. XVI.

52 Trezzini and Curtolo, *Oltre le quinte*, pp. 44, 62–3, 84, 88, 98; Buonassisi, *Musicista*, pp. 88–92; Cantarano, *Codice*, pp. 767–72; Nicolodi, 'Sistema produttivo', pp. 221–2; correspondence with Liduino Bonardi of Agenzia Lirica Concertistica Italiana, ATLaF Lettere 1950–1.

53 Correspondence of Nino Cattozzo, superintendent of La Fenice, 1950, ATLaF Lettere 1950–1. The information about fees in this file is, however, incomplete.

54 Schwarzkopf, *On and Off the Record*, p. 195; J. Culshaw, *Putting the Record Straight*, London, 1981, pp. 331–3.

55 R. Gelatt, *The Fabulous Phonograph*, London, 1956, pp. 80–6. This is still the main guide to an under-researched area; but see P. Martland, 'A business history of the Gramophone Company Ltd, 1897–1980', University of Cambridge Ph.D. thesis, 1992.

56 Lauri-Volpi, *Equivoco*, pp. 82–4, 110–11.

57 G. Richeri, 'Italian broadcasting and fascism 1924–1937', *Media, Culture and Society* 2 (1980), p. 50.

58 R. Celletti, *Carlo Galeffi e la Scala*, Milan, 1977, p. 34.

59 H. Greenfeld, *Caruso*, New York, 1983, pp. 208–9; Gigli, *Memorie*, pp. 291–3.

60 D. Forgacs, *Italian Culture in the Industrial Era 1880–1980*, Manchester, 1990, pp. 24, 81; G. Gualerzi and C. Marinelli Roscioni, *50 anni di opera lirica alla RAI 1931–1980*, Turin, 1981, pp. 7–19; Feliciotti, *Adriana Guerrini*; Battaglia, *Arte del canto in Romagna*, pp. 140–1; Buonassisi, *Musicista*, p. 31.

61 G. Lanza Tomasi in *Musica e industria in Italia*, ed. C. Martelli and C. Fontana, Milan, 1980, pp. 104–6.

62 Interview with Sir John Tooley, 10 Aug. 1988.

NOTE ON FURTHER READING

This is the first book on the subject defined by its title and subtitle. It has been preceded by a fine essay, S. Durante, 'Il cantante', in L. Bianconi and G. Pestelli, eds., *Storia dell'opera italiana*, Turin, 1987– , IV, pp. 349–415 (English translation expected from the University of Chicago Press).

Many earlier books have dealt with star singers. They are of very uneven quality; among the best general works are R. Christiansen, *Prima Donna*, London, 1984, and H. Pleasants, *The Great Singers*, New York, 1966. There are also a number of biographical and musical dictionaries, not always reliable. The most useful are K. J. Kutsch and L. Riemens, *Grosses Sängerlexikon*, Bern-Stuttgart, 2 vols., 1987, and, within their narrower compass, F. Regli, *Dizionario biografico dei più illustri poeti e artisti melodrammatici . . . in Italia dal 1800 al 1860*, Turin, 1860, and G. Berutto, *I cantanti piemontesi*, Turin, 1972. There are many biographies of singers in *The New Grove*, ed. S. Sadie, London, 20 vols., 1980, and still more in its offshoot *The New Grove Dictionary of Opera*, ed. Sadie, London, 1992. Many in *The Concise Oxford Dictionary of Opera*, ed. H. Rosenthal and J. Warrack, Oxford, 1964, still have value as embodying the editors' personal experience.

Individual biographies and autobiographies are legion. A useful bibliography is A. Farkas, ed., *Opera and Concert Singers*, New York, 1985. Though very full it is inevitably incomplete; Prof. Farkas promises a revised edition.

Few biographies or memoirs can be singled out as both reliable and illuminating. Perhaps because the genre has been thought little of in Italy, the best tend to be by non-Italians: 'Eine Selbstbiographie von Gertrud Elisabeth Mara', *AMZ* 10, 1875, L. Quicherat, *Adolphe Nourrit*, Paris, 3 vols., 1867, G.-L. Duprez, *Souvenirs d'un chanteur*, Paris, 1884, C. Santley, *Student and Singer*, London, 1892, Francis Walker, *Letters of a Baritone*, London, 1895 – the work of a singer made clear-sighted by failure, as is Viola Tree, *Castles in the Air*, London, 1926. Lilli Lehmann shows true Germanic serious-mindedness in *My Path through Life*, New York, 1914; the letters of Lillian

Nordica and her mother give documentary value to *Lillian Nordica's Hints to Singers*, ed. W. Armstrong, New York, 1923; and R. Ponselle and J. A. Drake, *Ponselle*, Garden City, 1982, conveys the Italian-American background of one of the greatest of singers.

On individual singers of early opera there are good scholarly essays, best found by using the index and notes of this book. Among later singers Titta Ruffo stands out for the liveliness of his autobiography, *La mia parabola*, Milan, 1937; there are a new edition with fresh material (Rome, 1977) and an English-language anthology: *Titta Ruffo*, ed. A. Farkas, Westport, Conn., 1984. Some of the best accounts of Italian singers are the least pretentious, e.g. the pamphlets on *Francesco Tamagno* by E. De Amicis (Palermo, 1902) and on *Galliano Masini* by M. Calvetti (Leghorn, 1979). Yet the most thorough biography of any singer, M. E. Henstock, *Fernando De Lucia*, London, 1990, sets a new scholarly standard.

The history of opera singing as an art and a discipline over the period 1600 to 1850 is best dealt with by R. Celletti, *Storia del belcanto*, Fiesole, 1983. For the earliest period H. Goldschmidt, *Die italienische Gesangsmethode des XVII. Jahrhunderts und ihre Bedeutung für die Gegenwart*, Breslau, 1890, is still important, as, for the castrati, is F. Haböck, *Die Kastraten und ihre Gesangskunst*, Stuttgart, 1927; A. Heriot, *The Castrati in Opera*, London, 1956, follows Haböck closely. Of the many treatises on singing the fundamental one is P. F. Tosi, *Opinioni de' cantori antichi e moderni o sieno osservazioni sopra il canto figurato*, Bologna, 1723, Eng. transl. by J. E. Galliard as *Observations on the Florid Song*, London, 1742, reprinted 1967. Formal musical education in Italy has to be studied in Italian-language monographs on particular institutions.

Since 1900 we can hear what most well-known singers sounded like; much has been published by and for devotees of old recordings. Detailed analytical guides are R. Celletti, *Le grandi voci*, Rome, 1964, and J. B. Steane, *The Great Tradition*, London, 1974.

The subject of this book overlaps with the history of Italian opera as a genre and a business. For the former as a whole, see D. Kimbell, *Italian Opera*, Cambridge, 1991; for the eighteenth century, M. F. Robinson, *Naples and Neapolitan Opera*, Oxford, 1972, and, for the nineteenth, the general chapters in each of the three volumes of J. Budden, *The Operas of Verdi*, London, 1973–81.

Robinson's and Budden's are both penetrating studies, but the liveliest sense of opera as a world of active professionals may come from a reading of the letters of Pietro Metastasio, in his *Tutte le opere*, ed. B. Brunelli, Milan, 5 vols., 1953, those of Mozart, ed. and transl. E. Anderson, London, 1985[3], and those of Verdi (a number of collections, all to be superseded by the critical edition launched by the Istituto di Studi Verdiani at Parma in 1988 with the first volume of *Carteggio Verdi-Ricordi*; there is, in English, a selection of *Letters of Giuseppe Verdi*, ed. and transl. C. Osborne, London, 1971). Knowledgeable first-hand evidence comes from Charles Burney, *Music, Men and Manners in France and Italy 1770*, ed. H. E. Poole, London, 1959, from the last part of his *A General History of Music*, ed. F. Mercer, London, 1935 (he had no doubt that Italian opera was the most important kind of modern music), and from the novelist Stendhal, on this subject always lively though at times eccentric: see his *Life of Rossini*, ed. and transl. R. N. Coe, London, 1956, and *Rome, Naples et Florence*, 1826² (several modern editions). Just as lively as Stendhal's is the criticism of George Bernard Shaw (several collections now brought together as *Shaw's Music*, ed. D. H. Laurence, London, 1989).

Opera as a business and a system of production over four centuries is dealt with in essays by F. Piperno, by me, and by F. Nicolodi in *Storia dell'opera italiana*, ed. Bianconi and Pestelli, IV. An important essay on the early period is L. Bianconi and T. Walker, 'Production, consumption and political function of seventeenth-century opera', *Early Music History* 4, 1984, pp. 209–96. On the period 1780–1930 there are my *The Opera Industry in Italy from Cimarosa to Verdi. The Role of the Impresario*, Cambridge, 1984, and 'The opera business and the Italian immigrant community in Latin America 1820–1930: the example of Buenos Aires', *Past & Present* no. 127, May 1990. On the period since 1920 Italian authors tend to be taken up with legislation (in modern Italy, it has been said, nothing can happen unless a law on the subject has been passed). Useful though their studies are, it is refreshing to come upon exceptions like M. Labroca, *L'usignolo di Boboli*, Venice, 1959, and P. Rattalino, *L'ente lirico va in trasferta*, Milan, 1983, lively reminiscences by men experienced in opera management.

Much can be got from histories of individual opera houses. This is another uneven genre, but among modern examples two stand out: A. Basso, ed., *Storia del Teatro Regio di Torino*, Turin, 5 vols., 1976–82, and N. Mangini, *I teatri di Venezia*, Milan, 1978.

Students wishing to work on unpublished material will find plenty of sources – more than are used in this book. The problem is to find material that is both consistently useful and accessible. Singers' letters are scattered through many libraries and archives, largely as a result of autograph collecting; but they are not always interesting, and if, as sometimes happens, catalogues are uninformative and you have to apply for one letter at a time, the result can be time-wasting. Fortunately the richest collections have good working conditions: these are the Museo Teatrale alla Scala/Biblioteca Livia Simoni, Milan, the Piancastelli collections at the Biblioteca Comunale, Forlì (both rich in nineteenth-century holdings), the Civico Museo Bibliografico Musicale, Bologna (mainly eighteenth-century correspondence, especially that of Padre Martini), and the Library of Performing Arts, Lincoln Center, New York (collections of letters of Giuditta Pasta and her family, Adelina Patti, Mathilde Marchesi, and a scattering of others).

Archives of impresarios are remarkably few. The only substantial ones open to the public are the much-used papers of the seventeenth-century impresario Marco Faustini in the Archivio di Stato, Venice, Scuola Grande di S. Marco b. 188, 194, two vast nineteenth-century collections of Alessandro Lanari's papers, in the Biblioteca Nazionale Centrale, Florence, and a smaller one of Carlo Balochino's papers in the Vienna Stadtbibliothek. The archive of the early eighteenth-century Florence impresario Luca Casimiro degli Albizzi is in private hands; it is the basis of a forthcoming study by William C. Holmes. The most important composer's archive is that of Verdi at his country house, Sant'Agata; it too is private, but it seems to be becoming gradually more accessible through the Istituto di Studi Verdiani at Parma.

The other chief source is the archives of governments and officials, including those of law courts and notaries. Judicial and notarial archives can provide remarkably detailed evidence, but working on them is time-consuming and they may be inaccessible: at Bologna, for more than a century the headquarters of the profession, there were, when I last heard, 18,500 volumes of court proceedings under the old papal government that were unusable because they had never been catalogued. In the old Italian states the supervisory boards (usually known as Deputazione or Soprintendenza dei Pubblici Spettacoli) had exceedingly detailed archives a number of which have survived, not as a rule complete. This kind of source tends to dry up under united Italy, partly because of less state intervention and partly because of the deteriorating quality of the paper used. With renewed state intervention from 1920 there are no doubt vast archives accumulating, but after the fascist period they are seldom accessible.

Fewer opera houses have archives than one might think. Among the more important ones are those of La Fenice, Venice (now in the Fondazione Levi, Venice), of the Teatro Regio, Parma, of the Théâtre-Italien, Paris (part of the Paris Opera archives, now in the Archives Nationales, Paris; detailed published catalogue by B. Labat-Poussin), and of the Metropolitan Opera, New York.

INDEX